CASENOTE® Legal Briefs®

CONSTITUTIONAL LAW

Keyed to Courses Using

Levinson, Balkin, Amar, Siegel, and Rodríguez's Processes of Constitutional Decisionmaking: Cases and Materials Eighth Edition

Authored by: Publisher's Editorial Staff

ASPEN PUBLISHING

This publication is designed to provide accurate and authoritative information in regard to the subject matter covered. It is sold with the understanding that the publisher is not engaged in rendering legal, accounting, or other professional services. If legal advice or other expert assistance is required, the services of a competent professional person should be sought.

— From a Declaration of Principles adopted jointly by a Committee of the American Bar Association and a Committee of Publishers and Associates

To contact Customer Service, e-mail customer.service@aspenpublishing.com, call 1-800-950-5259, or mail correspondence to:

Aspen Publishing
Attn: Order Department
P.O. Box 990
Frederick, MD 21705

Printed in the United States of America.

1 2 3 4 5 6 7 8 9 0

ISBN 978-1-5438-4145-9

SUSTAINABLE FORESTRY INITIATIVE Certified Chain of Custody At Least 10% Certified Forest Content www.sfiprogram.org SFI-01028

About Aspen Publishing

Aspen Publishing is a leading provider of educational content and digital learning solutions to law schools in the U.S. and around the world. Aspen provides best-in-class solutions for legal education through authoritative textbooks, written by renowned authors, and breakthrough products such as Connected eBooks, Connected Quizzing, and PracticePerfect.

The Aspen Casebook Series (famously known among law faculty and students as the "red and black" casebooks) encompasses hundreds of highly regarded textbooks in more than eighty disciplines, from large enrollment courses such as Torts and Contracts to emerging electives such as Sustainability and the Law of Policing. Study aids such as the *Examples & Explanations* and the *Emanuel Law Outlines* series, both highly popular collections, help law students master complex subject matter.

Major products, programs, and initiatives include:

- **Connected eBooks** are enhanced digital textbooks and study aids that come with a suite of online content and learning tools designed to maximize student success. Designed in collaboration with hundreds of faculty and students, the Connected eBook is a significant leap forward in the legal education learning tools available to students.

- **Connected Quizzing** is an easy-to-use formative assessment tool that tests law students' understanding and provides timely feedback to improve learning outcomes. Delivered through CasebookConnect.com, the learning platform already used by students to access their Aspen casebooks, Connected Quizzing is simple to implement and integrates seamlessly with law school course curricula.

- **PracticePerfect** is a visually engaging, interactive study aid to explain commonly encountered legal doctrines through easy-to-understand animated videos, illustrative examples, and numerous practice questions. Developed by a team of experts, PracticePerfect is the ideal study companion for today's law students.

- The **Aspen Learning Library** enables law schools to provide their students with access to the most popular study aids on the market across all of their courses. Available through an annual subscription, the online library consists of study aids in e-book, audio, and video formats with full text search, note-taking, and highlighting capabilities.

- Aspen's **Digital Bookshelf** is an institutional-level online education bookshelf, consolidating everything students and professors need to ensure success. This program ensures that every student has access to affordable course materials from day one.

- **Leading Edge** is a community centered on thinking differently about legal education and putting those thoughts into actionable strategies. At the core of the program is the Leading Edge Conference, an annual gathering of legal education thought leaders looking to pool ideas and identify promising directions of exploration.

Format for the Casenote® Legal Brief

Nature of Case: This section identifies the form of action (e.g., breach of contract, negligence, battery), the type of proceeding (e.g., demurrer, appeal from trial court's jury instructions) or the relief sought (e.g., damages, injunction, criminal sanctions).

Fact Summary: This is included to refresh your memory and can be used as a quick reminder of the facts.

Rule of Law: Summarizes the general principle of law that the case illustrates. It may be used for instant recall of the court's holding and for classroom discussion or home review.

Facts: This section contains all relevant facts of the case, including the contentions of the parties and the lower court holdings. It is written in a logical order to give you a clear understanding of the case. The plaintiff and defendant are identified by their proper names throughout and are always labeled with a (P) or (D).

Issue: The issue is a concise question that brings out the essence of the opinion as it relates to the section of the casebook in which the case appears. Both substantive and procedural issues are included if relevant to the decision.

Palsgraf v. Long Island R.R. Co.

Injured bystander (P) v. Railroad company (D)

N.Y. Ct. App., 248 N.Y. 339, 162 N.E. 99 (1928).

NATURE OF CASE: Appeal from judgment affirming verdict for plaintiff seeking damages for personal injury.

FACT SUMMARY: **Helen Palsgraf (P) was injured on R.R.'s (D) train platform when R.R.'s (D) guard helped a passenger aboard a moving train, causing his package to fall on the tracks. The package contained fireworks which exploded, creating a shock that tipped a scale onto Palsgraf (P).**

RULE OF LAW
The risk reasonably to be perceived defines the duty to be obeyed.

FACTS: Helen Palsgraf (P) purchased a ticket to Rockaway Beach from R.R. (D) and was waiting on the train platform. As she waited, two men ran to catch a train that was pulling out from the platform. The first man jumped aboard, but the second man, who appeared as if he might fall, was helped aboard by the guard on the train who had kept the door open so they could jump aboard. A guard on the platform also helped by pushing him onto the train. The man was carrying a package wrapped in newspaper. In the process, the man dropped his package, which fell on the tracks. The package contained fireworks and exploded. The shock of the explosion was apparently of great enough strength to tip over some scales at the other end of the platform, which fell on Palsgraf (P) and injured her. A jury awarded her damages, and R.R. (D) appealed.

ISSUE: Does the risk reasonably to be perceived define the duty to be obeyed?

HOLDING AND DECISION: (Cardozo, C.J.) Yes. The risk reasonably to be perceived defines the duty to be obeyed. If there is no foreseeable hazard to the injured party as the result of a seemingly innocent act, the act does not become a tort because it happened to be a wrong as to another. If the wrong was not willful, the plaintiff must show that the act as to her had such great and apparent possibilities of danger as to entitle her to protection. Negligence in the abstract is not enough upon which to base liability. Negligence is a relative concept, evolving out of the common law doctrine of trespass on the case. To establish liability, the defendant must owe a legal duty of reasonable care to the injured party. A cause of action in tort will lie where harm, though unintended, could have been averted or avoided by observance of such a duty. The scope of the duty is limited by the range of danger that a reasonable person could foresee. In this case, there was nothing to suggest from the appearance of the parcel or otherwise that the parcel contained fireworks. The guard could not reasonably have had any warning of a threat to Palsgraf (P), and R.R. (D) therefore cannot be held liable. Judgment is reversed in favor of R.R. (D).

DISSENT: (Andrews, J.) The concept that there is no negligence unless R.R. (D) owes a legal duty to take care as to Palsgraf (P) herself is too narrow. Everyone owes to the world at large the duty of refraining from those acts that may unreasonably threaten the safety of others. If the guard's action was negligent as to those nearby, it was also negligent as to those outside what might be termed the "danger zone." For Palsgraf (P) to recover, R.R.'s (D) negligence must have been the proximate cause of her injury, a question of fact for the jury.

ANALYSIS

The majority defined the limit of the defendant's liability in terms of the danger that a reasonable person in defendant's situation would have perceived. The dissent argued that the limitation should not be placed on liability, but rather on damages. Judge Andrews suggested that only injuries that would not have happened but for R.R.'s (D) negligence should be compensable. Both the majority and dissent recognized the policy-driven need to limit liability for negligent acts, seeking, in the words of Judge Andrews, to define a framework "that will be practical and in keeping with the general understanding of mankind." The Restatement (Second) of Torts has accepted Judge Cardozo's view.

Quicknotes

FORESEEABILITY A reasonable expectation that change is the probable result of certain acts or omissions.

NEGLIGENCE Conduct falling below the standard of care that a reasonable person would demonstrate under similar conditions.

PROXIMATE CAUSE The natural sequence of events without which an injury would not have been sustained.

Party ID: Quick identification of the relationship between the parties.

Concurrence/Dissent: All concurrences and dissents are briefed whenever they are included by the casebook author.

Analysis: This last paragraph gives you a broad understanding of where the case "fits in" with other cases in the section of the book and with the entire course. It is a hornbook-style discussion indicating whether the case is a majority or minority opinion and comparing the principal case with other cases in the casebook. It may also provide analysis from restatements, uniform codes, and law review articles.

Holding and Decision: This section offers a clear and in-depth discussion of the rule of the case and the court's rationale. It is written in easy-to-understand language and answers the issue presented by applying the law to the facts of the case. When relevant, it includes a thorough discussion of the exceptions to the case as listed by the court, any major cites to the other cases on point, and the names of the judges who wrote the decisions.

Quicknotes: Conveniently defines legal terms found in the case.

Note to Students

Aspen Publishing is proud to offer *Casenote® Legal Briefs*—continuing thirty years of publishing America's best-selling legal briefs.

Casenote® Legal Briefs are designed to help you save time when briefing assigned cases. Organized under convenient headings, they show you how to abstract the basic facts and holdings from the text of the actual opinions handed down by the courts. Used as part of a rigorous study regimen, they can help you spend more time analyzing and critiquing points of law than on copying bits and pieces of judicial opinions into your notebook or outline.

Casenote® Legal Briefs should never be used as a substitute for assigned casebook readings. They work best when read as a follow-up to reviewing the underlying opinions themselves. Students who try to avoid reading and digesting the judicial opinions in their casebooks or online sources will end up shortchanging themselves in the long run. The ability to absorb, critique, and restate the dynamic and complex elements of case law decisions is crucial to your success in law school and beyond. It cannot be developed vicariously.

In addition to *Casenote® Legal Briefs*, Aspen Publishing offers the following study aids:

- *Casenote® Legal Briefs*
- *Emanuel® Law Outlines*
- Emanuel® *Law in a Flash* Flash Cards
- Emanuel® *CrunchTime® Series*

Each of these series is designed to provide you with easy-to-understand explanations of complex points of law. Each volume offers guidance on the principles of legal analysis and, consulted regularly, will hone your ability to spot relevant issues. We have titles that will help you prepare for class, prepare for your exams, and enhance your general comprehension of the law along the way.

To find out more about our law school tools for success, visit us at *www.AspenPublishing.com* or e-mail us at *customer.service@aspenpublishing.com*. We'll be happy to assist you.

How to Brief a Case

A. Decide on a Format and Stick to It

Structure is essential to a good brief. It enables you to arrange systematically the related parts that are scattered throughout most cases, thus making manageable and understandable what might otherwise seem to be an endless and unfathomable sea of information. There are, of course, an unlimited number of formats that can be utilized. However, it is best to find one that suits your needs and stick to it. Consistency breeds both efficiency and the security that when called upon you will know where to look in your brief for the information you are asked to give.

Any format, as long as it presents the essential elements of a case in an organized fashion, can be used. Experience, however, has led *Casenote® Legal Briefs* to develop and utilize the following format because of its logical flow and universal applicability.

NATURE OF CASE: This is a brief statement of the legal character and procedural status of the case (e.g., "Appeal of a burglary conviction").

There are many different alternatives open to a litigant dissatisfied with a court ruling. The key to determining which one has been used is to discover *who is asking this court for what.*

This first entry in the brief should be kept as *short as possible.* Use the court's terminology if you understand it. But since jurisdictions vary as to the titles of pleadings, the best entry is the one that addresses who wants what in this proceeding, not the one that sounds most like the court's language.

RULE OF LAW: A statement of the general principle of law that the case illustrates (e.g., "An acceptance that varies any term of the offer is considered a rejection and counteroffer").

Determining the rule of law of a case is a procedure similar to determining the issue of the case. Avoid being fooled by red herrings; there may be a few rules of law mentioned in the case excerpt, but usually only one is *the* rule with which the casebook editor is concerned. The techniques used to locate the issue, described below, may also be utilized to find the rule of law. Generally, your best guide is simply the chapter heading. It is a clue to the point the casebook editor seeks to make and should be kept in mind when reading every case in the respective section.

FACTS: A synopsis of only the essential facts of the case, i.e., those bearing upon or leading up to the issue.

The facts entry should be a short statement of the events and transactions that led one party to initiate legal proceedings against another in the first place. While some cases conveniently state the salient facts at the beginning of the decision, in other instances they will have to be culled from hiding places throughout the text, even from concurring and dissenting opinions. Some of the "facts" will often be in dispute and should be so noted. Conflicting evidence may be briefly pointed up. "Hard" facts must be included. Both must be *relevant* in order to be listed in the facts entry. It is impossible to tell what is relevant until the entire case is read, as the ultimate determination of the rights and liabilities of the parties may turn on something buried deep in the opinion.

Generally, the facts entry should not be longer than three to five *short* sentences.

It is often helpful to identify the role played by a party in a given context. For example, in a construction contract case the identification of a party as the "contractor" or "builder" alleviates the need to tell that that party was the one who was supposed to have built the house.

It is always helpful, and a good general practice, to identify the "plaintiff" and the "defendant." This may seem elementary and uncomplicated, but, especially in view of the creative editing practiced by some casebook editors, it is sometimes a difficult or even impossible task. Bear in mind that the *party presently* seeking something from this court may not be the plaintiff, and that sometimes only the cross-claim of a defendant is treated in the excerpt. Confusing or misaligning the parties can ruin your analysis and understanding of the case.

ISSUE: A statement of the general legal question answered by or illustrated in the case. For clarity, the issue is best put in the form of a question capable of a "yes" or "no" answer. In reality, the issue is simply the Rule of Law put in the form of a question (e.g., "May an offer be accepted by performance?").

The major problem presented in discerning what is *the* issue in the case is that an opinion usually purports to raise and answer several questions. However, except for rare cases, only one such question is really the issue in the case. Collateral issues not necessary to the resolution of the matter in controversy are handled by the court by language known as *"obiter dictum"* or merely *"dictum."* While dicta may be included later in the brief, they have no place under the issue heading.

To find the issue, ask *who wants what* and then go on to ask *why did that party succeed or fail in getting it.* Once this is determined, the "why" should be turned into a question.

The complexity of the issues in the cases will vary, but in all cases a single-sentence question should sum up the issue. *In a few cases,* there will be two, or even more rarely, three issues of equal importance to the resolution of the case. Each should be expressed in a single-sentence question.

Since many issues are resolved by a court in coming to a final disposition of a case, the casebook editor will reproduce the portion of the opinion containing the issue or issues most relevant to the area of law under scrutiny. A noted law professor gave this advice: "Close the book; look at the title on the cover." Chances are, if it is Property, you need not concern yourself with whether, for example, the federal government's treatment of the plaintiff's land really raises a federal question sufficient to support jurisdiction on this ground in federal court.

The same rule applies to chapter headings designating sub-areas within the subjects. They tip you off as to what the text is designed to teach. The cases are arranged in a casebook to show a progression or development of the law, so that the preceding cases may also help.

It is also most important to remember to *read the notes and questions* at the end of a case to determine what the editors wanted you to have gleaned from it.

HOLDING AND DECISION: This section should succinctly explain the rationale of the court in arriving at its decision. In capsulizing the "reasoning" of the court, it should always include an application of the general rule or rules of law to the specific facts of the case. Hidden justifications come to light in this entry: the reasons for the state of the law, the public policies, the biases and prejudices, those considerations that influence the justices' thinking and, ultimately, the outcome of the case. At the end, there should be a short indication of thedisposition or procedural resolution of the case (e.g., "Decision of the trial court for Mr. Smith (P) reversed").

The foregoing format is designed to help you "digest" the reams of case material with which you will be faced in your law school career. Once mastered by practice, it will place at your fingertips the information the authors of your casebooks have sought to impart to you in case-by-case illustration and analysis.

B. Be as Economical as Possible in Briefing Cases

Once armed with a format that encourages succinctness, it is as important to be economical with regard to the time spent on the actual reading of the case as it is to be economical in the writing of the brief itself. This does not mean "skimming" a case. Rather, it means reading the case with an "eye" trained to recognize into which "section" of your brief a particular passage or line fits and having a system for quickly and precisely marking the case so that the passages fitting any one particular part of the brief can be easily identified and brought together in a concise and accurate manner when the brief is actually written.

It is of no use to simply repeat everything in the opinion of the court; record only enough information to trigger your recollection of what the court said. Nevertheless, an accurate statement of the "law of the case," i.e., the legal principle applied to the facts, is absolutely essential to class preparation and to learning the law under the case method.

To that end, it is important to develop a "shorthand" that you can use to make marginal notations. These notations will tell you at a glance in which section of the brief you will be placing that particular passage or portion of the opinion.

Some students prefer to underline all the salient portions of the opinion (with a pencil or colored underliner marker), making marginal notations as they go along. Others prefer the color-coded method of underlining, utilizing different colors of markers to underline the salient portions of the case, each separate color being used to represent a different section of the brief. For example, blue underlining could be used for passages relating to the rule of law, yellow for those relating to the issue, and green for those relating to the holding and decision, etc. While it has its advocates, thecolor-coded method can be confusing and time-consuming (all that time spent on changing colored markers). Furthermore, it can interfere with the continuity and concentration many students deem essential to the reading of a case for maximum comprehension. In the end, however, it is a matter of personal preference and style. Just remember, whatever method you use, underlining must be used sparingly or its value is lost.

If you take the marginal notation route, an efficient and easy method is to go along underlining the key portions of the case and placing in the margin alongside them the following "markers" to indicate where a particular passage or line "belongs" in the brief you will write:

N	(NATURE OF CASE)
RL	(RULE OF LAW)
I	(ISSUE)
HL	(HOLDING AND DECISION, relates to the RULE OF LAW behind the decision)
HR	(HOLDING AND DECISION, gives the RATIONALE or reasoning behind the decision)
HA	(HOLDING AND DECISION, applies the general principle(s) of law to the facts of the case to arrive at the decision)

Remember that a particular passage may well contain information necessary to more than one part of your brief, in which case you simply note that in the margin. If you are using the color-coded underlining method instead of marginal notation, simply make asterisks or checks in the margin next to the passage in question in the colors that indicate the additional sections of the brief where it might be utilized.

The economy of utilizing "shorthand" in marking cases for briefing can be maintained in the actual brief writing process itself by utilizing "law student shorthand" within the brief. There are many commonly used words and phrases for which abbreviations can be substituted in your briefs (and in your class notes also). You can develop abbreviations that are personal to you and which will save you a lot of time. A reference list of briefing abbreviations can be found on page x of this book.

C. Use Both the Briefing Process and the Brief as a Learning Tool

Now that you have a format and the tools for briefing cases efficiently, the most important thing is to make the time spent in briefing profitable to you and to make the most advantageous use of the briefs you create. Of course, the briefs are invaluable for classroom reference when you are called upon to explain or analyze a particular case. However, they are also useful in reviewing for exams. A quick glance at the fact summary should bring the case to mind, and a rereading of the rule of law should enable you to go over the underlying legal concept in your mind, how it was applied in that particular case, and how it might apply in other factual settings.

As to the value to be derived from engaging in the briefing process itself, there is an immediate benefit that arises from being forced to sift through the essential facts and reasoning from the court's opinion and to succinctly express them in your own words in your brief. The process ensures that you understand the case and the point that it illustrates, and that means you will be ready to absorb further analysis and information brought forth in class. It also ensures you will have something to say when called upon in class. The briefing process helps develop a mental agility for getting to the *gist* of a case and for identifying, expounding on, and applying the legal concepts and issues found there. The briefing process is the mental process on which you must rely in taking law school examinations; it is also the mental process upon which lawyers rely in serving their clients and in making a living.

Abbreviations for Briefs

acceptance	acp
affirmed	aff
answer	ans
assumption of risk	a/r
attorney	atty
beyond a reasonable doubt	b/r/d
bona fide purchaser	BFP
breach of contract	br/k
cause of action	c/a
common law	c/l
Constitution	Con
constitutional	con
contract	K
contributory negligence	c/n
cross	x
cross-complaint	x/c
cross-examination	x/ex
cruel and unusual punishment	c/u/p
defendant	D
dismissed	dis
double jeopardy	d/j
due process	d/p
equal protection	e/p
equity	eq
evidence	ev
exclude	exc
exclusionary rule	exc/r
felony	f/n
freedom of speech	f/s
good faith	g/f
habeas corpus	h/c
hearsay	hr
husband	H
injunction	inj
in loco parentis	ILP
inter vivos	I/v
joint tenancy	j/t
judgment	judgt
jurisdiction	jur
last clear chance	LCC
long-arm statute	LAS
majority view	maj
meeting of minds	MOM
minority view	min
Miranda rule	Mir/r
Miranda warnings	Mir/w
negligence	neg
notice	ntc
nuisance	nus
obligation	ob
obscene	obs
offer	O
offeree	OE
offeror	OR
ordinance	ord
pain and suffering	p/s
parol evidence	p/e
plaintiff	P
prima facie	p/f
probable cause	p/c
proximate cause	px/c
real property	r/p
reasonable doubt	r/d
reasonable man	r/m
rebuttable presumption	rb/p
remanded	rem
res ipsa loquitur	RIL
respondeat superior	r/s
Restatement	RS
reversed	rev
Rule Against Perpetuities	RAP
search and seizure	s/s
search warrant	s/w
self-defense	s/d
specific performance	s/p
statute	S
statute of frauds	S/F
statute of limitations	S/L
summary judgment	s/j
tenancy at will	t/w
tenancy in common	t/c
tenant	t
third party	TP
third party beneficiary	TPB
transferred intent	TI
unconscionable	uncon
unconstitutional	unconst
undue influence	u/e
Uniform Commercial Code	UCC
unilateral	uni
vendee	VE
vendor	VR
versus	v
void for vagueness	VFV
weight of authority	w/a
weight of the evidence	w/e
wife	W
with	w/
within	w/i
without	w/o
without prejudice	w/o/p
wrongful death	wr/d

Table of Cases

CHAPTER 1

The Bank of the United States: A Case Study

Quick Reference Rules of Law

McCulloch v. Maryland [The First Question]

Bank cashier (D) v. State (P)

17 U.S. (4 Wheat.) 316 (1819)

NATURE OF CASE: Appeal by writ of error from state's highest court's judgment that upheld the state's taxation of a bank chartered by the federal government.

FACT SUMMARY: McCulloch (D), the cashier of a Maryland (P) branch of the Second Bank of the United States (U.S. Bank), which was chartered by the United States government, refused to pay a tax imposed on the U.S. Bank by Maryland (P), and challenged the validity of the tax and the penalty for not paying it after Maryland's (P) courts upheld the tax and penalty.

RULE OF LAW

Congress has the power to incorporate a bank as an exercise of its implied powers under the Necessary and Proper Clause, notwithstanding that such power is not expressly enumerated in the Constitution.

FACTS: McCulloch (D), the cashier of a Maryland (P) branch of the Second Bank of the United States (U.S. Bank), which was chartered by the United States government, refused to pay a $15,000 tax imposed by Maryland (P) on banks not chartered by it. The law was acknowledged to have targeted the U.S. Bank in attempt to eliminate competition for state-chartered banks, as the U.S. Bank was the only bank in Maryland (P) not chartered by its legislature. Maryland (P) successfully sued McCulloch (D) in its courts for payment of the penalty for failure to pay the tax, and McCulloch (D) challenged the penalty and validity of the tax, by a writ of error, in the United States Supreme Court.

ISSUE: Does Congress have the power to incorporate a bank as an exercise of its implied powers under the Necessary and Proper Clause, notwithstanding that such power is not expressly enumerated in the Constitution?

HOLDING AND DECISION: (Marshall, C.J.) Yes. Congress has the power to incorporate a bank as an exercise of its powers under the Necessary and Proper Clause, notwithstanding that such power is not expressly enumerated in the Constitution. Although the Constitution technically was enacted by the states, who convened the Constitutional Convention, that does not mean, as argued by Maryland (P), that the states have superior sovereignty over the Constitution. Instead, since the states were acting on behalf of their citizens, the federal government is a creation of the people, and is a government of, and for, those people—not the states. Therefore, although the federal government's powers are limited by the Constitution, the Constitution is supreme over the laws of the states. The Constitution itself says so when it says that it is the "supreme law of the land," and, accordingly, any state constitutions or laws that conflict with the Union's laws or Constitution must cede to the federal laws. There is nothing in the Constitution that excludes incidental or implied powers. However, given that a constitution is effectively a broad outline of powers, it may be inferred that it grants the powers to execute the enumerated powers. It does not require that everything be granted expressly and minutely described. To have so required would have entirely changed the character of the Constitution and made it into a lengthy and complex legal code beyond the scope of comprehension of most citizens. The enumerated powers given to the government imply the ordinary means of execution. Although the Constitution does not expressly grant Congress the power to incorporate a bank, the power of creating a corporation may be implied as a sovereign power incidental to other powers or used as a means of executing them. The power of creating a corporation such as a bank is never used for its own sake, but for purpose of effecting something else. There is no good reason, then, why such a power may not be used as a means of executing those powers that are expressly granted. But reason alone is not all that supports this proposition; the Necessary and Proper Clause gives Congress the power to make "all laws which shall be necessary and proper for carrying into execution" the powers vested by the Constitution in the U.S. government. Maryland (P) argues that the word "necessary" limits Congress's power to passing laws for the execution of the granted powers to those that are indispensable. However, in common usage "necessary" frequently means convenient, useful, and essential. Considering the word's common usage, its usage in another part of the Constitution (art. 1, § 10), and its inclusion among the powers given to Congress, rather than among the limitations imposed upon Congress, it cannot be held to restrain Congress. To hold otherwise, and impose the extremely narrow construction proposed by Maryland (P), would have the effect of vitiating many federal government functions, such as those of the court system, or the postal system, and would abridge, and almost annihilate, Congress's useful and necessary right to select the means to perform the duties imposed on it so as to benefit the people. As long as the end is legitimate and within the scope of the Constitution, any means that are appropriate (or "proper" as the Constitution indicates), which are plainly adapted to that end, and which are not prohibited by the Constitution, but are consistent with its

Continued on next page.

spirit, are constitutional. The Constitution did not need to expressly mention corporations, since they are vehicles to achieving different ends. For example, the territorial government is a corporation, but its constitutionality is not questioned. Similarly, a bank is a convenient, useful, and essential instrument for handling national finances, and is necessary for carrying out Congress's enumerated powers. Moreover, there is nothing in the Constitution that would make the federal government dependent on the state governments, or on any means not within its control. Therefore, Congress in its discretion may choose a federal bank over a state bank for achieving its legislative ends. Hence, it is within Congress's power to enact a law incorporating a U.S. bank. [Reversed.]

ANALYSIS

Federalism is the basis of the Constitution's response to the problem of governing large geographical areas with diverse local needs. The success of federalism depends upon maintaining the balance between the need for the supremacy and sovereignty of the federal government and the interest in maintaining independent state government and curtailing national intrusion into intrastate affairs. The U.S. federal structure allocates powers between the nation and the states by enumerating the powers delegated to the national government and acknowledging the retention by the states of the remainder. The Articles of Confederation followed a similar scheme. The Constitution expanded the enumerated national powers to remedy weaknesses of the Articles. The move from the Articles to the Constitution was a shift from a central government with fewer powers to one with more powers.

Quicknotes

ENUMERATED POWERS Those powers expressly delegated by the United States Constitution to a particular branch of government.

FEDERALISM A scheme of government whereby the power to govern is divided between a central and localized governments.

IMPLIED POWERS Powers impliedly delegated to the various branches of government that, while not expressly stated in the United States Constitution, are necessary to effectuate the enumerated powers.

NECESSARY AND PROPER CLAUSE Article I, § 8 of the Constitution; it enables Congress to make all laws that may be "necessary and proper" to execute its other, enumerated powers.

McCulloch v. Maryland [The Second Question]

Bank cashier (D) v. State (P)

17 U.S. (4 Wheat.) 316 (1819)

NATURE OF CASE: Appeal by writ of error from state's highest court's judgment that upheld the state's taxation of a bank chartered by the federal government.

FACT SUMMARY: McCulloch (D), the cashier of a Maryland (P) branch of the U.S. Bank, which was chartered by the United States government, refused to pay a tax imposed on the U.S. Bank by Maryland (P), and challenged the validity of the tax and the penalty for not paying it after Maryland's (P) courts upheld the tax and penalty.

RULE OF LAW

A state may not constitutionally tax an instrumentality of the federal government used in the execution of its powers.

FACTS: McCulloch (D), the cashier of a Maryland (P) branch of the U.S. Bank, which was chartered by the United States government, refused to pay a $15,000 tax imposed by Maryland (P) on banks not chartered by it. The law was acknowledged to have targeted the U.S. Bank in attempt to eliminate competition for state-chartered banks, as the U.S. Bank was the only bank in Maryland (P) not chartered by its legislature. Maryland (P) successfully sued McCulloch (D) in its courts for payment of the penalty for failure to pay the tax, and McCulloch (D) challenged the penalty and validity of the tax, by a writ of error, in the United States Supreme Court.

ISSUE: May a state constitutionally tax an instrumentality of the federal government used in the execution of its powers?

HOLDING AND DECISION: (Marshall, C.J.) No. A state may not constitutionally tax an instrumentality of the federal government used in the execution of its powers. The federal Constitution and the laws made pursuant to it are the supreme law of the land, and, even though the states have sovereign powers that they exercise concurrently with the federal government, such as the taxing power, the Constitution's sweep is sufficiently broad to remove those powers from the states in certain defined circumstances where the states' exercise of those powers would conflict with those of the Union and impede the federal government. The federal powers, being superior to those of the states, cannot be subordinated to the states' powers, lest the federal government's powers be destroyed. Maryland (P) is incorrect in its assertion that the states may exercise their sovereign powers on instrumentalities of the federal government. Although a state's powers extend to everything that exists by its own authority, or is introduced by its permission, that power is limited to the powers that its own constituents have to give it. The Constitution derives its authority from the people of many states, not from the states themselves. Thus, any attempt to extend state powers over federal instrumentalities would be a usurpation of powers that the people of a single state cannot give. Citizens of one state would not trust citizens of another state to control any aspect of their government, and, similarly, there is no reason to suppose that people of any one state would be willing to trust those of another with a power to control the operations of a government to which they have confided their most important and most valuable interests. Citizens of all states are represented in Congress alone, so that Congress alone can be trusted by the people with the power of controlling measures that concern all, in the confidence that it will not be abused. Here, Maryland's (P) statute taxes the operation of the U.S. Bank, a bank properly created within Congress's power. The power to tax involves the power to destroy. Here it is in opposition to the supreme congressional power to create a bank. If the states may tax one instrument, employed by the government in the execution of its powers, they may tax any and every other instrument. This was not intended by the American people. They did not design to make their government dependent on the states. If the states could tax federal instrumentalities, the Constitution's declaration that it is the supreme law of the land would be rendered a meaningless nullity. When a state taxes an instrument created by the Union, it acts upon an institution created by people over whom it claims no control; it acts upon the measures of a government created by others as well as its own citizens, for the benefit of others in common with themselves. Such an attempted extension of a state's power, however, is impermissible. The states have no power, by taxation or otherwise, to impede, burden, or in any manner control the operations of constitutional laws enacted by Congress. The Maryland (P) statute is, therefore, unconstitutional and void. [Reversed.]

ANALYSIS

McCulloch is a landmark decision that firmly established not only the supremacy of the Constitution and Congress's powers under it, but also established that constitutional construction by the Court extended beyond the mere words of the Constitution. Although the decision strongly upheld the principle of

Continued on next page.

intergovernmental tax immunities, it did not resolve all issues surrounding the boundaries of those immunities, or the ability of states to tax or to regulate federal instrumentalities, and those issues are still being litigated to this day.

Quicknotes

ENUMERATED POWERS Those powers expressly delegated by the United States Constitution to a particular branch of government.

FEDERALISM A scheme of government whereby the power to govern is divided between a central and localized governments.

IMPLIED POWERS Powers impliedly delegated to the various branches of government that, while not expressly stated in the United States Constitution, are necessary to effectuate the enumerated powers.

NECESSARY AND PROPER CLAUSE Article I, § 8 of the Constitution; it enables Congress to make all laws that may be "necessary and proper" to execute its other, enumerated powers.

CHAPTER 2

The Constitution in the Early Republic

Quick Reference Rules of Law

Chisholm v. Georgia

Estate's executor from one state (P) v. A different state (D)

2 U.S. (2 Dall.) 419 (1793)

NATURE OF CASE: Action to determine whether a state has sovereign immunity from suit brought by a citizen of a different state. [The procedural posture of the case is not presented in the casebook extract.]

FACT SUMMARY: The State of Georgia (D) claimed that it had sovereign immunity from a suit brought by Chisholm (P), a citizen of South Carolina, to enforce a debt against Georgia (D).

RULE OF LAW

Under the Constitution, a state is subject to suit by a citizen of a different state notwithstanding that the state has not waived its sovereign immunity.

FACTS: During the Revolutionary War, Farquhar, a South Carolina citizen, had supplied the State of Georgia (D) with goods. Chisholm (P), the executor of Farquhar's estate, brought suit in the United States Supreme Court to enforce payment of the resulting debt owed to the estate by Georgia (D). Georgia (D), contending that it had sovereign immunity, refused to appear before the Court.

ISSUE: Under the Constitution, is a state subject to suit by a citizen of a different state notwithstanding that the state has not waived its sovereign immunity?

HOLDING AND DECISION: (Jay, C.J.) Yes. Under the Constitution, a state is subject to suit by a citizen of a different state notwithstanding that the state has not waived its sovereign immunity. Article III provides that "The Judicial Power shall extend to . . . Controversies . . . between a State and Citizens of another State," thus making explicit that a state such as Georgia (D) may be sued by a citizen, such as Chisholm (P), from a different state. The sovereignty that flowed from the British monarchy was eradicated by the Revolution. American citizens are now their own sovereigns, albeit sovereigns without subjects, and they have made it their will that the states are bound by the Constitution. All the country's citizens are equal when it comes to civil rights, so that an American citizen can sue a state, which is at heart a collection of other American citizens. This raises the question of whether a citizen may sue the United States—which, is also a collection of all its citizens—but this question does not have to be answered here. What can be said regarding that question is that when a citizen sues a state or another citizen, the national court is supported by the executive branch, but such support is lacking when a citizen sues the United States.

HOLDING AND DECISION: (Wilson, J.) Yes. Under the Constitution, a state is subject to suit by a citizen of a different state notwithstanding that the state has not waived its sovereign immunity. Just as a free person may bind himself to laws and the jurisdiction of courts established by those laws; so too, a state can bind itself, since a state is an aggregation of free persons. A dishonest state dishonors its contracts and is subject to the courts' jurisdictions; it cannot assert "sovereignty" to avoid its obligations. The Constitution does not recognize "sovereigns." Under the Constitution, there are citizens, including the citizens of Georgia, who, for purposes of forming the United States, have reserved to themselves supreme powers. Because such powers reside in the people, not in the states per se, Georgia cannot be a sovereign state under the Constitution. To effect the purposes of the Constitution, the people vested executive, legislative, and judicial powers through the Constitution, and those vested powers can bind the states. This conclusion can also be deduced from the Constitution's preamble and structure. One of the purposes of the Constitution was to form a more perfect union than the union that previously held the 13 states together. The previous union could not enforce its legislative power over the states. Accordingly, the Constitution established executive and judicial powers for the purpose of enforcing such legislative powers. Another listed purpose of the Constitution was to establish justice. From this, it can be deduced that there is to be a judicial authority, and that such authority can be exercised over the states, especially since the Constitution also provides that the states shall not pass any laws that impair contractual obligations. This provision would be meaningless if a state could pass a law impairing its contractual obligations without having to answer to a controlling judicial power. Finally, and more persuasively than these deductions, the Constitution plainly mandates that "The judicial power of the United States shall extend to controversies, between a state and citizens of another state."

DISSENT: (Iredell, J.) The common law, carried over from England, remains the basic law of each of the states. Also, the states have not given up their sovereignty to the extent they have reserved it and not given it up to the United States. Thus, the states' residual sovereignty means that they possess the same common-law immunity from suit as enjoyed by the British monarchy. Because the Crown could not be sued, even upon a debt it itself had assumed, except by its permission, so the states cannot be sued unless they consent to be sued.

Continued on next page.

ANALYSIS

The Eleventh Amendment, which was the first Constitutional amendment adopted after the Bill of Rights, and which gave states sovereign immunity from suits by citizens of other states and foreign nations, was a direct response to the Supreme Court's decision in *Chisholm.*

Quicknotes

COMMON LAW A body of law developed through the judicial decisions of the courts as opposed to the legislative process.

ELEVENTH AMENDMENT The Eleventh Amendment to the United States Constitution prohibits the extension of the judicial powers of the federal courts to suits brought against a state by citizens of another state, or of a foreign state, without the state's consent.

JURISDICTION The authority of a court to hear and declare judgment in respect to a particular matter.

SOVEREIGNTY The absolute power conferred to the state to govern and regulate all persons located and activities conducted therein.

Stuart v. Laird

Real property disputant (D) v. Real property disputant (P)

5 U.S. (1 Cranch) 299 (1803)

NATURE OF CASE: Appeal from judgment for plaintiff in land dispute, on the grounds, inter alia, that repeal of the Judiciary Act of 1801 was unconstitutional, that justices of the United States Supreme Court could not constitutionally ride circuit because they did not have specific commissions to do so, and that the Justices could not be required to ride circuit in the first instance.

FACT SUMMARY: After Laird (P) obtained a judgment against Stuart (D) in a land dispute, Stuart (D) argued that the judgment was unenforceable in a reconstituted circuit staffed by a United States Supreme Court justice, after repeal of the Judiciary Act of 1801, because it was unconstitutional to deprive the judges of the former circuits of their life tenure, because justices of the United States Supreme Court could not constitutionally ride circuit because they did not have specific commissions to do so, and because the justices could not be required to ride circuit in the first instance.

RULE OF LAW

(1) Congress may constitutionally cause an action to be transferred from one inferior federal judicial tribunal to another federal judicial tribunal.

(2) Members of the United States Supreme Court have authority to ride circuit without specific commissions as circuit judges.

FACTS: Laird (P) sued Stuart (D) in federal circuit court and obtained a judgment against Stuart (D). Thereafter, the Judiciary Act of 1801 was repealed and the circuit in which the judgment had been obtained was abolished and reconstituted with a new circuit staffed by a United States Supreme Court Justice riding circuit. The judges of the old circuit were let go. Stuart (D) appealed, arguing that the judgment was unenforceable because it was unconstitutional to deprive the judges of the former circuits of their life tenure, because justices of the United States Supreme Court could not constitutionally ride circuit because they did not have specific commissions to do so, and because the justices could not be required to ride circuit in the first instance. The United States Supreme Court heard the appeal.

ISSUE:

(1) May Congress constitutionally cause an action to be transferred from one inferior federal judicial tribunal to another federal judicial tribunal?

(2) Do members of the United States Supreme Court have authority to ride circuit without specific commissions as circuit judges?

HOLDING AND DECISION: (Paterson, J.)

(1) Yes. Congress may constitutionally cause an action to be transferred from one inferior federal judicial tribunal to another federal judicial tribunal. Under the Constitution, Congress has the authority to establish from time to time such inferior tribunals as it believes are proper; and to transfer an action from one such tribunal to another. Nothing in the Constitution prohibits or restrains the exercise of such legislative power.

(2) Yes. Members of the United States Supreme Court have authority to ride circuit without specific commissions as circuit judges. The "practice and acquiescence under it for a period of several years," since the beginning of the organization of the judiciary under the Constitution, has been that United States Supreme Court justices may ride circuit. That accepted practice is sufficient to resolve the issue without further analysis.

ANALYSIS

Justice Paterson avoided Stuart's (D) argument that repeal of the Judiciary Act of 1801 was unconstitutional because, under Article III of the Constitution, once circuit judges had received their commission, they had life tenure that could not constitutionally be abolished. His opinion thus effectively upheld the constitutionality of the repeal of the Judiciary Act and therefore acquiesced in (and gave constitutional blessing to) the Jeffersonian purge of the Federalist circuit judges. By so doing, the United States Supreme Court avoided a very serious political confrontation, and, arguably, thereby ensured the Court's continuation.

Quicknotes

ARTICLE III, CONSTITUTION OF THE UNITED STATES Limits federal judicial power to cases and controversies.

INTER ALIA Among other things.

Marbury v. Madison

Justice (P) v. Secretary of State (D)

5 U.S. (1 Cranch) 137 (1803)

NATURE OF CASE: Writ of mandamus to compel delivery of commission.

FACT SUMMARY: President Jefferson's Secretary of State, Madison (D), refused to deliver a commission granted to Marbury (P) by former President Adams.

RULE OF LAW

The United States Supreme Court has the power, implied from Article VI, § 2 of the Constitution, to review acts of Congress and, if they are found repugnant to the Constitution, to declare them void.

FACTS: On March 2, 1801, the outgoing President of the United States, John Adams, named 42 justices of the peace for the District of Columbia under the Organic Act passed the same day by Congress. William Marbury (P) was one of the justices named. The commissions of Marbury (P) and other named justices were signed by Adams on his last day in office, March 3, and signed and sealed by the Acting Secretary of State, John Marshall. However, the formal commissions were not delivered by the end of the day. The new President, Thomas Jefferson, treated those appointments that were not formalized by delivery of the papers of commission prior to Adams leaving office as a nullity. Marbury (P) and other affected colleagues brought this writ of mandamus to the United States Supreme Court to compel Jefferson's Secretary of State, James Madison (D), to deliver the commissions. John Marshall, the Chief Justice of the United States Supreme Court, delivered the opinion.

ISSUE: Does the Constitution give the United States Supreme Court the authority to review acts of Congress and declare them, if repugnant to the Constitution, to be void?

HOLDING AND DECISION: (Marshall, C.J.) Yes. The United States Supreme Court has the power, implied from Article VI, § 2 of the Constitution, to review acts of Congress and, if they are found repugnant to the Constitution, to declare them void. The government of the United States is a government of laws, not of men. The President, bound by these laws, is given certain political powers by the Constitution that he may use at his discretion. To aid him in his duties, he is authorized to appoint certain officers to carry out his orders. Their acts as officers are his acts and are never subject to examination by the courts. However, where these officers are given by law specific duties on which individual rights depend, any individual injured by breach of such duty may resort to his country's laws for a remedy. Here, Marbury (P) had a right to the commission, and Madison's (D) refusal to deliver it violated that right. The present case is clearly one for mandamus. However, should the Supreme Court be the court to issue it? The Judiciary Act of 1789 established and authorized United States courts to issue writs of mandamus to courts or persons holding office under U.S. authority. Secretary of State Madison (D) comes within the Act. If the Supreme Court is powerless to issue the writ of mandamus to him, it must be because the Act is unconstitutional. Article III of the Constitution provides that the Supreme Court shall have original jurisdiction in all cases affecting ambassadors, other public ministers and consuls, and where a state is a party. In all other cases, the Supreme Court shall have appellate jurisdiction. Marbury (P) urged that since Article III contains no restrictive words, the power to assign original jurisdiction to the courts remains in the legislature. But if Congress is allowed to distribute the original and appellate jurisdiction of the Supreme Court, as in the Judiciary Act, then the constitutional grant of Article III is form without substance. But no clause in the Constitution is presumed to be without effect. For the Court to issue a mandamus, it must be an exercise of appellate jurisdiction. The grant of appellate jurisdiction is the power to revise and correct proceedings already instituted; it does not create the cause. To issue a writ of mandamus ordering an executive officer to deliver a paper is to create the original action for that paper. This would be an unconstitutional exercise of original jurisdiction beyond the power of the court. It is the province and duty of the judicial department to say what the law is. And any law, including acts of the legislature, which is repugnant to the Constitution, is void. Rule discharged.

ANALYSIS

Judicial review of legislative acts was a controversial subject even before the Constitution was ratified and adopted. Alexander Hamilton upheld the theory of judicial review in the Federalist Papers. He argued that the judiciary, being the most vulnerable branch of the government, was designed to be an intermediary between the people and the legislature. Since the interpretation of laws was the responsibility of the judiciary, and the Constitution the supreme law of the land, any conflict between legislative acts and the Constitution were to be resolved by the court in favor of the Constitution. But

Continued on next page.

other authorities have attacked this position. In the case of *Eakin v. Raub*, 12 Serg. & Rawle 330 (1825), Justice Gibson dissented, stating that the judiciary's function was limited to interpreting the laws and should not extend to scrutinizing the legislature's authority to enact them. Judge Learned Hand felt that judicial review was inconsistent with the separation of powers. But history has supported the authority of judicial review of legislative acts. The United States survives on a tripartite government. Theoretically, the three branches should be strong enough to check and balance the others. To limit the judiciary to the passive task of interpretation would be to limit its strength in the tripartite structure. *Marbury* served to buttress the judiciary branch making it equal to the executive and legislative branches.

Quicknotes

APPELLATE JURISDICTION The power of a higher court to review the decisions of lower courts.

JUDICIAL REVIEW The authority of the courts to review decisions, actions, or omissions committed by another agency or branch of government.

ORIGINAL JURISDICTION The power of a court to hear an action upon its commencement.

WRIT OF MANDAMUS A court order issued commanding a public or private entity, or an official thereof, to perform a duty required by law.

Fletcher v. Peck

Grantee (P) v. Grantor (D)

10 U.S. (6 Cranch) 87 (1810)

NATURE OF CASE: Action alleging breach of warranty of title.

FACT SUMMARY: The land Peck (D) deeded to Fletcher (P) had been part of the Yazoo land-grant scandal, which saw the 1795 Georgia legislature practically give away state land to private companies and the 1796 Georgia legislature act in effort to rescind the grant.

RULE OF LAW

Once a state passes a law that is in its nature a contract, it cannot divest those absolute rights that have vested under that contract by repealing the law.

FACTS: The suit Fletcher (P) brought against Peck (D), alleging breach of warranty of title, came about because of the Yazoo land-grant scandal. Bribes had persuaded a majority of the 1795 Georgia legislature to pass a law allowing the cheap sale of 35,000,000 acres of state land to private companies. Much of the land had already been resold to innocent purchasers by the time the 1796 Georgia legislature passed an act attempting to rescind the 1795 conveyance. Fletcher (P) contended that the state was without power to rescind its contract with Peck (D), who held title pursuant to the land grant.

ISSUE: Can a state, having passed a law that is in its nature a contract, later divest those absolute rights that have vested under that contract by repealing the law?

HOLDING AND DECISION: (Marshall, C.J.) No. Once a state passes a law that is in its nature a contract, it cannot divest those absolute rights that have vested under that contract by repealing the law. This is so whether one looks to the general principles that are common to our free institutions or to the constitutional provision prohibiting states from passing any law impairing the obligation of contracts. A grant, in its own nature, amounts to an extinguishment of the right of the grantor and implies a contract not to reassert that right. A grant is a contract executed, the obligation of which still continues and cannot be impaired by action of the Georgia legislature. Thus, the statute it passed was ineffective to cancel the original conveyance to Peck's (D) predecessor in interest.

CONCURRENCE AND DISSENT: (Johnson, J.) I agree that a state does not possess the power to revoke its own grants, but I do not base this conclusion on the provision in the Constitution relative to laws impairing the "obligation" of contracts. A grant of conveyance by no means necessarily implies the continuance of an obligation, beyond the moment of executing it.

ANALYSIS

A complete understanding of the Contract Clause of Article I, § 10 of the Constitution requires some understanding of the historical factors that helped shape it. Just after the Revolutionary War, there was a depression. A number of states enacted debtor relief laws that altered existing contractual obligations or procedures creditors could use to enforce existing obligations. The Contract Clause was supposed to prevent this from happening again.

Quicknotes

CONTRACT An agreement pursuant to which a party agrees to act, or to forbear from acting, in exchange for performance on the part of the other party.

CONTRACT CLAUSE Article I, § 10 of the United States Constitution prohibiting states from passing any "law impairing the Obligation of Contracts."

RESCIND To cancel an agreement and return the parties to their positions prior to the formation of the contract.

Calder v. Bull

Heir (P) v. Beneficiary under will (D)

3 U.S. (3 Dall.) 386 (1798)

NATURE OF CASE: Appeal from probate decision.

FACT SUMMARY: Calder (P) claimed that a state legislature's resolution, setting aside a probate court's decree disapproving a will under which Bull (D) would have taken as beneficiary, was an unconstitutional ex post facto law. The Court ruled it was not, since it was not a criminal regulation. However, Justice Chase explored the question of whether the legislature could deprive a citizen of a vested property right.

RULE OF LAW

A state legislature may not deprive a citizen of a vested property right, even where such act is not expressly prohibited in the Constitution.

FACTS: A state probate court disapproved a will designating Bull (D) as beneficiary, thus allowing Calder (P) to inherit as decedent's heirs at law. In response, the state legislature passed a resolution setting aside the decree and granting a new hearing, at which the will was approved. The United States Supreme Court, on appeal, ruled that the legislative act was not an unconstitutional ex post facto law violative of Article I, § 10, which, the Court ruled, was limited to criminal legislation. However, Justice Chase explored the question of whether the legislature could deprive a citizen of a vested property right.

ISSUE: May a state legislature deprive a citizen of a vested property right, even where such act is not expressly prohibited in the Constitution?

HOLDING AND DECISION: (Chase, J.) No. A state legislature may not deprive a citizen of a vested property right, even where such act is not expressly prohibited in the Constitution. A state legislature's power is not unlimited, even if its powers are not expressly limited by the Constitution. The nature and ends of legislative power, necessarily limit its exercise. There are acts that neither the federal nor state legislatures can do without exceeding their authority. An act of the legislature contrary to the fundamental principles of the social compact on which our government is based, cannot be considered a rightful exercise of legislative authority. These principles include the protection of personal property. Thus, a law that takes property from A and gives it to B is beyond the legislature's power. While the legislature "may enjoin, permit, forbid, and punish; they may declare new crimes; and establish rules of conduct for all its citizens in future cases; they may command what is right, and prohibit what is wrong; but they cannot change the right of private property." To hold otherwise would be a "political heresy, altogether inadmissible in our free republican governments." Here, however, the probate court's decree did not vest a right in Calder (P), so that the legislature's act did not constitute a deprivation of a vested property right. Affirmed.

DISSENT: (Iredell, J.) Under a government of natural laws, such as that posited by Justice Chase, no court would have the power to declare a legislative act contrary to natural law. Instead, the federal and state constitutions define with precision the scope of legislative power and limit it within marked and settled boundaries. If a legislative act is contrary to a constitutional provision, then it is void. However, if a legislature passes a law that is within its constitutional power, the Court cannot hold that it is void, merely because in its opinion it violates natural justice. "The ideas of natural justice are regulated by no fixed standard: the ablest and the purest men have differed upon the subject; and all that the Court could properly say, in such an event, would be, that the Legislature (possessed of an equal right of opinion) had passed an act which, in the opinion of the judges, was inconsistent with the abstract principles of natural justice."

ANALYSIS

The vested rights doctrine, espoused by the Supreme Court in this case, originally developed and grew in the state courts. As this case points out, under that doctrine, not all rights were considered vested. For example, mere expectations were not considered vested. Only if an expectation became a title, whether legal or equitable, to the present or future enjoyment of property, or to enforcement of a demand, would it be considered vested. The doctrine assumed that the basic structure of entitlements was determined by common law as modified by legislation.

Quicknotes

CONTRACT CLAUSE Article I, § 10 of the United States Constitution prohibiting states from passing any "law impairing the Obligation of Contracts."

EX POST FACTO After the fact; a law that makes criminal activity or increases the punishment for a crime that occurred or eliminates a defense that was available to the defendant, prior to its passage.

VESTED RIGHT Rights in pension or other retirement benefits that are attained when the employee satisfies the minimum requirements necessary in order to be entitled to the receipt of such benefits in the future.

Gibbons v. Ogden

Navigator (D) v. Navigator (P)

22 U.S. (9 Wheat.) 1 (1824)

NATURE OF CASE: Action for an injunction to restrain violation of state-granted monopoly navigation right.

FACT SUMMARY: Ogden (P) was given exclusive navigation rights on a watercourse between New York and New Jersey by New York; Gibbons (D) claimed a right to navigate the same watercourse under a federal licensing statute.

RULE OF LAW
The Commerce Clause gives Congress plenary power to regulate interstate commerce, including navigation within one state that affects other states.

FACTS: Livingston and Fulton received from the New York state legislature a grant of the exclusive right to navigate the waters of the state by steamboats for a number of years. From this monopoly, Ogden (P) was assigned the right to navigate between New York City and New Jersey. Gibbons (D) was using in navigation between New York and New Jersey two steamboats licensed under the federal Coasting Act. Ogden (P) secured an injunction in a New York state court to prevent Gibbons (D) from violating his monopolistic right. Gibbons (D) appealed, arguing that the power of Congress to regulate commerce under the Commerce Clause, art. I, § 8, cl. 3 (which grants to Congress the power "to regulate commerce with the foreign nations and among the several states, and with the Indian tribes") is exclusive. Ogden (D) claimed that a concurrent power existed between the federal government and the states.

ISSUE: Does Congress have plenary power, under the Commerce Clause, to regulate commerce within one state that affects other states?

HOLDING AND DECISION: (Marshall, C.J.) Yes. There are three main questions that must be addressed in determining the scope of Congress's power over commerce. First, what does the term "commerce" include? Commerce, undoubtedly, is traffic, but it is something more—it is intercourse. It comprehends not only the buying and selling or the interchange of commodities but navigation as well. Second, to what extent does this power reach commerce within the separate states? While the completely internal commerce of a state is immune against federal regulation, the power of Congress does not stop at the jurisdictional lines of the several states. The power of Congress may be exercised within a state if a foreign voyage may commence or terminate at a port within that state. Congress, thus, may regulate all navigation that may affect more states than one. This power, like all others vested in Congress, is complete in itself, may be exercised to its utmost extent, and acknowledges no limitations other than are prescribed in the Constitution. Third, may the states severally exercise the same power within their respective jurisdictions? It has been suggested that the New York monopoly in question here is not inconsistent with Congress's power and thus should give way only to the extent required to give effect to the federal Coastal Act. However, unlike in instances of state taxation and inspection laws, when a state proceeds to regulate interstate commerce, it is exercising the very power that is granted to Congress and is doing the very thing Congress is authorized to do. In the examples of taxation and inspection, the state derives its power from some residual power that remains with the state; its exercise of power is on subjects acknowledged to be within its control. This Court, therefore, has the authority to inquire whether a particular state law collides with an act of Congress to regulate interstate commerce. Should a collision exist, it is immaterial that the state law was passed in virtue of a concurrent power. Accordingly, the grant of the monopolistic navigation right to Ogden (P), affecting as it did intercourse between New York and New Jersey, cannot stand in light of the federal Coastal Act. The injunction was improperly issued. Reversed.

CONCURRENCE: (Johnson, J.) The power to regulate commerce resides exclusively with Congress. This power finds its origin in history. The states, when they became independent, finally obtained the commerce power of which they had long been deprived. However, in their unrestricted exercise of such power, they began passing regulations that were destructive to the harmony of the states and fatal to their commercial interests abroad. This was the immediate cause that led to the formation of the Constitutional convention. Thus, in the Constitution, the "power to regulate commerce" means the power that the states previously enjoyed, i.e., a sovereign power over commerce. Such a power must by definition be exclusive. With regard to the coasting license even if the licensing act were repealed, the outcome would be the same—Congress has plenary power to regulate commerce. Certain state laws that regulate health and other non-commercial state interests, while seemingly regulating the same subject matter as Congress's regulation of commerce, are not regulations of commerce. Thus, the

Continued on next page.

laws are not concurrent, even though seemingly regulating the same matter. The guarded provisions of Article 1, § 10 support such a conclusion. Although inspection laws must combine municipal with commercial regulations, and the power of inspection is yielded to the states, it should not be inferred from this yielding that the power to regulate commerce resides in the states. Instead, Article 1, § 10 "negatives the exercise of that power to the States, as to the only two objects which could ever tempt them to assume the exercise of that power, to wit, the collection of a revenue from imposts and duties on imports and exports; or from a tonnage duty." As to imposts and duties, Congress's approval must be obtained before they may be imposed, and the monies must be paid to the federal government. Furthermore, all such laws may be modified or repealed by Congress.

ANALYSIS

Chief Justice Marshall's opinion in *Gibbons*, by failing to clearly hold that Congress had exclusive power over interstate commerce, left unsettled the important question of whether the states, in the absence of federal regulation, retained any concurrent power. One commentator has suggested that this omission was deliberate since Marshall may have felt that there conceivably might be some state regulation that would have merely had an incidental effect on interstate commerce. Also, by leaving the question open, Marshall hoped to enlarge the Unites States Supreme Court's jurisdiction in future cases to balance state and federal regulation.

Quicknotes

COMMERCE CLAUSE Article I, § 8, cl. 3 of the United States Constitution granting Congress the power to regulate commerce with foreign countries and between the states.

CONTRACT CLAUSE Article I, § 10 of the United States Constitution prohibiting states from passing any "law impairing the Obligation of Contracts."

INTERSTATE COMMERCE Commercial dealings between two parties located in different states or located in one state and accomplished through a point in another state or a foreign country; commercial dealings transacted between two states.

PLENARY POWER The complete authority of a court to hear and determine cases pertaining to specified subject matter or particular parties.

Arizona v. United States

State (D) v. Federal government (P)

132 S. Ct. 2492 (2012)

NATURE OF CASE: Appeal in action brought by the federal government to preempt a state's laws governing immigration. [The procedural posture of the case is not presented in the casebook excerpt.]

FACT SUMMARY: [The United States (P) sought to enjoin, on preemption grounds, several provisions of Arizona's (D) statute, S.B. 1070, which, inter alia, made failure to comply with federal alien-registration requirements a state misdemeanor (§ 3), made it a misdemeanor for an unauthorized alien to seek or engage in work in the state (§ 5(C)), and authorized state and local officers to arrest without a warrant a person believed to have committed any public offense that made the person removable from the United States (§ 6).]

RULE OF LAW

A state law will be preempted by federal law where, even though the state law does not directly conflict with federal law, the state law complements, or is an obstacle to, the regulatory system chosen by Congress in a field completely occupied by Congress.

FACTS: [The United States (P) sought to enjoin, on preemption grounds, several provisions of Arizona's (D) statute, S.B. 1070, which, inter alia, made failure to comply with federal alien-registration requirements a state misdemeanor (§ 3), made it a misdemeanor for an unauthorized alien to seek or engage in work in the state (§ 5(C)), and authorized state and local officers to arrest without a warrant a person believed to have committed any public offense that made the person removable from the United States (§ 6).]

ISSUE: Will a state law be preempted by federal law where, even though the state law does not directly conflict with federal law, the state law complements, or is an obstacle to, the regulatory system chosen by Congress in a field completely occupied by Congress?

HOLDING AND DECISION: (Kennedy, J.) Yes. A state law will be preempted by federal law where, even though the state law does not directly conflict with federal law, the state law complements, or is an obstacle to, the regulatory system chosen by Congress in a field completely occupied by Congress. The United States (P) has broad, undoubted power over the subject of immigration and the status of aliens, as immigration policy has nationwide impacts on trade, investment, tourism, diplomatic relations, and reciprocal treatment of U.S. citizens by other countries. As to § 3, which effectively adds a state-law penalty for conduct proscribed by federal law, the federal government has occupied the field of alien registration through its comprehensive alien registration regime. Where Congress occupies an entire field, as it has in the field of alien registration, even complementary or parallel state regulation is impermissible. Permitting Arizona to impose its own penalties for the federal offenses here would conflict with the careful framework Congress adopted. Accordingly, § 3 is preempted. As to § 5(C), Arizona (D) enacts a criminal prohibition where no federal counterpart exists. The Immigration Reform and Control Act of 1986's (IRCA's) express preemption provision, which in most instances bars states from imposing penalties on employers of unauthorized aliens, is silent about whether additional penalties may be imposed against the employees themselves. However, the existence of this express preemption provision does not bar the ordinary working of conflict preemption principles. One of these principles is the well-settled proposition that a state law is preempted where it "stands as an obstacle to the accomplishment and execution of the full purposes and objectives of Congress." Section 5(C) would interfere with the careful balance struck by Congress with respect to unauthorized employment of aliens. Although § 5(C) attempts to achieve one of the same goals as federal law—the deterrence of unlawful employment—it involves a conflict in the method of enforcement. Such a conflict in technique can be fully as disruptive to the system Congress enacted as conflict in overt policy. Because it is clear Congress determined that it would be inappropriate to impose criminal penalties on aliens who seek or engage in unauthorized employment, a state law to the contrary is an obstacle to the regulatory system Congress chose. Accordingly, § 5(C) is preempted. By authorizing state and local officers to make warrantless arrests of certain aliens suspected of being removable, § 6 too creates an obstacle to federal law. Section 6 attempts to provide state officers with even greater arrest authority on basis of possible removability than Congress has given to trained federal immigration officers, and the officers could exercise such authority with no instruction from the federal government. This is not the system Congress created. Federal law specifies limited circumstances in which state officers may perform an immigration officer's functions. By authorizing state officers to decide whether an alien should be detained for being removable, § 6 violates the principle that the removal process is entrusted to the discretion of the federal government. A decision on removability requires a determination whether it is

Continued on next page.

appropriate to allow a foreign national to continue living in the United States; such decisions implicate foreign relations and must be made with one voice.

ANALYSIS

The three types of preemption recognized by the Court in this case, and in the Court's precedents, are: (1) Express preemption, where the federal statute expressly refers to preemption and identifies the state laws supplanted by the federal statute. This form of preemption was not at issue in this case. (2) Field preemption, where federal regulation in the area is so extensive it gives rise to the inference that Congress left no room for the states to supplement federal law. The Court relied on this type of preemption to rule that § 3 is preempted. (3) Conflict preemption, where compliance with both federal and state regulations is a physical impossibility, and those instances where the challenged state law stands as an obstacle to the accomplishment and execution of the full purposes and objectives of Congress. The Court relied on this type of preemption to rule that § 5(C) was preempted.

Quicknotes

FEDERALISM A scheme of government whereby the power to govern is among central and localized governments.

PREEMPTION Doctrine holding that matters of national interest take precedence over matters of local interest; the federal law takes precedence over state law.

STATE SOVEREIGNTY The absolute power of self-government possessed by a state.

CHAPTER 3

Are We a Nation? The Jacksonian Era to the Civil War, 1835–1865

Quick Reference Rules of Law

Mayor of the City of New York v. Miln

City (P) v. Ship master (D)

36 U.S. (11 Pet.) 102 (1837)

NATURE OF CASE: Action to exact fines for violation of a state law.

FACT SUMMARY: Miln (D) charged that the New York state law he had violated was itself unconstitutional because it intruded on Congress's allegedly exclusive power to regulate commerce.

RULE OF LAW

The powers of internal police being among those not surrendered by the states, a state retains complete, unqualified, and exclusive authority to enact police measures.

FACTS: A New York State law passed in 1824 required the master of any ship arriving in New York from another state or country to furnish information on the passengers, to post security for the maintenance of immigrants and their children who became wards of the city, and to remove any noncitizen whom the mayor (P) determined might become such a ward. Miln (D), in fighting the attempt to assess a $15,000 penalty for his violation of the law, insisted that the law was unconstitutional because it interfered with Congress's power to regulate commerce, a power he claimed was exclusive.

ISSUE: Does a state retain complete and exclusive authority to enact police measures?

HOLDING AND DECISION: (Barbour, J.) Yes. Under the Constitution, the states did not give up their police powers but rather retained exclusive powers of internal police. The state law at issue here was passed in the exercise of that police power. It is not a regulation of commerce. Persons are not the subject of commerce. Being a properly enacted police measure, the state law at issue is not unconstitutional.

CONCURRENCE: (Thompson, J.) The law is valid if viewed as a police measure, but it is also constitutional if viewed as a regulation of commerce. The power to regulate commerce may be exercised by the states until Congress assumes the exercise. There is no existing federal law with which the New York law comes into conflict. Thus, the law is constitutional even if it involves a regulation of commerce.

DISSENT: (Story, J.) The power Congress has to regulate commerce is an exclusive one. Congress has passed federal laws regulating passenger ships and vessels and has authorized not only the transportation but the introduction of passengers into the country. New York's law is unconstitutional because it attempts to achieve a valid state object—preventing the introduction of paupers into the state—by an invalid means, i.e., the regulation of commerce.

ANALYSIS

The importance of determining if states could regulate commerce in the absence of federal regulation was much greater during the historical period in which this decision, which sidestepped the issue, was rendered. At that time, Congress was not inclined to take positive regulatory steps, which meant that there was likely to be no regulation at all if the states could not step in and regulate.

Quicknotes

COMMERCE POWER The power delegated to Congress by the United States Constitution to regulate interstate commerce.

POLICE POWERS The power of a state or local government to regulate private conduct for the health, safety, and welfare of the general public.

Cooley v. Board of Wardens

Ship owner (D) v. Board (P)

53 U.S. (12 How.) 299 (1851)

NATURE OF CASE: Action for violation of a state local pilot law.

FACT SUMMARY: Cooley (D) violated a Pennsylvania law requiring all ships using the port of Philadelphia to engage a local pilot.

RULE OF LAW

The states may regulate those areas of interstate commerce that are local in nature and do not demand one national system of regulation by Congress.

FACTS: In 1803, Pennsylvania passed a law that required every ship entering or leaving the port of Philadelphia to use a local pilot. The law imposed a penalty of half the pilotage fee that was paid to the Board of Wardens (P) and put in a fund for retired pilots and their dependents. Cooley (D), who was a consignee of two ships that had left the port without a local pilot, was held liable under the law. Cooley (D) challenged the right of the state to impose regulations on pilots because it interfered with interstate commerce. The Board of Wardens (P) relied on an act of Congress in 1789 that stated that all pilots in the rivers, harbors, and ports of the United States shall continue to be regulated in conformity with the existing laws of the states and such laws as the states shall enact for that purpose until Congress enacts legislation to the contrary.

ISSUE: May the states regulate those areas of interstate commerce that are local in nature and do not demand one national system of regulation by Congress?

HOLDING AND DECISION: (Curtis, J.) Yes. The states may regulate those areas of interstate commerce that are local in nature and do not demand one national system of regulation by Congress. It is evident from the Congressional Act of 1789 that Congress recognized that the states may, in some areas, enact regulations that effect interstate commerce. Some subjects of commerce demand a single uniform national rule, and, therefore, Congress has exclusive jurisdiction over those areas. However, there are some subjects that are primarily local in nature and therefore require many different rules to meet the local necessities. The problem concerning pilots is local in nature, and, therefore, Congress does not have exclusive power over this area. In the Act that Congress passed allowing the states to regulate pilots, Congress has recognized that the problems involved with pilots do not demand one uniform rule and thus allowed the states to regulate pilots. The Court held that the grant of the power over commerce to Congress did not imply a prohibition on the states to exercise the same power, but it is the exercise of the power by Congress that may make the exercise of the same power by the states unlawful. The Court noted that its decision in this case applied only to its facts and did not attempt to delineate the dividing line between those subjects of commerce that were primarily local and those which were primarily national in scope. The decision of the lower courts upholding Cooley's (D) fine was affirmed.

DISSENT: (McLean, J.) The regulation of pilots was solely vested with Congress under the Commerce Clause, and Congress could not grant to the states power by which they could enact their own legislation in this area, and, therefore, the Act of 1789 allowing the states to regulate pilots was not valid.

ANALYSIS

The local interest versus the national interest test is still used by the Court today. In applying this test, the Court balances the national interest against the local interest and determines if the local regulation discriminates against interstate commerce. If the local interest outweighs the national interest and the regulation does not discriminate against interstate commerce, the states are allowed to regulate that subject of commerce. If it appears that the state regulation has placed a burden on interstate commerce, the Court has drawn the line and refused to hold the state regulations valid even though a local subject may be involved.

Quicknotes

COMMERCE CLAUSE Article I, § 8, cl. 3 of the United States Constitution, granting Congress the power to regulate commerce with foreign countries and between the states.

INTERSTATE COMMERCE Commercial dealings between two parties located in different states or located in one state and accomplished through a point in another state or a foreign country; commercial dealings transacted between two states.

Corfield v. Coryell

[Parties not identified.]

F. Cas. No. 3,230 (D. Pa. 1823)

NATURE OF CASE: Action challenging as violative of the Privileges and Immunities Clause of the Constitution a state statute forbidding anyone not "an actual inhabitant and resident" of the state to gather clams and oysters from the state's waters. [The procedural posture of the case is not presented in the casebook extract.]

FACT SUMMARY: A nonresident of New Jersey challenged as unconstitutional a New Jersey statute forbidding anyone not "an actual inhabitant and resident" of the state to gather clams and oysters from the state's waters.

RULE OF LAW

The Privileges and Immunities Clause does not require that a state accord a citizen of a different state every benefit it accords its own citizens.

FACTS: New Jersey had a statute forbidding anyone not "an actual inhabitant and resident" of the state to gather clams and oysters from the state's waters. A nonresident challenged the statute as violative of the Constitution's Privileges and Immunities Clause. The nonresident argued that any citizen of the United States could enjoy all the rights enjoyed by citizens of a particular state. The circuit court considered the action. [The procedural posture of the case is not presented in the casebook extract.]

ISSUE: Does the Privileges and Immunities Clause require that a state accord a citizen of a different state every benefit it accords its own citizens?

HOLDING AND DECISION: (Washington, J.) No. The Privileges and Immunities Clause does not require that a state accord a citizen of a different state every benefit it accords its own citizens. Instead, the privileges and immunities of U.S. citizenship are those that are fundamental and that belong to citizens of all free nations. Some of these include: protection by the government; the right to acquire and possess property; and the right to pursue and obtain happiness and safety, subject to police power. They do not include all rights that are enjoyed by citizens of a particular state, such as rights in the common property of that state. [The procedural posture of the case is not presented in the casebook extract.]

ANALYSIS

Justice Washington's rationale has been cited frequently and continues to support the contemporary interpretation of the Privilege and Immunities Clause. For example it is on the basis of *Corfield* state universities can prefer in-state residents to out-of-staters or even completely disallow any access by nonresidents.

Quicknotes

PRIVILEGES AND IMMUNITIES CLAUSE Article IV, section 2, clause 1 of the U.S. Constitution, which states that a state cannot favor its own citizens by discriminating against other states' citizens who may come within its borders.

Crandall v. Nevada

Stagecoach company agent (D) v. State (P)

73 U.S. (6 Wall.) 35 (1868)

NATURE OF CASE: Appeal from conviction for violation of a state statute requiring the collection and payment of a capitation tax imposed on persons leaving the state via a normal mode of transportation. [The procedural posture of the case is not presented in the casebook extract.]

FACT SUMMARY: Crandall (D), a stagecoach company agent, contended that a state statute imposing a capitation tax on all persons leaving the state via a normal mode of transportation was unconstitutional.

RULE OF LAW

A state may not constitutionally impose a tax on all persons leaving the state by a normal mode of transportation.

FACTS: A Nevada (P) statute imposed a capitation tax of one dollar upon every person leaving the state by any railroad, stagecoach, or other vehicle engaged or employed in the business of transporting passengers for hire, and it required the carrier to collect the tax and turn it over to the state. Crandall (D), a stagecoach company agent, was convicted of failing to pay the tax. Crandall (D) argued that the statute violated the Constitution's Article I, § 10, prohibition on states imposing taxes on imports and exports, as well as the Commerce Clause. The United States Supreme Court heard the appeal. [The procedural posture of the case is not presented in the casebook extract.]

ISSUE: May a state constitutionally impose a tax on all persons leaving the state by a normal mode of transportation?

HOLDING AND DECISION: (Miller, J.) No. A state may not constitutionally impose a tax on all persons leaving the state by a normal mode of transportation. Because citizens travelling from one state to another are neither imports nor exports, there is no violation of Article I, § 10, of the Constitution. As to whether the statute violates the Commerce Clause, Congress has not passed any statute on this matter. Moreover, given that the tax does not affect national commerce, and has no operation over the country as a whole, it is difficult to see how it implicates the Commerce Clause. Nevertheless, the statute is unconstitutional. First, citizens of the county may be called to serve in various government roles, and no state may obstruct a citizen in rendering such public service. Second, citizens have the right to come to the seat of government to assert their claims against, and transact business with, the government. Moreover, citizens may go to various government offices and ports, and no state may impede such movement by placing obstacles before citizens who exercise these rights who must travel through the state. Thus, the tax imposed by Nevada's (P) statute is itself illegitimate, since it operates to impede persons residing in the state who may wish to get out of it, as well as persons not residing in it who may have occasion to pass through it. As members of the same national community, citizens must have the right to pass and repass through every part of it without interruption, as freely as they may in their own states. Finally, such a tax undermines the objectives that the Union was intended to achieve. The statute is invalid. [The disposition of the case is not presented in the casebook extract.]

ANALYSIS

Two dissenting justices (Justice Clifford and Chief Justice Chase) would have invalidated the statute at issue on the ground it was commercial in nature—i.e., a tax on the carrier—and therefore violated the Commerce Clause. Justice Miller rejected this position, finding that, ultimately, the tax was on the passengers.

Quicknotes

COMMERCE CLAUSE Article I, § 8, cl. 3 of the United States Constitution, granting Congress the power to regulate commerce with foreign countries and among the states.

Groves v. Slaughter

[Parties not identified.]

40 U.S. (15 Pet.) 449 (1841)

NATURE OF CASE: Action challenging, as an impermissible restriction of interstate commerce, the constitutionality of a state constitution's provision prohibiting the importation into the state of slaves for sale. [The procedural posture of the case is not presented in the casebook extract.]

FACT SUMMARY: Mississippi's constitution prohibited the importation into the state of slaves for sale. This provision was challenged as violating the Commerce Clause as an impermissible restriction of interstate commerce. [The complete factual background and procedural posture of the case are not presented in the casebook extract.]

RULE OF LAW

[In an opinion written by Justice Thompson, the Court sidestepped the constitutional issue presented, holding that activating legislation was necessary to implement the Mississippi constitution's provision at issue. A rule of law is not presented by the casebook extract.]

FACTS: Mississippi's constitution prohibited the importation into the state of slaves for sale. This provision was challenged as violating the Commerce Clause as an impermissible restriction of interstate commerce. The issue reached the United States Supreme Court. [In an opinion written by Justice Thompson, the Court sidestepped the constitutional issue, holding that activating legislation was necessary to implement the Mississippi constitution's provision at issue. However, three Justices addressed the constitutional issue in their concurrences. Extracts from those concurrences are presented in the casebook.] [The complete factual background and procedural posture of the case are not presented in the casebook extract.]

ISSUE: Does a state's prohibition on the importation into the state of slaves for sale violate the Commerce Clause as an impermissible regulation of interstate commerce?

HOLDING AND DECISION: (Thompson, J.) The constitutional issue is avoided, because activating legislation is necessary to implement the Mississippi constitution's provision at issue.

CONCURRENCE: (McLean, J.) Notwithstanding that some states consider slaves items of commerce, slaves cannot be merchandise since the Constitution gives them a "leading and controlling quality of persons." Nevertheless, states are free to deal with slavery as they see fit, because the matter is one of local concerns, and the state may protect itself and its citizens from the ill effects of slavery. The right of the states to govern this issue goes beyond the Constitution, since it touches on matters of self-preservation.

CONCURRENCE: (Taney, C.J.) The power to regulate slavery resides exclusively with the states, and Congress may not regulate slavery, either through its commerce power or any other power.

CONCURRENCE: (Baldwin, J.) Slaves are items of commerce, and Congress may regulate the interstate slave trade by virtue of its commerce power. Each state may decide for itself whether slaves are property. If, however, a state decides that slaves are property, Congress may regulate the commerce in those slaves to the extent permitted by the Constitution. Congress may not, for example, in violation of the Fifth Amendment, cause slaves to be taken without just compensation to their owners. While states can regulate their internal slave trades as they please, if such regulation purports to extend to other states or their citizens, it is limited by the Privileges and Immunities Cause, so that if a state allows its own citizens to traffic in slaves, then it must allow out-of-state slaveholders to bring in slaves for the purpose of selling them. If a state has abolished slavery, then none of its residents may become slaves. But, if slaves are merely being transported through such a state from one slave state to another, the slaves do not become free, but retain their character as property. For these reasons, the Mississippi provision at issue is unconstitutional. Moreover, to consider slaves as persons, and not as property, is the first step to undermining the federal system currently in place.

ANALYSIS

Although this case did not establish significant precedent, it demonstrates the Court's difficulty—and different approaches—in grappling with the slavery issues of the time, with the justices attempting to reconcile their notions of slaves, slavery, and federalism.

Quicknotes

COMMERCE CLAUSE Article I, § 8, cl. 3 of the United States Constitution, granting Congress the power to regulate commerce with foreign countries and between the states.

PRIVILEGES AND IMMUNITIES CLAUSE Article IV, section 2, clause 1 of the U.S. Constitution, which states that a state cannot favor its own citizens by discriminating against other states' citizens who may come within its borders.

Prigg v. Pennsylvania

Slave owner's agent (D) v. State (P)

41 U.S. (16 Pet.) 536 (1842)

NATURE OF CASE: Appeal from a state criminal conviction for violation of an antislavery statute.

FACT SUMMARY: Prigg (D) violated a Pennsylvania (P) law designed to keep slave owners from using self-help measures to recapture their fugitive slaves.

RULE OF LAW

Since Congress has exclusive power to legislate regarding a slave owner's constitutional right to reclaim his slave, a state has no power to pass laws that interfere with or obstruct the owner's rights or the remedies Congress prescribes to aid and enforce same.

FACTS: Prigg (D), agent for a slave owner, asked a Pennsylvania (P) magistrate to issue a certificate for removal of an escaped slave back to Maryland. Federal statute provided for a federal judge or state magistrate to issue a certificate in proper cases, but the magistrate refused. When Prigg (D) went ahead and forcibly removed the slave to Maryland, he was convicted of violating a Pennsylvania (P) law making it a crime to remove a Black person from the state into slavery.

ISSUE: Since Congress has exclusive power to legislate regarding a slave owner's constitutional right to reclaim his slave, does a state have the power to pass laws that interfere with or obstruct the owner's rights or the remedies Congress prescribes to aid and enforce same?

HOLDING AND DECISION: (Story, J.) No. Since Congress has exclusive power to legislate regarding a slave owner's constitutional right to reclaim his slave, a state has no power to pass laws that interfere with or obstruct the owner's rights or the remedies Congress prescribes to aid and enforce same. Article IV of the Constitution protects a slave owner's right to reclaim his slave and specifies that a slave cannot be discharged from service or labor in consequence of any state law or regulation. The power of legislation on this subject must be exclusive to Congress. To give the states concurrent power to legislate in this area, in the absence of legislation by Congress, would have been to give them the power to destroy the very rights of the slave owner that the Constitution specifically protects. States have the right to enact valid police power regulations affecting fugitive slaves, but they cannot interfere with or obstruct the just and constitutionally protected rights of an owner to reclaim his slave or with the remedies prescribed by Congress to aid and enforce the same. Reversed.

CONCURRENCE: (Taney, C.J.) The prohibition is only on state laws impairing the slave owner's right, not on state laws protecting the owner's right and aiding him in recovering his property.

DISSENT: (McLean, J.) The magistrate had a duty to obey the federal statutes (despite conflicting state laws), but his refusal to do so does not justify bypassing the statutory procedure to reclaim a slave. Prigg (D) should have taken the fugitive slave before one of the two federal judges residing in the state and obtained the proper certificate.

ANALYSIS

This decision intimated that the slave owner could rely only on self-help and the federal courts, i.e., that state courts were precluded from becoming involved in slave recapture. Justice Story's son claimed that this was his father's way of sabotaging the federal fugitive slave law—federal judges being too few and too distant to be of help to most slave owners.

Quicknotes

AGENT An individual who has the authority to act on behalf of another.

POLICE POWER The power of a government to impose restrictions on the rights of private persons, provided those restrictions are reasonably related to the promotion and protection of public health, safety, morals, and the general welfare.

Dred Scott v. Sandford

Former slave (D) v. Administrator (P)

60 U.S. (19 How.) 393 (1857)

NATURE OF CASE: Action in trespass.

FACT SUMMARY: Dred Scott (P) claimed to have been freed from his slave status by his travels to free states with his master, but Sanford (P) insisted Scott (D) could not bring a federal court action pressing the point because former slaves and their descendants are not "citizens."

RULE OF LAW

Black people who were slaves in this country, or who are the descendants of such slaves, are not "citizens" in the sense in which that word is used in the Constitution and are thus not entitled to maintain an action in federal court.

FACTS: Dred Scott (P), a slave, was taken along on his master's sojourns to the free state of Illinois and the free part of the Missouri Territory (according to the Missouri Compromise). It was after they returned to the slave state of Missouri that the master died, and Sandford (D) became the administrator of the master's estate. Scott (P) attempted to bring a diversity action in federal court based on his claim that his "residence" in the aforementioned free jurisdictions had liberated him from his status as a slave. He was, he insisted, thus properly considered a "citizen" of Missouri and was therefore entitled to bring suit in federal court against Sandford (D), who was a citizen of another state (New York). Sandford (D) argued that a former slave could not be considered a citizen of the United States or of Missouri. The lower court agreed with Sandford (D). Scott (P) appealed.

ISSUE: Are Black people who were slaves in this country, or who are the descendants of such slaves, "citizens" in the sense in which that word is used in the Constitution and thus entitled to maintain an action in federal court?

HOLDING AND DECISION: (Taney, C.J.) No. Black people who were slaves in this country, or who are the descendants of such slaves, are not "citizens" in the sense in which that word is used in the Constitution and are thus not entitled to maintain an action in federal court. A review of history reveals quite readily that neither that class of persons who had been imported as slaves nor their descendants, whether they had become free or not, were acknowledged as part of the "people" but were rather considered as mere property. They simply were not among those who were "citizens" of the several states when the Constitution was adopted, and that is the time frame that must be utilized in determining who was included as a "citizen" in the Constitution. Because he is not a "citizen," Scott (P) cannot maintain this action. Affirmed.

DISSENT: (Curtis, J.) At the time the Constitution was adopted, free persons descended from Africans held in slavery were considered by several of the states to be citizens thereof, and, in my opinion, every free person born on the soil of a state who is a citizen of that state by force of its constitution or laws is also a citizen of the United States. The majority opinion rests upon an untenable assumption—that no one can be deemed a citizen of the United States who is not entitled to enjoy all the privileges and franchises that are conferred on any citizen. In all the states, numerous persons, though citizens, cannot vote or cannot hold office either on account of their age or sex or want of the necessary legal qualifications.

ANALYSIS

The justices all knew this was a historically important case; each one took the time to write an opinion. In addition to the primary opinion by Chief Justice Taney, there were six concurring and two dissenting opinions. No longer doctrinally important because of subsequent amendments to the Constitution resolving of the slavery issues, this case still serves as a prime example of the view that the Constitution, as Chief Justice Taney put it, forever speaks "not only in the same words, but with the same meaning and intent with which it spoke when it came from the hands of the framers." It is a view that has been roundly criticized as too rigid and formalistic an approach to take toward a document that must be flexible enough to provide effective and operable guidelines and governing principles for an ever-evolving society.

Quicknotes

DIVERSITY ACTION An action commenced by a citizen of one state against a citizen of another state or against an alien, involving an amount in controversy set by statute, over which the federal court has jurisdiction.

TRESPASS Unlawful interference with, or damage to, the real or personal property of another.

Texas v. White

State (P) v. Bond broker (D)

7 Wall. 700 (1869)

NATURE OF CASE: Action by a State seeking return of bonds that had been transferred by the State's previous secessionist government.

FACT SUMMARY: Texas (P) sought the return of bonds that it claimed had been wrongfully transferred by its previous secessionist government, asserting that the secessionist government had been without legal authority to do so.

RULE OF LAW
A state may not constitutionally secede from the Union unilaterally.

FACTS: Texas (P) sought the return of bonds that it claimed had been wrongfully transferred by its previous secessionist government, asserting that the secessionist government had been without legal authority to do so. It brought suit in the United States Supreme Court under the Court's original jurisdiction.

ISSUE: May a state constitutionally secede from the Union unilaterally?

HOLDING AND DECISION: (Chase, C.J.) No. A State may not constitutionally secede from the Union unilaterally. Through the Articles of Confederation, and under the Constitution, the States formed a Union that is indissoluble, for purpose of creating a perpetual "more perfect Union." A State's relationship to the Union is not one of contract, but rather one of incorporation into an existing indissoluble political body. Thus, all the obligations of a perpetual Union, and all the guaranties of a republican government in the Union, attach at once to the State. This perpetual relationship cannot be severed unilaterally by a State, except through revolution, or with the permission of the other States in the Union. However, it should be noted that a State does not lose its sovereignty upon entering the Union. To the contrary, the preservation of the States, and the maintenance of their governments, are as much within the design and care of the Constitution as the preservation of the Union and the maintenance of the National government. The Constitution, in all its provisions, looks to an indestructible Union, composed of indestructible States. [The secessionist government, therefore, was illegal and had no authority to sell the bonds.]

DISSENT: (Grier, J.) This case should be decided on basis of political fact, not legal fiction. Taking account of Texas's (P) history, it cannot be said that Texas (P) continues to be part of the United States.

ANALYSIS

Some criticized this decision on the grounds only a State could invoke the Supreme Court's original jurisdiction, and the decision of whether Texas (P) was indeed a State at the time it brought the action was a political decision that should have been decided by Congress, not the Court. Nevertheless, this decision stands as a significant judicial bar to secession as a matter of law.

Prize Cases

Federal government (P) v. Ship owners (D)

67 U.S. (2 Black) 635 (1863)

NATURE OF CASE: Action to determine presidential military powers.

FACT SUMMARY: President Lincoln declared a blockade of southern ports prior to Congress declaring war against the southern states, and the owners of the seized ships contested the seizure of their ships as beyond the power of the President.

RULE OF LAW

Congress can delegate to the President the power to use military force to suppress insurrection against the government of the United States and, pursuant thereto, can take all measures necessary to this end.

FACTS: Pursuant to the Acts of Congress of 1795 and 1807, the President was authorized to call out the militia and use military and naval forces of the United States to suppress insurrection against the government of the United States. In April 1861, President Lincoln declared a blockade of southern ports and ordered Union ships to seize merchant vessels and cargoes of foreign neutrals and residents of the southern states. Congress had not, as of that date, declared war against the Confederacy.

ISSUE: Does the President have the power and authority to institute a blockade of enemy ports, which neutrals are bound to respect?

HOLDING AND DECISION: (Grier, J.) Yes. The President can be delegated the power and authority to institute a blockade of enemy ports, which neutrals are bound to respect, by an act of Congress. The President does not have the power to initiate or declare war but, pursuant to the Acts of Congress of 1795 and 1807, the President can use military force to suppress insurrection against the government of the United States. Here, Congress had not declared war against the Confederacy, but President Lincoln could order a blockade of southern ports based on their insurrection against the North.

DISSENT: (Nelson, J.) The Congressional Acts of 1795 and 1807 could not constitutionally confer on the President the power to declare war against a state of the Union or of deciding that war existed and, upon that ground, declare a blockade and seize property of the state found on the waters.

ANALYSIS

The decrees of condemnation were affirmed except for certain cargoes that were bought and paid for in the South before the war broke out. This was a 5-4 decision with the dissent emphasizing that only Congress has the power to declare war and that the President could not be constitutionally given such power. Throughout the years the President has been given more and more emergency powers at the time of war.

Ex parte Merryman

[Parties not identified.]

17 F. Cas. 144 (1861)

NATURE OF CASE: Petition for habeas corpus.

FACT SUMMARY: Merryman's lawyer argued that President Lincoln did not have the authority to suspend the writ of habeas corpus.

RULE OF LAW
The President has neither the discretionary authority under the Constitution to suspend the writ of habeas corpus nor to delegate such authority.

FACTS: Merryman was arrested and his lawyer filed a writ of habeas corpus, which President Lincoln had authorized his military Commanding General to suspend. The writ was ignored, and Chief Justice Taney, sitting as a circuit judge, decided whether the President had the authority to suspend the writ of habeas corpus.

ISSUE: Does the President have the discretionary authority under the Constitution to suspend the writ of habeas corpus or to delegate such authority?

HOLDING AND DECISION: [Judge not stated in casebook excerpt.] No. The President has neither the discretionary authority under the Constitution to suspend the writ of habeas corpus nor to delegate such authority. It has been understood that the writ of habeas corpus may be suspended only by Congress. The clause of the Constitution that authorizes the suspension of the privilege of the writ of habeas corpus is in the ninth section of the first article, which is devoted exclusively to the legislative department of the United States and makes no reference to the executive department. It is the Constitution's second article that deals with the executive power, and if the great power of suspending the writ of habeas corpus was intended to be conferred on the President, such power would appear in the second article. However, there is no mention of that power in the second article. The President's power is to ensure that "the laws shall be faithfully executed." He is not authorized to execute them himself, or through agents or officers, civil or military, appointed by himself. Thus, the President must support the judiciary. In exercising such power, the President acts in subordination to judicial authority, assisting it to execute its process and enforce its judgments. The President does not faithfully execute the laws if he takes it upon himself to exercise a power reserved to Congress, nor is he aiding the judicial power when he does so. This is true even in times of emergency, tumult, or danger. "The government of the United States is one of delegated and limited powers; it derives its existence and authority altogether from the constitution, and neither of its branches—executive, legislative, or judicial—can exercise any of the powers of government beyond those specified and granted." According to Blackstone, a positive attribute of the Constitution is that it does not leave to the President the decision as to what constitutes sufficient danger to warrant suspending the writ of habeas corpus, and instead only empowers Congress to do so, for a short and limited time.

ANALYSIS

A few months after Justice Taney's decision, Congress retroactively approved all of President Lincoln's acts, proclamations, and orders, including the suspension of the writ of habeas corpus. Two years later, Congress passed a habeas corpus act that provided that during the Civil War, whenever the President deemed it necessary for public safety, he could suspend the privilege of the writ of habeas corpus. Thus, Congress gave President Lincoln the power he could not constitutionally take as his own.

Quicknotes

WRIT OF HABEAS CORPUS A proceeding in which a defendant brings a writ to compel a judicial determination of whether he is lawfully being held in custody.

Ex parte Milligan

[Parties not identified.]

71 U.S. (1 Wall.) 2 (1866)

NATURE OF CASE: Appeal from conviction by military commission.

FACT SUMMARY: Milligan, a civilian, argued that he should have been tried before a jury rather than before a military commission.

RULE OF LAW

A civilian citizen charged with a crime may not be tried before a military commission where a court of law is available.

FACTS: Milligan and other critics of the Civil War were arrested by U.S. military officials in Indiana and charged with planning an armed uprising to seize Union weapons, liberate Confederate prisoners of war, and kidnap Indiana's governor. Indiana was not a theater of military operations, but Milligan was tried and convicted before a military commission. The court of appeals split on its decision, which, therefore was sent to the United States Supreme Court.

ISSUE: May a civilian citizen charged with a crime be tried before a military commission where a court of law is available?

HOLDING AND DECISION: (Davis, J.) No. A civilian citizen charged with a crime may not be tried before a military commission where a court of law is available. Article II, § 2, of the Constitution, provides that all crimes, except in cases of impeachment, shall be tried by jury. Only in cases of foreign invasion or civil war, where courts are closed, and it is necessary to provide a substitute for an overthrown civil authority, may the military govern by martial rule and crimes be tried before a military commission. Martial rule can never exist where the courts are open. Here, martial rule was not justified, because the Indiana courts were open and no actual war was occurring in that state. Thus, Milligan was entitled to be tried by a federal court.

CONCURRENCE: (Chase, C.J.) Congress has the power to authorize trial by military commission, such as the one that tried Milligan. Its powers over the army and navy give it the power to provide for trial and punishment by military courts without a jury. Not only does Congress have the power to raise and support and govern armies, it also has the power to declare war. This power necessarily extends to all legislation essential to the prosecution of war with vigor and success. This power, which is limited to times of war, encompasses establishing military tribunals for trying crimes without a jury to ensure the security of the armed forces as well as public safety. Here, Indiana was a military district and had been threatened with invasion. Therefore, Congress could have provided for trials by military commissions. The fact that Congress chose not to, because the federal courts were open, and Congress regarded that as a sufficient reason for not exercising its power, could not deprive Congress of the right to exercise such power if it chose to, even if the courts were open.

ANALYSIS

This case has contemporary significance, in that it raises the issue of whether a U.S. citizen detained in the United States because of suspicions that he or she is linked to terrorism must be tried in a civilian court, as opposed to a military tribunal (assuming the courts are open), or whether the suspect's right to trial by jury depends on whether Congress has authorized the President to forego such trials during the "war" on terrorism.

Hepburn v. Griswold

[Debtor (D) v. Creditor (P)]

8 Wall. 603 (1870)

NATURE OF CASE: Appeal in action raising the constitutionality of Congress's authority to make paper money legal tender for debts preexisting the date such money was authorized by Congress. [The procedural posture of the case is not presented in the casebook excerpt.]

FACT SUMMARY: [The specific facts giving rise to the case are not presented in the casebook excerpt.] In 1862, Congress passed the Legal Tender Act (the Act) making paper money legal tender for all debts, including those preexisting the date of the Act's passage. The constitutionality of the Act was challenged.

RULE OF LAW

Congress does not have the power under the Constitution to make paper money legal tender for all debts that preexisted the creation of such money.

FACTS: [The specific facts giving rise to the case are not presented in the casebook excerpt.] In 1862, Congress passed the Legal Tender Act (the Act) making paper money legal tender for all debts, including those preexisting the date of the Act's passage, when only gold and silver coins were deemed legal tender. The paper money became greatly devalued as compared with gold and silver coins, and the constitutionality of the Act was challenged as exceeding Congress's authority under the Constitution. The United States Supreme Court granted review to decide the issue.

ISSUE: Does Congress have the power under the Constitution to make paper money legal tender for all debts that preexisted the creation of such money?

HOLDING AND DECISION: (Chase, C.J.) No. Congress does not have the power under the Constitution to make paper money legal tender for all debts that preexisted the creation of such money. First, the Constitution does not expressly grant to Congress the power to make any kind of credit currency legal tender in payment of debts. Second, no such power can be implied. The argument that such power is necessary for Congress to carry out those general powers that are expressly enumerated in the Constitution, such as the power to make war, is rejected. The argument takes the doctrine of implied powers too far, since anything Congress does effectively involves money, so that anything done to promote an express general power may be done in the exercise of an implied power. If Congress wanted to raise money, it could have done so by issuing notes backed by government bonds; there was no need to make the notes legal tender. Even if it would be advantageous in some way for making paper notes legal tender under new contracts, it does not follow that there is such an advantage in compelling creditors to accept such notes in satisfaction of preexisting debts. Therefore, if there is no added utility to using notes in connection with a general power, the making of such notes legal tender cannot be justified. Moreover, there is no justification for the use of notes as legal tender where doing so would impair the use of currency. Further, legislation enacted by Congress must not be prohibited by the Constitution, but must be consistent with it. One of the Constitution's cardinal principles is the preservation of contractual obligations. The Act at bar, however, impairs such obligations, and, therefore, is contrary to the Constitution's spirit. It is contrary to the spirit of the Fifth Amendment's Just Compensation Clause, which prohibits the taking of private property by the government without just compensation for the benefit of all. If such takings must be compensated, it is difficult to see how private property can be taken by the government for the benefit of private citizens without just compensation. An act that compels all those all those who hold contracts for the payment of gold and silver money to accept in payment a currency of inferior value deprives such persons of property without due process of law. The Act does not incidentally impact the value of property, such as the value of stock in a company that is adversely impacted by legislation, but does so directly by forcing citizens to accept money that is worth significantly less than what is owed on a contract. That amounts to a taking of private property without due process.

CONCURRENCE: (Grier, J.) As a matter of statutory construction, the Legal Tender Act by its language does not apply to preexisting debts, but if it was construed to apply to such debts, it would be unconstitutional.

DISSENT: (Miller, J.) The Legal Tender Act was deemed a necessary means by Congress for the urgent purpose of raising armies and suppressing insurrections that were necessary to the nation's survival. Therefore, it was a means justified under the Constitution. The majority's Fifth Amendment argument is too vague as to how a great public measure, such as the Act, effects a taking of private property without compensation or due process, by depreciating the value of lands, or stock, or contracts. Under the majority's logic, a declaration of war with another nation would be unconstitutional if the Navy's ships lost their value along with those of private citizens. Under such logic, the abolition of tariffs would

Continued on next page.

be unconstitutional, as would every successive issue of government bonds during a war, because the increase of public debt would lessen the value of bonds already in private hands. Another danger of the majority's opinion is that it permits this Court to effectively legislate, by substituting the Court's views regarding vague notions of the Constitution's spirit for judicial construction, by substituting an undefined code of ethics for the Constitution, and by substituting itself for Congress. This is not the Court's proper role. The Court should not be declaring void a law that Congress and many courts deemed necessary and appropriate to legitimate ends. If the act to be considered is in any sense essential to the execution of an acknowledged power, the degree of that necessity is for the legislature and not for the court to determine.

ANALYSIS

This decision was expressly overruled a year later, in 1871, by *Knox v. Lee,* 79 U.S. (12 Wall.) 457 (1871), which held that the 1862 Legal Tender Act was constitutional as to all debts, whether prospective or preexisting. It did so on the grounds that the legal tender provisions were justified by the crisis, and threat to the Union, presented by the Civil War. The *Knox* decision also introduced for the first time in the Court's jurisprudence the principle that the federal government's power does not have to be traced to a single specified constitutional power, but may derive from several, or even all, of such express powers.

Quicknotes

IMPLIED POWERS Powers delegated to the various branches of government that, while not expressly stated in the Constitution, are necessary to effectuate the enumerated powers.

JUST COMPENSATION The right guaranteed by the Fifth Amendment to the United States Constitution that when property is taken for public use by the state, a person is to receive adequate compensation in order to restore him or her to the position he or she enjoyed prior to the appropriation.

CHAPTER 4

From Reconstruction to the New Deal: 1866–1934

Quick Reference Rules of Law

United States v. Hall

Federal government (P) v. Ku Klux Klan member indicted of committing federal crime (D)

26 F. Cas. 79 (C.C. Ala 1871)

NATURE OF CASE: Challenge to federal indictment of conspiring to violate murdered victims' First Amendment rights in violation of the Enforcement Act of 1870.

FACT SUMMARY: Hall (D), a member of the Ku Klux Klan who participated in killing two persons and who was indicted by a federal jury for conspiring to violate the First Amendment rights of the victims in violation of the Enforcement Act of 1870, argued that the indictment was defective on the grounds that the First Amendment was not a privilege or immunity of United States citizens under the Fourteenth Amendment.

RULE OF LAW

The First Amendment is a privilege or immunity of United States citizens under the Fourteenth Amendment.

FACTS: Hall (D), a member of the Ku Klux Klan who participated in killing two persons, was indicted by a federal jury for conspiring to violate the First Amendment rights of the victims in violation of the Enforcement Act of 1870, which made it a crime to "injure, oppress, threaten, or intimidate any citizen with intent to prevent or hinder his free exercise and enjoyment of any right or privilege granted or secured to him by the Constitution or laws of the United States." Hall (D) contended that the indictment was defective on the grounds that the First Amendment is not a privilege or immunity of United States citizens under the Fourteenth Amendment.

ISSUE: Is the First Amendment a privilege or immunity of United States citizens under the Fourteenth Amendment?

HOLDING AND DECISION: (Woods, J.) Yes. The First Amendment is a privilege or immunity of United States citizens under the Fourteenth Amendment. The Fourteenth Amendment provides that all persons born or naturalized in the United States are citizens thereof. Persons thus no longer have to obtain state citizenship as a condition of U.S. citizenship, as they did prior to the passage of the Fourteenth Amendment. Therefore, anyone born or naturalized in the United States is entitled to all the privileges and immunities secured by the Constitution to U.S. citizens. The question that follows is what constitutes such privileges and immunities. The answer is that they are fundamental rights that belong to citizens of all free states and that have been enjoyed by citizens of the states that make up the United States since its inception. Among these are rights secured to the people by the Constitution as against the action of the federal or state governments. These include the right of freedom of speech and the right peaceably to assemble. The federal government is prohibited from impairing these rights by the First Amendment, and the state governments are prohibited from impairing these rights by the Fourteenth Amendment. Additionally, under the Fourteenth Amendment, Congress, through appropriate legislation, has the power to protect U.S. citizens from state legislation or inaction that abridges such privileges and immunities, or that denies equal protection of the laws to U.S. citizens. Because Congress may not interfere directly with state laws and cannot compel state officials to act, the legislation that is appropriate to protecting the privileges and immunities of U.S. citizens is legislation that operates directly on offenders and offenses that violate U.S. citizens' fundamental rights. If such legislation interferes with state laws or the administration thereof, such interference must be tolerated for the protection of federal rights. In sum, the right of freedom of speech and the other rights enumerated in the first eight amendments to the Constitution, are the privileges and immunities of United States citizens that Congress has the power protect.

ANALYSIS

This decision was one of the first to construe the Fourteenth Amendment and find that the Bill of Rights applied to the states through the Privileges or Immunities Clause. However, this approach to the Fourteenth Amendment was short lived, as five years later, in *United States v. Cruikshank*, 92 U.S. 542 (1876), the Supreme Court rejected incorporation of the First Amendment against the states. This holding had the effect of reversing criminal convictions for the civil rights violations committed in aid of anti-Reconstruction murders, and was a significant blow to federal efforts to protect the civil rights of African Americans.

Quicknotes

FIRST AMENDMENT RIGHTS Rights conferred by the First Amendment to the U.S. Constitution prohibiting Congress from enacting any law respecting an establishment of religion or prohibiting the free exercise of religion; abridging freedom of speech or of the press; the right of

Continued on next page.

peaceful assembly; and the right to petition for a redress of grievances.

FOURTH AMENDMENT Provides that persons be secure as to their person and private belongings against unreasonable searches and seizures.

IMMUNITY Exemption from a legal obligation.

INDICTMENT A formal written accusation made by a prosecutor and issued by a grand jury, charging an individual with a criminal offense.

PRIVILEGE A benefit or right conferred upon a person or entity beyond those conferred upon the general public.

The Slaughterhouse Cases

Slaughterhouses (P) v. State (D)

83 U.S. (16 Wall.) 36 (1873)

NATURE OF CASE: Appeal of ruling upholding a state-imposed slaughterhouse monopoly.

FACT SUMMARY: The State of Louisiana granted a monopoly to a certain slaughterhouse, and this was challenged as being contrary to the Fourteenth Amendment.

RULE OF LAW

The Privileges and Immunities Clause of the Fourteenth Amendment guarantees only those federal rights protected as of the time of the amendment's adoption.

FACTS: The State of Louisiana (D) conferred by statute a monopoly in the slaughterhouse business on a certain slaughterhouse. Competing slaughterhouses (P) challenged this as an abridgement of the right to own and use property, which the plaintiffs contended was a right guaranteed by the Privileges and Immunities Clause of the Fourteenth Amendment. The lower courts upheld the statute.

ISSUE: Does the Privileges and Immunities Clause of the Fourteenth Amendment guarantee only those federal rights protected as of the time of the amendment's adoption?

HOLDING AND DECISION: (Miller, J.) Yes. The Privileges and Immunities Clause of the Fourteenth Amendment guarantees only those federal rights protected as of the time of the amendment's adoption. The amendment must be interpreted in light of its purpose. The first section overrules the *Dred Scott* decision, 60 U.S. (19 How.) 393 (1857), by conferring both national and state citizenship on those born in the United States. It would be a major leap to presume, however, that the amendment was intended to change the nature of the privileges granted by the United States vis-à-vis the states. Certain federally guaranteed rights do exist, but, by and large, the extent to which individual freedoms and rights have been granted is a matter of state prerogative, and the Court is not inclined to hold that the amendment alters that. Affirmed.

DISSENT: (Field, J.) The amendment should be construed as guaranteeing basic freedoms for all U.S. citizens. Even holding, as the Court does, that the clause goes no further than the Privileges and Immunities Clause of Article IV, the result should be different. The freedom to engage in one's livelihood is a basic freedom.

DISSENT: (Bradley, J.) The right to follow one's employment of choice is the most basic of rights and should be protected by the clause.

DISSENT: (Swayne, J.) Having been adopted after the Civil War, and intended to protect against oppression by the States, the clause must be given its intended effect. The language in the clause is deliberately and knowingly unqualified in its scope and must be applied to all citizens and all people, regardless of race or color—the Court has no authority to impose a limitation on that scope that is neither express nor implied.

ANALYSIS

The Slaughterhouse Cases represent the first major Supreme Court pronouncement on the Fourteenth Amendment. It was argued that the Privileges and Immunities Clause applied the Bill of Rights to the states and this was rejected. The Court has, of course, largely done this by using the Equal Protection and Due Process Clauses. Some have said that the Court would have been more honest in applying the Bill of Rights to the states by overruling *The Slaughterhouse Cases*, but it has not seen fit to do this.

Quicknotes

DUE PROCESS CLAUSE Language found in the Fifth and Fourteenth Amendments to the United States Constitution providing that no person shall be deprived of "life, liberty, or property without due process of law."

EQUAL PROTECTION CLAUSE A constitutional provision that each person be guaranteed the same protection of the laws enjoyed by other persons in like circumstances.

FOURTEENTH AMENDMENT Declares that no state shall make or enforce any law that shall abridge the privileges and immunities of citizens of the United States. No state shall deny to any person within its jurisdiction the equal protection of the laws.

PRIVILEGES AND IMMUNITIES CLAUSE Article IV, section 2, clause 1 of the U.S. Constitution, which states that a state cannot favor its own citizens by discriminating against other states' citizens who may come within its borders.

United States v. Cruikshank

Federal government (P) v. Convicted mob member (D)

92 U.S. 542 (1876)

NATURE OF CASE: Appeal from conviction of violating the 1870 Enforcement Act, which made it a crime to conspire to deny citizens of rights secured by the federal Constitution or laws. [The procedural posture of the case is not presented in the casebook extract.]

FACT SUMMARY: Members of a mob (D) that killed hundreds of innocent Black people, in an event known as the Colfax Massacre of April 1873, contended that their indictments and convictions under the 1870 Enforcement Act, which made it a crime to conspire to deny citizens of rights secured by the federal Constitution or laws, had to be overturned because the Act applied only to the federal government. [The complete factual background and procedural posture of the case are not presented in the casebook extract.]

RULE OF LAW

The Fourteenth Amendment does not incorporate the provisions of the Bill of Rights against the states.

FACTS: Following disputed state elections in Louisiana in 1872 that produced parallel governments, Whites supporting the Democratic candidate seized the village of Colfax and slaughtered hundreds of innocent Black people who included supporters of the Republican candidate. This violent event, which was one of the deadliest of Reconstruction, came to be known as the April 1983 Colfax Massacre. Members of the White mob (D) were indicted and convicted of violating the 1870 Enforcement Act, which made it a crime to conspire to deny citizens of rights secured by the federal Constitution or laws. The mob members (D) appealed, arguing that the Bill of Rights applied only to the federal government, not to the states or private parties. Accordingly, they argued that the indictments charging conspiracy to violate Black peoples' rights to assemble peacefully, petition, and bear arms were insufficient. The United States Supreme Court heard the appeal. [The complete factual background and procedural posture of the case are not presented in the casebook extract.]

ISSUE: Does the Fourteenth Amendment incorporate the provisions of the Bill of Rights against the states?

HOLDING AND DECISION: (Waite, C.J.) No. The Fourteenth Amendment does not incorporate the provisions of the Bill of Rights against the states. As to the right of assembly, that right was not created by the First Amendment, and the right is protected, if at all, by the states. The power over the right of assembly was never ceded by the states to the federal government. As to the right to bear arms, that right also is not granted by the Constitution. The Second Amendment merely protects that right from being infringed by Congress. Further, the indictments charging conspiracy to violate rights to life and liberty must fail because these are natural rights protected by the states, not the federal government. Similarly, indictments charging conspiracy to violate the right to vote also must fail since that right is also a state right. Finally, most of the indictments failed to allege racial discrimination, and the few that so alleged failed to specify the rights violated. For all these reasons, the indictments and convictions are overturned. Judgment for the defendants.

ANALYSIS

In addition to making clear that the United States Supreme Court would not apply the Bill of Rights against the states, this case was a major blow to the enforcement of civil rights in the South during Reconstruction.

Quicknotes

BILL OF RIGHTS Refers to the first ten Amendments to the United States Constitution, setting forth individual rights and liberties.

FOURTEENTH AMENDMENT Declares that no state shall make or enforce any law that shall abridge the privileges and immunities of citizens of the United States. No state shall deny to any person within its jurisdiction the equal protection of the laws.

Bradwell v. Illinois

Female bar applicant (P) v. State (D)

83 U.S. 130 (1873)

NATURE OF CASE: Appeal in action challenging as a violation of the Privileges or Immunities Clause the denial of a license to practice law to an applicant solely on the ground she was a woman. [The procedural posture of the case is not presented in the casebook extract.]

FACT SUMMARY: Bradwell (P), a female applicant to the Illinois (D) bar, challenged as a violation of the Privileges or Immunities Clause the denial by the Illinois Supreme Court of her application to practice law solely on the ground she was a woman. [The complete factual background and procedural posture of the case are not presented in the casebook extract.]

RULE OF LAW

The right to practice law is neither a privilege nor immunity of federal citizenship protected and made applicable to the states by the Fourteenth Amendment.

FACTS: Bradwell (P), a woman, applied to be admitted to the Illinois (D) bar. The Illinois Supreme Court denied her application solely on the ground she was a female; she was qualified in all other respects. She argued that the right to labor in one's chosen profession was a privilege or immunity of federal citizenship, as enumerated by the Declaration of Independence. The United States Supreme Court heard Bradwell's (P) appeal.

ISSUE: Is the right to practice law a privilege or immunity of federal citizenship protected and made applicable to the states by the Fourteenth Amendment?

HOLDING AND DECISION: (Miller, J.) No. The right to practice law is neither a privilege nor immunity of federal citizenship protected and made applicable to the states by the Fourteenth Amendment. Citizenship of any kind, whether federal or state, is not required for admission to the bar. Even if it were, states have the power to regulate admission to their bars, and this power was never ceded to the federal government. Judgment for Illinois (D).

CONCURRENCE: (Bradley, J.) The right of females to pursue any lawful employment, including practicing law, is not and never has been a privilege of immunity of females. The law, reflecting nature, has always recognized a wide difference in the respective spheres and destinies of man and woman. The harmony of interests and views that belong to the family institution is repugnant to the idea of a woman adopting a distinct and independent career from her husband. Historically women had no legal existence, and a married woman was incapable of making binding contracts without her husband's consent. This factor played heavily in the Supreme Court of Illinois' decision, since, as a married woman, Bradwell (D) would not be able to enter into binding contracts, which would render her incompetent fully to perform the duties and trusts that belong to the office of an attorney and counselor. The paramount destiny of women is to fulfill the noble and benign offices of wife and mother. Not every citizen of every age, sex, and condition is qualified for every calling and position, and it is the prerogative of the state legislature to prescribe regulations founded on nature, reason, and experience for the due admission of qualified persons to professions and callings.

DISSENT: (Chase, C.J.) Justice Miller and the concurring justices are wrong.

ANALYSIS

Justice Bradley conceded that the contractual restrictions applicable to married women did not apply to unmarried women, but also indicated that this was the exception, and that society's rules should not be based on exceptions, but rather on the general condition of things. Nevertheless, Justice Bradley's reasoning would seem to permit unmarried women to practice law, if they were otherwise qualified to do so, regardless of their gender, since they would be able to enter into binding contracts, thus meeting their professional obligations.

Quicknotes

FOURTEENTH AMENDMENT Declares that no state shall make or enforce any law that shall abridge the privileges and immunities of citizens of the United States. No state shall deny to any person within its jurisdiction the equal protection of the laws.

PRIVILEGES OR IMMUNITIES CLAUSE Section 1 of the Fourteenth Amendment of the U.S. Constitution; prohibits state laws that abridge the privileges or immunities of U.S. citizens.

Minor v. Happersett

Woman (P) v. State official (D)

82 U.S. 162 (1874)

NATURE OF CASE: Appeal from denial of request to register to vote.

FACT SUMMARY: Minor (P), an adult woman, argued that female adult citizens have a constitutional right to vote.

RULE OF LAW

Female adult citizens do not have a constitutional right to vote.

FACTS: Minor (P), an adult female citizen, attempted to register to vote. The state denied her request and she sued, claiming the Constitution granted women the right to vote. The state courts affirmed the denial, and the United States Supreme Court granted review.

ISSUE: Do female adult citizens have a constitutional right to vote?

HOLDING AND DECISION: (Waite, C.J.) No. Female adult citizens do not have a constitutional right to vote. Women are citizens, but the Constitution, which does not define privileges and immunities, does not make suffrage a necessary privilege of citizenship. When the Constitution was adopted, there was not one state in which all citizens had the right to vote. Instead, all the states had a property requirement to vote. If suffrage is necessarily a part of citizenship, then the citizens of each state would have to be entitled to vote in any state, with the same rights as that state's citizens. This means that they could retain their original citizenship but still vote in another state. This proposition, however, has never been asserted. Moreover, the Fifteenth Amendment, which prohibits denying the right to vote on the basis of race, would be superfluous if any citizen had the absolute right to vote. Looking outside the Constitution, no new state has ever been admitted to the Union that conferred the right to vote on women, and this has never been considered a valid objection to a state's admission into the Union. This, too, is true of the insurgent states, which although not granting the right to vote to women, have all been restored to their original position as states in the Union. Furthermore, some non-citizens have the right to vote. For nearly 90 years the people have acted upon the idea that the Constitution, when it conferred citizenship, did not necessarily confer the right of suffrage. "If uniform practice long continued can settle the construction of so important an instrument as the Constitution of the United States confessedly is, most certainly it has been done here." Affirmed.

ANALYSIS

This unanimous decision avoids altogether any public policy arguments about why women should, or should not, have the right to vote. Chief Justice Waite says, "No argument as to women's need of suffrage can be considered. We can only act upon her rights as they exist. It is not for us to look at the hardship of withholding. Our duty is at an end if we find it is within the power of a State to withhold." One argument, for example, was that women who owned property and did not have the right to vote would be taxed without being represented—taxation without representation was a principal motivator of the Revolution.

Quicknotes

RIGHT OF SUFFRAGE The right to vote.

Elk v. Wilkins

American Indian (P) v. Municipal election registrar (D)

112 U.S. 94 (1884)

NATURE OF CASE: Appeal in action challenging the refusal of a municipal election registrar to accept an application for voter registration. [The procedural posture of the case is not presented in the casebook excerpt.]

FACT SUMMARY: John Elk (P), an American Indian born in a tribe within the United States who had voluntarily given up his tribal membership, contended that he was a citizen of the United States under the Fourteenth Amendment for voter registration purposes. [The procedural posture of the case is not presented in the casebook excerpt.]

RULE OF LAW

An American Indian who is born a member of one of the American Indian tribes within the United States and who then gives up membership in that tribe and takes up residence among United States citizens is not considered a citizen of the United States within the meaning of the Fourteenth Amendment merely by reason of having been born within the United States.

FACTS: John Elk (P), who is an American Indian born in an American Indian tribe within the United States who had voluntarily given up his tribal membership and who took up residence in the municipality of Omaha, Nebraska, contended that he was a citizen of the United States under the Fourteenth Amendment, notwithstanding that he had not been naturalized as a citizen. Therefore, Elk (P) contended that Wilkins (D), the registrar of elections for Omaha, erred by not accepting his claim for voter registration on the grounds that he was not a U.S. citizen by birth. [The procedural posture of the case is not presented in the casebook excerpt.]

ISSUE: Is an American Indian who is born a member of one of the American Indian tribes within the United States and who then gives up membership in that tribe and takes up residence among United States citizens considered a citizen of the United States within the meaning of the Fourteenth Amendment merely by reason of having been born within the United States?

HOLDING AND DECISION: (Grey, J.) No. An American Indian who is born a member of one of the American Indian tribes within the United States and who then gives up membership in that tribe and takes up residence among United States citizens is not considered a citizen of the United States within the meaning of the Fourteenth Amendment merely by reason of having been born within the United States. Even though Elk (P) desires to be a U.S. citizen, there is no statute or treaty that entitles him to become one. Since the Founding, members of American Indian tribes have not been considered citizens of the United States, as they do not pay taxes and are not naturalized. Absent assent by the United States, as by statute or treaty in particular cases, members of American Indian tribes cannot be U.S. citizens. The Fourteenth Amendment settled the question of citizenship of freed African American slaves. However, American Indians born within the territorial limits of the United States, members of, and owing immediate allegiance to, one of the American Indian tribes (which are an alien though dependent power) although in a geographical sense born in the United States, are no more "born in the United States and subject to the jurisdiction thereof," within the meaning of the first section of the Fourteenth Amendment, than the children of subjects of any foreign government born within the domain of that government, or the children born within the United States of ambassadors or other public ministers of foreign nations. This view is confirmed by the second section of the Amendment, which provides that "representatives shall be apportioned among the several states according to their respective numbers, counting the whole number of persons in each state, excluding Indians not taxed." Because American Indians are not counted for purposes of representation, and are expressly and absolutely excluded from such representation, they cannot, and are not, considered citizens by birth. The only way an American Indian can become a U.S. citizen is by naturalization pursuant to treaty or statute. For these reasons, Elk (P) is not a U.S. citizen and is not entitled to be registered to vote.

DISSENT: (Harlan, J.) Implicit in the language of Article I, § 3 of the Constitution, excluding "Indians not taxed," is that there were, at that time, in the United States, American Indians who were taxed, since American Indians not taxed were tribal members who were not subject to any state's authority. This language is retained in the Fourteenth Amendment, and American Indians who live in states that tax them are counted for purposes of representation in Congress. The Civil Rights Act of 1866 (the Act) effectively provides that American Indians, other than those who are not taxed, are U.S. citizens. This Act reaches American Indians not in tribal relations, notwithstanding that such individuals, when born, were tribal members. The Fourteenth Amendment

Continued on next page.

was approved for adoption by the states during the same session of Congress in which the Act was passed, and the legislative history shows that Congress intended to grant national citizenship to every American Indian who was unconnected with any tribe, and who resided, in good faith, outside of any reservations and within one of the states or U.S. territories. This legislative history is entitled to great weight in determining the meaning and scope of the Fourteenth Amendment.

ANALYSIS

The majority's view was that no one can become a citizen of a nation without its consent, and, therefore, that a member of an American Indian tribe could not at will be alternately a citizen of the United States and a member of the tribe absent a statute or treaty that consented, via naturalization, to such individual becoming a citizen. It was not until 40 years after this case was decided that Congress passed legislation, at 8 U.S.C. § 140(a)(s), naturalizing all "Indians born within the territorial limits of the United States." This statute was repealed and replaced in 1952 with 8 U.S.C. § 1401(b), which states that "a person born in the United States to a member of an Indian, Eskimo, Aleutian, or other aboriginal tribe" is a U.S. national and citizen at birth.

Quicknotes

FOURTEENTH AMENDMENT Declares that no state shall make or enforce any law that shall abridge the privileges and immunities of citizens of the United States. No state shall deny to any person within its jurisdiction the equal protection of the laws.

NATURALIZATION The process pursuant to which a person becomes a citizen of a country.

Strauder v. West Virginia

Criminal defendant (D) v. State (P)

100 U.S. 303 (1880)

NATURE OF CASE: Appeal from conviction for murder.

FACT SUMMARY: Strauder (D), a Black man, was convicted of murder by a jury from which Black people were excluded.

RULE OF LAW

A state may not prevent Black people from serving on juries.

FACTS: Strauder (D), a Black man, was indicted for murder in the Circuit Court of Ohio County, West Virginia, on October 20, 1874, and after a trial was convicted of the charge. The judgment was affirmed by the state supreme court. On appeal, Strauder (D) argued that at the trial he was denied rights to which he was entitled under the Constitution and laws of the United States because under state law Black people were ineligible to serve on the grand or petit jury.

ISSUE: May a state prevent Black people from serving on juries?

HOLDING AND DECISION: (Strong, J.) No. A state may not prevent Black people from serving on juries. The Fourteenth Amendment is one of a series of constitutional provisions having a common purpose: namely, securing to a race recently emancipated, a race that through many generations had been held in slavery, all the civil rights that the superior race enjoys. The Fourteenth Amendment declares that the law in the states shall be the same for Black people as for the White people; that all persons, whether black or white, shall stand equal before the laws of the states, and, in regard to Black people, for whose protection the amendment was primarily designed, that no discrimination shall be made against them by law because of their color. The words of the amendment, it is true, are prohibitory, but they contain a necessary implication of a positive right to exemption from unfriendly legislation that implies inferiority in civil society. Here, the West Virginia statute respecting juries is clearly discriminatory. The very fact that Black people are singled out and expressly denied by a statute all right to participate in the administration of the law, as jurors, because of their color, though they are citizens, and may be in other respects fully qualified, is practically a brand upon them, and a stimulant to that race prejudice which is an impediment to securing to individuals of the race that equal justice which the law aims to secure to all others. The judgment of the West Virginia Supreme Court is reversed.

ANALYSIS

This case, one of the earliest decisions interpreting the Fourteenth Amendment, discusses two themes that later became significant in determining whether a group constituted a suspect classification, and whether the legislation in question violates constitutional prohibitions. The first is whether the class, as in the case of Black people, is one that has historically been the victim of societal discrimination. The second is whether the legislation in question tends to stigmatize that class in the eyes of society.

Quicknotes

FOURTEENTH AMENDMENT Declares that no state shall make or enforce any law that shall abridge the privileges and immunities of citizens of the United States. No state shall deny to any person within its jurisdiction the equal protection of the laws.

MURDER The unlawful killing of another person either with deliberation and premeditation or by conduct demonstrating a reckless disregard for human life.

STRICT SCRUTINY The method by which courts determine the constitutionality of a law, when a law affects a fundamental right. Under the test, the legislature must have a compelling interest to enact the law, and measures prescribed by the law must be the least restrictive means possible to accomplish its goal.

The Civil Rights Cases

Excluded citizens (P) v. Institutions (D)

109 U.S. 3 (1883)

NATURE OF CASE: Review of criminal and civil prosecutions under the 1875 Civil Rights Act.

FACT SUMMARY: In the 1875 Civil Rights Act, Congress sought to prohibit private discrimination under the Fourteenth and Thirteenth Amendments.

RULE OF LAW

Civil rights guaranteed by the Constitution cannot be impaired by the wrongful acts of individuals unless such acts are sanctioned or authorized by the state.

FACTS: Congress in 1875 passed the federal Civil Rights Act (the Act) prohibiting private citizens from excluding other citizens from inns, public transportation, and places of amusement based on race. The Act was passed under the authority of the Thirteenth and Fourteenth Amendments. In four criminal prosecutions and one civil lawsuit involving exclusion of Black people from hotels, theaters, and railroads, those prosecuted challenged the constitutionality of the Act.

ISSUE: Can civil rights guaranteed by the Constitution be impaired by the wrongful acts of individuals if such acts are not sanctioned or authorized by the state?

HOLDING AND DECISION: (Bradley, J.) No. Civil rights guaranteed by the Constitution cannot be impaired by the wrongful acts of individuals unless such acts are sanctioned or authorized by the state. Accordingly, Congress may not prohibit private discrimination under the Thirteenth and Fourteenth Amendments. The Fourteenth Amendment provides that no state shall deprive a person of equal protection or due process. It does not, by its terms, purport to affect private citizens' actions. While Congress does have the power to enforce the Amendment through appropriate legislation, such legislation cannot go so far as to turn an Amendment that limits states' rights into one that affects private parties. The Thirteenth Amendment, by prohibiting slaveholding, does regulate private citizens. However, racial segregation is not a "badge of slavery" sufficient to bring the Thirteenth Amendment into operation. Consequently, Congress exceeded its authority under these amendments in its 1875 legislation.

DISSENT: (Harlan, J.) To deny a citizen equal participation due to race is a vestige of slavery sufficient to invoke the Thirteenth Amendment.

ANALYSIS

The United States Supreme Court's narrow reading of § 1 of the Fourteenth Amendment stands to this day. Although subsequent decisions have chipped away at it to some extent, the rule remains that the Fourteenth Amendment affects only state action. The major civil rights legislation of the 1960s came about, not through the Fourteenth Amendment, but through the seemingly unlikely jurisdictional basis of the Commerce Clause of Article III.

Quicknotes

EQUAL PROTECTION A constitutional guarantee that no person shall be denied the same protection of the laws enjoyed by other persons in life circumstances.

STATE ACTION Actions brought pursuant to the Fourteenth Amendment claiming that the government violated the plaintiff's civil rights.

THIRTEENTH AMENDMENT The constitutional provision that abolished slavery in the United States.

Plessy v. Ferguson

Passenger (D) v. State (P)

163 U.S. 537 (1896)

NATURE OF CASE: Appeal from criminal prosecution for violating a state railway accommodation segregation law.

FACT SUMMARY: Plessy (D) was arrested for trying to sit in a railroad car that was designated "for whites only."

RULE OF LAW

Segregation of the races is reasonable if based upon the established custom, usage, and traditions of the people in the state.

FACTS: Plessy (D), who was 7/8 White and whose skin color was white, was denied a seat in a "for whites only" railroad car. When Plessy (D) resisted, he was arrested for violating a state law that provided for segregated "separate but equal" railroad accommodations. Plessy (D) appealed the conviction on the basis that separation of the races stigmatized Black people and stamped them with the badge of inferiority. He claimed that segregation violated the Thirteenth and Fourteenth Amendments. The trial court found Plessy (D) guilty on the basis that the law was a reasonable exercise of the state's police powers based upon custom, usage, and tradition in the state.

ISSUE: May the state segregate the races in "separate but equal" facilities or accommodations?

HOLDING AND DECISION: (Brown, J.) Yes. This is a valid exercise of the state's police power. Where this has been the established custom, usage, or tradition in the state, it may continue to require such segregation as is reasonable to preserve order and the public peace. Such decisions have been continuously upheld. This is not a badge of slavery under the Thirteenth Amendment, and it violates no provision of the Fourteenth Amendment. The enforced separation of the races is not a badge of servitude or inferiority, regardless of how Plessy (D) and other Black people deem to treat it. The conviction is sustained.

DISSENT: (Harlan, J.) The statute interferes with the personal freedom of individuals to freely associate with others. The Constitution is color-blind. All citizens should and must be treated alike. Black people are not subordinate or inferior things. They are citizens and are entitled to all the privileges this entails. Enforced separation is an impermissible burden on these privileges and freedoms. The conviction should be overturned.

ANALYSIS

Plessy is of importance only for its historical perspective. Later cases borrowed the "separate but equal" phraseology and turned it around 180 degrees. In *Brown v. Board of Education*, 347 U.S. 483 (1954), the Court, 58 years after *Plessy*, held that separate could never be considered equal. It, thus, expressly overruled *Plessy*.

Quicknotes

FOURTEENTH AMENDMENT Declares that no state shall make or enforce any law that shall abridge the privileges and immunities of citizens of the United States. No state shall deny to any person within its jurisdiction the equal protection of the laws.

POLICE POWERS The power of a state or local government to regulate private conduct for the health, safety, and welfare of the general public.

SEGREGATION The use of separate institutions and facilities for persons of different races.

THIRTEENTH AMENDMENT The constitutional provision that abolished slavery in the United States.

Buchanan v. Warley

White property seller (P) v Black property buyer (D)

245 U.S. 60 (1917)

NATURE OF CASE: Appeal in action for specific performance of a real estate contract challenging the constitutionality of a municipal ordinance restricting real estate sales by race. [The procedural posture of the case is not presented in the casebook excerpt.]

FACT SUMMARY: Buchanan (P), a White person, sought specific performance of a contract for the sale of a house from Warley (D), a Black person. Warley (D) defended by asserting the contract was illegal because a municipal ordinance prohibited Black persons from residing in blocks where the majority of houses were occupied by White persons, and vice versa. Buchanan (P) responded by asserting the ordinance was unconstitutional under the Due Process Clause of the Fourteenth Amendment.

RULE OF LAW

An ordinance that restricts the sale of real estate in residential districts on the basis of race for the purpose of keeping persons of different races separated on account of their color violates the Due Process Clause of the Fourteenth Amendment.

FACTS: Buchanan (P), a White person, entered into a contract for the sale of a house to Warley (D), a Black person. The house was located in a residential district of Louisville, Kentucky, where the majority of houses were occupied by White persons. A Louisville ordinance prohibited Black persons from residing in a block in which a majority of houses were occupied by White persons, and also prohibited White persons from residing in a block in which a majority of the houses were occupied by Black persons. The purpose of the ordinance was to segregate Black persons from White persons. When Buchanan (P) brought suit for specific performance of the contract, Warley (D) defended by claiming the Louisville ordinance rendered the contract illegal. Buchanan (P) then challenged the ordinance, arguing it violated the Due Process Clause of the Fourteenth Amendment. The United States Supreme Court granted certiorari in the case. [The procedural posture of the case is not presented in the casebook excerpt.]

ISSUE: Does an ordinance that restricts the sale of real estate in residential districts on the basis of race for the purpose of keeping persons of different races separated on account of their color violate the Due Process Clause of the Fourteenth Amendment?

HOLDING AND DECISION: (Day, J.) Yes. An ordinance that restricts the sale of real estate in residential districts on the basis of race for the purpose of keeping persons of different races separated on account of their color violates the Due Process Clause of the Fourteenth Amendment. The Louisville ordinance violates the Fourteenth Amendment and the Civil Rights Acts of 1866 and 1870, pursuant to which a Black man may acquire property without restrictions based solely on the color of his skin. This is not a case where an accommodation is being provided equally to persons of both races. Instead, the ordinance under consideration seeks to destroy the right of an individual to acquire, enjoy, and dispose of the individual's real property. Although there is hostility between the races, the solution is not to deprive citizens of their constitutional rights and privileges. The argument that the ordinance is necessary to maintain the purity of the races is unavailing, since Black servants are permitted in White families, and Black persons reside close to White persons, albeit not in the same blocks. Also unavailing is the argument that the ordinance is necessary for promoting public peace by preventing race conflicts. Even though such a goal is desirable, it cannot be achieved by denying rights protected under the federal Constitution. Lastly, the argument that permitting Black people to purchase property in neighborhoods where White people reside will result in lower property values also does not save the ordinance, since allowing undesirable White persons, or White persons who put the property to undesirable uses, similarly leads to lower property values. Therefore, the ordinance fails as a legitimate exercise of the police power.

ANALYSIS

Justice Day distinguished *Plessy v. Ferguson,* 163 U.S. 537 (1896), from the case at bar on the grounds that *Plessy* addressed a law that regulated social rights, whereas the case at bar addressed a law that regulated property rights. *Plessy* held that a Louisiana statute that required railroads carrying passengers within the state to "provide equal but separate accommodations for the white and colored races," did not violate the Thirteenth or Fourteenth Amendments. Although Justice Brown in *Plessy* had stated that "[l]aws permitting, and even requiring, [the races'] separation in places where they are liable to be brought into contact do not necessarily imply the inferiority of either race to the other, and have been generally, if not universally, recognized as within the competency of the state legislatures in the exercise of their police power," Justice Day emphasized

Continued on next page.

that the classification of accommodations in *Plessy* was permitted on the grounds that both races were equally accommodated as to their social rights, but that the Louisville ordinance could not render such "equal but separate" treatment because property "is more than the mere thing which a person owns" but also includes the right to acquire, use, and dispose of it. Because, in Justice Day's view, the Fourteenth Amendment and the Civil Rights Acts expressly provided that all citizens of the United States in any state had the same right to purchase property as was enjoyed by White citizens and because Black persons were citizens of the United States, they had the right to purchase property and enjoy and use the property without laws discriminating against them solely on account of color. The decision was unanimous, and was the first decision by the Court to break with a line of cases that upheld state-mandated racial segregation. Although some view the case as merely vindicating property rights, others view the case as the Court's first step, as the renowned sociologist W.E.B. Du Bois termed it, in breaking "the backbone of segregation."

Quicknotes

FOURTEENTH AMENDMENT Declares that no state shall make or enforce any law that shall abridge the privileges and immunities of citizens of the United States. No state shall deny to any person within its jurisdiction the equal protection of the laws.

FOURTEENTH AMENDMENT DUE PROCESS CLAUSE Provides that protections mandated by the U.S. Constitution and observed by the federal government are equally applicable, and therefore must be observed by the States.

ORDINANCE Law or statute usually enacted by a municipal government.

POLICE POWER The power of a government to impose restrictions on the rights of private persons, so long as those restrictions are reasonably related to the promotion and protection of public health, safety, morals, and the general welfare.

SPECIFIC PERFORMANCE An equitable remedy whereby the court requires the parties to perform their obligations pursuant to a contract.

Giles v. Harris

African American (P) v. [State official (D)]

189 U.S. 475 (1903)

NATURE OF CASE: Appeal in action seeking to enjoin systematic disenfranchisement of Black people. [The procedural posture of the case is not presented in the casebook extract.]

FACT SUMMARY: Giles (P), a Black man, sought to enjoin the systematic disenfranchisement of Black people in Alabama, contending that such disenfranchisement violated the Constitution. [The complete factual background and procedural posture of the case are not presented in the casebook extract.]

RULE OF LAW

[The Court avoided rendering an opinion on the legal/constitutional issue by indicating such an opinion would be futile to effect the change sought by Giles (P).]

FACTS: Giles (P), a Black man, who was literate and had voted many times, sought to enjoin the systematic disenfranchisement of himself and many other Black people in Alabama, through provisions in the state's constitution, contending that such disenfranchisement violated the federal Constitution. He sought to have disenfranchised Black people placed on the voter registration rolls. [The complete factual background and procedural posture of the case are not presented in the casebook extract.]

ISSUE: [The legal/constitutional issue is not presented in the casebook extract.]

HOLDING AND DECISION: (Holmes, J.) [The Court avoided rendering an opinion on the legal/constitutional issue by indicating such an opinion would be futile to effect the change sought by Giles (P).] Even if the facts are assumed to be true, there is no relief the Court can grant that, as a practical matter, will affect the political changes sought by Giles (P). Merely ordering the placement of names of disenfranchised Black people on the voting registration rolls would be an empty gesture. Unless the Court is prepared to supervise all voting in Alabama, a court order will do nothing to change the current situation. That change must be made politically, through the state itself, or through Congress.

ANALYSIS

The practical effect of the Court's decision was to uphold the constitutionality of the disenfranchising provisions of the southern states' constitutions, and to promote discrimination against Black people. It was not until many years later that the Court effectively overturned *Giles* in a series of cases that affirmed that the right to vote was protected by the Equal Protection Clause of the Fourteenth Amendment, and that the federal courts are empowered to reverse constitutional rights violations within the states.

Quicknotes

EQUAL PROTECTION CLAUSE A constitutional provision that each person be guaranteed the same protection of the laws enjoyed by other persons in like circumstances.

FOURTEENTH AMENDMENT Declares that no state shall make or enforce any law that shall abridge the privileges and immunities of citizens of the United States. No state shall deny to any person within its jurisdiction the equal protection of the laws.

Downes v. Bidwell

Merchant (P) v. Duties collector (D)

182 U.S. 244 (1901)

NATURE OF CASE: Appeal in action challenging as unconstitutional duties collected on imports from Puerto Rico. [The procedural posture of the case is not presented in the casebook extract.]

FACT SUMMARY: Downes (P), a merchant, challenged duties collected on behalf of the government by Bidwell (D) on oranges imported from Puerto Rico, a U.S. territory, arguing that the duties violated Article I, § 8, cl. 1 of the Constitution.

RULE OF LAW

U.S. territories (as opposed to states) are not subject to the Constitution's revenue clauses, including Article I, § 8, cl. 1.

FACTS: Downes (P), a merchant, challenged duties collected on behalf of the government by Bidwell (D) on oranges imported from Puerto Rico, a U.S. territory, arguing that the duties violated Article I, § 8, cl. 1 of the Constitution. That clause provides that "all duties, imposts, and excises shall be uniform throughout the United States." The duties were collected pursuant to the Foraker Act of April 12, 1900, which temporarily provided a civil government and sources of revenue for administration of Puerto Rico when that island became part of the United States after the ratification of the treaty with Spain that ended the Spanish-American War. The United States Supreme Court heard the appeal. [The procedural posture of the case is not presented in the casebook extract.]

ISSUE: Are U.S. territories (as opposed to states) subject to the Constitution's revenue clauses, including Article I, § 8, cl. 1?

HOLDING AND DECISION: (Brown, J.) No. U.S. territories (as opposed to states) are not subject to the Constitution's revenue clauses, including Article I, § 8, cl. 1. It has been determined that Puerto Rico is no longer a sovereign nation but is a territory of the United States. There is nothing in the original Constitution that indicates it applies to territories. Instead, the Constitution as written applies to the states. The Thirteenth Amendment shows that there are places subject to the United States' jurisdiction that are not part of the Union. The Fourteenth Amendment extends citizenship only to those who are born or naturalized in the United States; but does not extend citizenship to those born in territories subject to the jurisdiction of the United States. Further in connection with the purchase of the Louisiana Territory, French and Spanish ships were allowed to enter the port of New Orleans upon the same terms, and paying the same duties, as American ships bringing goods from French and Spanish territories. This treatment by Congress presumed that ports of territories are not ports of a state within the meaning of the Constitution, so that such treatment would not violate Article I, § 9, of the Constitution, which provides that no preference shall be given by any regulation of commerce or revenue to the ports of one state over those of another. Similar treatment has been made in subsequent territorial acquisitions. Similarly, in organizing the Louisiana Territory, Congress did not assume that the Constitution applied by its own force to that territory, but instead enacted legislation making the Constitution applicable therein. The Court's decisions as to this issue have hitherto not been consistent. Some indicate that the Constitution does not reach territories absent enabling legislation, whereas others suggest that the Constitution takes immediate effect upon a territory coming under U.S. jurisdiction. The *Dred Scott* decision [*Dred Scott v. Sandford,* 60 U.S. 393 (1857)] seemed to say that the Constitution did not permit the United States to permanently hold territories but could only govern such territories with the expectation that they would become states, which the Constitution would reach. That case is distinguishable, however, because it was based on incorrect notions of property, holding that slaves were just like any other form of property, instead of an exceptional class of property. Attempts by the Senate to extend the Constitution's reach to the territories also failed. To reach the result that some aspects of the Constitution do not reach the territories, it is not necessary to conclude that all provisions of the Constitution do not operate in territories. Those provisions that go to the root of congressional power, regardless of time or place, reach the territories, whereas those that are operative only "throughout the United States" or among the several states may not reach the territories. The question in the latter case becomes whether the territory is a part of the United States for constitutional purposes, notwithstanding that the territory is under U.S. jurisdiction. Regarding Article I, § 8, the text and purpose of that section makes clear that it was meant to apply only to the states. Only once a territory becomes a state do the provisions of this Article apply automatically. Until that point, the Constitution may apply only if Congress extends it to the territory legislatively. This applies equally to the status of territory inhabitants; it is up to Congress to determine whether those inhabitants will become full U.S. citizens

Continued on next page.

or not, and the inhabitants do not automatically become U.S. citizens. Congress may make this decision based on the differences of race, habits, laws, and customs of the people in the various outlying, remote, non-contiguous territories. Nevertheless, Congress's power in this regard is not limitless, and even the inhabitants of territories who remain aliens are still entitled to natural rights protected by the Constitution; "they are entitled under the principles of the Constitution to be protected in life, liberty, and property." In the case of Puerto Rico, Congress determined that it would be best to raise revenue for the territory through duties, rather than by imposition of an internal revenue system. The Framers obviously did not anticipate the vast expansion of territories since the Constitution was written. Otherwise, they would have addressed the Constitution to such expansion. However, as written, the Constitution only addresses itself to the states of the Union. If the Unites States may acquire foreign territories, it must be assumed that it has the same powers as any other sovereign nations to govern such territories. The states could only delegate to Congress such powers as they themselves possessed, and as they had no power to acquire new territory they had none to delegate in that connection. The logical inference from this is that if Congress has power to acquire new territory, its power to govern the territory is not hampered by the Constitution, and Congress may in so governing take into account the differences from our own of the inhabitants' religions, customs, laws, methods of taxation, and modes of thought. For these reasons, Puerto Rico belongs to the United States, but is not part of the Unites States for purposes of the Constitution's revenue provisions. [The procedural disposition of the case is not presented in the casebook extract.]

CONCURRENCE: (White, J.) The United States may acquire foreign territories, and it has the same powers as any other sovereign nations to govern such territories. However, because the Constitution absolutely bars Congress from depriving people of property and liberty, and "limitations of this character cannot be under any circumstances transcended," Congress may locally govern Puerto Rico, but without depriving its inhabitants of freedom and justice. The issue is whether the form of the tax imposed was repugnant to the Constitution. The answer to that question depends on whether Puerto Rico is incorporated into the United States or is unincorporated. It is inconceivable that a treaty alone can incorporate an alien people into the United States without the express or implied approval of Congress. If such were the potential power of treaties, "then millions of inhabitants of alien territory, if acquired by treaty, [could], without the desire or consent of the people of the United States speaking through Congress, be immediately and irrevocably incorporated into the United States, and the whole structure of the government be overthrown." As to the treaty regarding Puerto Rico, it did not incorporate the island, but left to Congress's discretion the civil rights and political status of the island's inhabitants. Because Puerto Rico has not been incorporated into the United States, Congress was not bound by Article I, § 8 in legislating for the island.

DISSENT: (Fuller, C.J.) It has been previously held that under the Fourteenth Amendment the United States includes its territories for purposes of citizenship. Also, residency in a territory would count toward the time needed to be eligible for the Office of the President. Further, the Fifteenth Amendment's prohibition on the abridgement of the voting right would seem to be especially pertinent to the residents of territories. Additionally, the Thirteenth Amendment's prohibition on slavery would operate in the territories even if the language "any place subject to their jurisdiction" following "within the United States" had not been added to the Amendment. No satisfactory reason has been given for restricting the words "throughout the United States," as qualifying the power to impose duties, to the states. Instead, the majority's interpretation rests on the dangerous assumption that Congress's power over the territories is unlimited. However, the government's powers come from, and are enumerated in, the Constitution. These powers are not enlarged when the domain over which the government has authority expands. The government is the agent of the people, and when there is a restriction on that agent's power, that is the end of the inquiry. To hold otherwise would overthrow the constitutional form of government and uphold the erroneous proposition that the states—not the people—created the government. The majority would give Congress unbridled power over commerce with U.S. territories, without regard to the Constitution. Because Congress's power emanates from the Constitution, it does not matter, contrary to the majority's construct, whether a territory is "incorporated" or "unincorporated." The concurring opinion recognizes the fact that Congress, in dealing with the people of new territories or possessions, is bound to respect the fundamental guarantees of life, liberty, and property, but assumes that Congress is not bound, in those territories or possessions, to follow the rules of taxation prescribed by the Constitution. And yet, the power to tax involves the power to destroy, and the levy of duties touches all people in all places under the jurisdiction of the government. The effect of this dichotomy is that the republican form of government is replaced with a government of absolute power and dominion when it comes to acquired territories. The majority contends that such absolute power is necessary when dealing with remote territories, but there is no authority for such absolute power in the Constitution.

Continued on next page.

DISSENT: (Harlan, J.) Whether a foreign people will assimilate with our people and can do so without danger to our institutions and within the confines of the Constitution, is a matter to be considered before their territory is acquired by treaty—not after, as the majority suggests. If a mistake is made in such acquisition, this is not grounds to ignore or violate the Constitution. Whether the Constitution is followed does not depend on a momentary crisis; it is the supreme law of the land and is to be followed at all times. When a territory is acquired, the Constitution necessarily becomes the supreme law of such new territory, and no power exists in any department of the government to make "concessions" that are inconsistent with its provisions. To hold otherwise implies that the government may ignore the Constitution under special or embarrassing circumstances. However, no such authority is granted in the Constitution itself, and, therefore, the government does not have such power. If the country is to become a world power, and if the government needs additional powers in conjunction with the country's expansion, such increased powers must be obtained through constitutional amendment, in the manner set forth in the Constitution itself. The Founding Fathers did not contemplate that a change in our system of government could be made through judicial interpretation, as the majority now does with respect to a domestic "territory of the United States" having a civil government established by the authority of the United States. The concurring opinion also fails to explain what is meant by "incorporation" and how such incorporation is achieved. While it is clear, as per the Constitution, that a territory cannot become a state without Congress's approval, it is an entirely different question whether a territory acquired by the United States, with a civil government established by Congress, is for all purposes of government under the complete jurisdiction of the United States and therefore a part of, and incorporated into, the United States, subject to all the authority that the federal government may exert over any territory or people. If judicial interpretation can permit Congress to go outside the Constitution as soon as a territory is acquired, it is meaningless to claim that no power can be exercised under and by authority of the United States except in accordance with the Constitution. Accordingly, Congress could not with regard to Puerto Rico abandon the rule of uniformity set forth in the Constitution.

ANALYSIS

This case is one of what are known as the "Insular Cases," which established how the Constitution would apply to island territories that were acquired during the Spanish-American War. As this five to four ruling demonstrates, providing Congress with power unfettered by the Constitution, except as to basic civil liberties, over the island, was, at the time, a close call. It has been suggested that the Court was following the country's expansionist, empire-building momentum in rendering its decision. Although it seemed that the Insular Cases were overturned by *Reid v. Covert,* 354 U.S. 1 (1957), which held that the Constitution supersedes international treaties ratified by the United States Senate, the Court in *United States v. Verdugo-Urquidez,* 494 U.S. 259 (1990), declared that the Insular Cases still govern the extent to which the Constitution applies to island territories.

Quicknotes

FOURTEENTH AMENDMENT Declares that no state shall make or enforce any law that shall abridge the privileges and immunities of citizens of the United States. No state shall deny to any person within its jurisdiction the equal protection of the laws.

Chae Chan Ping v. United States

Returning Chinese laborer (P) v. Federal government (D)

130 U.S. 581 (1889)

NATURE OF CASE: Appeal from denial of writ of habeas corpus.

FACT SUMMARY: Chae Chan Ping (P), a Chinese laborer who had lived in the United States for 12 years, contended that his being denied reentry into the country was unlawful and violated U.S. treaties with China.

RULE OF LAW

A statute regulating immigration is not unconstitutional because it conflicts with a treaty between the United States and another country.

FACTS: Chae Chan Ping (P), a Chinese laborer, had lived in San Francisco for 12 years. Before leaving to visit China, he had obtained a certificate entitling him to reenter the country. When he returned on October 8, 1888, the certificate was dishonored on the ground a week earlier Congress had passed an amendment to the Chinese Exclusion Act of 1882, which had prohibited Chinese laborers from entering the country. Under the legislation, the certificate had been annulled and his right to land had been abrogated. Because he was denied entry, the captain of the steamship on which he had arrived took custody of him. Chae Chan Ping (P) then filed for a writ of habeas corpus in federal court, which denied the writ, concluding that he had neither been unlawfully detained nor deprived of his liberty. He appealed to the United States Supreme Court, which heard his case.

ISSUE: Is a statute regulating immigration unconstitutional because it conflicts with a treaty between the United States and another country?

HOLDING AND DECISION: (Field, J.) No. A statute regulating immigration is not unconstitutional because it conflicts with a treaty between the United States and another country. The legislation at issue was passed in response to national concerns about the presence of Chinese nationals on the West Coast, especially after the commencement of the Gold Rush in 1848, when they represented significant competition to U.S. citizens in all manner of employment. This eventually caused great irritation to, and conflict with, U.S. citizens and the vast influx of Chinese nationals was seen as a threat to our civilization. The states and inhabitants of the West Coast petitioned Congress to address the problem. Notwithstanding that the United States and China had entered into a treaty in 1868 that supported the movement of people between the two nations, by 1880 the countries entered into a new supplemental treaty that acknowledged the United States had the right to limit or suspend immigration from China but could not abolish it altogether. The treaty also provided that Chinese laborers who already resided in the United States would be allowed to go and come of their own free will and accord. In May 1882, an act of Congress made the supplemental treaty effective, and provided that a 10-year suspension on the immigration of Chinese laborers would be inapplicable to those laborers who were in the United States on the effective date of the treaty. The collectors of customs at American ports were charged with supplying exempt laborers with appropriate certificates of residence. However, as a result of numerous cases of fraud in the issuance of such certificates, Congress passed the act at issue in this case. That act, of October 1, 1888, provided that laborers who held such certificates, but who were outside the United States after passage of the act, would be denied reentry and their certificates deemed annulled. This act concededly violated the treaty of 1868 and the supplemental treaty of 1880, as well as the enabling legislation that gave those treaties effect. However, the act is not therefore unconstitutional or otherwise invalid, because the treaties were of no greater legal obligation than the 1888 act. If a treaty operates by its own force, and relates to a subject within Congress's power, it can be deemed in that regard only the equivalent of a legislative act, to be repealed or modified at Congress's pleasure. Circumstances and unexpected events or emergencies may require the United States to breach its treaty obligations, and Congress has the authority to change policy as it sees fit, within the constitutional limits of its powers. It is not for the courts to judge whether such change is advisable, but only to determine of the new legislation's legality. Here, nothing in the treaties at issue impaired Congress's ability to act, so the remaining question is whether there was any other impairment to Congress's passing the act of 1888, e.g., where Congress did not have the power to regulate the immigration of Chinese laborers. The question must be answered in the negative, since it is settled that Congress may exclude aliens from the country. "The jurisdiction of the nation within its own territory is necessarily exclusive and absolute." The only limitation on such power is the Constitution and considerations of public policy and justice that control, more or less, the conduct of all civilized nations. Thus, Congress may enact legislation that serves to preserve its independence and security, including excluding invading hordes of foreigners who threaten the nation's peace and security, even in the absence of war. "The power of exclusion

Continued on next page.

of foreigners being an incident of sovereignty belonging to the government of the United States as a part of those sovereign powers delegated by the Constitution, the right to its exercise at any time when, in the judgment of the government, the interests of the country require it, cannot be granted away or restrained on behalf of any one." Accordingly, whatever rights Chinese laborers were granted to reenter the country prior to the act of 1888, were revocable at any time by the government, and the wisdom of such revocation is not a proper subject of judicial review. Finally, any arguments that the Alien Act of 1798 was unconstitutional have no bearing here, as that act is distinguishable from the act at bar. The act of 1888 is valid, as is the exclusion of Chae Chan Ping (P) from the country. Affirmed.

ANALYSIS

This case, known as the Chinese Exclusion Case, is still vitally important today, as it is followed for the proposition that the national government has the inherent, plenary, and sovereign right to control its borders. Such control over immigration, while nowhere expressly granted by the Constitution, is deemed to derive from the very nature of sovereignty itself.

Quicknotes

SOVEREIGNTY The absolute power conferred to the state to govern and regulate all persons located and activities conducted therein.

WRIT OF HABEAS CORPUS A proceeding in which a defendant brings a writ to compel a judicial determination of whether he is lawfully being held in custody.

In re Debs

[Parties not identified.]

158 U.S. 564 (1895)

NATURE OF CASE: Appeal from conviction for contempt of court for violating an injunction prohibiting a union strike of a railroad company. [The complete procedural posture of the case is not presented in the casebook extract.]

FACT SUMMARY: Eugene V. Debs, the leader of American Railway Union, contended that the federal courts did not have the power to enjoin his union's strike, so that his conviction for contempt of court for disregarding an injunction ordering his union workers back to work should have been overturned.

RULE OF LAW

The federal courts have the power to enjoin a strike that interferes with interstate commerce and the federal postal service.

FACTS: Eugene V. Debs was the leader of the American Railway Union, which was striking the railroads. A federal court issued an injunction ordering the union workers back to work, on the grounds the strike was interfering with interstate commerce and the operation of the federal postal service. The federal government contended that the 22 railroad companies affected by the strike annually carried 12 million people to and from Chicago; carried many millions of tons of freight; carried the federal mails, and as such were post roads; and could be called upon at any time to carry military troops and supplies therefor. It was claimed that the union was engaged in a conspiracy to thwart interstate commerce and would greatly harm the inhabitants of Chicago. The injunction was ignored, and Debs and other union leaders were found in contempt of court and sentenced to jail time. They contended that the federal courts did not have the authority to enjoin the strike. The United States Supreme Court heard their appeals.

ISSUE: Do the federal courts have the power to enjoin a strike that interferes with interstate commerce and the federal postal service?

HOLDING AND DECISION: (Brewer, J.) Yes. The federal courts have the power to enjoin a strike that interferes with interstate commerce and the federal postal service. The national government has the express power to regulate interstate commerce and to maintain a post-office system. Accordingly, the national government may prevent any unlawful and forcible interference with interstate commerce and the postal system. One way in which it can deal with such interference is through congressional legislation criminalizing it. The executive branch could also use force, through the military, to prevent such interference, especially if prosecuting the crime of obstructing interstate commerce and mail transportation would be of no avail, given the numbers of those disregarding the law in this regard. However, use of force is not the only alternative in such situations; the federal courts may also be appealed to for a peaceful judicial determination of the matter and an exercise of their powers to prevent any interference. If a court thus issues an injunction prohibiting the obstruction of interstate commerce and the transportation of the mails, and the injunction is ignored, the resulting contempt order does not violate the constitutional right to a jury, because when a court enforces its own orders, it is not enforcing the criminal laws of the land. Although it is true that during times of war or rebellion, judicial process has little efficacy, the strike here does not rise to the level of a rebellion or revolution, so that judicial process may be resorted to, and must be respected. [The disposition of the case is not presented in the casebook extract.]

ANALYSIS

It should be noted that in this case, Justice Brewer simply assumed that, in the service of the federal government's sovereignty, the President (executive branch) would have the inherent power to use force to break the strike, and that the federal courts had power to issue injunctive relief and issue contempt citations without a statutory cause of action. Presumably, Congress could also have used force, under Article I, § 8, of the Constitution, to break the strike.

Quicknotes

CONTEMPT OF COURT Conduct that is intended to obstruct the court's effective administration of justice or to otherwise disrespect its authority.

ENJOIN The ordering of a party to cease the conduct of a specific activity.

INTERSTATE COMMERCE Commercial dealings between two parties located in different states or located in one state and accomplished through a point in another state or a foreign country; commercial dealings transacted between two states.

Lochner v. New York

Employer bakery (D) v. State (P)

198 U.S. 45 (1905)

NATURE OF CASE: Appeal from conviction for violation of a labor law.

FACT SUMMARY: A state labor law prohibited employment in bakeries for more than 60 hours a week or more than 10 hours a day. Lochner (D) permitted an employee in his bakery to work over 60 hours in one week.

RULE OF LAW

A state law regulating the hours bakery employees may work is not a valid exercise of state police power.

FACTS: Lochner (D) was fined for violating a state labor law. The law prohibited employment in bakeries for more than 60 hours a week or more than 10 hours a day. Lochner (D) permitted an employee to work in his bakery for more than 60 hours in one week and was convicted for doing that.

ISSUE: Is a state law regulating the hours bakery employees may work a valid exercise of state police power?

HOLDING AND DECISION: (Peckham, J.) No. A state law regulating the hours bakery employees may work is not a valid exercise of state police power. The general right to make a contract in relation to one's business is part of the liberty of the individual protected by the Fourteenth Amendment. The right to purchase or sell labor is part of the liberty protected by this amendment. However, the states do possess certain police powers relating to the safety, health, morals, and general welfare of the public. If the contract is one that the state in the exercise of its police power has the right to prohibit, the Fourteenth Amendment will not prevent the state's prohibition. When, as here, the state acts to limit the right to labor or the right to contract, it is necessary to determine whether the rights of the state or the individual shall prevail. The Fourteenth Amendment limits the state's exercise of its police power, otherwise the state would have unbounded power once it stated that legislation was to conserve the health, morals, or safety of its people. It is not sufficient to assert that the act relates to public health. Rather, it must have a more direct relation, as a means to an end, to an appropriate state goal, before an act can interfere with an individual's right to contract in relation to his labor. In this case, there is no reasonable foundation for holding the act to be necessary to the health of the public or of bakery officials. Statutes such as this one are merely meddlesome interferences with the rights of the individual. They are invalid unless there is some fair ground to say that there is material danger to the public health or to the employees' health if the labor hours are not curtailed. It cannot be said that the production of healthy bread depends upon the hours that the employees work. Nor is the trade of a baker an unhealthy one to the degree that would authorize the legislature to interfere with the rights to labor and of free contract. Lochner's (D) conviction is reversed.

DISSENT: (Harlan, J.) Whether or not this is wise legislation is not a question for this Court. It is impossible to say that there is not substantial or real regulation between the statute and the state's legitimate goals. This decision brings under the Court's supervision matters that supposedly belonged exclusively to state legislatures.

DISSENT: (Holmes, J.) The word "liberty" in the Fourteenth Amendment should not invalidate a statute unless it can be said that a reasonable person would say that the statute infringes fundamental principles of our people and our law. A reasonable person might think this statute valid. Citizens' liberty is regulated by many state laws that have been held to be valid, i.e., the Sunday laws, the lottery laws, laws requiring vaccination.

ANALYSIS

From the *Lochner* decision in 1905 to the 1930s the Court invalidated a considerable number of laws on substantive due process grounds, such as laws fixing minimum wages, maximum hours, and prices and laws regulating business activities. The modern Court claims to have rejected the *Lochner* doctrine. It has withdrawn careful scrutiny in most economic areas but has maintained and increased intervention with respect to a variety of non-economic liberties. However, not only economic regulations were struck down under *Lochner*. That doctrine formed the basis for absorbing rights such as those in the First Amendment into the Fourteenth Amendment concept of liberty. *Lochner* also helped justify on behalf of other non-economic rights such as the right to teach in a foreign language (*Meyers v. Nebraska*, 262 U.S. 390). *Meyers* was to be relied upon in the birth control decision *Griswold v. Connecticut*, 318 U.S. 479 (1965).

Continued on next page.

Quicknotes

FOURTEENTH AMENDMENT Declares that no state shall make or enforce any law that shall abridge the privileges and immunities of citizens of the United States. No state shall deny to any person within its jurisdiction the equal protection of the laws.

POLICE POWERS The power of a state or local government to regulate private conduct for the health, safety, and welfare of the general public.

SUBSTANTIVE DUE PROCESS A constitutional safeguard limiting the power of the state, irrespective of how fair its procedures may be; substantive limits placed on the power of the state.

Coppage v. Kansas

Employer (D) v. State (P)

236 U.S. 1 (1915)

NATURE OF CASE: Appeal in action challenging as unconstitutional a statute that prohibited employers from requiring employees to enter agreements that they would not join a union ("yellow dog contracts") as a condition of employment. [The procedural posture of the case is not presented in the casebook excerpt.]

FACT SUMMARY: Kansas (P) made it illegal for an employer to require an employee to sign an agreement promising not to join a union ("yellow dog contract") as a condition of employment. Coppage (D), an employer, challenged the Kansas (P) law as violating the Fourteenth Amendment.

RULE OF LAW

A statute that prohibits an employer from requiring, as a condition of employment, that an employee sign an agreement that the employee will not join a union ("yellow dog contract") violates the Due Process Clause of the Fourteenth Amendment.

FACTS: Kansas (P) made it illegal for an employer to require an employee to sign an agreement promising not to join a union ("yellow dog contract") as a condition of employment. Coppage (D), an employer, challenged the Kansas (P) law as violating the Due Process Clause of the Fourteenth Amendment. [The procedural posture of the case is not presented in the casebook excerpt.]

ISSUE: Does a statute that prohibits an employer from requiring as a condition of employment that an employee sign an agreement that the employee will not join a union ("yellow dog contract") violate the Due Process Clause of the Fourteenth Amendment?

HOLDING AND DECISION: (Pitney, J.) Yes. A statute that prohibits an employer from requiring, as a condition of employment, that an employee sign an agreement that the employee will not join a union ("yellow dog contract") violates the Due Process Clause of the Fourteenth Amendment. Employers as well as employees are equally free to contract for conditions of employment, and any legislation that disturbs that equality is an arbitrary interference with freedom of contract that cannot justify the state's exercise of police power. Although there tends to be a natural inequality in the bargaining positions of employers and employees, as there typically is in many contract situations, to uphold freedom of contract, as well as property rights, it is necessary to hold that such inequalities are a legitimate result of that freedom of contract and exercise of property rights. The Fourteenth Amendment recognizes that "liberty" and "property" are co-equal rights, and prohibits the states from interfering with either. Accordingly, a state may not use its police power to strike down contracts, such as the one at bar, in the name of the public good by attempting to remedy the inequalities that are a normal and inevitable result of freedom of contract. Although there are situations in which a state may use its police powers for the public good by restricting the making of certain types of contracts, that is not the case here because the statute at issue does not aim to promote health, safety, morals, or public welfare other than by equalizing the bargaining positions of freely contracting parties. In other words, "an interference with the normal exercise of personal liberty and property rights is the primary object of the statute, and not an incident to the advancement of the general welfare." And it is precisely such interference that the Constitution prohibits.

ANALYSIS

In dissent, Justice Holmes argued that the Constitution does not expressly prohibit a statute such as the one Kansas enacted, so that such a law should be upheld, and he was also of the view that equality of bargaining position is the starting point of freedom of contract, so that enforcing such equality could be a justified exercise of the police power. In a separate dissent, Justice Day indicated that although the right of contract should be protected against arbitrary legislative restrains, it should be left to the legislature to decide whether a law, such as the Kansas law at issue, promotes the public welfare. Justice Day also indicated that, as a matter of public policy, a person may not be allowed to "barter away . . . substantial rights."

Quicknotes

FOURTEENTH AMENDMENT DUE PROCESS CLAUSE Provides that protections mandated by the U.S. Constitution and observed by the federal government are equally applicable, and therefore must be observed by the States.

FREEDOM OF CONTRACT The doctrine that parties have the right to bind themselves legally without outside interference from government.

LABOR UNION A group of employees formed for the purpose of obtaining more favorable working conditions or wages.

Continued on next page.

POLICE POWER The power of a government to impose restrictions on the rights of private persons, so long as those restrictions are reasonably related to the promotion and protection of public health, safety, morals, and the general welfare.

STATUTE A law enacted pursuant to the legislature's power and consistent with specified procedure so that it regulates a particular activity.

Jacobson v. Massachusetts

Vaccination objector (D) v. State (P)

197 U.S. 11 (1905)

NATURE OF CASE: Appeal in action challenging as unconstitutional a state compulsory vaccination law. [The procedural posture of the case is not presented in the casebook excerpt.]

FACT SUMMARY: Jacobson (D) asserted that a Massachusetts (P) law that required everyone except children with a medical exemption to be vaccinated or pay a fine was an unconstitutional infringement of liberty.

RULE OF LAW

A law that requires everyone except children with a medical exemption to be vaccinated against smallpox or pay a fine is not an unconstitutional infringement of liberty where there is an overwhelming consensus in the medical profession that the smallpox vaccine is safe and effective.

FACTS: Massachusetts (P) enacted a compulsory vaccination law, enforced by a monetary fine, that required everyone except children who had a medical exemption to be vaccinated against smallpox. Jacobson (D), who believed the smallpox vaccine was dangerous, asserted that putting him to the choice of being vaccinated or paying a fine unconstitutionally infringed his liberty. At the time, there was overwhelming consensus in the medical profession that the smallpox vaccination was safe and effective. The United States Supreme Court granted certiorari in the case. [The procedural posture of the case is not presented in the casebook excerpt.]

ISSUE: Is a law that requires everyone except children with a medical exemption to be vaccinated against smallpox or pay a fine an unconstitutional infringement of liberty where there is an overwhelming consensus in the medical profession that the smallpox vaccine is safe and effective?

HOLDING AND DECISION: (Harlan, J.) No. A law that requires everyone except children with a medical exemption to be vaccinated against smallpox or pay a fine is not an unconstitutional infringement of liberty where there is an overwhelming consensus in the medical profession that the smallpox vaccine is safe and effective. The liberty guaranteed by the Constitution is not absolute, as there are many restraints to which everyone is subject for the common good. If that were not so, and everyone had absolute liberty to do as they wanted, an organized society that is safe for its members could not exist, and instead there would be disorder and anarchy. Although Jacobson (D) presented evidence of those in the medical profession who do not believe that vaccination is a valid means of preventing the spread of smallpox, the overwhelming consensus in that profession, to the contrary, is that the smallpox vaccination is safe and effective. The state's legislature, being aware of these opposing views, chose the latter view to protect the public from an epidemic that threatened the entire population. The Court's task is not to make that legislative decision, but, upon review, it must determine if there is a relation between the means prescribed by the legislature and the ends sought to be effected. In light of the experience of this country and other countries that have dealt with smallpox, it cannot be said that there is no real or substantial connection between vaccination and the protection of public health and safety. A minority of the population, or even a single individual, cannot be allowed, in the name of their liberty, to endanger the majority of the population of which they are a part. "We are unwilling to hold it to be an element in the liberty secured by the Constitution ... that one person, or a minority of persons, residing in any community and enjoying the benefits of local government, should have the power ... to dominate the majority when supported in their action by the authority of the state."

ANALYSIS

Justices Peckham and Brewer dissented without opinion in *Jacobson*. Justice Harlan recognized in *Jacobson* that there could be "extreme cases" where, given a person's particular health conditions, it would be cruel and inhuman treatment to subject that person to vaccination, as where doing so would seriously impair that person's health, or even lead to the person's death. However, Justice Harlan also observed that there was no reason to believe that the Massachusetts (P) legislature intended the vaccination statute to be applied in such a case, or, if it were so intended, that the judiciary would not be competent to interfere and protect the health and life of the individual concerned, since all laws should be construed reasonably so that their application does not "lead to injustice, oppression, or an absurd consequence." Finding that the case at bar was not an "extreme" case, and that Jacobson (D) likely would not be harmed by vaccination, the Court held that, as applied to him, the Massachusetts (P) statute was a constitutional exercise of the police power.

Continued on next page.

Quicknotes

POLICE POWER The power of a government to impose restrictions on the rights of private persons, so long as those restrictions are reasonably related to the promotion and protection of public health, safety, morals, and the general welfare.

Muller v. Oregon

Employer (D) v. State (P)

208 U.S. 412 (1908)

NATURE OF CASE: Appeal from conviction for violating a state law that prohibited employers from requiring women to work more than ten hours a day.

FACT SUMMARY: Muller (D) was convicted of violating a state law that prohibited employers from requiring women to work more than ten hours a day. He appealed the conviction on the ground that it deprived him of the freedom to contract under the Fourteenth Amendment.

RULE OF LAW

A state law that prohibits employers from requiring women to work more than ten hours a day does not violate the freedom to contract guaranteed by the Fourteenth Amendment.

FACTS: Oregon (P) had a statute that required that no female could be employed for more than ten hours during any one day and that made it a misdemeanor to violate the statute. Muller (D), a supervisor at a laundry shop, was convicted of allowing one of his female employees to work more than ten hours per day. He appealed the conviction on the ground that it violated his constitutional right to freedom of contract. The Oregon Supreme Court affirmed the conviction, and the United States Supreme Court granted review.

ISSUE: Does a state law that prohibits employers from requiring women to work more than ten hours a day violate the freedom to contract guaranteed by the Fourteenth Amendment?

HOLDING AND DECISION: (Brewer, J.) No. A state law that prohibits employers from requiring women to work more than ten hours a day does not violate the freedom to contract guaranteed by the Fourteenth Amendment. There is no absolute freedom of contract, although any laws abridging such freedom must be justified by the existence of exceptional circumstances. Here those circumstances exist in the inherent difference between the two sexes, and a public interest in protecting women, who depend on men and whose "physical structure and the performance of the maternal functions place her at a disadvantage in the struggle for subsistence." Such legislation would not be necessary for men. Thus, the limits placed by the law on a woman's freedom of contract are not just for her benefit, but for the benefit of all of society.

ANALYSIS

Other than being a prime example of the Court's paternalism during the *Lochner* era (see *Lochner*, 198 U.S. 45 [1905]), this case is notable for the brief filed in the case by Louis Brandeis, who would later become a Supreme Court Justice. The brief, explicitly mentioned in the opinion, was a detailed, 113-page brief that purported to document that women's reproductive health required limiting nondomestic work. This type of brief, which used social science data to show the need for a particular law, came to be known as the "Brandeis brief."

Quicknotes

FOURTEENTH AMENDMENT Declares that no state shall make or enforce any law that shall abridge the privileges or immunities of citizens of the United States. No state shall deny to any person within its jurisdiction the equal protection of the laws.

FREEDOM OF CONTRACT A basic freedom guaranteed by Article I, § 10, clause 1, of the U.S. Constitution and which may not be denied by the state.

Adkins v. Children's Hospital

Government official (D) v. Employer (P)

261 U.S. 525 (1923)

NATURE OF CASE: Appeal from order enjoining enforcement of a law prescribing minimum wages for women.

FACT SUMMARY: Congress enacted a law that prescribed minimum wages for women working in the District of Columbia. Children's Hospital (P) challenged the law on the ground it violated the Fifth Amendment's due process guarantees.

RULE OF LAW

A law that prescribes minimum wages for women violates the Due Process Clause of the Fifth Amendment.

FACTS: Congress passed a law that fixed minimum wages for women (and children) in the District of Columbia. Children's Hospital (P), which employed many women, challenged the law as a violation of the Fifth Amendment's due process guarantees, and sued to enjoin enforcement of the law. The Supreme Court of the District (the trial court) denied the requested injunctive relief, but the Court of Appeals for the District reversed. The United States Supreme Court granted review.

ISSUE: Does a law that prescribes minimum wages for women violate the Due Process Clause of the Fifth Amendment?

HOLDING AND DECISION: (Sutherland, J.) Yes. The Due Process Clause of the Fifth Amendment guarantees the freedom of contract. Employment contracts are covered by that freedom and the parties thereto have an equal right to obtain from each other the best terms they can. And although freedom of contract is not absolute, it is the rule, not the exception, and for a law to abridge that freedom requires exceptional circumstances. Here, there are no such exceptional circumstances. The differences between the two sexes have diminished to the point of vanishing, as evidenced by passage of the Nineteenth Amendment [guaranteeing the vote for women], and emancipated women do not need to have their freedom of contract restricted to protect them, any more than men do. Also, the argument that without minimum wage women would be forced to earn money in an immoral manner is unfounded because it cannot be shown that well-paid women safeguard their morality any more than less-paid women. The law favors the employee but does not take into account employer's needs. The law exacts from the employer an arbitrary payment that is not connected to the employer's business or the kind of work the employee does. Although it is said that the regulation of wages is needed for social justice, the common good is better served by protecting society's members from the arbitrary restraint of their liberties. For these reasons, the law violates the Constitution's due process requirements.

DISSENT: (Holmes, J.) If it is constitutional to regulate maximum hours of work for women, as the Court has held, then it is likewise constitutional to regulate the minimum wages for that work, since the employment bargain entered is equally affected regardless of which half of the bargain is regulated. A minimum wage law does not compel the payment of anything, but merely forbids payment below what is necessary for health and "right living" for work performed. This is similar in effect to hundreds of regulations that have been upheld as a valid exercise of the police power, and it is not for the Court to determine, as a matter of constitutional law, whether such a regulation is for the public good or not.

ANALYSIS

Although the Court reaffirmed *Adkins* in 1936, in *Morehead v. New York ex rel. Tipaldo*, 298 U.S. 587 (1936), which also declared unconstitutional a state minimum-wage law for women on the grounds that it impermissibly interfered with the freedom of contract because it did not serve a valid state police purpose, President Roosevelt's threat to pack the Court convinced the Court to change course, and, in *West Coast Hotel Company v. Parrish*, 300 U.S. 379 (1937), the Court upheld a minimum wage law.

Quicknotes

DUE PROCESS CLAUSE Language found in the Fifth and Fourteenth Amendments to the U.S. Constitution providing that no person shall be deprived of "life, liberty, or property without due process of law."

FREEDOM OF CONTRACT A basic freedom guaranteed by Article I, § 10, clause 1, of the U.S. Constitution and which may not be denied by the state.

Champion v. Ames (The Lottery Case)

Conspirator (D) v. Federal government (P)

188 U.S. 321 (1903)

NATURE OF CASE: Petition for writ of habeas corpus.

FACT SUMMARY: Champion (D) was indicted for conspiracy to violate a federal law prohibiting the transportation of lottery tickets from one state to another by any means.

RULE OF LAW

As a means of executing the power to regulate interstate commerce, Congress may make it a criminal offense to cause lottery tickets to be carried from one state to another.

FACTS: An 1895 congressional act prohibited importing, mailing, or transporting from one state to another any lottery ticket. Champion (D), who had allegedly conspired to ship by Wells Fargo Express a box containing lottery tickets, was indicted thereunder. He filed a petition for a writ of habeas corpus, charging that the law was not a constitutional exercise of Congress's power to regulate interstate commerce.

ISSUE: Does Congress's power to regulate interstate commerce allow it to prohibit transportation of lottery tickets from one state to another?

HOLDING AND DECISION: (Harlan, J.) Yes. As a state may, for the purpose of guarding the morals of its own people, forbid all sales of lottery tickets within its limits, so Congress, for the purpose of guarding the people of the United States against the "widespread pestilence of lotteries," *Phalen v. Virginia*, 49 U.S. (8 How.) 163, 168 (1850), and to protect the commerce which concerns all the states, may exercise its power to regulate interstate commerce by prohibiting the carrying of lottery tickets from one state to another. This Court should hesitate long before adjudging that an evil of such appalling character, carried on through interstate commerce, cannot be met and crushed by the only power competent to that end. Congress alone has the power to occupy the complete sphere of interstate commerce, through legislation.

DISSENT: (Fuller, C.J.) Lottery tickets, like insurance policies, are personal contracts that do not constitute a part of the commerce between the states. If a lottery ticket is not an article of commerce, how can it become so when placed in a box and transported by an express company? By the ruling in this case, an invitation to dine or a note of introduction would become articles of commerce once deposited with an express company for transportation. Such a notion is absurd.

ANALYSIS

This was the first in a whole series of cases validating Congress's use of its commerce power as a device to achieve a strictly social goal—providing interstate commerce in things deemed socially harmful. For example, the Mann Act, making it a felony to transport a woman from one state to another for immoral purposes, was upheld.

Quicknotes

COMMERCE POWER The power delegated to Congress by the United States Constitution to regulate interstate commerce.

CONSPIRACY Concerted action by two or more persons to accomplish some unlawful purpose.

INTERSTATE COMMERCE Commercial dealings between two parties located in different states or located in one state and accomplished through a point in another state or a foreign country; commercial dealings transacted between two states.

WRIT OF HABEAS CORPUS A proceeding in which a defendant brings a writ to compel a judicial determination of whether he is lawfully being held in custody.

Hammer v. Dagenhart

Employment (D) v. Parent (P)

247 U.S. 251 (1918)

NATURE OF CASE: Appeal from a decree enjoining enforcement of the Child Labor Act.

FACT SUMMARY: Congress passed a law that prohibited the shipment in interstate commerce of any products of any mills, mines, or factories that employed children.

RULE OF LAW

Congress, under its commerce power, may not pass a law prohibiting the transportation in interstate commerce of products of companies that employed children as laborers in violation of the terms of the law.

FACTS: A congressional act prohibited the shipment in interstate commerce of the product of any mine or quarry that employed children under the age of 16. It prohibited the shipment in such commerce of the product of any mill, cannery, workshop, or factory that employed children under the age of 14 or employed children between the ages of 14 and 16 for more than eight hours a day, or more than six days a week, or before 6 A.M. or after 7 P.M. Dagenhart (P) brought this action on behalf of his two minor children after being informed by the company where they worked of their impending discharge on the effective date of the act. Hammer (D), the U.S. Attorney General, and the company that had employed Dagenhart's (P) children were named as defendants.

ISSUE: Can Congress, under its commerce power, pass a law prohibiting the transportation in interstate commerce of products of companies that employed children as laborers in violation of the terms of the law?

HOLDING AND DECISION: (Day, J.) No. Congress, under its commerce power, may not pass a law prohibiting the transportation in interstate commerce of products of companies that employed children as laborers in violation of the terms of the law. It is argued that the power of Congress to regulate commerce includes the power to prohibit the transportation of ordinary products in commerce. However, in cases such as the *Lottery* case, 188 U.S. 321 (1903), the power to prohibit the carrying of lottery tickets is as to those particular objects the same as the exertion of the power to regulate. In those cases, the use of interstate commerce was necessary to the accomplishment of harmful results. Regulation over commerce could only be accomplished by prohibiting the use of interstate commerce to affect the evil intended. Here, the thing intended to be accomplished by this act is the denial of interstate commerce facilities to those employing children within the prohibited ages. The goods shipped are of themselves harmless. The production of articles intended for interstate commerce is a matter of local regulation. The making of goods and the mining of coal are not commerce, nor does the fact that these things are to be afterwards shipped or used in interstate commerce make their production a part thereof. It is also argued that congressional regulation is necessary because of the unfair advantage possessed by manufacturers in states that have less stringent child labor laws. However, Congress has no power to require states to exercise their police powers to prevent possible unfair competition. The act is unconstitutional, and the decree enjoining its enforcement is affirmed.

DISSENT: (Holmes, J.) The *Lottery* case and others following it establish that a law is not beyond Congress's commerce power merely because it prohibits certain transportation. There is no legal distinction between the evils sought to be controlled in those cases and the evil of premature and excessive child labor. The Court has no right to substitute its judgment of which evils may be controlled.

ANALYSIS

After the *Hammer* decision, Congress sought to regulate child labor through the taxing power. That law was invalidated in *Bailey v. Drexel Furnishing Co.*, 259 U.S. 20 (1922). Subsequently, Congress submitted a proposed to the states a constitutional amendment that authorized national child labor law. The amendment has not been ratified, but the need for it has largely disappeared in view of *U.S. v. Darby*, 312 U.S. 100 (1941), which overruled *Hammer*.

Quicknotes

COMMERCE POWER The power delegated to Congress by the United States Constitution to regulate interstate commerce.

INTERSTATE COMMERCE Commercial dealings between two parties located in different states or located in one state and accomplished through a point in another state or a foreign country; commercial dealings transacted between two states.

POLICE POWERS The power of a state or local government to regulate private conduct for the health, safety and welfare of the general public.

TAXING POWER The authority delegated to Congress by the United States Constitution to impose taxes.

Bailey v. Drexel Furniture Co. (The Child Labor Tax Case)

Collector of Internal Revenue (D) v. Furniture company (P)

259 U.S. 20 (1922)

NATURE OF CASE: Constitutional challenge to federal law.

FACT SUMMARY: Congress enacted a bill imposing a special tax on those employing children under a certain age.

RULE OF LAW

Congress may not, under the pretext of enacting laws pursuant to its legitimate powers, pass laws to accomplish ends beyond its authority.

FACTS: Congress enacted the Child Labor Act (the Act), which applied a percentage of profit tax to any company employing children under a certain age. The Act also restricted the number of days per week and hours per day that could be worked. Both the Internal Revenue Service and the Department of Labor could enter and inspect the businesses covered under the Act. Drexel Furniture Co. (P) was assessed a tax for employing a factory boy under the age of 14 in violation of the Act. Drexel (P) appealed the tax assessment on the ground this was not a tax act and that Congress had no authority to regulate purely local conduct that was reserved to the states. Drexel (P) alleged that the Act was merely a sham to accomplish an end outside of Congress's power.

ISSUE: May Congress, under the pretext of enacting laws pursuant to its legitimate powers, pass laws to accomplish ends beyond its authority?

HOLDING AND DECISION: (Taft, C.J.) No. Congress may not, under the pretext of enacting laws pursuant to its legitimate powers, pass laws to accomplish ends beyond its authority. The Act herein is not a tax law. It is not designed to raise revenue, but to coerce businesses into abiding by national child labor laws. It excuses innocent conduct while punishing willful violations of the Act. The tax is not proportioned on the degree or frequency of violations. It is a penalty not a tax. The point herein is to order conduct, not raise revenue. The conduct sought to be regulated is local in nature and is beyond the power of Congress. The tax is unconstitutional.

ANALYSIS

The taxing and spending powers have close functional and doctrinal ties to the commerce power since the manner in which taxes are imposed can have significant regulatory impacts. As with commerce laws, taxing measures have been used to deal with "police" as well as economic problems. Regulation through taxing has been resorted to when the need for legislation seemed great and the direct regulatory authority through the Commerce Clause was "under constitutional clouds," such as in the cases of child labor and of New Deal legislation in the 1930s.

Quicknotes

COMMERCE CLAUSE Article I, § 8, cl. 3, of the United States Constitution, granting Congress the power to regulate commerce with foreign countries and between the states.

ENUMERATED POWERS Specific powers mentioned in, and granted by, the Constitution; e.g., the taxing power.

SPENDING POWER The power delegated to Congress by the United States Constitution to spend money in providing for the nation's welfare.

TAXING POWER The authority delegated to Congress by the United States Constitution to impose taxes.

Missouri v. Holland

State (P) v. Game warden (D)

252 U.S. 416 (1920)

NATURE OF CASE: An action in equity to enjoin the enforcement of the Migratory Bird Treaty Act.

FACT SUMMARY: Missouri (P) claimed that the Bird Treaty Act was an unconstitutional interference with the rights reserved to the states by the Tenth Amendment.

RULE OF LAW

Congress can constitutionally enact a statute under Article I, § 8 to enforce a treaty created under Article II, § 2, even if the statute by itself is unconstitutional.

FACTS: On December 8, 1916, the United States entered into a treaty with Great Britain to protect birds that migrated between Canada and the United States. Congress passed a statute to enforce the Migratory Bird Treaty, which allowed the Secretary of Agriculture to formulate regulations to enforce the treaty. The State of Missouri (P) filed a bill in equity to prevent Holland (D), the game warden of the United States, from enforcing the treaty. Missouri (P) claimed that the statute was an unconstitutional interference with the rights reserved to the states by the Tenth Amendment and that the state had a pecuniary interest as owner of the wild birds, which were being interfered with. Before the treaty had been entered into, Congress had attempted to regulate the killing of migratory birds within the states and that statute, standing by itself, had been declared unconstitutional. The United States (P) contended that Congress had the power to enact the statute to enforce the treaty and that the statute and treaty were the supreme law of the land.

ISSUE: Can Congress validly enact a statute to enforce a treaty if the statute standing by itself would be unconstitutional because it interfered with the rights reserved to the states by the Tenth Amendment?

HOLDING AND DECISION: (Holmes, J.) Yes. Article II, § 2 grants the President the power to make treaties and Article VI, § 2 declares that treaties shall be part of the supreme law of the land. If a treaty is a valid one, Article I, § 8 gives Congress the power to enact legislation that is a necessary and proper means to enforce the treaty. While acts of Congress are the supreme law of the land only when they are made in pursuance of the Constitution, treaties are valid when made under the authority of the United States. The Court stated that there were qualifications to the treaty-making power but felt that the qualifications must be determined by looking at the facts of each case. There are situations that require national action which an act of Congress could not deal with, but which a treaty enforced with a congressional act could. Because Missouri (P) did not have the power to adequately control the problem connected with the migratory birds (nor did any other state acting alone), this was a situation that required national action. Therefore, even though Missouri (P) would have been able to establish regulations pertaining to the birds if Congress had not already done so, Congress could establish regulations in conjunction with the treaty without infringing on the rights reserved to the states by the Tenth Amendment. The Court rejected Missouri's (P) claim that it had a pecuniary interest as an owner when the birds were in the state. There is no ownership until there is possession and the birds never came into the possession of the state of Missouri (P). Congress can, therefore, constitutionally enact a statute under Article I, § 8, to enforce a treaty even if the statute by itself would be unconstitutional. Treaty and statute upheld.

ANALYSIS

Many people were upset with the decision in this case because they feared that the Court had interpreted the treaty power so broadly that all constitutional limitations could be overridden by use of treaties and accompanying congressional legislation. In 1954, the Bricker Amendment was narrowly defeated. It required that a treaty could only become effective as internal law in the United States through legislation that would be valid in the absence of the treaty. This would have, in effect, overruled the decision in this case, because the congressional act was not valid when standing by itself. Several other similar proposals were made during the following three years, which also failed.

Quicknotes

EQUITY Fairness; justice; the determination of a matter consistent with principles of fairness and not in strict compliance with rules of law.

TENTH AMENDMENT The Tenth Amendment to the United States Constitution reserves those powers therein, not expressly delegated to the federal government or prohibited to the states, to the states or to the people.

TREATY An agreement between two or more nations for the benefit of the general public.

Hans v. Louisiana

State's citizen (P) v. State (D)

134 U.S. 1 (1890)

NATURE OF CASE: Appeal in action brought in federal court by a citizen of a state against the state that arose under the Constitution or laws of the United States. [The procedural posture of the case is not presented in the casebook extract.]

FACT SUMMARY: Hans (P), a citizen of Louisiana (D), contended that he was entitled to sue Louisiana (D) in federal court on a claim that arose under the Constitution or the laws of the United States. [The procedural posture and complete factual background of the case are not presented in the casebook extract.]

RULE OF LAW

A citizen of a state may not sue the state in federal court, absent the state's consent, in an action that arises under the Constitution or laws of the United States.

FACTS: Hans (P), a citizen of Louisiana, sued Louisiana (D) in federal court in an action involving bonds issued by the state, which action involved a claim under the federal Constitution or the laws of the United States. An 1875 statute had given federal courts jurisdiction over cases involving such claims. Hans (P) lost, and the United States Supreme Court heard his appeal. [The procedural posture and complete factual background of the case are not presented in the casebook extract.]

ISSUE: May a citizen of a state sue the state in federal court, absent the state's consent, in an action that arises under the Constitution or laws of the United States?

HOLDING AND DECISION: (Bradley, J.) No. A citizen of a state may not sue the state in federal court, absent the state's consent, in an action that arises under the Constitution or laws of the United States. If only the plain text of the Eleventh Amendment were to control this case, Hans (P) would be correct in asserting that the Eleventh Amendment only bars suits in federal court brought against states by citizens of other states or of other countries and does not bar his suit. However, so reading the amendment leads to the anomalous result that a state, absent its consent, can be sued in federal court by its own citizens, but not by citizens of other states or countries. Such a result would be "startling and unexpected." The Court's earlier decision in *Chisholm v. Georgia,* 2 U.S. (2 Dall.) 419 (1793), which permitted a citizen of one state to sue a different state, was decided incorrectly, and it is no surprise that the Eleventh Amendment was enacted in response to that decision. The correct view of the Constitution then, and now, is that states have sovereign immunity from suits brought by individuals. To think that the Eleventh Amendment would have been adopted if it had included a proviso that citizens of a state could sue their state is absurd.

CONCURRENCE: (Harlan, J.) The majority's reliance on *Chisholm v. Georgia* is misplaced, since that case was correctly decided based on the Constitution as it was then written. Otherwise, the majority's basic holding is correct.

ANALYSIS

Hans continues to be good law, and it has been used to support a number of decisions that have expanded sovereign immunity, despite the Eleventh Amendment's narrow wording. It has also been criticized on the ground it has created significant—if not insurmountable—difficulties for individuals attempting to hold the states accountable for violations of the Constitution and other federal laws.

Quicknotes

ELEVENTH AMENDMENT The Eleventh Amendment to the United States Constitution prohibits the extension of the judicial powers of the federal courts to suits brought against a state by citizens of another state, or of a foreign state, without the state's consent.

SOVEREIGN IMMUNITY Immunity of government from suit without its consent.

CHAPTER 5

The New Deal and the Civil Rights Era

Quick Reference Rules of Law

CHAPTER 5

Home Building & Loan Association v. Blaisdell (The Minnesota Mortgage Moratorium Case)

Mortgagee (P) v. Mortgagor (D)

290 U.S. 398 (1934)

NATURE OF CASE: Appeal to determine the constitutionality of a state statute.

FACT SUMMARY: In 1933, Minnesota passed the Mortgage Moratorium Law, which provided for a delay in the final foreclosure of mortgages.

RULE OF LAW
The Contract Clause of the Constitution does not "absolutely" bar a state from passing any law that will impair the obligations of contracts.

FACTS: In 1933, Minnesota passed the Mortgage Moratorium Law, to remain in effect during the emergency created by the Depression. This law provided that the period for redemption from foreclosure sales could be extended for a specified time (i.e., foreclosure of mortgages could be delayed) if the mortgagor obtained an order requiring him to pay a reasonable value of the income of the property or its fair rental value to the mortgagee. After passage of this law, the Blaisdells (D) secured an order delaying the final foreclosure of their mortgage on the condition that they pay the property's reasonable rental value to the Home Building & Loan Assn. (Home Building) (P), the mortgagee. Thereupon, Home Building (P) brought an action against the Blaisdells (D) to complete foreclosure. After the Minnesota Supreme Court held for the Blaisdells (D) on the basis that the Mortgage Moratorium Law was constitutional, Home Building (P) appealed.

ISSUE: Does the Contract Clause of the Constitution "absolutely" bar a state from passing any law that will impair the obligations of contracts?

HOLDING AND DECISION: (Hughes, C.J.) No. The Contract Clause of the Constitution does not "absolutely" bar a state from passing any law that will impair the obligations of contracts. The Contract Clause of the Constitution provides that no state shall pass any law impairing the obligations of contracts, but, even if such obligations will be impaired, a state may exercise its eminent domain power and/or its power to protect the public's health, safety, and welfare. These are essential attributes of sovereign power and, as such, must be retained by the states. Of course, though, they must be exercised reasonably (i.e., only those means appropriate to accomplish them can be used). Here, the Mortgage Moratorium Law is reasonably necessary under the circumstances to protect the public's welfare. Therefore, even though the Mortgage Moratorium Law impairs the obligations of contracts (i.e., by delaying mortgagee's rights under mortgage agreements), the Law is valid. Affirmed.

DISSENT: (Sutherland, J.) An examination of the history behind the adoption of the Impairment of Contracts Clause leaves no reasonable ground upon which to base a denial that the clause was meant to foreclose state action impairing the obligation of contracts primarily and especially in respect of such action aimed at giving relief to debtors in time of emergency. The time of emergency defense should not now succeed because it constitutes an effort to overthrow the constitutional provision by an appeal to facts and circumstances identical with those which brought it into existence.

UNPUBLISHED CONCURRENCE: (Cardozo, J.) The Industrial Revolution and tremendous population growth have resulted in social and economic changes that have made it necessary for government to do a thousand things beyond the experience and thought of the Founding Fathers. With the growing recognition of this need, courts have awakened to the truth that the Contract Clause is perverted from its proper meaning when it throttles the capacity of the states to exert their governmental power in response to crying needs. The adoption of the Fourteenth Amendment brought a dramatic change in the relationship of federal and state governments. The distinction between right and remedy diminished, and contracts were still to be preserved. But a promise exchanged between individuals was not to paralyze the state in its endeavor in times of direful crises to keep its lifeblood flowing.

ANALYSIS

This case illustrates the central limitation placed upon the Contract Clause of the Constitution. There are, however, other limitations. For example, the Clause applies only to state legislation (i.e., only a legislature can "pass" a law). As such, a state court can overrule a prior decision even though such a reversal may affect contracts. Note, also, that the Contract Clause does not apply to the federal government. However, the concept of due process in the Fifth Amendment has been interpreted in a manner that provides basically the same protection against the federal government.

Continued on next page.

Quicknotes

CONTRACT An agreement pursuant to which a party agrees to act, or to forbear from acting, in exchange for performance on the part of the other party.

DUE PROCESS CLAUSE Language found in the Fifth and Fourteenth Amendments to the United States Constitution providing that no person shall be deprived of "life, liberty, or property without due process of law."

EMINENT DOMAIN The governmental power to take private property for public use so long as just compensation is paid therefore.

MORTGAGE An interest in land created by a written instrument providing security for the payment of a debt or the performance of a duty.

West Coast Hotel Co. v. Parrish

Employer (D) v. Employee (P)

300 U.S. 379 (1937)

NATURE OF CASE: Appeal from money judgment favoring female employee (P) for the difference between wages paid to her by her employer (D) and minimum wages set by state law.

FACT SUMMARY: The State of Washington had a law that set the minimum wage for women. Parrish (P), a woman employed by West Coast Hotel Co. (D), brought suit to recover the difference between the wages paid to her and the minimum wages set by the state. West Coast Hotel Co. (D) challenged the minimum wage law as violating the Fourteenth Amendment's due process guaranties.

RULE OF LAW

A state minimum wage law for women does not violate the Fourteenth Amendment's due process guaranties.

FACTS: The State of Washington enacted a law entitled, "Minimum Wages for Women," that fixed minimum wages for women (and minors). West Coast Hotel Co. (D) was in the hotel business, and employed Parrish (P), a woman, as a chambermaid. Parrish (P) brought suit to recover the difference between the wages paid to her and the minimum wages set by the state. West Coast Hotel Co. (D) challenged the minimum wage law as violating the Fourteenth Amendment's due process guaranties. The supreme court of Washington, reversing the trial court, sustained the statute and directed judgment for Parrish (P). The United States Supreme Court granted review.

ISSUE: Does a state minimum wage law for women violate the Fourteenth Amendment's due process guaranties?

HOLDING AND DECISION: (Hughes, C.J.) No. A state minimum wage law for women does not violate the Fourteenth Amendment's due process guaranties. It is alleged that the law works as a deprivation of freedom of contract. However, the Constitution does not speak of freedom of contract. It speaks of liberty and prohibits the deprivation of liberty without due process of law. Regulation that is reasonable in its relation to its subject and is adopted in the interests of the community is due process. The freedom of contract may be restricted in the employment context for the protection of health and safety, and to ensure good work conditions and freedom from oppression. The safeguarding of women's health and their protection from unscrupulous employers is in the public interest. The state's legislature was entitled to consider the situation of women in employment—that they receive the least pay, they have weak bargaining power, and they are easily taken advantage of, or exploited at wages so low that they cannot meet the bare cost of living. The legislative response to these conditions is not arbitrary or capricious, and, therefore, the legislature's judgment must be deferred to. Moreover, the law reasonably furthers a legitimate public purpose because the denial of a living wage is not only detrimental to their health and well-being but casts a direct burden for their support upon the community. Affirmed and *Adkins v. Children's Hospital*, 261 U.S. 525 (1923), overruled.

ANALYSIS

This case expressly overruled *Adkins v. Children's Hospital*, 261 U.S. 525 (1923), which had held that a minimum wage law for women, much like the one in this case, was unconstitutional. *West Coast Hotel Co.* was one of the first cases that seemingly repudiated the entire principle of substantive due process and signaled an end to the *Lochner*, 198 U.S. 45 (1905), era's laissez-faire doctrines. With *West Coast Hotel Co.*, the Court introduced a more relaxed and deferential standard of review to measure the connection between legislative means and ends.

Quicknotes

DUE PROCESS CLAUSE Language found in the Fifth and Fourteenth Amendments to the United States Constitution providing that no person shall be deprived of "life, liberty, or property without due process of law."

United States v. Carolene Products Co.

Federal government (D) v. Milk producer (D)

304 U.S. 144 (1938)

NATURE OF CASE: An appeal of a decision sustaining a demurrer to an indictment of the Filled Milk Act.

FACT SUMMARY: Carolene Products (D) was attempting to have the Filled Milk Act declared unconstitutional.

RULE OF LAW

In cases challenging the constitutionality of legislation affecting ordinary commercial transactions, the Supreme Court will apply the rational basis test, which means that the person challenging the legislation has the burden of showing that a rational basis does not exist.

FACTS: Congress passed the Filled Milk Act (the Act), which prohibited the shipment in interstate commerce of skimmed milk compounded with any fat or oil other than milk fat. Carolene Products Co. (D) was indicted for violating the Act. The trial court sustained a demurrer to the indictment by Carolene Products Co. (D) and the Government (P) appealed to the United States Supreme Court. Carolene Products (D) claimed that the Filled Milk Act violated the Fifth Amendment because Congress had not attempted to regulate the interstate shipment of oleomargarine that substituted vegetable fats for butter fat. It also claimed that the Act was void on its face because it lacked a rational basis.

ISSUE: In cases challenging the constitutionality of legislation affecting ordinary commercial transactions, will the Supreme Court apply the rational basis test?

HOLDING AND DECISION: (Stone, J.) Yes. In cases challenging the constitutionality of legislation affecting ordinary commercial transactions, the Supreme Court will apply the rational basis test, which means that the person challenging the legislation has the burden of showing that a rational basis does not exist. Legislation is not unconstitutional because it does not attempt to correct all similar evils at the same time. Congress could properly choose to control shipments of milk substitutes without regulating butter substitutes in the same manner. In cases challenging the constitutionality of legislation affecting ordinary commercial transactions, the Court will apply a rational basis test. Congress had held many hearings prior to passing the Filled Milk Act and the Court held that Congress could rationally believe that the Act was necessary for the protection of the general public. In dealing with legislation such as this, there is a presumption that it is constitutional, and the Court stated that this presumption would be enough to sustain the Act. Carolene Products (D) had the burden to show that no rational basis existed for the Filled Milk Act and that burden had not been met. Therefore, the trial court was wrong in sustaining the demurrer to the indictment. Reversed.

ANALYSIS

One of the most important steps in constitutional litigation is the determination by the Court of the approach they will use in deciding a case. If they decide to apply the rational basis test, the burden of showing that the legislation does not have a rational basis is on the person attacking it. It is almost impossible to show that facts do not exist that support the validity of the legislation or that Congress could not reasonably believe that they exist. When the Court feels that the legislation impinges on a fundamental right, the burden is on the government to show a compelling governmental interest that supports the legislation. This is also a difficult burden to prove. In most cases, the approach the Court decides to use determines the outcome of the case.

Quicknotes

FIFTH AMENDMENT Provides that no person shall be compelled to serve as a witness against oneself, be subject to trial for the same offense twice, or be deprived of life, liberty, or property without due process of law.

FUNDAMENTAL RIGHT A liberty that is either expressly or impliedly provided for in the United States Constitution, the deprivation or burdening of which is subject to a heightened standard of review.

RATIONAL BASIS TEST A test employed by the court to determine the validity of a statute in equal protection actions, whereby the court determines whether the challenged statute is rationally related to the achievement of a legitimate state interest.

Williamson v. Lee Optical Co.

State (D) v. Optician (P)

348 U.S. 483 (1955)

NATURE OF CASE: Action to have a state law declared unconstitutional and enjoin its enforcement.

FACT SUMMARY: Lee Optical Co. (P) challenged the constitutionality of an Oklahoma law that, among other things, effectively prevented opticians from fitting or duplicating lenses without a prescription from an ophthalmologist or optometrist.

RULE OF LAW

A regulation enacted by a state is not beyond constitutional bounds unless it has no rational relation to a legitimate objective of the state.

FACTS: Oklahoma passed a law with provisions that: (1) effectively prohibited opticians from fitting old glasses into new frames or supplying new or duplicate lenses without a prescription from a licensed ophthalmologist or optometrist; (2) made it unlawful to solicit the sale of frames, mountings, or any other optical appliances; and (3) prevented anyone engaged in the business of retailing general merchandise to the public from renting space or subleasing departments to any person purporting to do eye examination or visual care. Lee Optical Co. (P) brought suit asking that the law be declared unconstitutional and state officials be enjoined from enforcing it. The district court held the aforementioned provisions unconstitutional as contrary to the Due Process Clause. The law was deemed to arbitrarily interfere with the optician's right to do business.

ISSUE: Is a regulation enacted by a state within constitutional bounds as long as it has a rational relation to a legitimate state objective?

HOLDING AND DECISION: (Douglas, J.) Yes. A regulation enacted by a state is not beyond constitutional bounds unless it has no rational relation to a legitimate objective of the state. It cannot be said that the regulations at issue in this case bear no rational relation to the legitimate objectives Oklahoma was pursuing. The regulations that Oklahoma imposed in an effort to advance its legitimate goals may exact a needless, wasteful requirement in many cases, e.g., those in which the optician can easily supply new frames or new lenses without reference to the old written prescription. But in some cases, the directions contained in the prescription are essential if the glasses are to be fitted to correct the particular defects of vision or alleviate the eye condition. It is for legislatures, not the courts, to balance the advantages and disadvantages of these new requirements. The regulations are constitutional. Reversed.

ANALYSIS

Resort to a "minimum rationality" approach was the Court's way of officially preserving the rational basis test while making its practical affect nil. Justice Black was among those who advocated the more forthright action of repudiating the basic notion that the Due Process Clause gave the courts the power to determine whether economic legislation had a "rational basis."

Quicknotes

DUE PROCESS CLAUSE Language found in the Fifth and Fourteenth Amendments to the United States Constitution providing that no person shall be deprived of "life, liberty, or property without due process of law."

RATIONAL BASIS TEST A test employed by the court to determine the validity of a statute in equal protection actions, whereby the court determines whether the challenged statute is rationally related to the achievement of a legitimate state interest.

Schechter Poultry Corp. v. United States

Slaughterhouse operator (D) v. Federal government (P)

295 U.S. 495 (1935)

NATURE OF CASE: Appeal in action challenging the constitutionality of a federal regulation of intrastate labor conditions. [The procedural posture of the case is not presented in the casebook extract.]

FACT SUMMARY: Schechter Poultry Corp. (D), a chicken slaughterhouse operator, which had been found to have violated federal labor regulations of wages and hours worked, contended that the regulations were unconstitutional as applied because Schechter Poultry's (D) operations were local in nature and only remotely affected interstate commerce. [The procedural posture and complete factual background of the case are not presented in the casebook extract.]

RULE OF LAW

The federal government does not have authority under the Commerce Clause to regulate employee wages and hours in an industry that conducts its business solely in one state.

FACTS: The National Industrial Recovery Act (NIRA) authorized the creation of business codes that regulated various industries. One such code, a "Live Poultry Code," attempted to ensure fair competition for the live poultry industry of the metropolitan area of New York City by regulating the wages and hours of poultry slaughterhouse employees. The poultry slaughterhouses, including Schechter Poultry Corp. (D), contended that the federal government lacked power under the Commerce Clause to authorize these regulations since, although most of the poultry were obtained outside the state, the slaughterhouses sold only to New York retailers. The Government (P) contended that the local wages and hours affected the interstate market price for poultry, which authorized the federal regulation thereof. Schechter Poultry (D), which had been found to have violated the regulations, appealed. The United States Supreme Court heard the case. [The procedural posture and complete factual background of the case are not presented in the casebook extract.]

ISSUE: Does the federal government have authority under the Commerce Clause to regulate employee wages and hours in an industry that conducts its business solely in one state?

HOLDING AND DECISION: (Hughes, C.J.) No. The federal government does not have authority under the Commerce Clause to regulate employee wages and hours in an industry that conducts its business solely in one state. Whether certain intrastate commercial transactions can be characterized as interstate varies from case to case and depends on the degree to which they affect interstate commerce, and whether their impacts are direct or indirect. Where the effects are indirect, the transactions remain within the domain of state power. If the Commerce Clause reached all indirect effects of intrastate transactions, the federal government would have power to regulate almost all human activity, and the states would not have any power to regulate transactions within their borders except with permission of the federal government. Persons employed in slaughtering and selling in local trade are not employed in interstate commerce, and their hours and wages have no direct relation to interstate commerce. If the impact of a local business's cost can be considered an interstate impact, then not only hours and wages are implicated, but other factors that impact cost, such as rents, marketing, number of employees, the processes of production and distribution, etc., could be regulated as interstate impacts. Such regulation would go beyond the federal government's power. [The disposition of the case is not presented in the casebook extract.]

CONCURRENCE: (Cardozo, J.) The Government's (P) view of causation would obliterate the distinction between what is national and what is local in the activities of commerce. The question is one of degree, and activities that are local in their immediacy do not become interstate and national because of remote repercussions. To hold otherwise would doom the federal system.

ANALYSIS

In *Schechter Poultry*, the Court not only struck down the National Industrial Recovery Act (NIRA) as a violation of the Commerce Clause, it also struck NIRA down on the grounds it constituted an unlawful delegation of legislative power to the President and private industry to create business codes.

Quicknotes

CAUSATION The aggregate effect of preceding events that bring about a tortious result; the causal connection between the actions of a tortfeasor and the injury that follows.

COMMERCE CLAUSE Article I, § 8, cl. 3 of the United States Constitution, granting Congress the power to regulate commerce with foreign countries and among the states.

Continued on next page.

INTERSTATE COMMERCE Commercial dealings between two parties located in different states or located in one state and accomplished through a point in another state or a foreign country; commercial dealings transacted between two states.

Carter v. Carter Coal Co.

Stockholder (P) v. Corporation (D)

298 U.S. 238 (1936)

NATURE OF CASE: Stockholder suit to enjoin company from complying with requirements of the Coal Conservation Act.

FACT SUMMARY: The Coal Conservation Act of 1935 (the Act) attempted to regulate certain aspects of coal production. Carter (P) brought suit to enjoin his company (D) from complying with the Act.

RULE OF LAW

Production or manufacture of goods that are later to be shipped out of state is not interstate commerce and is not subject to federal regulation.

FACTS: The Coal Conservation Act of 1935 (the Act) established a tax on coal production. Producers would receive a reduction of this tax by accepting coal codes that were to be formulated. These codes would establish minimum prices for coal, wages, and hours for workers, and would require that producers recognize their employees' right to organize and bargain collectively. Carter (P) brought this action to enjoin Carter Coal Co. (D) from complying with these requirements and from paying the tax.

ISSUE: Is the production of coal that may or may not be shipped across state lines "interstate commerce" that would allow federal regulation?

HOLDING AND DECISION: (Sutherland, J.) No. The attempted federal regulation of coal production is not sustainable as within Congress's power to regulate interstate commerce or as within a more general power to regulate for the public welfare. The preamble of the Coal Conservation Act of 1935 (the Act) states that the production of coal "directly affects interstate commerce" and that regulation is necessary to protect the public interest in maintaining an adequate supply of coal and promoting fair producer-employee relations. It has always been held that Congress can only exercise powers that were specifically delegated to it by the Constitution; therefore, this Act cannot be sustained merely on the ground it promotes the general welfare. The Act, then, can only be upheld if it is within the powers granted the federal government by the Commerce Clause. In manufacturing a product which it subsequently ships into interstate commerce, a manufacturer engages in two separate activities: first, the manufacture or production of a product (which is purely local and only subject to state regulation); second, the actual shipment of the goods across state lines, which is subject only to federal regulation. Since production is purely local, and this Act purports to regulate the employer/employee relationship in production, the Act is not a valid exercise of Congress's power to regulate interstate commerce and cannot be sustained.

ANALYSIS

The *Carter* case, like *Schechter Corp. v. United States*, 295 U.S. 495 (1935), is based on a strict geographical definition of interstate commerce. If the act in question, here the production of coal, takes place at all times within a single state, it cannot be interstate commerce and cannot be regulated. Although the Court admits coal production has an effect on interstate commerce, it was only an indirect, not a direct effect. The weakness of this argument is pointed out in the dissent—intrastate acts can have such a great influence on interstate commerce, even in the absence of a direct effect, that the literalistic direct/indirect distinction serves no purpose.

Quicknotes

COMMERCE CLAUSE Article I, § 8, cl. 3 of the United States Constitution, granting Congress the power to regulate commerce with foreign countries and between the states.

INTERSTATE COMMERCE Commercial dealings between two parties located in different states or located in one state and accomplished through a point in another state or a foreign country; commercial dealings transacted between two states.

United States v. Butler

Federal government (P) v. Receivers (D)

297 U.S. 1 (1936)

NATURE OF CASE: Action challenging the constitutionality of the Agricultural Adjustment Act of 1933.

FACT SUMMARY: The Agricultural Adjustment Act of 1933 states that there is a national economic emergency arising from the low price of agricultural products in comparison with other commodities. To remedy this situation, a tax will be collected from processors of an agricultural product. The revenue raised will be paid to farmers who curtail their production of that product.

RULE OF LAW

A tax on the processing of agricultural products is not valid where the revenue raised by the tax is to be paid to farmers who voluntarily curtail their production of crops.

FACTS: The Agricultural Adjustment Act of 1933 (the Act) declared that a national economic emergency had arisen due to the disparity between the prices of agricultural and other commodities, resulting in the destruction of farmers' purchasing power. To remedy this situation, a tax will be collected from processors of agricultural products. The revenue raised thereby will be paid to farmers who voluntarily curtail their production of those crops used by the processors. The Secretary of Agriculture is to determine the crops to which the Act's plan shall apply. In July 1933, the Secretary determined that the Act's plan should be applied to cotton. A tax claim was presented to Butler (D) as receivers of the Hoosac Mills Corp., as cotton processors. The district court held the tax unconstitutional.

ISSUE: Is a tax on the processing of agricultural products valid where the revenue raised by the tax is to be paid to farmers who voluntarily curtail their production of crops?

HOLDING AND DECISION: (Roberts, J.) No. A tax on the processing of agricultural products is not valid where the revenue raised by the tax is to be paid to farmers who voluntarily curtail their production of crops. First, Butler (D) has standing to question the validity of the tax because it is but a part of the unconstitutional plan of the Agricultural Adjustment Act (the Act). A tax, as the term is used by the Constitution, is an exaction for the support of the government. It has never been thought to mean the expropriation of money from one group for the benefit of another, as is attempted by the Act in question here. The Act is unconstitutional in that it invades the rights of the states. It is a statutory plan to regulate and control agriculture production, a matter beyond the power of the federal government. The Government (P), in attempting to defend the Act, places great reliance on the fact that the Act's plan is voluntary. However, the farmer who chooses not to comply with the plan loses benefits. "The power to confer or withhold unlimited benefits is the power to coerce or destroy." Even if the plan were truly voluntary, it would not be valid. "At best, it is a scheme for purchasing with federal funds submission to federal regulation of a subject reserved to the states." Contracts for the reduction of acreage and the control of production are not within Congress's power. Congress has no power to enforce the ends sought by this Act onto the farmer. Hence, it may not indirectly accomplish those ends by taxing and spending to enforce them. If this Act is valid, Congress could exercise its power to regulate all industry. It could extract money from one branch of an industry and pay it to another branch. Congress may not under the pretext of exercising the taxing power, accomplish prohibited ends. Affirmed.

DISSENT: (Stone, J.) Courts are to be concerned only with the power to enact statutes, not with their wisdom. The constitutional power of Congress to tax the processing of agricultural products is not questioned. The present tax is held to be invalid because the use to which its proceeds are to be put is disapproved. The tax is held to be invalid because it is a step in a plan to regulate agricultural production. The Court states that state powers are infringed by the expenditure of the proceeds of the tax to compensate farmers for the curtailment of their crop production. Such a limitation is contradictory and destructive of the power to appropriate for the public welfare and is incapable of practical application. Congress's spending power is not subordinate to its legislative powers. This independent grant of power presupposes freedom of selection among diverse ends and aims and the capacity to impose such conditions as will render the choice effective. It is contradictory to say that there is a power to spend for the national welfare, while rejecting any power to impose conditions reasonably adapted to the end which justifies the expenditure. "If appropriation in aid of a program of curtailment is constitutional, and it is not denied that it is, payment to farmers on condition that they reduce their crop acreage is constitutional."

ANALYSIS

The *Butler* decision contributed greatly to the pressure that produced the Court-packing plan a few months

Continued on next page.

later. It is called the landmark case in the area of federal regulation of local matters through taxation. However, if the tax and the appropriation provisions had not been so closely tied together, it is doubtful that the Court would have invalidated the tax. The tax appeared to have a valid revenue-raising purpose, and once separated from the taxing provisions, there would have been no one with standing to attack the appropriation.

Quicknotes

SPENDING POWER The power delegated to Congress by the United States Constitution to spend money in providing for the nation's welfare.

TAXING POWER The authority delegated to Congress by the United States Constitution to impose taxes.

NLRB v. Jones & Laughlin Steel Corp.

Labor board (P) v. Steel company (D)

301 U.S. 1 (1937)

NATURE OF CASE: Action alleging unfair labor practice under the National Labor Relations Act.

FACT SUMMARY: Jones & Laughlin Steel Corp. (Jones & Laughlin) (D), a manufacturing company with subsidiaries in several states and nationwide sales, was charged with an unfair labor practice under the National Labor Relations Act (the Act). In defense, Jones & Laughlin (D) claimed that the Act was an unconstitutional attempt to regulate intrastate production.

RULE OF LAW

Under the Commerce Clause, Congress has the power to regulate any activity, even intrastate production, if the activity has an appreciable effect, either direct or indirect, on interstate commerce.

FACTS: Pursuant to a complaint filed by a labor union, the National Labor Relations Board (the Board) (P) found that Jones & Laughlin Steel Corp. (Jones & Laughlin) (D) had engaged in unfair labor practices. The Board (P) issued a cease and desist order to Jones & Laughlin (D) to stop using discriminatory and coercive practices to prevent union organization at two steel plants in and around Pittsburgh. The company refused to comply and the Board (P) went to court for judicial enforcement of its order under the authority of the National Labor Relations Act of 1935. Jones and Laughlin (D) contended that the order was an unconstitutional exercise of the Board's (P) authority since the plants were not engaged in interstate commerce, being totally manufacturing facilities. The court of appeals upheld the company's position and refused enforcement of the order on the ground the order lay beyond the range of federal power.

ISSUE: Does Congress have the power to regulate any activity, even intrastate production, under the Commerce Clause if the activity has an appreciable effect, either directly or indirectly, on interstate commerce?

HOLDING AND DECISION: (Hughes, C.J.) Yes. Under the Commerce Clause, Congress has the power to regulate any activity, even intrastate production, if the activity has an appreciable effect, either direct or indirect, on interstate commerce. The National Labor Relations Board's (the Board's) (P) ordering Jones & Laughlin (D) to cease interfering with its employees' rights of self-organization and collective bargaining is an exercise of the congressional power to regulate interstate commerce. The definitions in the National Labor Relations Act of 1935 restrict the Board's (P) actions to protecting interstate commerce in the constitutional sense, and the Board (P) is given the power to determine if the practice in question affects commerce in such a way as to be subject to federal control. Congress has the power to protect interstate commerce by all appropriate types of legislation, and the controlling question is the effect on interstate commerce, not the source of the interference. Although such legislation may result in the regulation of acts that are intrastate in character, Congress still has the power to regulate if the intrastate acts bear such a close and substantial relation to interstate commerce that control is appropriate for the protection of commerce. Congress is forbidden only from regulating acts that have a remote and indirect effect on interstate commerce. Here, even though the application of the National Labor Relations Act results in the regulation of labor practices at Jones & Laughlin's (D) manufacturing plants, the circumstances indicate the required substantial effect on interstate commerce. If production were interrupted at one of the plants due to a labor dispute, the extensive nationwide operations of Jones & Laughlin (D) indicate there would necessarily be an immediate effect on interstate commerce. Therefore, the National Labor Relations Act as applied to the facts of this case is a proper exercise of Congress's power to regulate interstate commerce.

ANALYSIS

With this case the Supreme Court retreated from its strict geographical definition of interstate commerce and the direct/indirect approach that it used in *A.L.A. Schechter Poultry Corp. v. United States*, 295 U.S. 495 (1935), and *Carter v. Carter Coal Co.*, 298 U.S. 238 (1936). *Jones & Laughlin* states that under the Commerce Clause Congress has the power to regulate any activity that has a significant effect on interstate commerce, regardless of whether that effect is direct or indirect. This new concept is often called the "affectation doctrine." Although the court cited prior cases in its opinion and said it was not creating new law, *Jones & Laughlin* is, in effect, a reversal of the *Schechter* line of cases. The Court now bases its opinions on a combination of the Commerce Clause and the Necessary and Proper Clause—power to regulate interstate commerce extends to control over intrastate activities when necessary and appropriate to make regulation of interstate commerce effective.

Continued on next page.

Quicknotes

COLLECTIVE BARGAINING Negotiations between an employer and employee that are mediated by a specified third party.

COMMERCE CLAUSE Article I, § 8, cl. 3 of the United States Constitution, granting Congress the power to regulate commerce with foreign countries and between the states.

NATIONAL LABOR RELATIONS ACT Guarantees employees the right to engage in collective bargaining and regulates labor unions.

United States v. Darby

Federal government (P) v. Lumber manufacturer (D)

312 U.S. 100 (1941)

NATURE OF CASE: Criminal prosecution for violation of Fair Labor Standards Act.

FACT SUMMARY: Darby (D) was a lumber manufacturer, some of whose goods were later shipped in interstate commerce. He was indicted for violation of the wage and hour provisions of the Fair Labor Standards Act and defended on the ground as an intrastate producer he was not subject to federal regulation.

RULE OF LAW

Congress has the power to regulate the hours and wages of workers who are engaged in the production of goods destined for interstate commerce and can prohibit the shipment in interstate commerce of goods manufactured in violation of the wage and hour provisions.

FACTS: Darby (D) was a manufacturer of finished lumber, and a large part of the lumber he produced was shipped in interstate commerce. The purpose of the Fair Labor Standards Act (the Act) was to prevent the shipment in interstate commerce of certain products produced under substandard labor conditions. The Act set up minimum wages and maximum hours and punished the shipment in interstate commerce of goods produced in violation of the wage and hour requirements and also punished the employment of persons in violation of those requirements. Darby (D) was arrested for both shipment of goods in violation of the Act and employment of workers in violation of the Act. The trial court dismissed the indictment on the ground the Act was an unconstitutional regulation of manufacturing within the states.

ISSUE: Does Congress have the power to prohibit shipment in interstate commerce of goods produced in violation of the wage and hour provisions of the Fair Labor Standards Act and the power to prohibit employment of workers involved in the production of goods for interstate shipment in violation of the wage and hour provisions of the Fair Labor Standards Act?

HOLDING AND DECISION: (Stone, J.) Yes. Congress has the power to prohibit shipment in interstate commerce of goods produced in violation of wage and hour provisions of the Fair Labor Standards Act and the power to prohibit employment of workers involved in the production of goods for interstate shipment in violation of the wage and hour provisions of the Fair Labor Standards Act? Both prohibitions are a constitutional exercise of Congress's commerce power. Although manufacturing itself is not interstate commerce, the shipment of goods across state lines is interstate commerce, and the prohibition of such shipment is a regulation of commerce. Congress has plenary power to exclude from interstate commerce any article which it determines to be injurious to public welfare, subject only to the specific prohibitions of the Constitution. In the Fair Labor Standards Act, Congress has determined that the shipment of goods produced under substandard labor conditions is injurious to commerce and therefore has the power to prohibit the shipment of such goods, independent of the indirect effect of such prohibition on the states. The prohibition of employment of workers engaged in the production of goods for interstate commerce at substandard conditions is also sustainable, independent of the power to exclude the shipment of the goods so produced. The power over interstate commerce is not confined to the regulation of commerce among the states but includes regulation of intrastate activities that so affect interstate commerce as to make regulation of them an appropriate means to the end of regulating interstate commerce. Here, Congress has determined that the employment of workers in substandard conditions is a form of unfair competition injurious to interstate commerce since the goods so produced will be lower priced than the goods produced under adequate conditions. Such a form of competition would hasten the spread of substandard conditions and produce a dislocation of commerce and the destruction of many businesses. Since Congress has the power to suppress this form of unfair competition, and the Act is an appropriate means to that end, the wage/hour provisions are within Congress's power. It is irrelevant that only part of the goods produced will be shipped in interstate commerce; Congress has power to regulate the whole factory even though only a part of the products will have an effect on interstate commerce. *Hammer v. Dagenhart* 247 U.S. 251 (1918), overruled and judgment reversed.

ANALYSIS

Darby, like *Jones and Laughlin,* 301 U.S. 1 (1937), is an example of the application of the affectation doctrine. It had long been the law that Congress had the power to exclude from interstate commerce harmful objects or immoral activities, such as mismarked goods or lottery tickets. This case extends the power to exclude articles produced under conditions that Congress considered harmful to the national welfare. Even though production

Continued on next page.

of lumber was an entirely intrastate activity, it was a part of an economic process that led to the eventual sale of lumber across state limits, affecting interstate commerce. The federal commerce power extends to purely intrastate transactions; the effect on commerce, not the location of the regulated act, is the basis for the exercise of the federal power. This case overruled the earlier case of *Hammer v. Dagenhart*, 247 U.S. 251 (1918), which held unconstitutional an attempt by Congress to exclude articles made by child labor from interstate commerce.

Quicknotes

COMMERCE POWER The power delegated to Congress by the United States Constitution to regulate interstate commerce.

FAIR LABOR STANDARDS ACT Enacted in 1938, the statute establishes a minimum wage applicable to all employees of covered employers and provides for mandatory overtime payment for covered employees who work more than 40 hours a week. Executive, administrative, and professional employees paid on a salary basis are exempt from the statute.

INTERSTATE COMMERCE Commercial dealings between two parties located in different states or located in one state and accomplished through a point in another state or a foreign country; commercial dealings transacted between two states.

PLENARY POWER The complete authority of a court to hear and determine cases pertaining to specified subject matter or particular parties.

Wickard v. Filburn

Department of Agriculture (P) v. Farmer (D)

317 U.S. 111 (1942)

NATURE OF CASE: Action to enjoin enforcement of penalty provisions of the Agricultural Adjustment Act.

FACT SUMMARY: Filburn (D) was ordered to pay a penalty imposed by the Agriculture Adjustment Act for producing wheat in excess of his assigned quota. He argued that the federal regulations could not be constitutionally applied to his crops because part of his crop was intended for his own consumption, not for interstate commerce.

RULE OF LAW

Congress, under the Commerce Clause, has the power to regulate the production of wheat that is grown for home-consumption purposes rather than for sale in interstate commerce.

FACTS: The purpose of the Agriculture Adjustment Act (the Act) was to control the volume of wheat moving in interstate commerce to avoid surpluses and shortages that would result in abnormally high or low prices and thereby obstruct commerce. Under the Act, the Secretary of Agriculture would set a national acreage allotment for wheat production, which would be divided into allotments for individual farms. Filburn (D) was the owner and operator of a small farm. In the past he had grown a small amount of wheat of which he sold part, fed part to poultry and livestock (some of the livestock were later sold), used part in making flour for home consumption, and kept the rest for seeding the next year. In 1940, his wheat production exceeded the maximum he was allowed under the Act and he was assessed a penalty for the excess. Filburn (D) refused to pay on the ground the Act was unconstitutional in that it attempted to regulate purely local production and consumption that, at most, had an indirect effect on interstate commerce. The Government (P) argued that the Act regulated not production and consumption, but only marketing (which was defined in the Act to include the feeding of the wheat to livestock that was later sold), and even if interpreted to include production and consumption, it was a legitimate exercise of the Commerce Clause and the Necessary and Proper Clause.

ISSUE: Does Congress, under the Commerce Clause, have the power to regulate the production of wheat that is grown for home-consumption purposes rather than for sale in interstate commerce?

HOLDING AND DECISION: (Jackson, J.) Yes. Under the Commerce Clause, Congress has the power to regulate the production of wheat that is grown for home-consumption purposes rather than for sale in interstate commerce. Farm production that is intended for consumption on the farm is subject to Congress's commerce power, since it may have a substantial economic effect on interstate commerce. A local activity, such as production, may be reached under the Commerce Clause if it exerts a substantial economic effect on interstate commerce. The Agriculture Adjustment Act was enacted because of the problems of the wheat market: there had been a decrease in export in recent years, causing surpluses that in turn caused congestion in the market and lower prices. It has been repeatedly held that the commerce power of Congress includes the power to regulate prices and practices affecting prices. Wheat destined for home consumption has an effect on the interstate price of wheat and is, therefore, subject to regulation. As the market price of wheat climbs, farmers will sell more of their crop that was intended for home consumption on the market causing a decrease in prices. Even if the wheat is never sold, there still is a substantial effect on interstate commerce because it reduces demand for wheat; the wheat that Filburn (D) produces for his own use means that he will buy less wheat on the market. Although the actual effect of Filburn's (D) overproduction will be small, the combination of all such producers does cause a substantial effect on commerce.

ANALYSIS

Wickard is yet another application of the "affectation doctrine." The Court focuses not on the nature of the regulated activity (e.g., whether it is local) but on the final economic effect of that activity. Here, although the effect of Filburn's (D) excess wheat production was insignificant on the national market, there still was some effect, at least in theory, and thus regulation was allowed. The Court in *Wickard* expressly rejected the old formulas for determining the extent of the commerce power such as direct/indirect and production/commerce.

Quicknotes

COMMERCE POWER The power delegated to Congress by the United States Constitution to regulate interstate commerce.

NECESSARY AND PROPER CLAUSE Article I, § 8 of the United States Constitution; enables Congress to make all laws that may be "necessary and proper" to execute its other, enumerated powers.

Steward Machine Company v. Davis

Employer (P) v. Government (D)

301 U.S. 548 (1937)

NATURE OF CASE: Action challenging the constitutionality of the Social Security Act as applied to employers of eight or more.

FACT SUMMARY: The Social Security Act levies an excise tax on employers of eight or more. The proceeds go into the general treasury. However, if a taxpayer has made contributions to a state unemployment fund, such contributions can be credited against the federal tax. Between 1929 and 1936 the United States suffered from extreme unemployment.

RULE OF LAW

A federal unemployment insurance tax statute that provides for credit for contributions made to state unemployment funds is valid because Congress enacted it primarily to safeguard its own treasury, the proceeds of the tax are not earmarked for a special group but go into the general treasury, and the act is directed to an end for which Congress and the states may lawfully cooperate.

FACTS: The Social Security Act imposes an excise tax on employers of eight or more based on the wages paid. The proceeds go into the general treasury. However, if a taxpayer has made contributions to a state unemployment fund, such contributions can be credited against the federal tax, provided that the state law has been certified by the Social Security Board as satisfying certain minimum criteria. Between 1929 and 1936 there was an unprecedented number of unemployed in the United States, and the states were unable to give the requisite relief to the needy. Steward Machine Co. (P) paid a tax in accordance with the statute and filed a claim to recover the payment, asserting that the statute is unconstitutional.

ISSUE: Is a federal unemployment insurance tax statute that provides for credit for contributions made to state unemployment funds valid?

HOLDING AND DECISION: (Cardozo, J.) Yes. A federal unemployment insurance tax statute that provides for credit for contributions made to state unemployment funds is valid because Congress enacted it primarily to safeguard its own treasury, the proceeds of the tax are not earmarked for a special group but go into the general treasury, and the act is directed to an end for which Congress and the states may lawfully cooperate. First, in a crisis as extreme as the unemployment crisis, the use of the nation's moneys to relieve the unemployed and their dependents cannot be called a use for any purpose other than the promotion of the general welfare. By 1935, when Congress enacted the Social Security Act, the unemployment situation had become so severe that the states were unable to continue to help those in need. There was need of help from the nation if people were not to starve. Before Congress enacted the Social Security Act, few states had passed unemployment laws. Many held back for fear that the toll placed on industry by such legislation would put them at an economic disadvantage as compared with neighboring states. The purpose of Congress's intervention in enacting the Social Security Act was to safeguard its own treasury, and, as an incident to that protection, to place the states upon a footing of equal opportunity as to unemployment insurance. Unlike the Child Labor Tax, the Federal Unemployment Tax will be abated upon the doing of an act that will satisfy the fiscal need subserved by the tax. Unlike the tax in *United States v. Butler*, 297 U.S. 1 (1936), the proceeds from the federal unemployment tax are not earmarked for a special group but go into the general treasury. Also, the state unemployment law, which is a condition of the credit, has had the state's approval (and could not be a law without such approval). Nor is the condition linked to an irrevocable agreement. The state may choose to repeal its unemployment law, thereby terminating the credit; further, the credit condition is not directed to achieve an unlawful end but an end, the relief of unemployment, for which the nation and states may lawfully cooperate. Lastly, the statute does not call for a surrender by the states of powers essential to their quasi-sovereign existence. The condition requiring that the state laws meet the Social Security Board's criteria is suitable to assure that those who look to the laws for protection receive that protection. What is basic and essential may be assured by suitable conditions. The Social Security Act is constitutional.

ANALYSIS

Policy guidance via the spending power goes back to the beginning of the nation, as is pointed out in the majority opinion in *Steward*. The programs have increased considerably over the years, and there has been increasing opposition to narrow categorical grants-in-aid and advocacy of broader unrestricted grants to state and local governments. The Advisory Commission on Intergovernmental Relations was established in 1959. One of its major functions is the examination of the impact of national spending on the federal system. In its Annual Report for 1969 it stated, "unless state

Continued on next page.

and local governments are permitted 'free,' albeit limited, access to the prime power source—the Federal Income Tax—their positions within our federal systems are bound to deteriorate."

Quicknotes

SOCIAL SECURITY ACT Federal law creating the Social Security Administration, which is charged with the administration of a national program where contributions from employers and employees are held until the worker retires or is disabled, at which time they are paid out.

SPENDING POWER The power delegated to Congress by the United States Constitution to spend money in providing for the nation's welfare.

Heart of Atlanta Motel v. United States

Motel (P) v. Federal government (D)

379 U.S. 241 (1964)

NATURE OF CASE: Constitutional challenge to federal act.

FACT SUMMARY: Heart of Atlanta Motel (P) discriminated against Black people in violation of Title II of the Civil Rights Act of 1964.

RULE OF LAW

Congress may prohibit discrimination in public accommodations under its authority under the Commerce Clause.

FACTS: Heart of Atlanta Motel (the Motel) (P) was located within easy access to state and interstate highways. The Motel (P) solicited patronage through national advertising. Much of its patronage came from conventions and approximately three-quarters of its guests were from out-of-state. The Motel (P) discriminated against Black people. The Motel (P) brought a declaratory judgment action to declare that Title II of the Civil Rights Act of 1964 (the Act) was unconstitutional or had no effect on it. Title II prohibited discrimination or segregation in any place of public accommodation, including motels. The Motel (P) alleged that the Act was beyond the power of Congress. The Court upheld the Act.

ISSUE: May Congress prohibit discrimination in public accommodations under its Commerce Clause power?

HOLDING AND DECISION: (Clark, J.) Yes. Congress has the power to regulate interstate travel. Under this power it may reach purely local activities that may have a significant and harmful effect on travel. Millions of people travel each year. Black people are often subject to discrimination around the country. The inability to find accommodations has become acute. This has the effect of restricting the individual's right to travel. While the actions of a single motel may have no appreciable effect, cumulatively the effect on the right to interstate travel may be profound. The Commerce Clause covers both commercial and noncommercial travel. The Civil Rights Act of 1964 does not deprive the Motel (P) of a property right under the Fifth Amendment. Having made use of the products of interstate commerce and activities, the Motel (P) cannot complain of its regulation under the Commerce Clause. Affirmed.

ANALYSIS

In *Maryland v. Wirtz*, 392 U.S. 183 (1968), the Court conclusively settled the issue of whether Congress's power under the Commerce Clause extends to purely local activity. The Court held that Congress has the authority to declare that an entire class of activity affects commerce. The only question the court must decide is whether the class is within reach of federal power. The Court has no right to go beyond such a finding excising "trivial" activities.

Quicknotes

COMMERCE CLAUSE Article 1, § 8, cl. 3 of the United States Constitution, granting Congress the power to regulate commerce with foreign countries and between the states.

FIFTH AMENDMENT Provides that no person shall be compelled to serve as a witness against oneself, be subject to trial for the same offense twice, or be deprived of life, liberty, or property without due process of law.

Katzenbach v. McClung

[Parties not identified.]

379 U.S. 294 (1964)

NATURE OF CASE: Action seeking injunctive relief and attacking the validity of Title II of the Civil Rights Act of 1964 as applied to a restaurant.

FACT SUMMARY: Ollie's Barbecue refused sit-down service to Black people. The lower court found that a substantial portion of the food served in the restaurant had moved in interstate commerce.

RULE OF LAW

Although an activity is local and may not be regarded as commerce, it may still be reached by Congress if it exerts a substantial economic effect on interstate commerce.

FACTS: Ollie's Barbecue was a family-owned restaurant situated on a state highway, 11 blocks from an interstate highway and a somewhat greater distance from railroad and bus stations. It had a take-out service for Black people, but it refused to serve them in its dining rooms. The lower court found that a substantial portion of the food served in the restaurant had moved in interstate commerce. It was argued Congress legislated conclusive presumption that a racial discrimination in restaurants serving food, which had been transported in interstate commerce, affects such commerce. Congress made no formal findings on this issue.

ISSUE: Although an activity is local and may not be regarded as commerce, may it still be reached by Congress if it exerts a substantial economic effect on interstate commerce?

HOLDING AND DECISION: (Clark, J.) Yes. Although an activity is local and may not be regarded as commerce, it may still, whatever its nature, be reached by Congress if it exerts a substantial economic effect on interstate commerce. Further, although an individual defendant or plaintiff's own effect on commerce may be slight, if his contribution taken together with that of many others similarly situated is substantial, then that individual's activity may be regulated. Hence, although the amount of food served at Ollie's may be insignificant when compared with the amount of food transported in interstate commerce, and although Ollie's may appear to be local, Congress may still regulate it if there is a rational basis for its finding the Civil Rights Act (the Act) to be necessary to the protection of commerce. It is true that Congress did not make any formal findings as to the effect upon commerce of racial discrimination in restaurants. However, Congress did conduct prolonged hearings on the Act, and the record is replete with testimony of the burdens placed on commerce by discrimination in restaurants. Diminutive spending by Black people springing from discrimination practiced by restaurants, and the total loss of such people as customers has, regardless of the absence of direct evidence, a close connection to interstate commerce. Also, there was testimony that discrimination in restaurants had a direct and restrictive effect upon interstate travel by Black people. This testimony afforded ample basis for the conclusion that restaurants practicing discrimination sold less interstate food, travel was obstructed, and business in general suffered due to the practice of racial discrimination in restaurants. Hence, Congress had a rational basis for finding that such discrimination had a direct and adverse effect on the free flow of interstate commerce. The Act, as applied to restaurants, and to Ollie's, is constitutional.

ANALYSIS

Prior to the Civil Rights Act of 1964, the Court had found that general provisions of the Interstate Commerce Act prohibited racial discrimination by interstate carriers. *Henderson v. United States*, 339 U.S. 816 (1950), held that these provisions prohibited segregation in railroad dining cars. In *Boynton v. Virginia*, 364 U.S. 454 (1960), the Court reversed a trespass conviction of a Black interstate bus passenger who had been refused service at a bus terminal restaurant. Like the Interstate Commerce Act, the National Labor Relations Act and the Railway Labor Act contain no provisions specifically addressed to racial discrimination, and interpretations have made them applicable to the civil rights area. In *Steele v. Louisville and N.R.R.*, 323 U.S. 192 (1944), it was held that a union's status as exclusive bargaining agent under the Railway Labor Act carried the implied duty to represent all members in the bargaining unit without discrimination.

Quicknotes

INTERSTATE COMMERCE Commercial dealings between two parties located in different states or located in one state and accomplished through a point in another state or a foreign country; commercial dealings transacted between two states.

RATIONAL BASIS REVIEW A test employed by the court to determine the validity of a statute in equal protection actions, whereby the court determines whether the challenged statute is rationally related to the achievement of a legitimate state interest.

South Carolina v. Katzenbach

State (P) v. Federal government (D)

383 U.S. 301 (1966)

NATURE OF CASE: Constitutional challenge to Voting Rights Act of 1965.

FACT SUMMARY: South Carolina (P) and other states (P) challenged the validity of the Voting Rights Act of 1965.

RULE OF LAW

Congress may, under the Fifteenth Amendment, prescribe appropriate voter registration and election procedures to the states.

FACTS: The Voting Rights Act of 1965 (the Act) was enacted to eliminate various discriminatory devices used to disenfranchise Black people. States were prohibited from using literacy tests and similar devices for five years after a finding of discrimination. New devices had to be submitted to federal officials for review before they could be implemented. Federal election officials were to monitor state activities once past discrimination had been shown. These and other facets of the Act were challenged by South Carolina (P) and other states (P) which had been adjudged guilty of voting discrimination. It was argued that the Congress lacked the power to prescribe state election procedures, the Act violated the equality of states, utilized an invalid presumption, and involved the district courts in a situation where they had to issue advisory opinions.

ISSUE: May Congress prescribe rules and regulations concerning election procedures/voter's registration to the states?

HOLDING AND DECISION: (Warren, C.J.) Yes. Congress may, under the Fifteenth Amendment, prescribe appropriate voter registration and election procedures to the states. The Fifteenth Amendment declares that neither the states nor the federal government shall deny or abridge the rights of citizens to vote on basis of race, color, or previous condition of servitude. This is a self-executing provision that automatically invalidates statutes that are discriminatory on their face or in practice. The Fifteenth Amendment also grants to Congress the power to enforce it by appropriate legislation. If the end is legitimate and the means are constitutional, congressional acts may prescribe rules that are binding on the states. The Voting Rights Act of 1965 (the Act) is applied to states that have, in the past, utilized discrimination to disenfranchise various segments of their citizens. Past activities provide a reasonable inference of future evils and Congress may particularly address legislation to these offending states. The use of devices to discriminate in the past is adequate grounds for banning their use. Monitoring of local activities by federal officials merely assures compliance. The use of new voter registration restrictions by the district court is a reasonable requirement and is not an advisory opinion but an attempt to make certain that future discrimination does not occur. Congress has the power to enact legislation to prevent those states previously guilty of discrimination from continuing such practices and the means chosen under the Act are reasonably calculated to achieve this end. The Act is constitutional.

CONCURRENCE AND DISSENT: (Black, J.) While I concur with the majority's basic conclusions that the Voting Rights Act of 1965 (the Act) is constitutional, certain portions of it cannot survive careful scrutiny. The provision preventing states from amending their constitutions or laws relating to voting rights without prior federal approval violates the care and controversy requirement for jurisdiction. Secondly, we have overstepped the bounds of federalism and states rights under this provision. Section 5 of the Act is clearly unconstitutional.

ANALYSIS

Section 5 of the Voting Rights Act of 1965 has been interpreted by the Court to include within its purview attempts to change from district to at-large elections. *Allen v. State Board of Elections*, 393 U.S. 544 (1969). It also covered changes in boundary lines through annexation. *Perkins v. Matthews*, 400 U.S. 379 (1971). Section 5 has been read to reach any plan that dilutes the voting power of a state's citizens. *Reynolds v. Sims*, 377 U.S. 533 (1964).

Quicknotes

FEDERALISM A scheme of government whereby the power to govern is divided between a central and localized governments.

FIFTH AMENDMENT Provides that no person shall be compelled to serve as a witness against oneself, be subject to trial for the same offense twice, or be deprived of life, liberty, or property without due process of law.

Katzenbach v. Morgan

Registered voters (P) v. State Attorney General (D)

384 U.S. 641 (1966)

NATURE OF CASE: Challenge to constitutionality of federal statute.

FACT SUMMARY: As part of the Voting Rights Act, Congress inserted a provision that prohibited restrictions on the right to register to vote and the applicant's inability to read and write English where the applicant had at least a sixth-grade education in a Puerto Rican school where instruction was primarily in Spanish. New York had a statutory requirement of an ability to read and write English as a prerequisite to voter registration.

RULE OF LAW

A federal statute enacted pursuant to the Enabling Clause of the Fourteenth Amendment supersedes a conflicting state law by reason of the Supremacy Clause of the United States Constitution.

FACTS: New York had a statute that required all persons seeking to register to vote be able to read and write the English language. In the Voting Rights Act of 1965, Congress inserted a provision that prohibited a requirement of English reading and writing ability where the person seeking to vote had completed at least a sixth-grade education in Puerto Rico, where the language of instruction is primarily Spanish. This suit was instituted by a group of registered voters in New York who challenged that provision of the federal statute insofar as it would prohibit enforcement of the New York requirement. At issue were the several hundred thousand Puerto Rican immigrants in New York who were prevented from voting by the New York statute, but who would be qualified under the federal law. The Attorney General of New York filed a brief in which he argued that the federal legislation would supersede the state law only if the state law were found to violate the provisions of the Fourteenth Amendment without reference to the federal statute. Also advanced was the argument that the federal statute violated the Equal Protection Clause of the Fourteenth Amendment, since it discriminated between non-English-speaking persons from Puerto Rico and non-English-speaking persons from other countries.

ISSUE: Does a federal statute enacted pursuant to the Enabling Clause of the Fourteenth Amendment supersede a conflicting state law by reason of the Supremacy Clause of the United States Constitution?

HOLDING AND DECISION: (Brennan, J.) Yes. A federal statute enacted pursuant to the Enabling Clause of the Fourteenth Amendment supersedes a conflicting state law by reason of the Supremacy Clause of the United States Constitution. There is no need to determine if the New York English literacy law is violative of the Fourteenth Amendment Equal Protection Clause to validate the federal law respecting voter qualifications. If Congress were limited to restricting only those state laws that violated the amendment, there would be no need for the federal law, since the state law could be invalidated in the courts. Rather, the test must be whether the federal legislation is appropriate to enforcement of the Equal Protection Clause. Section 5 of the Fourteenth Amendment is to be read to grant the same powers as the Necessary and Proper Clause of Article I, § 8. Therefore, the federal statute must be examined to see if it is "plainly adapted to that end" and whether it is not prohibited by but is consistent with "the letter and spirit of the Constitution." It was well within congressional authority to say that the need to vote by the Puerto Rican community warranted intrusion upon any state interests served by the English literacy test. The federal law was "plainly adapted" to furthering the aims of the Fourteenth Amendment. There is a perceivable basis for Congress to determine that this legislation was a proper way to resolve an inequity resulting from Congress's evaluation that an invidious discrimination existed. As to the contention that the federal law itself violates the Equal Protection Clause, the law does not restrict anyone's voting rights, but rather extends the franchise to a previously ineligible group. This was a reform measure and, as we have previously held, Congress need not correct an entire evil with one law but may "take one step at a time, addressing itself" (*Williamson v. Lee Optical Co.*, 348 U.S. 483 (1955)) to that problem which seems most pressing. We hold, therefore, that the federal law was a proper exercise of the powers granted Congress by the Fourteenth Amendment and that the Supremacy Clause prevents enforcement of the New York statute insofar as it is inconsistent with the federal law.

DISSENT: (Harlan, J.) The majority has confused the question of legislative enforcement power with the area of proper judicial review. The question here is whether the state law is so arbitrary or irrational as to violate the Equal Protection Clause. And that is a judicial, not legislative, determination. The majority has validated a legislative determination by Congress that a state law is violative of the Constitution. There is no record of any evidence secured by Congress to support this determination. The judiciary is the ultimate arbiter of constitutionality, not Congress.

Continued on next page.

ANALYSIS

As has occurred before, there was a footnote to the decision that caused as much controversy as the decision itself. In this footnote, the Court stated that Congress could enact legislation giving force to the Fourteenth Amendment that expanded the rights provided in the Amendment, but could not dilute or restrict the Amendment by legislation. In other words, Congress can make determinations of constitutionality so long as they expand rights but cannot make those determinations if they restrict rights. However, there is serious debate as to whether allowing Congress to take an independent role in interpreting the Constitution can be justified under any circumstances in view of *Marbury v. Madison*, 5 U.S. (1 Cranch) 137 (1803). Once loosed in this area, can any restraint be thereafter imposed? Congress has traditionally tried to stay within judicially circumscribed bounds of constitutionality. But if it has an "independent role" in this area the restraints are removed. An example of this may be seen in the Omnibus Crime Control Act, wherein Congress made legislative inroads to judicially granted rights as expressed in the *Miranda* decision (*Miranda v. Arizona*, 384 U.S. 436 (1966)). The Court can always rule on these inroads, but is it not better that Congress not be encouraged to embark on them in the first instance?

Quicknotes

ENABLING CLAUSE OF THE FOURTEENTH AMENDMENT A constitutional provision giving the power to implement and enforce the law.

EQUAL PROTECTION CLAUSE A constitutional guarantee that no person should be denied the same protection of the laws enjoyed by other persons in like circumstances.

NECESSARY AND PROPER CLAUSE Article I, § 8 of the United States Constitution enables Congress to make all laws that may be "necessary and proper" to execute its other, enumerated powers.

PREEMPTION Doctrine stating that certain matters are of a national character so that federal laws preempt or take precedence over state or local laws.

SUPREMACY CLAUSE Article VI, § 2 of the United States Constitution, which provides that federal action must prevail over inconsistent state action.

Jones v. Alfred H. Mayer Co.

Buyer (P) v. Real estate company (D)

392 U.S. 409 (1968)

NATURE OF CASE: Certiorari review of private action of refusal of property owners to sell to a Black person.

FACT SUMMARY: Jones (P) brought suit in federal district court against the Alfred H. Mayer Co. (D) alleging that Mayer (D) refused to sell a home to him for the sole reason that Jones (P) was a Black person.

RULE OF LAW

Congress, pursuant to the authority vested in it by the Thirteenth Amendment, which clothes "Congress with power to pass all laws necessary and proper for abolishing all badges and incidents of slavery," may validly bar all racial discrimination, private as well as public, in the sale or rental of property.

FACTS: Relying upon 42 U.S.C. § 1982 (all citizens have the same right to inherit, purchase, lease, hold, and convey real and personal property as is enjoyed by White citizens), Jones (P) brought suit in federal district court against the Alfred H. Mayer Co. (Mayer) (D) alleging that Mayer (D) refused to sell a home to him for the sole reason that Jones (P) was a Black person.

ISSUE: May Congress, pursuant to the authority vested in it by the Thirteenth Amendment, which clothes "Congress with power to pass all laws necessary and proper for abolishing all badges and incidents of slavery," validly bar all racial discrimination, private as well as public, in the sale or rental of property?

HOLDING AND DECISION: (Stewart, J.) Yes. Congress, pursuant to the authority vested in it by the Thirteenth Amendment, which clothes "Congress with power to pass all laws necessary and proper for abolishing all badges and incidents of slavery," may validly bar all racial discrimination, private as well as public, in the sale or rental of property. Section 1982 is only a limited attempt to deal with discrimination in a select area of real estate transactions, even though, on its face, § 1982 appears to prohibit all discrimination against Black people in the sale or rental of property. If § 1982, originally enacted as § 1 of the Civil Rights Act of 1866, had been intended to grant nothing more than an immunity from governmental interference, then much of § 2 of the 1866 Act, which provides for criminal penalties where a person has acted "under color" of any law, would have been meaningless. The broad language of § 1982 was intentional. In 1866, Congress had before it considerable evidence showing private mistreatment of Black people. The focus of Congress, then, was on private groups (e.g., the Ku Klux Klan) operating outside the law. At the very least, the Thirteenth Amendment includes the freedom to buy whatever a White man can buy, and the right to live wherever a White man can live.

ANALYSIS

In *Sullivan v. Little Hunting Park, Inc.*, 396 U.S. 229 (1969), the Court invalidated a refusal by a homeowner's association to permit a member to assign his recreation share to a Black person. Once again, Justice Harlan in dissent questioned whether the Court should expand a century-old statute to encompass today's real estate transactions. After these two cases, it is questionable whether the Court will place any limits on its reading of the Thirteenth Amendment when reviewing legislation aimed at private discrimination.

Quicknotes

42 U.S.C. § 1982 "All citizens of the United States shall have the same right in every state at territory, as is enjoyed by white citizens thereof to inherit, purchase, lease, sell, hold, and convey real and personal property."

THIRTEENTH AMENDMENT The constitutional provision that abolished slavery in the United States.

Oregon v. Mitchell

State (P) v. Federal official (D)

400 U.S. 112 (1970)

NATURE OF CASE: Action challenging the constitutionality of a federal statute that would lower the minimum voting age from 21 to 18 for both federal elections and state and local elections.

FACT SUMMARY: Oregon (P) contended that a federal statute, the Voting Rights Act Amendments of 1970, which provided, inter alia, that the minimum voting age would be lowered from 21 to 18 for both federal elections and state and local elections, was unconstitutional.

RULE OF LAW

Congress does not have the power by statute to prevent age discrimination in voting at both the state and federal levels.

FACTS: Oregon (P) and other states challenged the constitutionality of the Voting Rights Act Amendments of 1970, which, inter alia, lowered the minimum age of voters in both state and local elections and federal elections from 21 to 18. In enacting this statute, Congress determined that setting the voting age at 21 or older denied and abridged the inherent constitutional rights of citizens 18 years of age but not yet 21 years of age to vote, which it found to be a particularly unfair treatment of such citizens in view of the national defense responsibilities imposed upon such citizens; had the effect of denying to citizens 18 years of age but not yet 21 years of age the due process and equal protection of the laws; and did not bear a reasonable relationship to any compelling state interest. The United States Supreme Court, exercising its original jurisdiction, heard the case, but there was no majority opinion. Four justices opined that the law should be upheld in its entirety; four other justices opined that the law as applied to both state and federal elections had to be struck down, and one justice—Justice Black—opined that Congress has the authority to permit 18-year-old citizens to vote in national elections, but not in state and local elections.

ISSUE: Does Congress have the power to prevent by statute age discrimination in voting at both the state and federal levels?

HOLDING AND DECISION: [Judge not listed in casebook excerpt.] No. Congress does not have the power by statute to prevent age discrimination in voting at both the state and federal levels.

OPINION: (Black, J.) Congress has the authority under Article 1, § 4 of the Constitution to set the age for voting in federal elections but lacks such power regarding state and local elections. The Civil War Amendments do not provide such power, since they were intended to prevent the states from discriminating on basis of race, not age; the statute at bar is not an attempt to prevent or eliminate racial discrimination by the states.

OPINION: (Douglas, J.) The authority of Congress to fix at 18 the minimum age for the civil right of voting in national elections derives from the Equal Protection Clause of the Fourteenth Amendment and the power to "enforce" granted by § 5 of that Amendment. Congress has an adequate basis for concluding that 18-year-olds are mature enough to vote and that to deprive them of the franchise would be a denial of equal protection. Election inequalities created by state laws and based on factors other than race may violate the Equal Protection Clause, and there is nothing in § 5 that restricts its applicability to matters of race alone.

OPINION: (Brennan, J., joined by Marshall, J. and White, J.) The issue is not whether the statute can withstand judicial scrutiny under the Equal Protection Clause (though it probably could), but instead it is whether Congress's determination in this regard must be respected. There was ample evidence to support Congress's conclusion that the exclusion of citizens 18 to 21 years of age from the franchise is unnecessary to promote any legitimate interest the states may have in assuring intelligent and responsible voting. Thus, the statute is a valid exercise of congressional power under § 5 of the Fourteenth Amendment. The nature of the judicial process makes it an inappropriate forum for the determination of complex factual questions of the kind so often involved in constitutional adjudication. Courts, therefore, will overturn a legislative determination of a factual question only if the legislature's finding is so clearly wrong that it may be characterized as "arbitrary," "irrational," or "unreasonable." This limitation of the judicial process, however, is inapplicable to Congress under § 5 of the Fourteenth Amendment, which expressly empowers Congress to enforce the Amendment and make its own determinations as to state discrimination. The core dispute here is between state and federal legislative determinations of the factual issues upon which depends decision of a federal constitutional question—the legitimacy, under the Equal Protection Clause, of state discrimination against persons between the ages of 18 and 21. It is well established that when state and federal claims come into

Continued on next page.

conflict, the primacy of federal power requires the federal findings of fact control. Because Congress's determination as to this issue is not clearly erroneous, and because Congress determined that no legitimate state interest was served in limiting voting to those 21 years of age or older, Congress has ample power under § 5 of the Fourteenth Amendment to forbid state discrimination in this regard.

OPINION: (Stewart, J., joined by Burger, C.J., and Blackmun, J.) Congress has no power to confer the right to vote in state or local elections on citizens from the ages of 18 to 21 since under the Constitution only the states have the power to set voting qualifications. Neither the Constitution, as amended, nor any precedent, gives Congress the power to nullify state laws requiring voters to be 21 years of age or older if Congress rationally concludes that such laws are not supported by a "compelling state interest." To use the compelling state interest test to deny the states of their unimpeachable right to establish a voting age is to effectively deprive of them of that right, since no state could demonstrate a "compelling interest" in drawing the line with respect to age at one point rather than another. The power to establish an age qualification must carry with it the power to choose 21 as a reasonable voting age, as most states have done. While Congress may impose on the states a remedy for a denial of equal protection in violation of the Constitution and may override state laws on the ground they in fact are being used as instruments of invidious discrimination, Congress does not have the power to determine what are and what are not "compelling state interests" for equal protection purposes. Here, the states have not engaged in invidious discrimination, and, hence, Congress does not have the authority to override them.

OPINION: (Harlan, J.) The Fourteenth Amendment was not intended to restrict the authority of the states to allocate their political power as they see fit, and neither this Amendment nor any other provision of the Constitution authorizes Congress to set voter qualifications in state or local elections. There is consensus that § 1 of the Fourteenth Amendment did not reach discriminatory voter qualifications. Moreover, the fact that other constitutional amendments were necessary to make law regarding other aspects of voting discrimination makes clear that the Fourteenth Amendment was never understood to empower Congress to legislate in these respects. Neither can the Court ignore the Constitution's commands, nor can it permit Congress to disregard those commands. Because under the Constitution the establishment of voting requirements is a matter left to the state legislatures, it is their decision that must be accorded judicial deference; to rely on Congress would make that body a judge in its own cause. The only power Congress has in this regard is to halt invidious discrimination, and there is no such discrimination that violates the Constitution being affected by the states. "[T]the suggestion members of the age group between 18 and 21 are threatened with unconstitutional discrimination, or that any hypothetical discrimination is likely to be affected by lowering the voting age, is little short of fanciful."

ANALYSIS

In direct response to this decision, the Twenty-Sixth Amendment was adopted in 1971. It provides that no person 18 or older may be denied the right to vote on the basis of age.

Quicknotes

COMPELLING STATE INTEREST Defense to an alleged Equal Protection Clause violation; that a state action was necessary to protect an interest the government is under a duty to protect.

EQUAL PROTECTION CLAUSE A constitutional provision that each person be guaranteed the same protection of the laws enjoyed by other persons in like circumstances.

CHAPTER 6

Federalism, Separation of Powers, and National Security in the Modern Era

Quick Reference Rules of Law

United States v. Lopez

Federal government (P) v. Student (D)

514 U.S. 549 (1995)

NATURE OF CASE: Appeal from order reversing federal firearms law violation conviction.

FACT SUMMARY: Lopez (D) was convicted under the 1990 federal Gun-Free School Zones Act, which prohibited guns near schools.

RULE OF LAW

The 1990 federal Gun-Free School Zones Act exceeds Congress's Commerce Clause regulatory powers.

FACTS: The 1990 federal Gun-Free School Zones Act made it a federal offense for a student to carry a gun onto campus. Lopez (D) was charged and convicted under the Act. On appeal, he contended that the Act was beyond Congress's powers under the Commerce Clause. The Fifth Circuit agreed and reversed. The Supreme Court granted review.

ISSUE: Did the 1990 Federal Gun-Free School Zones Act exceed Congress's Commerce Clause regulatory power?

HOLDING AND DECISION: (Rehnquist, C.J.) Yes. The 1990 federal Gun-Free School Zones Act exceeds Congress's Commerce Clause regulatory powers. It must be remembered that the federal government is one of limited, enumerated powers. For Congress to legislate, it must do so under an express constitutional provision. Since the 1930s, the Commerce Clause has been the source of most of Congress's legislative power. However, this clause is not a general grant of police power. A law passed under this Clause must relate to: (1) a channel of interstate commerce; (2) an instrumentality of interstate commerce; or (3) an activity having a substantial effect on interstate commerce. In this case, the regulated activity, carrying a gun to school, has no such effect. It is a purely local matter. Granted, if one is willing to accept a lengthy series of interferences and assumptions, such an activity may affect interstate commerce. Any activity can do so. However, if the concept of limited federal government is to have any meaning, Congress's legislative power must be cut off somewhere. That somewhere is the point at which a regulated activity does not substantially affect interstate commerce, and that point has been passed here. Affirmed.

CONCURRENCE: (Kennedy, J.) It is only with great care that this Court should intervene in matters relating to the Commerce Clause, as it is a matter best left to the political sectors of government. However, when an exercise of power under the Clause unduly upsets the balance of power between the states and the national government, as does the law at issue here, it is proper for the Court to intervene.

CONCURRENCE: (Thomas, J.) The substantial effects test is a New Deal innovation which goes far beyond the original intent of the Framers, who had a much narrower view of what was regulatable commerce. In fact, it grants Congress something approaching a general police power, a result clearly at odds with the Tenth Amendment.

DISSENT: (Stevens, J.) The education of our youth has a major impact on the national economy and is a proper subject for Commerce Clause regulation.

DISSENT: (Souter, J.) The Court's approach today constitutes a step backward towards the excessive judicial activism that characterized judicial review of congressional enactments during the first third of this century.

DISSENT: (Breyer, J.) In determining whether a regulated activity has a significant impact on interstate commerce, it is necessary to consider not a single example of the regulated activity, but rather the cumulative effects of all similar instances of that conduct. Here, it is clear the cumulative impact of the possession of weapons by students on campus will, over time, have a significant impact on the national economy.

ANALYSIS

Since 1937, the scope of congressional regulatory power under the Commerce Clause has grown enormously. By the 1960s, Congress's power under the Clause had increased to a level approaching a general police power. The present case represents the first significant break in this pattern and may signal a states' rights trend.

Quicknotes

COMMERCE CLAUSE Article I, § 8, cl. 3 of the United States Constitution, granting Congress the power to regulate commerce with foreign countries and between the states.

ENUMERATED POWERS Specific powers mentioned in and granted by the Constitution, e.g., the taxing power.

POLICE POWER The power of a government to impose restrictions on the rights of private persons, as long as these restrictions are reasonably related to the promotion and protection of public health, morals, safety, and the general welfare.

National Federation of Independent Business v. Sebelius (The Health Care Case)

Business group (P) v. Government official (D)

567 U.S. 519 (2012)

NATURE OF CASE: Appeal from judgment in action challenging the constitutionality of the "individual mandate" provision of the 2010 Patient Protection and Affordable Care Act. [The procedural posture of the case is not presented in the casebook extract.]

FACT SUMMARY: A coalition of plaintiffs (P) challenged the constitutionality of the "individual mandate" provision of the 2010 Patient Protection and Affordable Care Act. The Government (D) contended that the individual mandate was a valid exercise of Congress's authority under the Commerce Clause and the Necessary and Proper Clause.

RULE OF LAW

(1) The "individual mandate" provision of the Patient Protection and Affordable Care Act, which requires individuals to purchase health care insurance under certain circumstances, is not a valid exercise of Congress's power under the Commerce Clause.

(2) The "individual mandate" provision of the Patient Protection and Affordable Care Act, which requires individuals to purchase health care insurance under certain circumstances, is not a valid exercise of Congress's power under the Necessary and Proper Clause.

FACTS: In 2010, Congress enacted the Patient Protection and Affordable Care Act (the Act) to increase the number of Americans covered by health insurance and decrease the cost of health care. A key provision of the Act is the individual mandate, which requires most Americans to maintain "minimum essential" health insurance coverage. For individuals who are not exempt, and who do not receive health insurance through an employer or government program, the means of satisfying the requirement is to purchase insurance from a private company. Those who do not comply with the mandate must make a "shared responsibility payment" to the federal government based on income and subject to a statutory cap. A coalition of plaintiffs (P) challenged the individual mandate as unconstitutional. The Government (D) contended the individual mandate was a valid exercise of Congress's authority under the Commerce Clause and the Necessary and Proper Clause. The Government (D) asserted the health care market is characterized by a significant cost-shifting problem. This problem arises because, according to the Government (D), everyone will eventually need health care at a time and to an extent they cannot predict, but if they do not have insurance, they often will not be able to pay for it. Because state and federal laws nonetheless require hospitals to provide a certain degree of care to individuals without regard to their ability to pay, hospitals end up receiving compensation for only a portion of the services they provide. To recoup the losses, hospitals pass on the cost to insurers through higher rates, and insurers, in turn, pass on the cost to policyholders in the form of higher premiums. Congress estimated that the cost of uncompensated care raises family health insurance premiums, on average, by over $1,000 per year. To address this problem, at least in part, Congress included "guaranteed-issue" and "community-rating" provisions in the Act. These provisions together prohibit insurance companies from denying coverage to those with preexisting conditions or charging unhealthy individuals higher premiums than healthy individuals. The guaranteed-issue and community-rating reforms do not, however, address the issue of healthy individuals who choose not to purchase insurance to cover potential health care needs. In fact, the reforms sharply exacerbate that problem, by providing an incentive for individuals to delay purchasing health insurance until they become sick, relying on the promise of guaranteed and affordable coverage. The reforms also threaten to impose massive new costs on insurers, who are required to accept unhealthy individuals but prohibited from charging them rates necessary to pay for their coverage. This will lead insurers to significantly increase premiums on everyone. The individual mandate was Congress's solution to these problems. By requiring that individuals purchase health insurance, the mandate prevents cost-shifting by those who would otherwise go without it. In addition, the mandate forces into the insurance risk pool more healthy individuals, whose premiums on average will be higher than their health care expenses. This allows insurers to subsidize the costs of covering the unhealthy individuals the reforms require them to accept. The Government (D) contended the individual mandate is within Congress's power because the failure to purchase insurance "has a substantial and deleterious effect on interstate commerce" by creating the cost-shifting problem. The Government (D) also contended the mandate is an "integral part of a comprehensive scheme of economic regulation"—the guaranteed-issue and community-rating insurance

Continued on next page.

reforms—so Congress has the authority to enact the individual mandate under the Necessary and Proper Clause. The United States Supreme Court granted certiorari. [The procedural posture of the case is not presented in the casebook extract.]

ISSUE:

(1) Is the "individual mandate" provision of the Patient Protection and Affordable Care Act, which requires individuals to purchase health care insurance under certain circumstances, a valid exercise of Congress's power under the Commerce Clause?

(2) Is the "individual mandate" provision of the Patient Protection and Affordable Care Act, which requires individuals to purchase health care insurance under certain circumstances, a valid exercise of Congress's power under the Necessary and Proper Clause?

HOLDING AND DECISION: (Roberts, C.J.)

(1) No. The "individual mandate" provision of the Patient Protection and Affordable Care Act, which requires individuals to purchase health care insurance under certain circumstances, is not a valid exercise of Congress's power under the Commerce Clause. Congress has never attempted to rely on the commerce power to compel individuals not engaged in commerce to purchase an unwanted product—and with good reason. Congress is empowered to regulate commerce, which presupposes the existence of commercial activity to be regulated. If the power to "regulate" something included the power to create it, many of the provisions in the Constitution would be superfluous. The Constitution's language supports such a conclusion, as does the Court's precedent, which uniformly describes the commerce power as reaching "activity." The individual mandate, however, does not regulate existing commercial activity. It instead compels individuals to become active in commerce by purchasing a product, on the ground their failure to do so affects interstate commerce. Construing the Commerce Clause to permit Congress to regulate individuals precisely because they are doing nothing would open a new and potentially vast domain to congressional authority, as the Government's (D) logic would justify a mandatory purchase to solve almost any problem. People, for reasons of their own, often fail to do things that would be good for them or good for society. Those failures—joined with the similar failures of others—can readily have a substantial effect on interstate commerce. Under the Government's (D) logic, that authorizes Congress to use its commerce power to compel citizens to act as the Government (D) would have them act. Congress already possesses expansive power to regulate what people do. Upholding the Act under the Commerce Clause would give Congress the same license to regulate what people do not do. The Framers knew the difference between doing something and doing nothing. They gave Congress the power to regulate commerce, not to compel it. Ignoring that distinction would undermine the principle the federal government is a government of limited and enumerated powers. Contrary to the Government's (D) contention, the uninsured to be affected by the individual are not "active in the market for health care." In fact, the individual mandate's regulation of the uninsured as a class is particularly divorced from any link to existing commercial activity. The mandate primarily affects healthy, often young adults who are less likely to need significant health care and have other priorities for spending their money. It is precisely because these individuals, as an actuarial class, incur relatively low health care costs that the mandate helps counter the effect of forcing insurance companies to cover others who impose greater costs than their premiums are allowed to reflect. If the individual mandate is targeted at a class, it is a class whose commercial inactivity rather than activity is its defining feature. The Commerce Clause is not a general license to regulate an individual from cradle to grave, simply because he will predictably engage in particular transactions. Any police power to regulate individuals as such, as opposed to their activities, remains vested in the States. The individual mandate thus cannot be sustained under Congress's power to "regulate Commerce."

(2) No. The "individual mandate" provision of the Patient Protection and Affordable Care Act, which requires individuals to purchase health care insurance under certain circumstances, is not a valid exercise of Congress's power under the Necessary and Proper Clause. Each of this Court's prior cases upholding laws under that Clause involved exercises of authority derivative of, and in service to, a granted power. The individual mandate, by contrast, vests Congress with the extraordinary ability to create the necessary predicate to the exercise of an enumerated power and draw within its regulatory scope those who would otherwise be outside of it. This is in no way an authority that is "narrow in scope," or "incidental" to the exercise of the commerce power, as required by precedent. Rather, the Government's (D) conception of the Necessary and Proper Clause would work a substantial expansion of federal authority. No longer would Congress be limited to regulating under the Commerce Clause those who by some preexisting activity bring themselves within the sphere of federal regulation. Instead, Congress could reach beyond the natural limit of its authority and draw within its regulatory scope those who

Continued on next page.

otherwise would be outside of it. Thus, even if the individual mandate is "necessary" to the Act's other reforms, such an expansion of federal power is not a "proper" means for making those reforms effective. Accordingly, the individual mandate cannot be upheld as a "necessary and proper" component of the insurance reforms. Affirmed in part and reversed in part. [The procedural posture of the case is not presented in the casebook extract.]

CONCURRENCE AND DISSENT: (Ginsburg, J.) Beyond question, Congress could have provided a single-payer federal health care scheme similar to Social Security, whereby the federal government would be the only health care insurer. However, it chose to preserve a central role for private insurers and state governments. According to the majority opinion on this issue, authored by the Chief Justice, the Commerce Clause does not permit that preservation. This rigid reading of the Clause makes scant sense and is stunningly retrogressive. The problem the Act seeks to remedy with the individual mandate is that the uninsured heavily burden the national health care market. Those with health insurance subsidize the medical care of those without it, or, in the words of economists, the uninsured "free ride" on those who pay for health insurance. States cannot resolve the problem of the uninsured on their own. A state offering universal health care would place itself in a position of economic disadvantage as compared with neighbors or competitors, because it would have to raise taxes, private health-insurance companies would have to increase premiums, and higher taxes and increased insurance costs would, in turn, encourage businesses and healthy individuals to leave the state. Because the states cannot resolve this problem on their own, Congress stepped in with the Act to provide a national solution. However, Congress comprehended guaranteed-issue and community-rating laws alone will not work. When insurance companies are required to insure the sick at affordable prices, individuals can wait until they become ill to buy insurance. The result is those in need of immediate medical care—i.e., those who cost insurers the most—become the insurance companies' main customers. This "adverse selection" problem leaves insurers with two choices: They can either raise premiums dramatically to cover their ever-increasing costs or they can exit the market. This, in fact, is what happened in those states that implemented guaranteed-issue and community-rating laws without requiring universal acquisition of insurance coverage, and the results were disastrous. In the one state—Massachusetts—that succeeded, almost all residents were required to obtain a minimum level of health insurance. Congress passed the minimum coverage provision as a key component of the Act to address an economic and social problem that has plagued the country for decades: the large number of U.S. residents who are unable or unwilling to obtain health insurance. Congress had the prerogative to make this policy decision, which passes muster under the Commerce Clause and the Necessary and Proper Clause. As to the Commerce Clause, precedent holds Congress's authority under the Commerce Clause is dependent upon "practical" considerations, including "actual experience," and Congress is afforded the leeway "to undertake to solve national problems directly and realistically." When appraising Congress's social and economic legislation, the Court asks only (1) whether Congress had a "rational basis" for concluding the regulated activity substantially affects interstate commerce, and (2) whether there is a "reasonable connection between the regulatory means selected and the asserted ends." In answering these questions, it is presumed the statute under review is constitutional, and the Court may strike it down only on a "plain showing" Congress acted irrationally. Here, Congress had a rational basis for concluding the uninsured, as a class, substantially affect interstate commerce. The individual mandate, furthermore, bears a "reasonable connection" to Congress's goal of protecting the health care market from the disruption caused by individuals who fail to obtain insurance. By requiring those who do not carry insurance to pay a toll, the minimum coverage provision gives individuals a strong incentive to insure. This incentive, Congress had good reason to believe, would reduce the number of uninsured and, correspondingly, mitigate the adverse impact the uninsured have on the national health care market. Further, Congress also acted reasonably in requiring uninsured individuals, whether sick or healthy, either to obtain insurance or to pay the specified penalty. Because it is not disputed all U.S. residents participate in the market for health services over the course of their lives, contrary to the Chief Justice's position, Congress is not compelling individuals not engaged in commerce to purchase an unwanted product, even assuming the Chief Justice is correct that it is beyond Congress's power to compel individuals that way. Also contrary to the Chief Justice's position, the facts show an uninsured's consumption of health care is thus quite proximate: It is virtually certain to occur in the next five years and more likely than not to occur this year. It is Congress's role, not the Court's, to delineate the boundaries of the market Congress seeks to regulate. The Chief Justice defines the health care market as including only those transactions that will occur either in the next instant or within some (unspecified) proximity to the next instant. However, Congress could reasonably have viewed the market from a long-term perspective, encompassing all transactions virtually certain to occur over the next decade, not just those occurring here and now. Moreover, precedent directs that Congress may dictate the conduct of an individual today because of prophesied future activity.

Continued on next page.

Congress's actions in this case are rational, where the future activity (the consumption of medical care) is certain to occur, the sole uncertainty being the time the activity will take place. Thus, upholding the individual mandate on the ground that all are participants or will be participants in the health care market does not imply that Congress may use its commerce power to mandate individuals to buy products and services other than the ones they do or will buy at some point. Further, it is inaccurate to say, as does the Chief Justice, that the individual mandate compels individuals to purchase an unwanted product, given that virtually everyone will at some point or another seek medical care. In requiring individuals to obtain health insurance, Congress is therefore not mandating the purchase of a discrete, unwanted product. Rather, Congress is merely defining the terms on which individuals pay for an interstate good they consume. Additionally, contrary to the Chief Justice's view, the individual mandate is not an effort to have the young and healthy subsidize the health care of the unhealthy or infirm. Under the current health care system, healthy persons who lack insurance receive a benefit for which they do not pay: They are assured that, if they need it, emergency medical care will be available, although they cannot afford it. Those who have insurance bear the cost of this guarantee. By requiring the healthy uninsured to obtain insurance or pay a penalty structured as a tax, the minimum coverage provision ends the free ride these individuals currently enjoy. Viewed over a lifespan, the costs and benefits may even out, and everyone will be covered for catastrophic loss, even if not everyone will need to use that coverage; that is the nature of insurance. The Constitution's language and precedent also do not support the Chief Justice's interpretation that by enacting the individual mandate, Congress is not regulating something already in existence, but rather is bringing the subject of the regulation into existence. Requiring individuals to obtain insurance unquestionably regulates the interstate health insurance and health care markets, both in existence well before the Act's enactment. Thus, the "something to be regulated" was surely there when Congress created the minimum coverage provision. A long line of precedent also rejects the Chief Justice's formalistic distinction between activity and inactivity as a measure of the subject of Congress's commerce power. The fear the commerce power would be unlimited unless limited to regulating active participants in a commercial market is unfounded. Given the unique attributes of the health care market, upholding the individual mandate would not give Congress carte blanche to enact any and all purchase mandates. Nor would the commerce power be unbridled, absent an "activity" limitation, as Congress would remain unable to regulate noneconomic conduct that has only an attenuated effect on interstate commerce and is traditionally left to state law. The choice to self-insure, however, does not have an attenuated effect on commerce, but is an economic act with the requisite connection to interstate commerce. Also, the democratic process serves as another check on Congress's purchase-mandating behavior. Finally, merely because the individual mandate is a novelty is not a reason to override it. To the contrary, and as the Court has recognized for decades, Congress must be permitted to adapt to the changing "economic and financial realities."

The individual mandate is also a valid exercise of Congress's commerce power under the Necessary and Proper Clause. That Clause empowers Congress to enact laws in effectuation of its commerce power that are not within its authority to enact in isolation. It is undisputed the Congress has the power to eliminate the insurance industry's practice of charging higher prices or denying coverage to individuals with preexisting medical conditions. Without the individual mandate, however, this goal would be undercut and would lead to an adverse-selection death-spiral in the health-insurance market. Therefore, the individual mandate is an essential part of a larger regulation of economic activity that may be upheld under the Necessary and Proper Clause. Additionally, it is spurious to suggest, as does the Chief Justice, that the individual mandate improperly intrudes on "essential attributes of state sovereignty." First, the Act does not operate in an area such as criminal law enforcement or education where states historically have been sovereign. Second, and more importantly, the minimum coverage provision, along with the Act's other provisions, addresses the very sort of interstate problem that made the commerce power essential in our federal system. Instead of intruding on state's rights, the Act is an attempt to solve a problem the states cannot solve separately, on their own; the Act serves the general welfare of the people of the United States while retaining a prominent role for the states.

DISSENT: (Scalia, J., Kennedy, J., Thomas, J., Alito, J.) It is manifestly clear there are structural limitations on the commerce power and on what Congress can prescribe with respect to private conduct, and upon what it can impose upon the states. To say Congress's commerce power reaches inactivity would be to permit Congress to regulate virtually every aspect of human activity and inactivity. If the individual mandate regulates anything it is the failure to maintain minimum essential coverage. That failure is abstention from commerce, not commerce. One does not regulate commerce that does not exist by compelling its existence. The meaning of "regulate" at the time the Constitution was written was "[t]o adjust by rule, method or established mode." It can mean to direct the manner of something but it has never been understood to mean to direct that something come into being. When Congress provides citizens must buy an insurance

Continued on next page.

contract, it goes beyond "adjust[ing] by rule or method," or "direct[ing] according to rule;" it directs the creation of commerce. The fact the proposed regulations will impose great costs on the health insurance industry does not justify pressing into service healthy individuals who could be but are not customers of the relevant industry, to offset the undesirable consequences of the regulation. Congress's desire to force these individuals to purchase insurance is motivated by the fact they are further removed from the market than unhealthy individuals with preexisting conditions, because they are less likely to need extensive care in the near future. If Congress can reach out and command even those furthest removed from an interstate market to participate in the market, then the Commerce Clause becomes a font of unlimited power. Precedent makes clear the Commerce Clause, even when supplemented by the Necessary and Proper Clause, is not carte blanche for doing whatever will help achieve the ends Congress seeks by the regulation of commerce. The precedent on which the Government (D) relies to support the individual mandate is also distinguishable, as that precedent did not represent the expansion of the federal power to direct into a broad new field. The mandating of economic activity does, and since it is a field so limitless that it converts the Commerce Clause into a general authority to direct the economy, that mandating is inconsistent with the letter and spirit of the Constitution. Moreover, in that precedent, the prohibition was the only practicable way of achieving the desired outcome. Here, in contrast, there are many ways other than the individual mandate by which the regulatory scheme's goals of reducing insurance premiums and ensuring the profitability of insurers could be achieved. For example, those who did not purchase insurance could be subjected to a surcharge when they do enter the health insurance system, or they could be denied a full income tax credit given to those who do purchase the insurance. Also, the Government's (D) argument the individual mandate regulates activities having a substantial relation to interstate commerce must be rejected. The Government (D) argues the provision directs the manner, in which individuals purchase health care services and related goods, but the primary problem with this argument is it does not apply only to persons who purchase all, or most, or even any, of the health care services or goods the mandated insurance covers. Those persons—generally healthy and young—are not participants in the health care market the individual mandate purports to regulate. Because the decision to forgo participation in an interstate market is not itself commercial activity within Congress's power to regulate, the individual mandate cannot be justified by claiming it regulates such decisions because they have a substantial and deleterious effect on interstate commerce. If the Government (D) is permitted to regulate everyone who may at some point engage in commerce, there no longer will be any limits on the Government's (D) powers. Although Justice Ginsburg is correct in pointing out that Congress needs only a rational basis for concluding regulated activity substantially affects interstate commerce, she disregards the premise this test contains, which is that what is regulated is activity, not merely the failure to engage in commerce. If all inactivity affecting commerce is commerce, commerce is everything. The constitutional order is threatened by such an expansive reading of the commerce power, by which all private conduct (including failure to act) becomes subject to federal control, effectively destroying the Constitution's division of governmental powers. Contrary to Justice Ginsburg's treatment of the Constitution as an enumeration of problems Congress can address, the Constitution is not an enumeration of federally soluble problems, but federally available powers. Accordingly, the individual mandate is unconstitutional, and because it is not severable from the Act's other provisions, the Act in its entirety must be struck down.

DISSENT: (Thomas, J.) A "substantial effects" test under the Commerce Clause is inconsistent with the original understanding of Congress's powers and with the Court's early Commerce Clause cases. The Court's continued use of that test has encouraged the Government (D) to persist in its view the Commerce Clause has virtually no limits. Here, the Government's (D) unprecedented claim that it may regulate not only economic activity but also inactivity that substantially affects interstate commerce is a case in point.

ANALYSIS

The Court's former endeavors to impose categorical limits on the commerce power did not fare well. In several pre-New Deal cases, the Court attempted to cabin Congress's Commerce Clause authority by distinguishing "commerce" from activity once conceived to be noncommercial, notably, "production," "mining," and "manufacturing." The Court also sought to distinguish activities having a "direct" effect on interstate commerce, and for that reason, subject to federal regulation, from those having only an "indirect" effect, and therefore not amenable to federal control. These line-drawing exercises were untenable, and the Court long ago abandoned them. Accordingly, Justice Ginsburg opines the Chief Justice has failed to learn from history and instead "plows ahead" with his formalistic distinction between those who are "active in commerce," and those who are not. She also, therefore, warns hindering Congress's ability to address the health care problem is shortsighted, and predicts that if history is any guide, the Court's constriction of the Commerce Clause will not endure.

Continued on next page.

Quicknotes

COMMERCE CLAUSE Article I, § 8, cl. 3 of the United States Constitution, granting Congress the power to regulate commerce with foreign countries and among the states.

NECESSARY AND PROPER CLAUSE, Article I, § 8 of the United States Constitution enables Congress to make all laws that may be "necessary and proper" to execute its other, enumerated powers.

United States v. Comstock

Federal government (P) v. Sexually violent prisoner (D)

560 U.S. 126 (2010)

NATURE OF CASE: Appeal in action challenging as beyond Congress's power under the Necessary and Proper Clause a federal civil-commitment statute authorizing the federal government to civilly commit "sexually dangerous persons" beyond the date it lawfully could hold them on a charge or conviction for a federal crime. [The procedural posture of the case is not presented in the casebook extract.]

FACT SUMMARY: Congress enacted 18 U.S.C. § 4248, which authorizes the federal government to civilly commit "sexually dangerous persons" beyond the date it lawfully could hold them on a charge or conviction for a federal crime. The statute was challenged as beyond Congress's power under the Necessary and Proper Clause.

RULE OF LAW

Congress has power under the Necessary and Proper Clause to enact a law authorizing the federal government to civilly commit "sexually dangerous persons" beyond the date it lawfully could hold them on a charge or conviction for a federal crime.

FACTS: Congress enacted 18 U.S.C. § 4248, which authorizes the federal government to civilly commit "sexually dangerous persons" beyond the date it lawfully could hold them in the federal prison system on a charge or conviction for a federal crime. This statute would apply if neither the state of a prisoner's domicile nor the state in which the prisoner was tried was willing to assume the responsibility for the prisoner's custody, care, and treatment, and if that individual (1) previously "engaged or attempted to engage in sexually violent conduct or child molestation," (2) currently "suffers from a serious mental illness, abnormality, or disorder," and (3) "as a result of" that mental illness, abnormality, or disorder is "sexually dangerous to others," in that "he would have serious difficulty in refraining from sexually violent conduct or child molestation if released." The statute was challenged as beyond Congress's power under the Necessary and Proper Clause. [The procedural posture of the case is not presented in the casebook extract.]

ISSUE: Does Congress have power under the Necessary and Proper Clause to enact a law authorizing the federal government to civilly commit "sexually dangerous persons" beyond the date it lawfully could hold them on a charge or conviction for a federal crime?

HOLDING AND DECISION: (Breyer, J.) Yes. Congress has power under the Necessary and Proper Clause to enact a law authorizing the federal government to civilly commit "sexually dangerous persons" beyond the date it lawfully could hold them on a charge or conviction for a federal crime. The Clause grants Congress broad authority to pass laws in furtherance of its constitutionally enumerated powers. In determining whether the Clause authorizes a particular federal statute, there must be "means-ends rationality" between the enacted statute and the source of federal power. Although the Constitution nowhere grants Congress express power to create federal crimes beyond those specifically enumerated, to punish their violation, to imprison violators, or to provide appropriately for those imprisoned, Congress possesses broad authority to do each of those things under the Clause. The Government (P) has long been involved in the delivery of mental health care to federal prisoners, and has long provided for their civil commitment. As custodian of its prisoners, Congress has the constitutional power to act in order to protect nearby (and other) communities from the danger such prisoners may pose. Moreover, § 4248 is reasonably adapted to Congress's power to act as a responsible federal custodian. Congress could have reasonably concluded that federal inmates who suffer from a mental illness that causes them to have serious difficulty in refraining from sexually violent conduct would pose an especially high danger to the public if released, since Congress could have reasonably concluded that a reasonable number of such individuals would likely not be detained by the states if released from federal custody. The statute does not violate state sovereignty under the Tenth Amendment, since that Amendment does not reserve to the states those powers that are delegated to the federal Government (P) by the Constitution, including the powers delegated by the Necessary and Proper Clause. Moreover, § 4248 also does not otherwise invade state sovereignty. To the contrary, it seeks to accommodate state interests, since it requires the Attorney General to encourage the relevant states to take custody of the individual without inquiring into the "suitability" of their intended care or treatment, and to relinquish federal authority whenever a state asserts its own. Finally, contrary to the defendants' (D) contentions, when Congress legislates pursuant to the Necessary and Proper Clause, its authority does not have to be no more than one step removed from a specifically enumerated power. [The procedural outcome of the case is not presented in the casebook extract.]

Continued on next page.

CONCURRENCE: (Kennedy, J.) Under the Necessary and Proper Clause, application of a "rational basis" test should be at least as exacting as it has been in the Commerce Clause cases, which require a tangible link to commerce, not a mere conceivable rational relation. Thus, the link must be an empirically demonstrated link in fact. Also, while it is logically correct to say that if the federal Government (P) has a given power to act under the Necessary and Proper Clause then that power is not one reserved to the States, it is essential in determining whether the Government (P) has authority to exercise a given power in the first place to consider whether state sovereignty is compromised by the federal Government's (P) assertion of that power. If state sovereignty is compromised, that suggests that the power is not one properly within the reach of federal power.

CONCURRENCE: (Alito, J.) Despite the ambiguity in the standard established by the majority, it is clear that most federal criminal statutes rest upon a congressional judgment that, in order to execute one or more of the powers conferred on Congress, it is necessary and proper to criminalize certain conduct, and in order to do that it is obviously necessary and proper to provide for the operation of a federal criminal justice system and a federal prison system. Thus, it is necessary and proper for Congress to protect the public from dangers created by the federal criminal justice and prison systems. Given that it is necessary and proper for Congress to provide for the apprehension of escaped federal prisoners, it is similarly necessary and proper for Congress to provide for the civil commitment of dangerous federal prisoners who would otherwise escape civil commitment as a result of federal imprisonment. Further, studies have shown that states are very reluctant to accept the prisoners that are the subject of § 4248, so that the link between the statute and Congress' constitutional powers is very strong.

DISSENT: (Thomas, J.) The Government (P) identifies no specific enumerated power or powers as a constitutional predicate for § 4248, and none are readily discernible; and not even the Commerce Clause can justify federal civil detention of sex offenders. The settled understanding of Congress's power under the Necessary and Proper Clause is that Congress may act under that Clause only when its legislation carries into execution one of the federal Government's (P) enumerated powers. However, § 4248 does not execute any enumerated power, so it must, therefore, be unconstitutional. Moreover, the Court has long recognized that the power to care for the mentally ill and, where necessary, the power to protect the community from the dangerous tendencies of some mentally ill persons, are among the numerous powers that remain with the States. Regardless of whether the States are willing or able to use their police powers to commit released dangerous federal prisoners, those powers belong to the States alone. Thus, the majority's decision comes perilously close to transforming the Necessary and Proper Clause into a basis for the federal police power that the Court has always rejected. Further, the Necessary and Proper Clause does not provide Congress with authority to enact any law simply because it furthers other laws Congress has enacted in the exercise of its incidental authority; the Clause plainly requires a showing that every federal statute must carry into execution one or more of the federal Government's (P) enumerated powers. Civil detention under § 4248, however, lacks any such connection to an enumerated power.

ANALYSIS

One of the constitutional principles that the Court elaborated in this decision is that congressional authority under the Necessary and Proper Clause can be more than one step removed from an enumerated power. When the inquiry is whether a federal law has sufficient links to an enumerated power to be within the scope of federal authority, the analysis depends not on the number of links in the congressional-power chain but on the strength of the chain. Thus, concluding that a relation can be put into a verbal formulation that fits somewhere along a causal chain of federal powers is merely the beginning, not the end, of the constitutional inquiry.

Quicknotes

ENUMERATED POWERS Those powers expressly delegated by the U.S. Constitution to a particular branch of government.

NECESSARY AND PROPER CLAUSE, ART. I, § 8 OF THE CONSTITUTION Enables Congress to make all laws that may be "necessary and proper" to execute its other, enumerated powers.

POLICE POWER The power of a government to impose restrictions on the rights of private persons, so long as those restrictions are reasonably related to the promotion and protection of public health, safety, morals, and the general welfare.

National Federation of Independent Business v. Sebelius (The Health Care Case)

Business group (P) v. Government official (D)

567 U.S. 519 (2012)

NATURE OF CASE: Appeal from judgment in action challenging the constitutionality of the "individual mandate" provision of the 2010 Patient Protection and Affordable Care Act. [The procedural posture of the case is not presented in the casebook extract.]

FACT SUMMARY: A coalition of plaintiffs (P) challenged the constitutionality of the "individual mandate" provision of the 2010 Patient Protection and Affordable Care Act. The Government (D) contended, inter alia, that the individual mandate was a valid exercise of Congress's taxing power, since it provided individuals who did not purchase health care insurance would pay a penalty in the form of a tax.

RULE OF LAW

The "individual mandate" provision of the Patient Protection and Affordable Care Act, which requires that individuals who do not purchase health care insurance under certain circumstances must pay a penalty in the form of a tax, is a valid exercise of Congress's taxing power.

FACTS: In 2010, Congress enacted the Patient Protection and Affordable Care Act (the Act) to increase the number of Americans covered by health insurance and decrease the cost of health care. A key provision of the Act is the individual mandate, which requires most Americans to maintain "minimum essential" health insurance coverage. For individuals who are not exempt, and who do not receive health insurance through an employer or government program, the means of satisfying the requirement is to purchase insurance from a private company. Those who do not comply with the mandate must make a "shared responsibility payment" to the Internal Revenue Service (IRS) based on factors such as income, number of dependents, and joint filing status, and is subject to a statutory cap. A coalition of plaintiffs (P) challenged the individual mandate as unconstitutional. The Government (D) contended, inter alia, the individual mandate was a valid exercise of Congress's taxing power, since the Act provided the penalty would be paid to the IRS with an individual's taxes, and "shall be assessed and collected in the same manner" as tax penalties. The imposition of the individual mandate was expected to raise $4 billion per year by its third year. The United States Supreme Court granted certiorari. [The procedural posture of the case is not presented in the casebook extract.]

ISSUE: Is the "individual mandate" provision of the Patient Protection and Affordable Care Act, which requires that individuals who do not purchase health care insurance under certain circumstances must pay a penalty in the form of a tax, a valid exercise of Congress's taxing power?

HOLDING AND DECISION: (Roberts, C.J.) Yes. The "individual mandate" provision of the Patient Protection and Affordable Care Act, which requires that individuals who do not purchase health care insurance under certain circumstances must pay a penalty in the form of a tax, is a valid exercise of Congress's taxing power. The individual mandate must be construed as imposing a tax on those who do not have health insurance, if such a construction is reasonable. The most straightforward reading of the individual mandate is it commands individuals to purchase insurance. However, the Government's (D) alternative argument is that the mandate may be upheld as within Congress's power to "lay and collect Taxes." In pressing its taxing power argument, the Government (D) asks the Court to view the mandate as imposing a tax on those who do not buy a health insurance product. Granting the Act the full measure of deference owed to federal statutes, it can be so read, for the following reasons. First, the exaction imposed by the Act has many of the features of a tax, and is functionally like a tax, and it has the essential feature of a tax insofar as it raises revenue for the Government (D). Taking such a functional approach is confirmed by precedent. Second, taking such an approach, the exaction functions more like a tax than a penalty. For most Americans, the amount due will be far less than the price of insurance, and, by statute, it can never be more. Also, the individual mandate contains no scienter requirement. Further, the payment is collected solely by the IRS through the normal means of taxation—except the IRS is not allowed to use those means most suggestive of a punitive sanction, such as criminal prosecution. For these reasons, the exaction may be viewed as a tax and not as a penalty. Additionally, merely because the individual mandate is designed to regulate individual conduct and encourage the purchasing of health insurance does not mean it cannot be a valid exercise of the taxing power. To some extent, all taxes are regulatory in nature. Because it is estimated four million people each year will choose to pay the IRS rather than buy insurance, and because Congress apparently regards such extensive failure to comply with the mandate as tolerable, it seems Congress

Continued on next page.

did not think it was creating four million outlaws. It suggests instead the shared responsibility payment merely imposes a tax citizens may lawfully choose to pay in lieu of buying health insurance. Contrary to the joint dissenters' opinion, the individual mandate may be upheld as a tax notwithstanding Congress did not frame it as a tax. The mandate's substance is in the form of a tax, and that conclusion should not change simply because Congress used the word "penalty" to describe the payment. Thus, interpreting such a law to be a tax would not impose a tax through judicial legislation, but instead would give practical effect to Congress's enactment. The individual mandate also complies with the other requirements for taxes under the Constitution, as it is not a capitation, and is not a direct tax that is required to be apportioned among the states. A more fundamental objection to a tax on those who lack health insurance—similar to the objection to the individual mandate as exceeding the commerce power—is that it should be troubling to permit Congress to impose a tax for not doing something. There are three reasons why such a tax passes constitutional scrutiny. First, the Constitution does not guarantee that individuals may avoid taxation through inactivity, so that upholding the individual mandate under the Taxing Clause does not recognize any new federal power but is a determination Congress has used an existing one. Second, while Congress's taxing power has limits, so exactions cannot become punitive, it has already been explained the individual mandate passes muster as a tax and not as a punitive penalty. Accordingly, it comes within the strict limits within which Congress can tax. Third, Congress's authority under the taxing power is limited to requiring an individual to pay money to the federal government; the individual retains the choice whether to do or not do a certain act, so long as he or she is willing to pay a tax levied on that choice. The individual mandate also imposes a cost on the choice not to obtain health care insurance. Accordingly, the individual mandate comes within the Constitution's requirements. Case affirmed in part and reversed in part.

DISSENT: (Scalia, J., Kennedy, J., Thomas, J., Alito, J.) The individual mandate cannot be characterized as a tax. Therefore, there is no need to reach the issue of whether it comes within Congress's permissible taxing power.

ANALYSIS

The issue of whether the individual mandate comes within Congress's taxing power was reached only because the majority determined the Commerce Clause did not authorize the individual mandate's command to purchase insurance. Because the statute reads more naturally as a command to buy insurance than as a tax, and because the Court held the statute was unconstitutional as a command, the Court exercised its duty to construe the statute to save it, if possible, if it could be interpreted as a tax. Without deciding the Commerce Clause question, the Court would have found no basis to adopt such a saving construction. Through the exercise of its duty of statutory construction, the Court upheld the individual mandate's constitutionality, but only because the Court determined the statute could reasonably be read as a tax.

Quicknotes

TAXING POWER The authority delegated to Congress by the United States Constitution to impose taxes.

National Federation of Independent Business v. Sebelius (The Health Care Case)

Business group (P) v. Government official (D)

567 U.S. 519 (2012)

NATURE OF CASE: Appeal from judgment in action challenging the constitutionality of the "Medicaid expansion" provision of the 2010 Patient Protection and Affordable Care Act. [The procedural posture of the case is not presented in the casebook extract.]

FACT SUMMARY: A coalition of plaintiffs (P) challenged the constitutionality of the "Medicaid expansion" provision of the 2010 Patient Protection and Affordable Care Act, which expanded certain Medicaid benefits, but also threatened the states, which administer Medicaid, with the loss not only of funding for the increased coverage, but also the loss of all federal Medicaid funds.

RULE OF LAW

That part of the "Medicaid expansion" provision of the Patient Protection and Affordable Care Act that threatens the states with a loss of all federal Medicaid funding for failing to comply with the Act's expansion of Medicaid benefits and coverage, is not a valid exercise of Congress's power under the Spending Clause.

FACTS: In 2010, Congress enacted the Patient Protection and Affordable Care Act (the Act) to increase the number of Americans covered by health insurance and decrease the cost of health care. A key provision of the Act is the "Medicaid expansion." The current Medicaid program offers federal funding to states to assist pregnant women, children, needy families, the blind, the elderly, and the disabled in obtaining medical care. The Act would expand the scope of the Medicaid program and increases the number of individuals the states must cover. For example, the Act requires state programs to provide Medicaid coverage by 2014 to adults with incomes up to 133 percent of the federal poverty level, whereas many states now cover adults with children only if their income is considerably lower and do not cover childless adults at all. The Act increases federal funding to cover the states' costs in expanding Medicaid coverage, but if a state does not comply with the Act's new coverage requirements, it may lose not only the federal funding for those requirements, but all its federal Medicaid funds. A coalition of plaintiffs (P), including some states, challenged the Medicaid expansion as unconstitutionally exceeding Congress's spending power under the Spending Clause by coercing the states to enact the statute. The United States Supreme Court granted certiorari. [The procedural posture of the case is not presented in the casebook extract.]

ISSUE: Is that part of the "Medicaid expansion" provision of the Patient Protection and Affordable Care Act that threatens the states with a loss of all federal Medicaid funding for failing to comply with the Act's expansion of Medicaid benefits and coverage, a valid exercise of Congress's power under the Spending Clause?

HOLDING AND DECISION: (Roberts, C.J.) No. That part of the "Medicaid expansion" provision of the Patient Protection and Affordable Care Act (the Act) that threatens the states with a loss of all federal Medicaid funding for failing to comply with the Act's expansion of Medicaid benefits and coverage is not a valid exercise of Congress's power under the Spending Clause. There is no doubt the Act dramatically increases state obligations under Medicaid. In light of expansion in coverage mandated by the Act, the Government (D) estimates its Medicaid spending will increase by approximately $100 billion per year, nearly 40 percent above current levels. To be constitutional, Congress's power under the Spending Clause to secure state compliance with federal objectives rests on whether the state voluntarily and knowingly accepts the terms of the "contract" offered by the federal Government (D). The Constitution has never been understood to confer upon Congress the ability to require the states to govern according to Congress's instructions. Otherwise the two-government system established by the Framers would give way to a system that vests power in one central government, and individual liberty would suffer. Thus, Congress may use its spending power to create incentives for states to act in accordance with federal policies, but when pressure turns into compulsion, the legislation runs contrary to our system of federalism. That is true whether Congress directly commands a state to regulate or indirectly coerces a state to adopt a federal regulatory system as its own. Here, the plaintiffs (P) claim Congress has crossed the line from encouragement to coercion by structuring the Medicaid expansion so states that refuse the new conditions not only will not receive new funding but will lose all existing funding. The plaintiffs (P) claim this threat serves no purpose other than to force unwilling states to sign up for the dramatic expansion in health care coverage effected by the Act. Under the circumstances presented by the case, the plaintiffs (P) are correct—the Government's (D) "inducement" to participate is tantamount to a gun to the head. Respecting

Continued on next page.

some states, the loss of all Medicaid funding represents a loss of as much as 10 percent of the state's entire budget. This is economic coercion that leaves the states with no real option but to acquiesce in the Medicaid expansion. The states contend the expansion is in reality a new program and Congress is forcing them to accept it by threatening the funds for the existing Medicaid program. The Government (D) counters the Medicaid expansion is properly viewed merely as a modification of the existing program, and emphasizes the states agreed Congress could change the terms of Medicaid when they signed on in the first place. The issue is one of substance, not merely what Congress has labeled the program. Here, the Medicaid expansion accomplishes a shift in kind, not merely degree. The original program was designed to cover medical services for four particular categories of the needy. Previous amendments to Medicaid eligibility merely altered and expanded the boundaries of these categories. Under the Act, however, Medicaid is transformed into a program to meet the health care needs of the entire nonelderly population with income below 133 percent of the poverty level. It is no longer a program to care for the neediest among us, but rather an element of a comprehensive national plan to provide universal health insurance coverage. A state could hardly have anticipated when it signed on to the Medicaid program that Congress's reservation of the right to "alter" or "amend" the Medicaid program included the power to transform it so dramatically. The constitutional violation is fully remedied by precluding the Government (D) from withdrawing existing Medicaid funds for failure to comply with the requirements set out in the expansion. The other provisions of the Act are not affected. Congress would have wanted the rest of the Act to stand, had it known that states would have a genuine choice whether to participate in the Medicaid expansion. Case affirmed in part and reversed in part.

CONCURRENCE AND DISSENT: (Ginsburg, J.) Congress could have recalled the existing Medicaid legislation and replaced it with a new law making Medicaid as embracive of the poor as Congress chose. Congress should not have to take that route. Instead, Congress may expand by amendment the classes of needy persons entitled to Medicaid benefits. A ritualistic requirement that Congress repeals and reenacts spending legislation in order to enlarge the population served by a federally funded program would advance no constitutional principle and would scarcely serve the interests of federalism. Here, Medicaid, and Medicaid as amended by the Patient Protection and Affordable Care Act (the Act), are not two separate programs, but just one with a constant aim—to enable poor persons to receive basic health care when they need it. Moreover, the states are not entitled to Medicaid funding, and if they accept such funding, they must do so on Congress's terms. Here, there are no coercion concerns, because the expansion relates solely to the federally funded Medicaid program; if states choose not to comply, Congress has not threatened to withhold funds earmarked for any other program. Nor does the Act use Medicaid funding to induce states to take action Congress itself could not undertake. The Government (D) undoubtedly could operate its own health care program for poor persons, just as it operates Medicare for seniors' health care. Contrary to the Chief Justice's opinion, the Act does not affect a new program; it merely expands the number of people covered by the existing program. The aspects of the expansion cited by the Chief Justice as supporting his premise that the expansion creates a new program do not, in fact, support his premise. The Chief Justice's finding that the expansion took states by surprise is also unfounded. The precedent on which he relies merely requires conditions on federal funds be unambiguously clear at the time a state receives and uses the money—not at the time, perhaps years earlier, when Congress passed the law establishing the program. In any event, from the start, the Medicaid Act put states on notice the program could be changed, or even repealed. Thus, the states were on notice of the Act's proposed changes. Further, the Chief Justice does not announce a workable judicial standard for determining when a state is being coerced by the federal government. The coercion inquiry appears to involve political judgments that defy judicial calculation, and conceptions of when a state has been "coerced" are too amorphous to be judicially administrable. In sum, the Chief Justice and the joint-dissenters' position is that the states' reliance on federal funds limits Congress's authority to alter its spending programs. This gets things backwards: Congress, not the states, is tasked with spending federal money in service of the general welfare, and each successive Congress is empowered to appropriate funds as it sees fit. For all these reasons, the Medicaid expansion is within Congress's spending power.

DISSENT: (Scalia, J., Kennedy, J., Thomas, J., Alito, J.) Contrary to the Government's (D) argument, it is not enough to meet the anticoercion rule if states are free as a matter of law to turn down federal funds. This argument ignores the reality that when a heavy federal tax is levied to support a federal program that offers large grants to the states, states may, as a practical matter, be unable to refuse to participate in the federal program and to substitute a state alternative. This is because, as a practical matter, states would have to impose a huge tax on top of the heavy tax imposed by the federal government. Acceptance of the Government's (D) interpretation of the anticoercion rule would permit Congress to dictate policy in areas traditionally governed primarily at the state or local level. Further, the record shows Congress anticipated 100 percent state participation. The Government (D) asserts this expectation arose because the Patient

Continued on next page.

Protection and Affordable Care Act's (the Act's) offer to the states was a generous gift. If, however, that was true, why did more than half the states file this suit claiming the Medicaid expansion was coercive? Also, if the "gift" was so generous, Congress could have made just the new funding provided under the Act contingent on acceptance of the terms of the Medicaid expansion. Accordingly, the Medicaid expansion must fall, as it is not severable from the Medicaid extension.

ANALYSIS

It should be noted that the Court's decision does not strike down any provision of the Patient Protection and Affordable Care Act (the Act). It prohibits only the "application" of the Secretary of Health and Human Service's authority to withhold Medicaid funds from states that decline to conform their Medicaid plans to the Act's requirements. Thus, the Act's authorization of funds to finance the expansion remains intact and the Secretary's authority to withhold funds for reasons other than noncompliance with the expansion remains unaffected. The joint dissenters would have held the expansion was not severable from the Medicaid extension, and would have consequently held the entire expansion was invalid. Justice Ginsburg agreed with the Chief Justice that the Medicaid Act's severability clause determined the appropriate remedy. That clause provides that "[i]f any provision of [the Medicaid Act], or the application thereof to any person or circumstance, is held invalid, the remainder of the chapter, and the application of such provision to other persons or circumstances shall not be affected thereby." 42 U.S.C. § 1303.

Quicknotes

FEDERALISM A scheme of government whereby the power to govern is among central and localized governments.

SPENDING CLAUSE The power delegated to Congress by the Constitution to spend money in providing for the nation's welfare.

SPENDING POWER The power delegated to Congress by the Constitution to spend money in providing for the nation's welfare.

Bond v. United States

Convicted federal crimes offender (D) v. Federal government (P)

134 S. Ct. 2077 (2014)

NATURE OF CASE: Appeal from conviction for violation of the Chemical Weapons Convention Implementation Act of 1998. [The procedural posture of the case is not presented in the casebook extract.]

FACT SUMMARY: Bond (D) contended that her conviction for violation of the Chemical Weapons Convention Implementation Act of 1998 (the Implementation Act) had to be overturned because the Implementation Act was beyond Congress's power.

RULE OF LAW

The constitutionality of a statute will not be decided if there are other grounds upon which a case involving the statute can be disposed.

FACTS: The United States ratified the international Convention on the Prohibition of the Development, Production, Stockpiling, and Use of Chemical Weapons and on Their Destruction. To implement this convention, Congress enacted the Chemical Weapons Convention Implementation Act of 1998 (the Implementation Act). The statute forbade, among other things, any person knowingly possessing or using any chemical weapon, which was defined as a toxic chemical not used for any peaceful purpose related to an industrial, agricultural, research, medical, or pharmaceutical activity. Bond (D) sought revenge against Haynes—with whom her husband had carried on an affair—by spreading two toxic chemicals on Haynes's car, mailbox, and doorknob in hopes that Haynes would develop an uncomfortable rash. Haynes suffered a minor chemical burn that she treated by rinsing with water, but Bond's (D) attempted assaults were otherwise entirely unsuccessful. Federal prosecutors charged Bond (D) with violating the Implementation Act. Bond (D) moved to dismiss the chemical weapons charges on the ground the Act went beyond Congress's powers. The United States Supreme Court heard her appeal. [The procedural posture of the case is not presented in the casebook extract.]

ISSUE: Will the constitutionality of a statute be decided if there are other grounds upon which a case involving the statute can be disposed?

HOLDING AND DECISION: (Roberts, C.J.) No. The constitutionality of a statute will not be decided if there are other grounds upon which a case involving the statute can be disposed. Here, there is an ambiguity in the statute that derives from the improbably broad reach of the key statutory definition, given the term—"chemical weapon"—that is being defined, the deeply serious consequences of adopting such a boundless reading, and the lack of any apparent need to do so in light of the context from which the statute arose—a treaty about chemical warfare and terrorism, not about local assaults. Thus, the Court can reasonably insist on a clear indication that Congress intended to reach purely local crimes before interpreting the Implementation Act's expansive language in a way that intrudes on the states' police power. Thus, applying these principles of construction and federalism, there is no need to reach the constitutional issue that Bond (D) raises. [The disposition of the case is not presented in the casebook extract.]

CONCURRENCE: (Scalia, J.) The constitutional issue presented can and should be reached, since the Necessary and Proper Clause does not empower Congress to enact statutes that implement treaties. Under the Constitution, only the President and Senate are empowered to make treaties, but they are not empowered to enforce treaties. Thus, Congress has the power to help the President make treaties, but not a power to implement treaties already made.

CONCURRENCE: (Thomas, J.) The treaty power cannot be used to regulate purely domestic matters, and any treaty must relate to intercourse with other nations. While it is sometimes difficult to distinguish between matters of international intercourse and matters of purely domestic regulation, such difficulty is no reason for ignoring a constitutional limit on federal power.

CONCURRENCE: (Alito, J.) The treaty power is limited to agreements that address matters of legitimate international concern. Thus, the main focus of the Convention represents a legitimate exercise of the treaty power, but insofar as the Convention may be read to obligate the United States to enact domestic legislation criminalizing conduct of the sort at issue in this case, which typically is the sort of conduct regulated by the states, the Convention exceeds the scope of the treaty power.

ANALYSIS

To be able to reach the constitutional issue, the Court would have to decide that Bond's (D) conduct unambiguously came within the scope of the Implementation Act. Justice Scalia urged such an interpretation, saying that as sweeping and unsettling as the Chemical Weapons Convention Implementation Act of 1998 may be, it was clear beyond doubt that it covered what Bond

Continued on next page.

(D) did, and that the Court did not have the authority to judicially amend the statute, but only to determine whether the statute's application to Bond (D) was constitutional. He would have invalidated the statute precisely because, in his opinion, it swept too broadly and represented overreaching by Congress, through the statute's purported regulation of states' treatment of their own citizens.

Quicknotes

AMBIGUITY Language that is capable of being understood to have more than one interpretation.

FEDERALISM A scheme of government whereby the power to govern is among a central and localized governments.

POLICE POWER The power of a government to impose restrictions on the rights of private persons, so long as those restrictions are reasonably related to the promotion and protection of public health, safety, morals, and the general welfare.

City of Boerne v. Flores

Municipality (D) v. Church (P)

521 U.S. 507 (1997)

NATURE OF CASE: Review of judgment sustaining the constitutionality of the Religious Freedom Restoration Act of 1993.

FACT SUMMARY: A decision by zoning authorities in Boerne (D) to deny a church (P) a building permit was challenged under the Religious Freedom Restoration Act.

RULE OF LAW

The Religious Freedom Restoration Act (RFRA) unconstitutionally exceeds Congress's enforcement power under the Due Process Clause of the Fourteenth Amendment.

FACTS: The Religious Freedom Restoration Act (RFRA) prohibited the government from substantially burdening a person's exercise of religion, even if the burden is the result of a generally applicable law, unless the government has a compelling interest and is using the least restrictive means. Flores (P) sought a building permit to expand his church, a historic landmark. The City of Boerne (D) denied the permit and Flores (P) sued, invoking RFRA. The district court determined that RFRA exceeded congressional power, but the Fifth Circuit reversed, holding the Act constitutional. Boerne (D) appealed.

ISSUE: Does the Religious Freedom Restoration Act (RFRA) unconstitutionally exceed Congress's enforcement power under the Due Process Clause of the Fourteenth Amendment?

HOLDING AND DECISION: (Kennedy, J.) Yes. The Religious Freedom Restoration Act (RFRA) unconstitutionally exceeds Congress's enforcement power under the Due Process Clause of the Fourteenth Amendment. Here, Congress, with RFRA, attempts to replace, with the compelling interest test, this Court's decision in *Employment Div., Dept. of Human Resources of Ore. v. Smith*, 494 U.S. 872 (1990). *Smith* held that the compelling interest test is inappropriate in cases where general prohibitions are opposed by free exercise challenges. But RFRA violates the long tradition of separation of powers established by the Constitution. The judiciary is to determine the constitutionality of laws, and the powers of the legislature are defined and limited. While Congress can enact remedial, preventive legislation that deters violations, RFRA is not a preventive law. Instead, RFRA redefines the scope of the Free Exercise Clause and nothing in our history extends to Congress the ability to take such action. RFRA is so out of proportion to a supposed remedial or preventive object that it cannot be regarded as a response to unconstitutional behavior. Reversed.

CONCURRENCE: (Stevens, J.) The Religious Freedom Restoration Act is a "law respecting an establishment of religion" that violates the First Amendment to the Constitution.

DISSENT: (O'Connor, J.) *Smith* was wrongly decided and the Court should correct the misrepresentation.

DISSENT: (Souter, J.) I have serious doubts about the value of the *Smith* rule and world dismiss.

DISSENT: (Breyer, J.) The Court should set this case for reargument over the issue of whether *Smith* was correctly decided but need not reach the question of whether the Fourteenth Amendment would authorize Congress to enact The Religious Freedom Restoration Act.

ANALYSIS

The Religious Freedom Restoration Act (RFRA) was one of the four federal laws overturned by the United States Supreme Court during its 1997 term. Although the Court has endorsed judicial restraint in recent years, it has not hesitated to quash improper intrusions on its authority to set unconstitutional standards. The Court, however, chose not to revisit the religious freedom issue in its *Boerne* decision, leaving intact the ruling in *Smith* that inspired Congress to pass RFRA. In *Smith*, the Court approved Oregon's use of its ban on peyote to prohibit the drug's use in Native American religious rituals. RFRA was intended to guarantee religious observance a higher degree of statutory protection than the *Smith* Court thought necessary.

Quicknotes

FREE EXERCISE OF RELIGION The right to practice one's religious beliefs free from governmental conduct or interference.

SEPARATION OF POWERS DOCTRINE Each branch of government is precluded from interfering with the authority of another.

STRICT SCRUTINY The method by which courts determine the constitutionality of a law, when a law affects a

Continued on next page.

fundamental right. Under the test, the legislature must have a compelling interest to enact law, and measures prescribed by the law must be the least restrictive means possible to accomplish goal.

ZONING ORDINANCE A statute that divides land into defined areas and which regulates the form and use of buildings and structures within those areas.

United States v. Morrison

Federal government (P) v. Students (D)

529 U.S. 598 (2000)

NATURE OF CASE: Certiorari review of the constitutionality of the federal Violence Against Women Act. [The procedural posture of the case is not presented in the casebook extract.]

FACT SUMMARY: Brzonkala (P) brought suit against two football-playing male students (D) and Virginia Polytechnic University under the Violence Against Women Act (VAWA), 42 U.S.C. § 13981. The students and university contended VAWA was an unconstitutional exercise of Congress's remedial power under § 5 of the Fourteenth Amendment.

RULE OF LAW

Section 13891 of the Violence Against Women Act may not be upheld as a constitutional exercise of Congress's remedial power under § 5 of the Fourteenth Amendment.

FACTS: Brzonkala (P), a student at Virginia Polytechnic Institute, complained that football-playing students Morrison (D) and Crawford (D) assaulted and repeatedly raped her. Virginia Tech's Judicial Committee found insufficient evidence to punish Crawford (D) but found Morrison (D) guilty of sexual assault and sentenced him to immediate suspension for two semesters. The school's vice president set this aside as excessive punishment. Brzonkala (P) then dropped out of the university and brought suit against the school and the male students (D) under the Violence Against Women Act (VAWA), 42 U.S.C. § 13981, 42 U.S.C. § 13981, providing a federal cause of action for a crime of violence motivated by gender. The United States Supreme Court granted certiorari in the case. [The procedural posture of the case is not presented in the casebook extract.]

ISSUE: May § 13891 of the Violence Against Women Act be upheld as a constitutional exercise of Congress's remedial power under § 5 of the Fourteenth Amendment?

HOLDING AND DECISION: (Rehnquist, C.J.) No. Section 13891 of the Violence Against Women Act (VAWA) may not be upheld as a constitutional exercise of Congress's remedial power under § 5 of the Fourteenth Amendment. The argument that § 5 of the Fourteenth Amendment authorizes the cause of action provided for in VAWA under Congress's remedial power is based on the assertion that there is pervasive bias in various state justice systems against victims of gender-motivated violence. This argument is supported by a voluminous congressional record. It is argued that this bias denies victims of gender-motivated violence equal protection of the laws, and that Congress therefore acted appropriately by providing a remedy that would address such bias by the states and deter future instances of discrimination in the state courts. Although sex discrimination is one of the objects of the Fourteenth Amendment, the Amendment prohibits only state action, not private action, and Congress's ability to attack discriminatory conduct is limited to prevent the Fourteenth Amendment from obliterating the Constitution's careful balancing of power between the States and federal Government. This is a long-standing interpretation by the Court of the Fourteenth Amendment's provisions. Brzonkala (P) also argued that here there has been gender-disparate treatment by state officials, whereas in prior cases there was no indication of state action. This argument is also rejected. Section 13891 is unlike any of the § 5 remedies that previously have been upheld since it has no consequence on any public official involved in investigating or prosecuting an assault such as the one asserted by Brzonkala (P). It is not aimed at state laws that promote inequality, nor is it aimed at proscribing discrimination by any state or state actor. It is aimed only at individuals who have committed criminal acts motivated by gender bias. Section 13981 is also different from previously upheld remedies in that it applies uniformly throughout the Nation, even though Congress's findings indicate that the problem addressed does not exist in all, or even most, States. Congress's power under § 5, therefore, does not extend to the enactment of § 13891. [Affirmed.]

DISSENT: (Breyer, J.) The Court's reasoning rejecting Congress's source of authority under § 5 of the Fourteenth Amendment is questionable. Although it has long been held that § 5 does not authorize Congress to use the Fourteenth Amendment as a source of power to remedy the conduct of private parties, the argument here presented is that Congress is using § 5 to remedy the well-documented actions of States, which, through discriminatory design or the discriminatory conduct of their officials, has failed to provide adequate or any state remedies for women injured by gender-motivated violence. The Court has not addressed such a claim before. The majority responds directly to this "state actor" claim by finding that the present law lacks "congruence and proportionality" to the state discrimination that it purports to remedy because it is not specifically directed at any state or state actor. This Court, however, has held that Congress may enact remedial legislation that prohibits

Continued on next page.

conduct that is not itself unconstitutional. The remedy enacted by Congress intrudes little upon States or private parties, but it may lead state actors to improve their own remedial systems. It also imposes liability for private conduct that is already outlawed by state law. Therefore, the remedy is not "disproportionate." It is also not incongruent, given that it is a substitute for constitutionally inadequate state remedies. Additionally, although the majority asserts that the inadequacy of state remedies did not exist in all states, the record nowhere revealed that Congress concluded this was not a national problem. The majority for the first time thus holds that Congress must document the existence of a certain problem in every State prior to proposing a national solution. However, such a requirement is inappropriate given that under § 5, the Court must defer to Congress's chosen remedy.

ANALYSIS

The *Morrison* decision has been criticized on grounds it failed to seriously take into account the Fourteenth Amendment's history and the objectives the Reconstruction framers meant to achieve in giving Congress the power to enforce "equal protection of the laws" as well as basic guarantees of equal citizenship. One aspect of the Amendment's history is that it was enacted in response to states abdicating their responsibilities to ensure the most basic equality by turning a blind eye to their own laws that would have punished private violence against African Americans and those who supported them. The legislative history of the Amendment clearly indicates that the Amendment was intended to give Congress the power to stop such private violence in the face of patent state neglect.

Quicknotes

COMMERCE CLAUSE Article 1, section 8, clause 3 of the United States Constitution, granting Congress the power to regulate commerce with foreign countries and between the states.

EQUAL PROTECTION A constitutional guarantee that no person shall be denied the same protection of the laws enjoyed by other persons in like circumstances.

FOURTEENTH AMENDMENT No state shall deny to any person within its jurisdiction the equal protection of the laws.

REMEDIAL ACTION Actions taken pursuant to the Fourteenth and Fifteenth Amendments to provide remedies for violations of those amendments.

Board of Trustees of the University of Alabama v. Garrett

State employer (D) v. Disabled state employee (P)

531 U.S. 356 (2001)

NATURE OF CASE: Action to determine whether Congress validly abrogated the states' sovereign immunity under the Eleventh Amendment by providing for private actions for money damages against states that did not comply with Title I of the Americans with Disabilities Act of 1990. [The procedural posture of the case is not presented in the casebook extract.]

FACT SUMMARY: Title I of the Americans with Disabilities Act of 1990 (ADA), which prohibited the states and other employers from discriminating against employees with disabilities, provided for private actions for money damages against states that did not comply with the ADA. Alabama (D), against which such suits were brought by its disabled employees (P), contended that by providing for such actions, the ADA exceeded Congress's authority to abrogate the states' sovereign immunity under the Eleventh Amendment.

RULE OF LAW

Suits brought in federal court by state employees to recover money damages by reason of a state's failure to comply with Title I of the Americans with Disabilities Act of 1990 (ADA) are barred by the Eleventh Amendment.

FACTS: Disabled Alabama state employees (P) brought suit against Alabama (D) under Title I of the Americans with Disabilities Act of 1990 (ADA), which prohibited the states and other employers from discriminating against employees with disabilities, and which provided for private actions for money damages against states that did not comply with the ADA. Alabama (D) contended that by providing for such actions, the ADA exceeded Congress's authority to abrogate the states' sovereign immunity under the Eleventh Amendment. The United States Supreme Court granted certiorari in the case. [The procedural posture of the case is not presented in the casebook extract.]

ISSUE: Are suits brought in federal court by state employees to recover money damages by reason of a state's failure to comply with Title I of the Americans with Disabilities Act of 1990 (ADA) barred by the Eleventh Amendment?

HOLDING AND DECISION: (Rehnquist, C.J.) Yes. Suits brought in federal court by state employees to recover money damages by reason of a state's failure to comply with Title I of the Americans with Disabilities Act of 1990 (ADA) are barred by the Eleventh Amendment. Congress may subject nonconsenting states to federal-court suit when it does so pursuant to a valid exercise of its power under § 5 of the Fourteenth Amendment. Section 5 authorizes Congress to enforce the substantive guarantees contained in § 1 of the Fourteenth Amendment by enacting "appropriate legislation." Because it is the Court's responsibility, not Congress's, to define the substance of constitutional guarantees, § 5 legislation, to the extent it reaches beyond the precise scope of § 1's protections, must exhibit congruence and proportionality between the injury to be prevented or remedied and the means adopted to that end. The Fourteenth Amendment does not require states to make special accommodations for the disabled, so long as their actions toward such individuals are rational. They could quite hardheadedly—and perhaps hardheartedly—hold to job-qualification requirements that do not make allowance for the disabled. If special accommodations for the disabled are to be required, they must come from positive law and not through the Equal Protection Clause. However, the ADA's legislative history fails to show that Congress identified a history and pattern of irrational employment discrimination by the states against the disabled. Although the legislative record indicates that Congress found that discrimination against the disabled is pervasive throughout society, it did not specifically identify state action or activities. Even if it were to be determined that a few incidents of discrimination by the states were unconstitutional, these incidents taken together fall far short of even suggesting the pattern of unconstitutional discrimination on which § 5 legislation must be based. Additionally, the rights and remedies created by the ADA against the states raise concerns as to congruence and proportionality. For example, although it would be entirely rational (and therefore constitutional) for a state employer to conserve scarce financial resources by hiring employees able to use existing facilities, the ADA requires employers to make such facilities readily accessible to and usable by disabled individuals. Such an accommodation duty far exceeds what is constitutionally required. Congress is the final authority as to desirable public policy, but to authorize private individuals to recover money damages against the states, there must be a pattern of discrimination by the states that violates the Fourteenth Amendment, and the remedy imposed by Congress must be congruent and proportional to the targeted violation. Those requirements are not met here, and to uphold the Act's application to the states would allow

Continued on next page.

Congress to rewrite the Court's established Fourteenth Amendment law.

DISSENT: (Breyer, J.) Congress amassed a vast legislative record documenting massive, society-wide discrimination against persons with disabilities, and that record implicates every part of society, including the states. There were roughly 300 examples of discrimination by state governments themselves in the legislative record, and even if these examples were based on anecdote and opinion, Congress, unlike the courts, may rely on such evidence for its conclusions. A legislature is not a court of law, and Congress is not required to make the kind of extensive investigation of each piece of evidence that a court might have to make before reaching a decision—especially, where, as here, that evidence is not easily refuted. The issue, unlike that framed by the majority, is whether Congress's likely conclusions were reasonable, not whether there was adequate evidentiary support in the record for those conclusions. In any event, Congress found that the pervasive discrimination against disabled people in society is the kind outlawed by the Fourteenth Amendment—that such discrimination is arbitrary, and rests solely upon negative attitudes, fear, or irrational prejudice. Congress could have reasonably believed that the hundreds of examples of such unjustified discrimination, including discrimination by states and localities, represented signs of a widespread problem of an unconstitutional dimension. The Court's failure to find sufficient evidentiary support may well rest upon its decision to hold Congress to a strict, judicially created evidentiary standard, particularly in respect to lack of justification. However, limitations stemming from the nature of the judicial process have no application to Congress, and rational-basis review—with its presumptions favoring constitutionality—is a paradigm of judicial restraint that applies to lower courts, but not to Congress. There is absolutely no reason to require Congress, seeking to determine facts relevant to the exercise of its § 5 authority, to adopt rules or presumptions that reflect a court's institutional limitations. Congress is unlike the courts in its ability to gather national evidence and to gauge public sentiment. Most importantly, however, unlike judges, members of Congress are elected, and the Court itself has repeatedly stated that it may not sit as a superlegislature to judge the wisdom or desirability of legislative policy determinations. To apply a rule designed to restrict courts as if it restricted Congress's legislative power is to stand the underlying principle—a principle of judicial restraint—on its head. However, without the use of this burden of proof rule or some other unusually stringent standard of review, it is difficult to see how the Court can find the legislative record here inadequate. Although the majority argues in the alternative that the statute's damages remedy is not "congruent" with and "proportional" to the equal protection problem that Congress found, the Court has upheld disparate-impact standards in contexts where they were not constitutionally required. Even though the remedy at issue may exceed what is necessary to avoid a constitutional violation, it is that power to require more than the minimum that § 5 grants to Congress. The Court has repeatedly confirmed this power, which it has held is not confined to the enactment of legislation that merely parrots the precise wording of the Fourteenth Amendment. Rather, the Court has ruled that Congress can prohibit a somewhat broader swath of conduct, including that which is not itself forbidden by the Amendment's text. The ADA clearly imposes a burden on the states by removing their Eleventh Amendment protection from suit, thereby subjecting them to potential monetary liability, but rules for interpreting § 5 that would provide states with special protection run counter to the very object of the Fourteenth Amendment. By its terms, that Amendment prohibits states from denying their citizens equal protection of the laws. The Fourteenth Amendment and other Civil War Amendments were specifically designed as an expansion of federal power and an intrusion on state sovereignty. Thus, ironically, the greater the obstacle the Eleventh Amendment poses to the creation by Congress of the kind of remedy at issue here—the decentralized remedy of private damages actions—the more Congress, seeking to cure important national problems, such as the problem of disability discrimination before us, will have to rely on more uniform remedies, such as federal standards and court injunctions, which are sometimes draconian and typically more intrusive. In other words, the majority's decision does nothing to further any constitutionally based federalism interest.

ANALYSIS

One of the arguments those in support of the Americans with Disabilities Act's (ADA's) money-damages remedy made was that the inquiry as to unconstitutional discrimination should extend not only to states themselves, but to units of local governments, such as cities and counties. The majority rejected this argument, reasoning that since the Eleventh Amendment does not extend its immunity to units of local government, these entities are subject to private claims for damages under the ADA without Congress's ever having to rely on § 5 of the Fourteenth Amendment to render them so, so that it would make no sense to consider constitutional violations on their part, as well as by the states themselves, when only the states are the beneficiaries of the Eleventh Amendment. Justice Breyer, in his dissent, rejected this reasoning, concluding instead that the substantive obligation that the Equal Protection Clause creates applies to state and local governmental entities

Continued on next page.

alike, especially since local governments often work closely with, and under the supervision of, state officials, and in general, state and local government employers are similarly situated.

Quicknotes

DISPARATE TREATMENT Unequal treatment of employees or of applicants for employment without justification.

ELEVENTH AMENDMENT The Eleventh Amendment to the United States Constitution prohibits the extension of the judicial powers of the federal courts to suits brought against a state by citizens of another state, or of a foreign state, without the state's consent.

JUDICIAL RESTRAINT Self-imposed discipline by judges making decision without indulging their own personal views or ideas that may not be consistent with existing law.

SOVEREIGN IMMUNITY Immunity of government from suit without its consent.

Shelby County, Alabama v. Holder

State political subdivision (P) v. Federal government official (D)

570 U.S. 529 (2013)

NATURE OF CASE: Appeal from judgment upholding the constitutionality of §§ 4(b) and 5 of the Voting Rights Act of 1965. [The complete procedural posture of the case is not presented in the casebook extract.]

FACT SUMMARY: Shelby County, Alabama (P), which was covered by § 4(b) of the Voting Rights Act of 1965 (the Act), contended that §§ 4(b) and 5 of the Act were facially unconstitutional.

RULE OF LAW

The coverage formula in § 4(b) of the Voting Rights Act of 1965 is facially unconstitutional.

FACTS: The Voting Rights Act of 1965 (the Act) was enacted to address entrenched racial discrimination in voting. Only some jurisdictions are covered by some of the Act's provisions. Section 4(b) of the Act provides a "coverage formula," defining the "covered jurisdictions" as States or political subdivisions that maintained tests or devices as prerequisites to voting, and had low voter registration or turnout, in the 1960s and early 1970s. In those covered jurisdictions, § 5 of the Act provides that no change in voting procedures can take effect until approved by either the Department of Justice or a three-judge district court. Such approval is known as "preclearance." The coverage formula and preclearance requirement were initially set to expire after five years, but the Act has been reauthorized several times. In 2006, the Act was reauthorized for an additional 25 years, but the coverage formula was not changed. Coverage still turned on whether a jurisdiction had a voting test in the 1960s or 1970s and had low voter registration or turnout at that time. Shortly after the 2006 reauthorization, a Texas utility district sought to bail out from the Act's coverage and, in the alternative, challenged the Act's constitutionality. In *Northwest Austin Municipal Util. Dist. No. One v. Holder*, 557 U.S. 193 (2009), the Supreme Court avoided the constitutional issue on statutory grounds but expressed serious doubts about the Act's continued constitutionality. Shelby County (P), a covered jurisdiction in Alabama, sought a declaratory judgment that §§ 4(b) and 5 are facially unconstitutional, as well as a permanent injunction against their enforcement. The court of appeals upheld those sections constitutionality, and the United States Supreme Court granted certiorari. [The complete procedural posture of the case is not presented in the casebook extract.]

ISSUE: Is the coverage formula in § 4(b) of the Voting Rights Act of 1965 facially unconstitutional?

HOLDING AND DECISION: (Roberts, C.J.) Yes. The coverage formula in § 4(b) of the Voting Rights Act of 1965 (the Act) is facially unconstitutional. The Voting Rights Act "imposes current burdens and must be justified by current need," *Northwest Austin Municipal Util. Dist. No. One v. Holder*, 557 U.S. 193 (2009), and a departure from the fundamental principle of equal sovereignty requires a showing that a statute's disparate geographic coverage is sufficiently related to the problem that it targets. States retain broad autonomy in structuring their governments and pursuing legislative objectives, and the Tenth Amendment reserves to the states all powers not specifically granted to the federal government, including the power to regulate elections. The states are also equally sovereign, and under the principle and tradition of equal sovereignty, there must be an exceptional circumstance justifying disparate treatment of the states. The Act sharply departs from these basic principles. It requires states to beseech the federal government for permission to implement laws that they would otherwise have the right to enact and execute on their own. Despite the tradition of equal sovereignty, the Act applies to only nine States (and additional counties). That is why, in 1966, the Court described the Act as "stringent" and "potent." The Court nonetheless upheld the Act, concluding that such an uncommon exercise of congressional power could be justified by exceptional conditions. In 1966, these departures were justified by the blight of racial discrimination in voting that had infected the electoral process in parts of our country for nearly a century. At the time, the coverage formula made sense. The Act was limited to areas where Congress found evidence of actual voting discrimination, and the covered jurisdictions shared two characteristics: "the use of tests and devices for voter registration, and a voting rate in the 1964 presidential election at least 12 points below the national average." The Court explained that "[t]ests and devices are relevant to voting discrimination because of their long history as a tool for perpetrating the evil; a low voting rate is pertinent for the obvious reason that widespread disenfranchisement must inevitably affect the number of actual voters." For these reasons, the Court concluded that the coverage formula was rational in both practice and theory. Nearly 50 years later, things have changed dramatically. Largely because of the Voting Rights Act, voter turnout and registration rates in covered jurisdictions have approached parity. African American voter turnout is mostly equal to—or even exceeds—White

Continued on next page.

voter turnout. Blatantly discriminatory evasions of federal decrees are rare, and minority candidates hold office at unprecedented levels. The tests and devices that blocked ballot access have been forbidden nationwide for over 40 years. The Act, which undoubtedly has contributed to these significant changes, however, has not reflected the changes. It has not eased § 5's restrictions or narrowed the scope of § 4's coverage formula along the way. Instead, those extraordinary and unprecedented features have been reauthorized as if nothing has changed, and they have grown even stronger. In fact, Congress expanded the scope of § 5 coverage in 2006. Thus, the bar that covered jurisdictions must clear has been raised even as the conditions justifying that requirement have dramatically improved. Moreover, the fact that § 5's deterrence effect has contributed to salutary changes does not immunize it from scrutiny. Because § 5 applies only to those jurisdictions singled out by § 4, it must be determined whether that provision is constitutional in light of current conditions. Coverage today is based on decades-old data and eradicated practices and is no longer rational in theory and practice. The formula captures states by reference to literacy tests and low voter registration and turnout in the 1960s and early 1970s. The literacy tests have been banned for over 40 years, and voter registration and turnout numbers in covered states have risen dramatically. In 1965, the states could be divided into those with a recent history of voting tests and low voter registration and turnout and those without those characteristics. Notwithstanding that today the country is no longer divided along those lines, the Act continues to treat it as if it were. The Government (D) attempts to defend the formula on grounds that it is "reverse-engineered," i.e., that Congress identified the jurisdictions to be covered and then came up with criteria to describe them. The Court never sanctioned such an approach, reasoning instead that the coverage formula was rational because the "formula . . . was relevant to the problem." The Government's (D) fallback position is that because the formula was relevant in 1965, its continued use is permissible so long as any discrimination remains in the states identified in 1965. Such an approach does not look to current political conditions, instead relying on a comparison between the states in 1965. However, history did not end in 1965. In assessing the current need for a preclearance system treating states differently from one another today, history since 1965 cannot be ignored. The Fifteenth Amendment is not designed to punish for the past; its purpose is to ensure a better future. To serve that purpose, Congress—if it is to divide the States—must identify those jurisdictions to be singled out on a basis that makes sense in light of current conditions. The Government (D) also relies heavily on data from the record compiled by Congress before reauthorizing the Act. Regardless of how one looks at that record, no one can fairly say that it shows anything approaching the "pervasive," "flagrant," "widespread," and "rampant" discrimination that clearly distinguished the covered jurisdictions from the rest of the country in 1965. Still, a more fundamental problem remains: Congress did not use that record to fashion a coverage formula grounded in current conditions. It instead re-enacted a formula based on 40-year-old facts having no logical relation to the present day. Even if, as Congress found, there are second generation barriers constructed to prevent minority voters from fully participating in the electoral process, using the decades' old criteria found in § 4(b) is an irrational way to address those barriers. The dissent wrongly asserts that there are no serious constitutional issues with § 4's coverage formula, but that ignores the Court's decision in *Northwest Austin.* The dissent similarly ignores principles of equal sovereignty, and although *Northwest Austin* stated definitively that "current burdens" must be justified by "current needs," the dissent argues that the coverage formula can be justified by history, and that the required showing can be weaker on reenactment than when the law was first passed. For these reasons, § 4(b) is unconstitutional and must be struck down. That conclusion, however, does not affect the Act's other provisions, and Congress is free to draft another formula based on current conditions. Reversed.

CONCURRENCE: (Thomas, J.) Section 5 of the Act is also unconstitutional and should be struck down. The majority opinion compellingly demonstrates that Congress has failed to justify current burdens with a record demonstrating current needs, and it is just a matter of time before § 5 will be struck down; there is no need to prolong that inevitability.

DISSENT: (Ginsburg, J.) The majority usurps Congress's power to determine whether, as currently operative, § 5 remains justifiable. Congress decided that § 5 should continue in force because it would facilitate completion of the gains made thus far, and because it would prevent backsliding. Notwithstanding that the majority acknowledges discrimination exists today, it jettisons the very remedy that proved to be best suited to block that discrimination. The Act, through the preclearance mechanism, worked where other attempted remedies failed. Jurisdictions covered by the preclearance requirement continued to submit, in large numbers, proposed changes to voting laws that the Attorney General declined to approve, auguring that barriers to minority voting would quickly resurface were the preclearance remedy eliminated. There also are in place numerous second-generation barriers to minority voting that go beyond voter registration and involve vote dilution, and the Court has long recognized that vote dilution, when adopted with a discriminatory purpose, cuts down the right to vote as certainly as denial of access to the ballot. Congress studied the problem of racial discrimination prior to reauthorizing the Act and compiled a compelling

Continued on next page.

record that presents countless "examples of flagrant racial discrimination" since the last reauthorization; Congress also brought to light systematic evidence that "intentional racial discrimination in voting remains so serious and widespread in covered jurisdictions that section 5 preclearance is still needed." It is well established that Congress must be given substantial deference in enforcing the Fourteenth and Fifteenth Amendments. Congress's power is at its height when dealing with invidious discrimination, and the deference it is owed is a matter both of the Constitution's text and precedent. The Civil War Amendments armed Congress with the power and authority to protect all persons within the Nation from violations of their rights by the states, and in exercising that power, Congress may use "all means which are appropriate, which are plainly adapted" to the constitutional ends declared by these Amendments." Congress may use any rational means to effectuate the constitutional prohibition of racial discrimination in voting, and if the means is rational, the Court may not question whether it is wise and substitute its judgment for Congress's. Here, the 2006 reauthorization of the Act satisfies the minimal requirements of the rational-basis test, and constitutes a means "appropriate" and "plainly adapted to" a legitimate constitutional end. Congress received considerable evidence that preclearance was still effectively preventing discriminatory changes to voting laws, as well as that § 2 alone was an inadequate substitute for preclearance in the covered jurisdictions. Because § 2 is enforced through litigation, after the fact, preclearance reduces the monetary burden on minorities of pursuing such litigation, as well as on the covered jurisdictions themselves, because the preclearance process is far less costly than defending against a § 2 claim, and clearance by the Department of Justice (DOJ) substantially reduces the likelihood that a § 2 claim will be mounted. Prior to the reauthorization, there were numerous attempted electoral changes that were stopped through preclearance, suggesting that § 5 effectively protected minority voting rights. Congress noted that conditions in the South have impressively improved since passage of the Act, but also concluded that the Act was the driving force behind the improvement. But Congress also found that voting discrimination had evolved into subtler second-generation barriers, and that eliminating preclearance would risk loss of the gains that had been made. As to reauthorization of the coverage formula in § 4(b), Congress found that conditions in the covered jurisdictions demonstrated that the formula was still justified by "current needs," based on studies showing that racial discrimination in voting remains concentrated in the jurisdictions singled out for preclearance. Controlling for population, there were nearly four times as many successful § 2 cases in covered jurisdictions as there were in non-covered jurisdictions. The majority ignores these findings. The evidence before Congress, furthermore, indicated that voting in the covered jurisdictions was more racially polarized than elsewhere in the country. When voting is racially polarized, inevitably there is greater discrimination against minority groups. Thus, such places have a greater need for prophylactic measures to prevent purposeful race discrimination. The reauthorization also provided a mechanism for a covered jurisdiction to bail out—upon a showing that it had complied with the Act for ten years and had engaged in efforts to eliminate intimidation and harassment of voters. The reauthorization also provided for bail-in of jurisdictions not currently covered if it was determined they needed federal supervision. Congress was satisfied that the Act's bailout mechanism provided an effective means of adjusting its coverage over time. In fact, 200 jurisdictions have successfully bailed out; this belies the majority's portrayal of the Act as static and unchanged since 1965. Pursuant to a facial constitutional attack, a plaintiff must demonstrate that no set of circumstances exists under which the statute would be valid. Here, Shelby County (P) cannot meet this burden, because as applied to Shelby County (P), the Act's preclearance requirements are incontestable. Alabama has had the second highest rates of successful § 2 suits, and there have been numerous recent incidents of discrimination, so that this sorry history of § 2 violations alone provides sufficient justification for Congress's determination in 2006 that Alabama and its political subdivisions, including Shelby County (P), should remain subject to preclearance requirements. That determination alone should suffice to dispose of this case. Additionally, the Act's severability provision requires that unconstitutional applications be severed, leaving the Act in place for jurisdictions as to which its application does not transgress constitutional limits. Thus, permitting a facial attack by a jurisdiction that clearly comes within the Act is inappropriate under the Court's precedents. Further, the majority's use of the equal sovereignty principle in this case is misplaced. That principle has been unequivocally held to apply only to the terms upon which states are admitted to the Union. The majority's unprecedented extension of the equal sovereignty principle outside its proper domain—the admission of new states—is capable of much mischief, especially given that numerous federal statutes treat states disparately. Most significantly, Congress in its reauthorizations relied on the Court's equal sovereignty doctrine to believe that the Act's limited geographical scope would weigh in favor of, not against, the Act's constitutionality. Under the majority's holding, not only do defenders of the Act need to show a need for the preclearance regime in certain places, but also must disprove the existence of a comparable need elsewhere. There is no precedent for such a double burden on defenders of legislation. The majority should have left this matter in Congress's bailiwick. The majority's view is that preclearance does not meet current conditions—contrary to an overwhelming amount of evidence to the contrary. "Throwing out preclearance when it

Continued on next page.

has worked and is continuing to work to stop discriminatory changes is like throwing away your umbrella in a rainstorm because you are not getting wet." The majority insists that Congress must start from scratch, but Congress made ample evidentiary findings that the preclearance regime continued to be appropriate for many of the jurisdictions identified by the coverage formula. Congress had more than a reasonable basis to conclude the existing coverage formula was not out of sync with conditions on the ground in covered areas, and it is clear Shelby County (P) was no candidate for release through the mechanism Congress provided. The majority thus ignores what Congress actually did in reauthorizing the Act. The majority also utterly fails to grasp why the Act has proven effective. The majority appears to believe that the Act's success in eliminating the specific devices extant in 1965 means that preclearance is no longer needed. With that belief, and the argument derived from it, history repeats itself. The same assumption—that the problem could be solved when particular methods of voting discrimination are identified and eliminated—was indulged and proved wrong repeatedly prior to the Act's enactment. Unlike prior statutes, which singled out particular tests or devices, the Act is grounded in Congress's recognition of the "variety and persistence" of measures designed to impair minority voting rights. The evolution of voting discrimination into subtler second-generation barriers is powerful evidence that a remedy as effective as preclearance remains vital to protect minority voting rights and prevent backsliding. In sum, the majority errs egregiously by overriding Congress's judgment in this regard.

ANALYSIS

Although the Court purports to declare unconstitutional only the coverage formula set out in § 4(b), without that formula, § 5 is effectively immobilized. Thus, this decision essentially guts the Voting Rights Act's enforcement mechanism, and, with it, Congress's power (absent new legislation) to realize the goals of the Civil War Amendments.

Quicknotes

CERTIORARI A discretionary writ issued by a superior court to an inferior court to review the lower court's decisions; the United States Supreme Court's writ ordering such review.

DECLARATORY JUDGMENT A judgment of the court establishing the rights of the parties.

Brnovich v. Democratic National Committee

State official (D) v. Political party's national committee (P)

__U.S.__, 2021 WL 2690267 (2021)

NATURE OF CASE: Appeal in action challenging a state's time, place, and manner voting regulations as violating § 2 of the Voting Rights Act and the Fifteenth Amendment. [The procedural posture of the case is not presented in the casebook excerpt.]

FACT SUMMARY: The Democratic National Committee (P) challenged certain time, place, and manner voting regulations enacted by Arizona (D) as violating § 2 of the Voting Rights Act and the Fifteenth Amendment, contending that the regulations made it more difficult to vote and discriminated against minorities.

RULE OF LAW

A facially neutral state time, place, and manner voting regulation that incidentally has a disparate impact on minorities does not violate § 2 of the Voting Rights Act or the Fifteenth Amendment.

FACTS: The Democratic National Committee (P) challenged certain time, place, and manner voting regulations enacted by Arizona (D), such as the regulation of where and how long polls are open, when voters can register, rules for absentee ballots, and voter identification requirements, as violating § 2 of the Voting Rights Act and the Fifteenth Amendment, contending that the regulations made it more difficult to vote and discriminated against minorities. In 1982, Congress amended the language in § 2 that had been interpreted to require proof of discriminatory intent by a plurality of the Supreme Court in *Mobile v. Bolden*, 446 U.S. 55, (1980). In place of that language, § 2(a) now provides that: "No voting qualification or prerequisite to voting or standard, practice, or procedure shall be imposed or applied by any State or political subdivision in a manner which results in a denial or abridgement of the right . . . to vote on account of race or color." Section 2(b) in turn explains what must be shown to establish a § 2 violation. Section 2(b) states that § 2 is violated only where "based on the totality of the circumstances, it is shown that the political processes leading to nomination or election" are not "equally open to participation" by members of the relevant protected group "in that its members have less opportunity than other members of the electorate to participate in the political process and to elect representatives of their choice." In amending § 2, Congress sought to reject the intent test and substitute a test of fair equal opportunity to vote, focusing on the results of a state voting practice. *Thornburg v. Gingles*, 478 U.S. 30 (1986). The United States Supreme Court granted certiorari in the case. [The procedural posture of the case is not presented in the casebook excerpt.]

ISSUE: Does a facially neutral state time, place, and manner voting regulation that incidentally has a disparate impact on minorities violate § 2 of the Voting Rights Act or the Fifteenth Amendment?

HOLDING AND DECISION: (Alito, J.) No. A facially neutral state time, place, and manner voting regulation that incidentally has a disparate impact on minorities does not violate § 2 of the Voting Rights Act or the Fifteenth Amendment. The size of the burden imposed by a challenged voting regulation is highly relevant to determining whether it violates § 2. Voting necessarily requires some effort and compliance with some rules; thus, the concept of a voting system that is "equally open" and that furnishes equal "opportunity" to cast a ballot must tolerate the usual burdens of voting; mere inconvenience is insufficient. Another relevant consideration is the degree to which a voting rule departs from what was standard practice when § 2 was amended in 1982. The burdens associated with the rules in effect at that time are useful in gauging whether the burdens imposed by a challenged rule are sufficient to prevent voting from being equally "open" or furnishing an equal "opportunity" to vote in the sense meant by § 2. Based on that 1982 environment, it is doubtful Congress intended to uproot facially neutral time, place, and manner regulations that have a long pedigree or are in widespread use in the United States. Another important factor to consider is the size of any disparities in a rule's impact on members of different racial or ethnic groups. To the extent that minority and non-minority groups differ with respect to employment, wealth, and education, even neutral regulations may well result in disparities in rates of voting and noncompliance with voting rules. The mere fact that there is some disparity in impact does not necessarily mean that a system is not equally open or that it does not give everyone an equal opportunity to vote. The strength of the state interests—such as the strong and entirely legitimate state interest in preventing election fraud—served by a challenged voting rule is yet another important factor to consider. In determining whether a rule goes too far "based on the totality of circumstances," rules that are supported by strong state interests are less likely to violate § 2. Further, there is no footing in the text of § 2 that requires the Court to adopt a least-restrictive means requirement that would force a state to prove that the interest served by its voting rule could not be accomplished in any other less burdensome way. To do so would

Continued on next page.

have the effect of invalidating a great many neutral voting regulations with long pedigrees that are reasonable means of pursuing legitimate interests. It would also transfer much of the authority to regulate election procedures from the states to the federal courts. Notwithstanding any disparate burden caused by Arizona's (D) law, Arizona's (D) interest in preventing election fraud would save it from § 2 liability, since a state has a compelling interest in preserving the integrity of the election process. The dissent, however, looks only at disparate impact, rather than looking at the "totality" of the circumstances. Under the dissent's approach, states would be deprived of their authority to establish nondiscriminatory voting rules, and impermissibly effect a wholesale transfer of the authority to set voting rules from the states to the federal courts.

CONCURRENCE: (Gorsuch, J.) The majority decision leaves open the question of whether there is an implied cause of action under § 2.

DISSENT: (Kagan, J.) The majority undermines § 2 and the rights it was intended to provide by giving it a cramped reading. The majority then uses that very narrow reading to validate voting regulations that discriminate against minority voters. Instead of furthering the goal of § 2 to end discrimination in voting, the majority thwarts that goal. And, the majority does this in an era of voting-rights retrenchment, when many states and localities are restricting voting access in ways that will predictably deprive members of minority groups of equal access to voting. The majority clearly is wrong to think that what was standard practice when § 2 was amended in 1982 is a relevant consideration in a § 2 analysis. The 1982 state of the world is no part of the § 2 test. An election rule prevalent at that time may make voting harder for minority than for White citizens, so § 2 then covers such a rule, as it is supposed to cover any other. Contrary to the majority's unsupported speculation, Congress intended exactly that; Congress wanted the Voting Rights Act to eradicate the numerous practices and procedures that act as continued barriers to registration and voting. Section 2 was meant to disrupt the status quo, not to preserve it—to eradicate then-current discriminatory practices, not to "set them in amber." Throughout American history, election officials have asserted antifraud interests in using voter suppression laws. Poll taxes are a classic example. Poll taxes, which kept Black people from voting, were often justified as necessary for honest elections. There have been numerous such examples, so many, that it seems that states have always found it natural to wrap discriminatory policies in "election-integrity garb." Congress intended for § 2 to prevent such measures from working, and wanted it to apply to all laws, even facially neutral ones, that resulted in members of minority groups having unequal, and diminished, access to voting and the political process. The majority does not see it that way. Instead, it finds that a statute that would remove such discriminatory laws is "radical." It sees that such a statute would be an excessive, and undemocratic, transfer of authority to set voting rules from the states to the federal courts. However, in light of history, the majority is clearly wrong in its paean to state authority and its denigration of federal responsibility for ensuring voting rules that do not discriminate against minorities. The text of the Voting Rights Act does not uphold states' rights against federal courts; it upholds the right of every American, of every race, to have equal access to the ballot box. The majority undermines that right by refusing to apply the plain terms of the Act, by declaring some racially discriminatory burdens inconsequential, and by refusing to subject asserted state interests to serious means-end scrutiny. In sum, the majority enables voting discrimination.

ANALYSIS

Prior to deciding this case, the Court, in *Shelby County v. Holder,* 570 U.S. 529 (2013), held that a list of covered jurisdictions contained in § 4(b) of the Voting Rights Act was unconstitutional. Section 5 of the Act required that those jurisdictions, because of their history of enacting voting rules that discriminated against minorities, had to preclear any changes to their voting systems with the federal Department of Justice or a three-judge district court in Washington, D.C. By invalidating § 4(b), the Court effectively gutted § 5, which left only § 2 as a national guard against racial discrimination in voting. Justice Kagan, in her dissent, notes that almost immediately after *Shelby County* was handed down, states and localities put in place new restrictive voting laws and policies, with numerous barriers to voting, and with foreseeably adverse effects on minority voters. For these reasons, Justice Kagan sees that § 2, which Congress never meant to bear all of the weight of the Act's commitments, and which was supposed to be a backup to §§ 4(b) and 5, "is what voters have left." Given the majority's decision in *Brnovich,* it is unclear that even a weakened § 2 will be able to effectively prevent discrimination in voting throughout the nation.

Quicknotes

POLL TAX A tax imposed upon each person within a jurisdiction. Under the Twenty-fourth Amendment state and federal governments may not impose a poll tax as a condition to voting.

TIME, PLACE, AND MANNER RESTRICTION Certain types of regulations on speech that are permissible since they restrict only the time, place, and manner in which the speech may occur.

National League of Cities v. Usery

Organization of cities (P) v. Federal official (D)

426 U.S. 833 (1976)

NATURE OF CASE: Action challenging as unconstitutional amendments to the Fair Labor Standards Act purporting to extend to state and municipal employees the Act's minimum wage and maximum hour provisions.

FACT SUMMARY: [Congress sought to extend minimum wage and maximum hour provisions to state and local employees through amendments to the Fair Labor Standards Act. States (P) and municipalities (P) challenged the amendments as violative of the Tenth Amendment.]

RULE OF LAW

Congress may not constitutionally displace the states' abilities to structure employer-employee relationships in areas of traditional governmental functions.

FACTS: [Congress sought to extend minimum wage and maximum hour provisions to state and local employees through amendments to the Fair Labor Standards Act. States (P) and municipalities (P) challenged the amendments as violative of the Tenth Amendment.]

ISSUE: May Congress constitutionally displace the states' abilities to structure employer-employee relationships in areas of traditional governmental functions?

HOLDING AND DECISION: (Rehnquist, J.) No. Congress may not constitutionally displace the states' abilities to structure employer-employee relationships in areas of traditional governmental functions. The Tenth Amendment prohibits Congress from exercising its power in a manner that impairs the states' (P) integrity or ability to function effectively in a federal system. There are attributes of sovereignty attaching to every state government that may not be impaired by Congress, not because Congress lacks an affirmative grant of legislative authority to reach the matter, but because the Constitution prohibits it from exercising the authority in that manner. One clear attribute of state sovereignty is the states' (P) power to determine the wages that are to be paid to those whom they employ to carry out their governmental functions, what hours those persons will work, and what compensation will be provided where these employees may be called upon to work overtime. The amendments will alter or displace the states' (P) abilities to structure employer-employee relationships in such areas as fire prevention, police protection, sanitation, public health, and parks and recreation. If Congress can remove the states' (P) authority in this area, there will be little left of the states' (P) separate and independent existence. Therefore, insofar as the challenged amendments operate to directly displace the states' freedom (P) to structure integral operations in areas of traditional governmental functions, they are not within the authority granted Congress.

DISSENT: (Brennan, J.) Contrary to the majority's key premise, there is nothing in the 10th Amendment that constitutes a limitation on congressional exercise of powers delegated by the Constitution to Congress. The majority baldly asserts, without explanation or support, that the decision as to wages and hours is an "undoubted attribute of state sovereignty." Such a sweeping holding is ominous for constitutional jurisprudence.

DISSENT: (Stevens, J.) Numerous activities of states qua states are constitutionally subject to federal regulation, so it is unclear why the regulation of wages and hours is any different.

ANALYSIS

National League of Cities overruled *Maryland v. Wirtz*, 392 U.S. 183 (1968), which had upheld amendments to the Fair Labor Standards Act that extended wage and hour laws to the employees of hospitals, elementary and secondary schools, and institutions of higher education, including those owned and operated by states. In *Wirtz*, the Court upheld Congress's power under the Commerce Clause to regulate interstate commerce, even if, in doing so, it impaired the states' (P) ability to provide for the welfare or necessities of their inhabitants. With *National League of Cities*, the Court abandoned the reasoning it had applied in *Wirtz*, and instead emphasized fears of unchecked power expressed by Justice Douglas in his dissent in *Wirtz*. Nine years after *National League of Cities* was decided, the Court revisited the issue in *Garcia v. San Antonio Metropolitan Transit Authority*, 469 U.S. 528 (1985), and overruled *National League of Cities*, concluding that the "traditional governmental functions" test applied in *National League of Cities* was unsound and unworkable, as the courts had not come up with an analytically sound distinction between traditional and non-traditional governmental operations.

Continued on next page.

Quicknotes

FAIR LABOR STANDARDS ACT Enacted in 1938, the statute establishes a minimum wage applicable to all employees of covered employers and provides for mandatory overtime payment for covered employees who work more than 40 hours a week. Executive, administrative, and professional employees paid on a salary basis are exempt from the statute.

TENTH AMENDMENT The Tenth Amendment to the United States Constitution reserves those powers therein, not expressly delegated to the federal government or prohibited to the states, to the states, or to the people.

Garcia v. San Antonio Metropolitan Transit Authority

State department (P) v. Public transportation agency (D)

469 U.S. 528 (1985)

NATURE OF CASE: Appeal from denial of application of federal labor standards to state operations.

FACT SUMMARY: Garcia (P) appealed from a decision for San Antonio Metropolitan Transit Authority (SAMTA) (D) holding that municipal ownership and operation of a mass transit system is a traditional governmental function and thus, according to the test laid down in *National League of Cities v. Usery*, 426 U.S. 833 (1976), its system was immune from the requirements of the Fair Labor Standards Act.

RULE OF LAW

The test for determining state immunity from federal regulation under the Commerce Clause is not whether the state activity sought to be regulated is a traditional state function, but rather whether the regulation as applied to the state activity is destructive of state sovereignty or violative of any constitutional provision.

FACTS: San Antonio Metropolitan Transit Authority (SAMTA) (D) is the public mass transit authority that provides transportation in the San Antonio metropolitan area. The Wage and Hour Administration of the Department of Labor (P) found that SAMTA's (D) operations were not immune from the application of the minimum wage and overtime requirements of the Fair Labor Standards Act (FLSA). SAMTA (D) filed an action for declaratory judgment, seeking a ruling that pursuant to the earlier decision in *National League of Cities v. Usery*, 426 U.S. 833 (1976), its activities comprised a traditional governmental function and were thus immune from the requirements of the FLSA. During the appeals of this case, the United States Supreme Court decided a case that found that the provision of a commuter rail service was not a traditional governmental function and thus did not enjoy constitutional immunity from congressional regulation under the Commerce Clause. The case was remanded to the district court in light of this case, which adhered to its original view and entered judgment in favor of SAMTA (D). From this decision, Garcia (P) appealed.

ISSUE: Does the test for determining whether a state activity is immune from federal regulation under the Commerce Clause continue to include a determination of whether the activity is a traditional state governmental function?

HOLDING AND DECISION: (Blackmun, J.) No. The test for determining state immunity from federal regulation under the Commerce Clause is not whether the state activity sought to be regulated is a traditional governmental function, but rather whether the regulation as applied to the state activity is destructive of state sovereignty or violative of any constitutional provision. The prerequisite for governmental immunity under *National League of Cities v. Usery*, the federal statute tread on traditional governmental functions, has proved to be an unworkable standard. The *National League* case gave no indication of how to determine whether a function was a traditional or nontraditional one. The decisions of the lower courts, which have made elusive constitutional distinctions in order to find some functions traditional and others nontraditional, indicate the difficulty in applying the standard. This Court has previously rejected the notion that a governmental function could be determined to be traditional on a purely historical basis since this basis does not allow accommodating changes in the historical functions of states. Any distinction that purports to separate out important governmental functions is inconsistent with the role of federalism in a democratic society, which allows states to engage freely in any activity not forbidden to them under the Constitution, since allowing unelected federal judiciaries to determine which functions may be important disserves the principles of democratic self-government. The manner in which the states are insulated from congressional regulation under the Commerce Clause, is found in the limitations imposed by the Constitution under Article I and in the structure of the federal government itself, which in giving the states considerable influence over both branches of the Congress and the executive branch, affords the states protection against the unbridled regulation of the federal government under the Commerce Clause. The constitutional scheme developed to protect the "states as states" is thus one of process, not one of result. It is sufficient to say that in the present case the application of the minimum wage and overtime requirements of the Fair Labor Standards Act (FLSA) to SAMTA (D) is not destructive of state sovereignty or violative of any constitutional provision, and that therefore SAMTA (D) is not immune from the application of the FLSA. *National League of Cities v. Usery* is overruled. Reversed.

DISSENT: (Powell, J.) The Court in the present case works a substantial alteration of the federal government and the states, allowing Congress to assume a state's sovereign power free from judicial review.

Continued on next page.

DISSENT: (Rehnquist, J.) Either approach suggested by the dissents is preferable to the Court's actions in the present case, and under either approach, the judgment of the district court should be affirmed.

DISSENT: (O'Connor, J.) State autonomy should be weighed as a factor in the balance when determining whether the means chosen by Congress to regulate the states as states is appropriate. By abandoning *National League*, state sovereignty has been left at the mercy of Congress's as-of-yet undeveloped capacity for self-restraint.

ANALYSIS

The continuing validity of *National League of Cities v. Usery* had always been in doubt, and the scope of that particular opinion had uncertain limits. For example, it was not clear that Congress would be prohibited from affecting traditional governmental function of the states under various powers delegated to Congress, such as the war power or the civil rights enforcement power, and it was not clear whether that decision would apply to regulatory conditions attached to federal grants disbursed through the spending power.

Quicknotes

COMMERCE CLAUSE Article I, § 8, cl. 3 of the United States Constitution, granting Congress the power to regulate commerce with foreign countries and between the states.

FEDERALISM A scheme of government whereby the power to govern is divided between a central and localized governments.

PREEMPTION Doctrine stating that certain matters are of a national character so that federal laws preempt or take precedence over state or local laws.

SUPREMACY CLAUSE Article VI, § 2 of the United States Constitution, which provides that federal action must prevail over inconsistent state action.

Gregory v. Ashcroft

[Parties not identified.]

501 U.S. 452 (1991)

NATURE OF CASE: Challenge to constitutional validity of a state statute.

FACT SUMMARY: Two state judges challenged a state mandatory retirement rule as violative of the federal Age Discrimination in Employment Act and the Fourteenth Amendment's Due Process Clause.

RULE OF LAW

The Age Discrimination in Employment Act does not apply to the state's appointment of its most important officials.

FACTS: [The facts of the case are not stated in the casebook excerpt.]

ISSUE: Does the Age Discrimination in Employment Act apply to the state's appointment of its most important officials?

HOLDING AND DECISION: (O'Connor, J.) No. The Age Discrimination in Employment Act (ADEA) does not apply to the state's appointment of its most important officials. The ADEA makes it unlawful for an "employer" to discharge an individual who is at least 40 years old on account of that person's age. The term "employer" is defined to include a state or political subdivision of a state. The Constitution establishes a system of dual sovereignty between the state and the federal government. The federal government holds an advantage in this balance: the Supremacy Clause. Congress may impose its will on the states so long as it acts within those powers granted to it by the Constitution. Congress may legislate in areas traditionally regulated by the states. The present case involves a state constitutional provision through which the state establishes a qualification for its judges. Congressional interference with this type of decision would upset the constitutional balance of federal and state powers. Thus, the federal court must be certain of Congress's intent before finding that federal law overrides this balance. If Congress indeed intends to alter such balance, it must make that intent clear in the language of the statute. This Court has acknowledged the unique nature of state decisions that go to the heart of representative government. In several cases the Court has applied the "political function" exception to laws through which states exclude aliens from positions "intimately related to the process of democratic self-government." The cases recognize the authority of the states to determine the qualifications of their most important government officials. This authority is not without limit. In 1974 Congress extended the provisions of the ADEA to include the states as employers. This extension was valid exercise of Congress's powers under the Commerce Clause. In light of the ADEA's exclusion of most important public officials, it is ambiguous whether Congress intended that appointed judges be included. The qualification for judges was within the state's authority.

ANALYSIS

Section 630(f) of the Age Discrimination in Employment Act defines the term employee as "an individual employed by any employer except . . . any person elected to public office in any state or political subdivision of any state by the qualified voters thereof, or any person chosen by such officer to be on such officer's personal staff, or an appointee on the policymaking level or an intermediate advisor with respect to the exercise of the constitutional or legal powers of the office."

Quicknotes

DUE PROCESS CLAUSE Language found in the Fifth and Fourteenth Amendments to the United States Constitution providing that no person shall be deprived of "life, liberty, or property without due process of law."

EQUAL PROTECTION CLAUSE A constitutional guarantee that no person should be denied the same protection of the laws enjoyed by other persons in like circumstances.

New York v. United States

State (P) v. Federal government (D)

505 U.S. 144 (1992)

NATURE OF CASE: Appeal of dismissal of suit for declaratory judgment.

FACT SUMMARY: New York (P) sought a declaration that the Low-Level Radioactive Waste Policy Amendments Act was unconstitutional.

RULE OF LAW

The federal government may not order a state government to enact particular legislation.

FACTS: Three states had disposal sites for radioactive waste. After study and negotiation, the National Governors' Association (NGA) devised a plan that became the Low-Level Radioactive Waste Policy Amendments Act (the 1985 Act). The 1985 Act set deadlines for every state to join a regional waste compact, develop in-state disposal, or find another way to dispose of its own waste. The 1985 Act assured the sited states they would not have the entire nation's waste burden and gave the other 47 states seven more years of access to active sites. The 1985 Act provided three incentives for state compliance: (1) Congress authorized sited states to impose a surcharge, part of which would go into federal escrow, with funds to be returned to complying states; (2) Congress empowered sited states to deny access to states not in compliance; and (3) any state not in compliance by 1992 had to either take title to all waste generated in their state or else become liable to in-state waste generators for all damages. As of 1990 New York (P) had not joined a regional waste compact. Unable to settle on an in-state site, New York (P) sought to invalidate the 1985 Act as violative of state sovereignty principles of the Tenth Amendment. The sited states intervened as defendants. The district court dismissed, the court of appeals affirmed, and New York (P) appealed.

ISSUE: May the federal government order a state government to enact particular legislation?

HOLDING AND DECISION: (O'Connor, J.) No. The federal government may not order a state government to enact particular legislation. The federal government may provide incentives for states to regulate in a certain way by tying funding to acceptance of a federal plan or by giving states a choice between enacting a federal plan or having state law preempted by federal law. Here, the first incentive is a congressional exercise of Commerce Clause power (allowing sited states to impose a surcharge on interstate commerce and imposing a federal tax on that surcharge) combined with an exercise of Spending Clause power (making return of surcharges contingent on compliance with the federal plan). The second incentive is a routine exercise of the commerce power. If a state chooses not to follow the federal plan, generators of waste within that state become subject to federal regulation authorizing states with waste sites to deny access. The burden would fall on the waste generators, not on the state, and the state would not be forced to spend funds or accede to federal direction. The third incentive, however, crossed the line to coercion. Whether a state "chooses" to take title to waste or to accept liability for disposal, the burden of not enacting the federal plan falls on the state. The strength of the federal interest is irrelevant. Federal courts may issue directives to state officials, but the Constitution expressly grants that authority. Such authority is outside Congress's enumerated powers and, for that reason, also infringes on state sovereignty reserved by the Tenth Amendment. While the 1985 Act was a creation of and compromise among the states, the states may not constitutionally consent to give up their sovereignty. Affirmed as to the first two incentives, reversed as to the third.

CONCURRENCE AND DISSENT: (White, J.) The Acts were the product of cooperative federalism. The states bargained among themselves to solve an imminent crisis and achieve compromises for Congress to sanction. New York (P) reaped the benefits of the 1985 Act, an agreement it helped formulate, and should not be able to sue now. The majority wrongly finds that states cannot consent to relinquish some sovereignty. Tenth Amendment restrictions on the commerce power are procedural limits, designed to prevent federal destruction of state governments, not to protect substantive areas of state autonomy.

CONCURRENCE AND DISSENT: (Stevens, J.) The notion that Congress may not order states to implement federal legislation is incorrect and unsound. The federal government regulates state railroads, schools, prisons, and elections, and in time of war, Congress undoubtedly could command states to supply soldiers.

ANALYSIS

Under the Articles of Confederation, the federal government could only act by ordering states to enact legislation. The Framers decided that the federal government needed power to regulate citizens directly and

Continued on next page.

so drafted the Constitution. The Court interpreted the Framers' decision as a rejection of federal power to order states to enact legislation.

Quicknotes

COMMERCE CLAUSE Article I, § 8, cl. 3 of the United States Constitution, granting Congress the power to regulate commerce with foreign countries and between the states.

ENUMERATED POWERS Specific powers mentioned in, and granted by, the Constitution, e.g., the taxing power.

FEDERALISM A scheme of government whereby the power to govern is divided between a central and localized governments.

SPENDING CLAUSE The power delegated to Congress by the United States Constitution to spend money in providing for the nation's welfare.

STATE SOVEREIGNTY The absolute power of self-government possessed by a state.

TENTH AMENDMENT The Tenth Amendment to the United States Constitution reserving those powers therein, not expressly delegated to the federal government or prohibited to the states, to the states or to the people.

Printz v. United States

State officer (P) v. Federal government (D)

521 U.S. 898 (1997)

NATURE OF CASE: Review of decision upholding the constitutionality of the Brady Act.

FACT SUMMARY: State officer Printz (P) challenged the constitutionality of the Brady Act, which required state and local law enforcement officers to conduct background checks on potential handgun purchasers and perform other related tasks.

RULE OF LAW

The compelled enlistment of state officers for the administration of federal programs is unconstitutional.

FACTS: In 1993, Congress amended the Gun Control Act by enacting the Brady Act. In part, interim provisions of the Brady Act required state chief law enforcement officers (CLEOs) to conduct background checks and perform certain other duties before a dealer may sell a handgun to a purchaser. Printz (P), a CLEO, filed an action challenging these interim provisions of the Brady Act. The district court found the interim provisions unconstitutional, but severable from the rest of the Act. The Ninth Circuit reversed, declaring the entire Brady Act constitutional. Printz (P) appealed.

ISSUE: Is the compelled enlistment of state officers for the administration of federal programs unconstitutional?

HOLDING AND DECISION: (Scalia, J.) Yes. The compelled enlistment of state officers for the administration of federal programs is unconstitutional. Here, Congress has no particularized constitutional authority to command state executive officers. While certain instances in our constitutional history have allowed Congress to direct state judicial officers to follow its dictates, nothing in that same history authorizes such power over nonjudicial officers. Congress has the power to regulate individuals, not states, and its power would be unfairly augmented if it could enlist state police officers. States can and should regulate themselves. Even though the federal government (D) is not requiring state police officers to create policy in this case, compelling their service is still an unconstitutional infringement on state sovereignty.

CONCURRENCE: (O'Connor, J.) State and law enforcement may voluntarily continue to participate in the federal programs and Congress may provide for its continuance on a contractual basis.

CONCURRENCE: (Thomas, J.) The federal government's (D) authority does not extend to wholly intrastate, point-of-sale transactions.

DISSENT: (Stevens, J.) When Congress exercises its constitutional power, it may impose affirmative obligations on executive and judicial officers of state and local governments, as well as on ordinary citizens, especially when such imposition is for the benefit of the people of the nation.

DISSENT: (Souter, J.) When the federal government (D) commands state officers here, it is simply utilizing those officers as auxiliaries to the enforcement of federal laws. Such action is constitutional.

DISSENT: (Breyer, J.) Simply because there is a paucity of examples of direct federal assignment of duties to state officers does not mean that the Constitution is so inflexible as to prohibit certain assignments.

ANALYSIS

This case highlights the tension between state sovereignty and the Supremacy Clause. Article VI, § 2 of the United States Constitution provides that to the extent that Congress has exercised its powers, any inconsistent state laws are prohibited. The extent of congressional power, however, has been a serious cause of debate, culling arguments from the Tenth Amendment's exclusive state powers and the Constitution's other exclusive federal powers.

Quicknotes

STATE SOVEREIGNTY The absolute power of self-government possessed by a state.

SUPREMACY CLAUSE Article VI, § 2, of the United States Constitution, which provides that federal action must prevail over inconsistent state action.

United States v. Cox

[Parties not identified.]

342 F.2d 167 (5th Cir.), *cert. denied, sub nom. Cox v. Hauberg*, 381 U.S. 935 (1965)

NATURE OF CASE: Review of the constitutional validity of a district court order.

FACT SUMMARY: Hauberg and Katzenbach appealed from a district court order finding Hauberg guilty of civil contempt and ordering Katzenbach to appear to show-cause why he should not also be convicted of such contempt for failure to follow the grand jury's orders to present certain indictments.

RULE OF LAW

The signature of the government attorney is necessary to the validity of an indictment, and the affixing or withholding of the signature is a matter of executive discretion that cannot be coerced or reviewed by the courts.

FACTS: The United States District Court for the Southern District of Mississippi entered an order finding Hauberg guilty of civil contempt for refusal to obey an order of the grand jury to prepare certain indictments. The order also provided for a citation to issue to Acting Attorney General Katzenbach to appear before the court to show-cause why he should not be adjudged guilty of contempt for his instructions to disregard the court's orders. Hauberg and Katzenbach appealed.

ISSUE: Is the signature of the government attorney necessary to the validity of an indictment, and is the affixing or withholding of the signature a matter of executive discretion which cannot be coerced or reviewed by the courts?

HOLDING AND DECISION: (Jones, J.) Yes. The signature of the government attorney is necessary to the validity of an indictment, and the affixing or withholding of the signature is a matter of executive discretion that cannot be coerced or reviewed by the courts. The constitutional requirement of an indictment or presentment as a prerequisite to a prosecution for a capital or infamous crime has the primary purpose of protecting an individual from jeopardy except upon a finding of probable cause and is designed to safeguard against oppressive actions by a prosecutor or court. The constitutional provision is not to be read as conferring any rights or prerogatives on the grand jury. The Federal Rules of Criminal Procedure now provide the Attorney General or United States Attorney may, by leave of court, file a dismissal of an indictment. The purpose of the rule is to prevent harassment of the defendant. The role of the grand jury is restricted to a finding of whether there is probable cause to believe that an offense has been committed. The discretionary power of the attorney for the United States in determining whether to commence a prosecution may depend on policy matters independent of any issue of probable cause. While the attorney is a member of the court, he is also an executive official whom exercises discretion as to whether there should be a prosecution in a particular case. It follows as an incident of separation of powers that the courts may not interfere with the free exercise of the discretionary powers of such attorneys as to whether there will be a prosecution in a particular case. The requirement of Rule 7 that the attorney sign the indictment is a recognition of that power, in the absence of which there is no valid indictment. Reversed.

CONCURRENCE AND DISSENT: (Rives, J.) A federal grand jury has the unquestioned right to inquire into any matter within the jurisdiction involving violations of law and to return an indictment if it finds a reasonable probability that a crime has been committed. When the United States Attorney prepares and signs an indictment, he does not adopt, approve, or vouch for the charge, nor does he institute a criminal prosecution.

CONCURRENCE: (Brown, J.) I agree that the district attorney may not be compelled to sign the formal indictment but disagree that he may ignore the grand jury's efforts to the point of declining to prepare the indictment they have voted to return. The court may legally compel the district attorney to act as a legal scrivener to the grand jury and order him to prepare the indictment in legal form.

CONCURRENCE: (Wisdom, J.) The decision not to prosecute represents the exercise of a discretion analogous to the exercise of the executive privilege. The Attorney General has concluded that there is not sufficient evidence to prove perjury and that trial would have the effect of inhibiting Black people in Mississippi from registering to vote.

ANALYSIS

This case involves a conflict between society's interest in enforcing the law and national policy of outlawing racial discrimination. Wisdom's concurrence would take this discretion out of the province of the grand jury and properly place it within the executive functions of the President or the Attorney General.

Continued on next page.

Quicknotes

CIVIL CONTEMPT CITATION One party's failure to comply with a court order requiring that party to undertake an action for the benefit of another party to the action.

INDICTMENT A formal written accusation made by the prosecution to the grand jury under oath, charging an individual with a criminal offense.

PROBABLE CAUSE A reasonable basis for believing that a crime has been committed.

United States v. Nixon, President of the United States

Federal government (P) v. President of the United States (D)

418 U.S. 683 (1974)

NATURE OF CASE: Appeal from denial of a motion to quash a third-party subpoena duces tecum.

FACT SUMMARY: A subpoena duces tecum was issued by the special prosecutor directing Nixon (D), the President of the United States, to turn over taped presidential conversations and transcripts.

RULE OF LAW

Neither the doctrine of separation of powers nor the need for confidentiality of high-level communications alone can sustain an absolute, unqualified presidential privilege of immunity from judicial process under all circumstances.

FACTS: A grand jury indicted seven presidential advisors of conspiracy to defraud the United States (P) and to obstruct justice. Nixon (D), the President of the United States, although not indicted, was named as a co-conspirator. Upon motion of the special prosecutor, a third-party subpoena duces tecum was issued ordering Nixon (D) to turn over tape recordings and transcripts of certain presidential conversations relating to certain precisely identified meetings between Nixon (D) and others. Nixon (D) appealed specially seeking to quash the subpoena on grounds relating to a claim of absolute executive privilege. The motion to quash was denied, and this appeal followed.

ISSUE: Can either the doctrine of separation of powers or the need for confidentiality of high-level communications alone sustain an absolute, unqualified presidential privilege of immunity from judicial process under all circumstances?

HOLDING AND DECISION: (Burger, C.J.) No. Neither the doctrine of separation of powers nor the need for confidentiality of high-level communications alone can sustain an absolute, unqualified presidential privilege of immunity from judicial process under all circumstances. The court is the final arbiter of executive privilege. First, the courts had jurisdiction over the question because the district court's order was final. Second, the matter was justiciable because the mere assertion of a claim of an "intrabranch dispute" (the special prosecutor, an executive appointive, against the chief executive), without more, has never operated to defeat federal jurisdiction. Here, the executive was required to enforce its own regulation, which had the force of law, giving the special prosecutor his unique independence within the executive branch itself. Turning to the claim of privilege that doctrine of separation of powers does not preclude judicial review of a President's claim of privilege, it is for the court to interpret claims with respect to powers alleged to derive from enumerated powers. While the sovereign power of federal government has been divided amongst three coequal branches, the separate powers were not intended to operate with absolute independence. The legitimate needs of judicial process may outweigh presidential privilege. It is not denied that the shaping of government policy requires confidentiality that, in turn, requires a presumptive privilege of confidentiality for presidential communications. While this privilege has received utmost deference when based upon military or diplomatic secrecy, no case has given such deference to a President's generalized interest in confidentiality. Thus, "when the ground for asserting privilege as to subpoenaed materials sought for use in a criminal trial is based only on the generalized interest in confidentiality, it cannot prevail over the fundamental demands of due process of law in the fair administration of criminal justice."

ANALYSIS

This case can be summed up in the well-known saying, "No man is above the law." President Nixon's resignation from office followed shortly after announcement of this decision relating and arising out of the Watergate scandal. While President Nixon argued a claim of confidentiality, nowhere in the constitution is there any explicit reference to such a privilege. However, "to the extent (confidentiality) relates to the effective discharge of a President's powers, it is constitutionally based." Here, that privilege clashed with the specific constitutional rights of a defendant in a criminal trial "to be confronted with the witnesses against him" and "to have compulsory process for obtaining witnesses in his favor" and was overcome by those rights.

Quicknotes

CONSPIRACY Concerted action by two or more persons to accomplish some unlawful purpose.

DUE PROCESS CLAUSE Language found in the Fifth and Fourteenth Amendments to the United States Constitution providing that no person shall be deprived of "life, liberty, or property without due process of law."

EXECUTIVE PRIVILEGE The right of the executive branch to refuse to disclose confidential communications if such

Continued on next page.

exemption is necessary for the effective discharge of its official duties.

SEPARATION OF POWERS The system of checks and balances preventing one branch of government from infringing upon exercising the powers of another branch of government.

SUBPOENA DUCES TECUM A court mandate compelling the production of documents under a witness's control.

Trump v. Vance

President of the United States (P) v. Municipal district attorney (D)

140 S. Ct. 2412 (2020)

NATURE OF CASE: Appeal from affirmance of denial of injunction in action brought by sitting President of the United States to enjoin enforcement of grand jury subpoena for records related to the President and business organizations affiliated with him.

FACT SUMMARY: After the New York County District Attorney's Office—acting on behalf of a grand jury—served a subpoena duces tecum on Mazars USA, LLP (Mazars) (D), the personal accounting firm of President Donald Trump (Trump) (P), for financial records relating to Trump (P) and his businesses, Trump (P) sued the district attorney (D) and Mazars (D) to enjoin enforcement of the subpoena, arguing that a sitting President enjoys absolute immunity from state criminal process under Article II and the Supremacy Clause.

RULE OF LAW

(1) A sitting President does not under Article II or the Supremacy Clause categorically have absolute immunity from a state grand jury subpoena seeking the President's private papers.

(2) Neither Article II nor the Supremacy Clause requires a heightened standard for the issuance of a state criminal subpoena seeking the private papers of a sitting President.

FACTS: In 2019, the New York County District Attorney's Office—acting on behalf of a grand jury—served a subpoena duces tecum on Mazars USA, LLP (Mazars) (D), the personal accounting firm of President Donald J. Trump (Trump) (P), for financial records relating to Trump (P) and his businesses. Trump (P), acting in his personal capacity, sued the district attorney (D) and Mazars (D) in federal district court to enjoin enforcement of the subpoena, arguing that a sitting President enjoys absolute immunity from state criminal process under Article II and the Supremacy Clause. The district court denied injunctive relief, and the court of appeals affirmed. The United States Supreme Court granted certiorari.

ISSUE:

(1) Does a sitting President under Article II or the Supremacy Clause categorically have absolute immunity from a state grand jury subpoena seeking the President's private papers?

(2) Do either Article II or the Supremacy Clause require a heightened standard for the issuance of a state criminal subpoena seeking the private papers of a sitting President?

HOLDING AND DECISION: (Roberts, C.J.)

(1) No. A sitting President does not under Article II or the Supremacy Clause categorically have absolute immunity from a state grand jury subpoena seeking the President's private papers. In 1807, Chief Justice Marshall ruled that a sitting President is not exempt from the Sixth Amendment's guarantee that the accused have compulsory process for obtaining witnesses for their defense. *United States v. Burr*, 25 F.Cas. 30 (CC Va. 1807). Marshall also concluded that the Sixth Amendment's guarantee extended to the production of documents, since the propriety of introducing any documents depends on the nature of the document and not the character of the person who holds it, and since the court may decide whether introducing the document is appropriate after the document is produced. In the two centuries following *Burr*, successive Presidents accepted Marshall's ruling that the President is subject to subpoena, and uniformly agreed to testify when called in criminal proceedings. In 1974, the question whether to compel the disclosure of official communications over the President's objection came to a head when the Watergate Special Prosecutor secured a subpoena duces tecum directing President Nixon to produce, among other things, tape recordings of Oval Office meetings. The Court rejected Nixon's claim of an absolute privilege of confidentiality for all presidential communications. Recognizing that "compulsory process" was imperative for both the prosecution and the defense, the Court held that the President's "generalized assertion of privilege must yield to the demonstrated, specific need for evidence in a pending criminal trial." *United States v. Nixon*, 418 U.S. 683 (1974). President Nixon dutifully released the tapes. This history all involved federal criminal proceedings. Here, the President (P) claims that the Supremacy Clause gives a sitting President absolute immunity from state criminal subpoenas because compliance with such subpoenas would categorically impair the performance of the President's Article II functions. The Solicitor General, arguing on behalf of the United States, claims that a state grand jury subpoena for a sitting President's personal records

Continued on next page.

(it was agreed that the records at issue belonged to Trump (P) and that Mazars (D) was merely their custodian) must, at the very least, meet a heightened standard of need—a standard that according to the Solicitor General was not met here. It is well established that federal criminal subpoenas do not impermissibly impair the President's ability to perform the Executive's constitutionally mandated functions. Here, Trump (P) argues that state criminal subpoenas categorically impair that function and are impermissibly burdensome on grounds of diversion, stigma, and harassment. Trump (P) contends that complying with state criminal subpoenas would necessarily distract the Chief Executive from the Executive's duties. Trump (P) grounds that concern in *Nixon v. Fitzgerald,* 457 U.S. 731 (1982), which recognized a President's "absolute immunity from damages liability predicated on his official acts." However, contrary to Trump's (P) suggestion, that case did not hold that distraction was sufficient to confer absolute immunity. Indeed, the Court expressly rejected immunity based on distraction alone 15 years later in *Clinton v. Jones,* 520 U.S. 681 (1997), when President Clinton sought absolute immunity from civil liability for private acts. As the Court explained, *Fitzgerald's* principal concern was not mere distraction but the distortion of the Executive's "decisionmaking process." The prospect that a President may become "preoccupied by pending litigation" did not ordinarily implicate constitutional concerns. Two centuries of experience likewise confirm that a properly tailored criminal subpoena will not normally hamper the performance of a President's constitutional duties. The President (P) claims this case is different. He believes that he is under investigation and argues that the toll will necessarily be heavier in that circumstance. But Trump (P) is not seeking immunity from the diversion occasioned by the prospect of future criminal liability. He concedes that he may be investigated while in office. His objection is instead limited to the additional distraction caused by the subpoena itself. That argument, however, runs up against the 200 years of precedent establishing that Presidents, and their official communications, are subject to judicial process, even when the President is under investigation. Trump (P) next claims that the stigma of being subpoenaed will undermine his leadership at home and abroad. However, even if a tarnished reputation were a cognizable impairment, there is nothing inherently stigmatizing about a President performing the citizen's normal duty of furnishing information relevant to a criminal investigation. Nor can the risk of association with persons or activities under criminal investigation absolve a President of such an important public duty. The consequences for a President's public standing will likely increase if he is the one under investigation, but Trump (P) concedes that such investigations are permitted under Article II and the Supremacy Clause. Additionally, the receipt of a subpoena would not seem to categorically magnify the harm to Trump's (P) reputation. Additionally, in the grand jury context, longstanding secrecy rules aim to prevent the very stigma Trump (P) anticipates. Finally, Trump (P) argues that subjecting Presidents to state criminal subpoenas will make them targets for harassment. The Court rejected a nearly identical argument in *Clinton,* concluding that the risk posed by harassing civil litigation was not "serious" because federal courts have the tools to deter and dismiss vexatious lawsuits. Harassing state criminal subpoenas could, under certain circumstances, threaten the independence or effectiveness of the Executive, but the law already seeks to protect against such abuse. First, grand juries are prohibited from engaging in "arbitrary fishing expeditions" or initiating investigations "out of malice or an intent to harass," and federal courts may intervene in state proceedings that are motivated by or conducted in bad faith. *Huffman v. Pursue, Ltd.,* 420 U.S. 529, 611 (1975). Second, because the Supremacy Clause prohibits state judges and prosecutors from interfering with a President's official duties, any effort to manipulate a President's policy decisions or to retaliate against a President for official acts through issuance of a subpoena would be unconstitutional. Finally, federal law allows a President to challenge any such allegedly unconstitutional influence in a federal forum. Given these safeguards and the Court's precedents, absolute immunity from a state grand jury subpoena seeking a President's private papers for a sitting President is neither necessary not appropriate under Article II or the Supremacy Clause.

(2) No. Neither Article II nor the Supremacy Clause requires a heightened standard for the issuance of a state criminal subpoena seeking the private papers of a sitting President. First, although a President cannot be treated as an "ordinary individual" when executive communications are sought, *Burr* teaches that, with regard to private papers, a President is similarly situated to any other individual. Second, there has been no showing here that heightened protection against state subpoenas is necessary for the Executive to fulfill Article II functions. Finally, absent a need to protect the Executive, the public interest in fair and effective law enforcement cuts in favor of comprehensive access to evidence. Rejecting a heightened need standard does not leave Presidents without recourse. A President may take advantage of the same

Continued on next page.

protections available to every other citizen, including the right to challenge the subpoena on any grounds permitted by state law, which usually include bad faith and undue burden or breadth. When the President invokes such protections, the high respect that is owed to the President's office should inform the conduct of the entire proceeding, including the timing and scope of discovery. In addition, a President can raise subpoena-specific constitutional challenges in either a state or a federal forum. For example, a President can challenge the subpoena as an attempt to influence the performance of the President's official duties, in violation of the Supremacy Clause. In addition, a President can argue that compliance with a particular subpoena would impede the President's constitutional duties. Affirmed and remanded.

CONCURRENCE: (Kavanaugh, J.) *United States v. Nixon*, 418 U.S. 683 (1974), requires that a prosecutor establish a "demonstrated, specific need" for privileged executive branch information, including a President's information. This requirement accommodates the interests of the criminal process and the Article II interests of the Executive, and seeks to avoid diversion or harassment of a sitting President by a state prosecutor. The majority did not apply the *Nixon* requirement to this case, but it should have. Nonetheless, the majority accounted for some of the important concerns that were raised in *Nixon* and explained existing constraints on a prosecutor issuing a subpoena to a sitting President. Moreover, there is unanimity of opinion on the Court that a President may raise objections to a state criminal subpoena not just in state court, but also in federal court. Regardless whether in the future the majority's standard is applied, or *Nixon's* "demonstrated, specific need" standard is used, a court will have to first delve into why the state wants the information; why and how much the state needs the information, including whether the state could obtain the information elsewhere; and whether compliance with the subpoena would unduly burden or interfere with a President's official duties.

DISSENT: (Thomas, J.) There is no dispute that a President is not entitled to absolute immunity from the issuance of a state criminal subpoena, but a President may be entitled to relief against the subpoena's enforcement, if the President can demonstrate that presidential duties require all of the President's time—until the end of the President's term or until the President is removed from office. This standard applies with equal force to federal and state subpoenas, and a federal court may provide injunctive and declaratory relief to stay enforcement of a state subpoena when a President meets this standard. Here, Trump (P) has requested such relief. Accordingly, the Court should have vacated and remanded (instead of affirming and remanding) so the district court could determine whether Trump (P) has met this standard, and, thus, whether enforcement of the subpoena should be enjoined. As to the issue of whether a grand jury must make a showing of heightened need, under a heightened-need standard, a grand jury with only the usual need for particular information would be refused the information when the President is perfectly able to comply, whereas a grand jury with a heightened need would be entitled to the information even if compliance would place undue obligations on the President. This result makes little sense and lacks any basis in the original understanding of the Constitution. The questions of the grand jury's need should thus be left to state law.

DISSENT: (Alito, J.) This case raises important constitutional issues, and the specific issue before the Court cannot be answered without considering the broader question of whether the Constitution restricts a state's use of its criminal law enforcement powers against a sitting President. One consideration is that there is not always a clear line between a President's personal and official affairs. Another is that a President must be able to carry out the responsibilities of the office at all times. Although the states retain many powers under the Constitution, they may not block or interfere with the federal government's lawful work. It is clear, based on these considerations and well-established principles, that a state may not prosecute a sitting President. This conclusion is bolstered by the Constitution's impeachment provisions. However, these considerations apply not only to a state's prosecution of a sitting President, but also to any legal proceedings against a sitting President. The key is that the responsibilities and demands of the Executive Office must be taken into account; the nature of the office demands in some instances that the application of laws be adjusted at least until the person's term in office ends. This should be true of subpoenas issued to a sitting President, and a uniform rule should be articulated regarding such issuance. Such a rule should take into account both the effect of subpoenas on the functioning of the presidency and the risk that they will be used for harassment. First, even if a President suspects that he may be criminally prosecuted, that alone will sap the President's energy and impair his ability to perform their constitutional duties. Second, the use by local prosecutors of a criminal subpoena aimed at the President could be a political strategy, which would undermine the constitutional structure. The majority's approach relegates a President to the "meager defenses" that are available to all citizens when an ordinary grand jury subpoena is challenged. Instead, the presidency deserves greater protection. For these reasons, a prosecutor should be required (1) to provide at least a general description of the possible offenses that are under investigation, (2) to outline how the subpoenaed records relate

Continued on next page.

to those offenses, and (3) to explain why it is important that the records be produced and why it is necessary for production to occur while the President is still in office. The prosecutor's response must be detailed and specific and must address concerns for the President's ability to carry out the President's official duties, before a subpoena will be enforced during the President's term. In sum, the Court's decision threatens to impair the functioning of the presidency and provides the presidency no real protection against the use of the subpoena power by the nation's more than 2,300 local prosecutors.

ANALYSIS

The assertion that President Trump (P) made in this case was extraordinary. Had his claim of absolute immunity from criminal process prevailed, there potentially would have been limitless immunity from criminal process not only for a President during the President's term of office, but also for the President's family members and associates. As the district court observed, presidential immunity would stretch to cover every phase of criminal proceedings, including investigations, grand jury proceedings and subpoenas, indictment, prosecution, arrest, trial, conviction, and incarceration. Such immunity presumably would encompass any conduct, at any time, in any forum, whether federal or state, and whether the President acted alone or in concert with other individuals. The President's exemption from criminal proceedings would extend not only to matters arising from performance of the President's duties and functions in the President's official capacity, but also to matters arising from the President's private affairs, financial transactions, and all other conduct undertaken by the President as an ordinary citizen, both during and before the President's tenure in office. The practical implications and actual effects of such categorical immunity could be far-reaching. In some circumstances, applicable statutes of limitations could run, barring further investigation and prosecution of serious criminal offenses, thus potentially enabling both the President and any accomplices to escape being brought to justice. Temporally, such immunity would operate to frustrate the administration of justice by insulating from criminal law scrutiny and judicial review, whether by federal or state courts, not only matters occurring during the President's tenure in office, but potentially also records relating to transactions and illegal actions the President and others may have committed before the President assumed the presidency. However, Trump's (P) claim did not prevail. All the courts to review the claim, as well as all the Supreme Court justices, agreed that there is nothing in the Constitution, in the constitutional balance of power between the respective branches of government, or in the Supreme Court's precedents that absolutely immunizes a sitting President from criminal process during the President's term. As Chief Justice Roberts notes in the majority opinion, the Founders shunned the concept of the inviolability of the King of England and the bounds of the monarch's protective screen covering the Crown's actions from legal scrutiny, and, therefore, disclaimed any notion that the Constitution generally conferred similarly all-encompassing immunity upon the President. The wisdom of that view has been tested before the courts on various occasions and has been roundly and consistently reaffirmed by the Supreme Court and lower courts, which, in numerous rulings, have circumscribed claims of presidential immunity in multiple ways. As the district court put it, the proposition advanced by President Trump (P) is "repugnant to the nation's governmental structure and constitutional values." *Trump v. Vance,* 395 F. Supp. 3d 283, 290 (S.D.N.Y. 2019).

Quicknotes

GRAND JURY A group summoned to investigate, inform, and accuse persons of crimes when sufficient evidence exists to do so.

IMMUNITY Exemption from a legal obligation.

INJUNCTIVE RELIEF A court order issued as a remedy, requiring a person to do, or prohibiting that person from doing, a specific act.

SUBPOENA DUCES TECUM A court mandate compelling the production of documents under a witness' control.

SUPREMACY CLAUSE Article VI, ¶ 2 of the U.S. Constitution, which provides that federal action must prevail over inconsistent state action.

Trump v. Mazars USA, LLP

President of the United States (P) v. President's personal accounting firm (D)

140 S. Ct. 2019 (2020)

NATURE OF CASE: Appeal in action brought by the sitting President in a personal capacity contesting the enforcement of subpoenas issued by the U.S. House of Representatives (the House) seeking information about his finances, his children, and his business affiliates, on the grounds that the subpoenas exceeded the House's constitutional authority. [The procedural posture of the case is not presented in the casebook excerpt.]

FACT SUMMARY: The U.S. House of Representatives (the House) issued subpoenas seeking information about the finances of President Donald Trump (Trump) (P), his children, and affiliated businesses, asserting the information it sought was for legislative purposes. Trump (P) contended that the subpoenas exceeded the House's constitutional authority.

RULE OF LAW

When Congress issues a subpoena, purportedly in furtherance of legislative purposes, for the President's personal, nonprivileged papers, a court being asked to enforce such a subpoena must take into account the significant separation of powers concerns implicated by such a subpoena by inquiring, at the least, as to whether: (1) the asserted legislative purpose warrants the significant step of involving the President and the President's papers; (2) the subpoena is no broader than reasonably necessary to support Congress's legislative objective; (3) the evidence offered by Congress to establish that a subpoena advances a valid legislative purpose is detailed and substantial; and (4) the burdens imposed on the President are excessive.

FACTS: Three committees of the U. S. House of Representatives (the House) issued four subpoenas seeking information about the finances of President Donald Trump (Trump) (P), his children, and affiliated businesses. The House Committee on Financial Services issued a subpoena to Deutsche Bank seeking any document related to account activity, due diligence, foreign transactions, business statements, debt schedules, statements of net worth, tax returns, and suspicious activity identified by Deutsche Bank. It issued a second subpoena to Capital One for similar information. The Permanent Select Committee on Intelligence issued a subpoena to Deutsche Bank that mirrored the subpoena issued by the Financial Services Committee, and the House Committee on Oversight and Reform issued a subpoena to Trump's (P) personal accounting firm, Mazars USA, LLP (Mazars) (D), demanding information related to Trump (P) and several affiliated businesses. Although each of the committees sought overlapping sets of financial documents, each supplied different justifications for the requests, explaining that the information would help guide legislative reform in areas ranging from money laundering and terrorism to foreign involvement in U.S. elections. Trump (P) in his personal capacity, along with his children and affiliated businesses, contested the subpoenas, contending that they were issued to harass Trump (P), expose Trump's (P) personal matters, and conduct law enforcement activities beyond the House's authority, thus exceeding the House's constitutional authority. The United States Supreme Court granted certiorari in the case. [The procedural posture of the case is not presented in the casebook excerpt.]

ISSUE: When Congress issues a subpoena, purportedly in furtherance of legislative purposes, for the President's personal, nonprivileged papers, must a court being asked to enforce such a subpoena take into account the significant separation of powers concerns implicated by such a subpoena by inquiring, at the least, as to whether: (1) the asserted legislative purpose warrants the significant step of involving the President and the President's papers; (2) the subpoena is no broader than reasonably necessary to support Congress's legislative objective; (3) the evidence offered by Congress to establish that a subpoena advances a valid legislative purpose is detailed and substantial; and (4) the burdens imposed on the President are excessive?

HOLDING AND DECISION: (Roberts, C.J.) Yes. When Congress issues a subpoena, purportedly in furtherance of legislative purposes, for the President's personal, nonprivileged papers, a court being asked to enforce such a subpoena must take into account the significant separation of powers concerns implicated by such a subpoena by inquiring, at the least, as to whether: (1) the asserted legislative purpose warrants the significant step of involving the President and the President's papers; (2) the subpoena is no broader than reasonably necessary to support Congress's legislative objective; (3) the evidence offered by Congress to establish that a subpoena advances a valid legislative purpose is detailed and substantial; and (4) the burdens imposed on the President are excessive. Historically, for over two centuries, disputes over congressional demands for presidential documents have been resolved by the political branches through negotiation and compromise without ever before

Continued on next page.

involving the Court. This is the first time such a dispute reaches the Court and represents a significant departure from historical practice. Because in the past Congress and Presidents have been able to resolve such disputes without the Court's intervention, the Court must tread very carefully to ensure that it does not needlessly disturb the compromises and working arrangements previously reached by those branches of government. Although Congress has no enumerated constitutional power to conduct investigations or issue subpoenas, the Court has held that each House of Congress has the power to secure needed information for the purpose of legislating. This power is "indispensable" because, without information, Congress would be unable to legislate wisely or effectively. Nevertheless, because this power is justified solely as an adjunct to the legislative process, it is subject to several limitations. Most importantly, a congressional subpoena is valid only if it is related to, and in furtherance of, a legitimate task of the Congress, and the subpoena must serve a valid legislative purpose. Also, Congress may not issue a subpoena for the purpose of law enforcement, because that power is assigned to the President and the judiciary. Finally, recipients of congressional subpoenas retain their constitutional rights and various privileges throughout the course of an investigation. Trump (P) contends, as does the Solicitor General on behalf of the United States, that these usual rules for congressional subpoenas should not apply in a case such as the one at bar that involves the President's papers, and that a more exacting standard should be applied. That standard, which the Court has applied where the President asserts executive privilege, would require Congress to show that the requested information satisfies a "demonstrated, specific need," and is "demonstrably critical" to a legislative purpose. Because executive privilege safeguards the public interest in candid, confidential deliberations within the executive branch, information subject to the privilege deserves the greatest protection consistent with the fair administration of justice. However, such protection is not necessary in cases involving nonprivileged, private information, which by definition does not implicate sensitive executive branch deliberations, and such a heightened standard, if applied outside the context of privileged information, would risk seriously impeding Congress in carrying out its responsibilities, giving short shrift to its important interests in conducting inquiries to obtain information needed to legislate effectively. On the other hand, the separation of powers issues raised when Congress seeks the President's nonprivileged papers requires more than applying the rules already in place for legislative subpoenas. Otherwise, there would be essentially no limits on the congressional power to subpoena the President's personal records. A limitless subpoena power could transform the established practice of the political branches and allow Congress to aggrandize itself at the President's expense. These separation of powers concerns are unmistakably implicated by the subpoenas here, which represent not a run-of-the-mill legislative effort but rather a clash between rival branches of government over records of intense political interest for all involved. The interbranch conflict does not vanish simply because the subpoenas seek personal papers or because the President has sued in a personal capacity. Nor are separation of powers concerns less palpable because the subpoenas are issued to third parties. Neither side identifies an approach that adequately accounts for these weighty separation of powers concerns. Such concerns require a balanced approach. Therefore, in assessing whether a subpoena directed at a President's personal information is "related to, and in furtherance of, a legitimate task of the Congress," courts must take adequate account of the separation of powers principles at stake, including both the significant legislative interests of Congress and the unique position of the President. Several special considerations inform such an analysis. First, courts should carefully assess whether the asserted legislative purpose warrants the significant step of involving the President and the President's papers. Because occasions for constitutional confrontation between the two branches should be avoided whenever possible, Congress may not rely on the President's information if other sources could reasonably provide Congress the information it needs in light of its particular legislative objective. Second, to narrow the scope of possible conflict between the branches, courts should insist on a subpoena no broader than reasonably necessary to support Congress's legislative objective, and the specificity of the subpoena's request should serve as an important safeguard against unnecessary intrusion into the operation of the office of the President. Third, courts should be attentive to the nature of the evidence offered by Congress to establish that a subpoena advances a valid legislative purpose—the more detailed and substantial, the better. That is particularly true when Congress contemplates legislation that raises sensitive constitutional issues, such as legislation concerning the presidency. Fourth, courts should assess the burdens imposed on the President by a subpoena, particularly because they stem from a rival political branch that has an ongoing relationship with the President and incentives to use subpoenas for institutional advantage. Other considerations may be pertinent as well; one case every two centuries does not afford enough experience for an exhaustive list. Vacated and remanded.

DISSENT: (Thomas, J.) Congress lacks the power to issue a subpoena for private documents, regardless of whether they belong to the President or anyone else because the scope of its implied powers is very limited. As a matter of history, at the time of the founding, such power was not included by necessary implication in any

Continued on next page.

of Congress's legislative powers, and there is no support in the Constitution for Congress to issue subpoenas for nonofficial documents. Congress argues that at the time of the founding, Congress had the same investigatory powers that the British Parliament had. However, Parliament was supreme, whereas Congress is not, and the protections of the Bill of Rights, such as the prohibition on unreasonable searches and seizures, constrain Congress's power to compel documents from private citizens. Also, as a matter of history, the colonial legislatures did not issue subpoenas for private, nonofficial documents. The first the time the Court considered such a subpoena, the Court declined to uphold it because it failed to see how such a subpoena was necessary for Congress to carry out its legislative duties and because the subpoena impermissibly sought to inquire into the private affairs of citizens. A half a century later, in 1927, in *McGrain v. Daugherty*, 273 U.S. 135 (1927), the Court ruled that Congress has the power to issue subpoenas for private documents, but only if they are relevant to a legislative power. That case was decided incorrectly, as it had no support in the Constitution's text or in historical practice. Following *McGrain*, the Court pared back Congress's authority to compel testimony and documents. Instead of trying to compensate for *McGrain*, as the majority does with its four-part test, the Court should discard it altogether as unsupported precedent.

DISSENT: (Alito, J.) Legislative subpoenas are inherently suspicious because they are rarely used for considering potential legislation, but can easily be used for improper non-legislative purposes. Accordingly, courts must be highly sensitive to separation of powers issues when asked to approve the enforcement of such subpoenas, especially when the subpoena is issued to a third party. In such instances, Congress must be required to provide more than a perfunctory explanation of its legislative need and how the requested documents will further the stated legislative goals. To that end, Congress should be required to specify the type of legislation being considered, its authority to enact such legislation, and why the subpoenaed information, rather than information available from other sources, is necessary. These are the types of questions the district court should be required to make on remand, and, absent a satisfactory showing by Congress regarding such questions, enforcement of the subpoenas should not be ordered.

ANALYSIS

The majority in this case affirmed Congress's broad power to investigate, and also affirmed that the scope of that power is coextensive with the scope of Congress's power to legislate. In *Watkins v. United States*, 354 U.S. 178 (1957), the Court held that Congress's power to investigate encompasses "inquiries concerning the administration of existing laws as well as proposed or possibly needed statutes" and "surveys of defects in our social, economic, or political system for the purpose of enabling the Congress to remedy them." The majority further affirmed that Congress's broad investigatory powers permit it to investigate the executive branch and even the President where such investigation is related to legitimate legislative purposes. In this case, for example, the House Oversight Committee asserted that it issued its subpoena after it received information that President Trump (P) might have failed to disclose certain financial holdings in his required federal disclosures, so that Congress had an interest in obtaining more information about his finances to guide its consideration about whether to strengthen financial disclosure laws and impose new restrictions on presidential conflicts of interest. Under the Court's precedents, such a purpose clearly serves a legitimate legislative interest.

Quicknotes

SEPARATION OF POWERS The system of checks and balances preventing one branch of government from infringing upon exercising the powers of another branch of government.

SUBPOENA A command issued by court to compel a witness to appear at trial.

Morrison v. Olson

Independent counsel (P) v. Government official (D)

487 U.S. 654 (1988)

NATURE OF CASE: Appeal from reversal of denial of motion to quash subpoenas.

FACT SUMMARY: Morrison (P) appealed from a decision reversing a district court decision upholding the constitutionality of the independent counsel provisions of the Ethics in Government Act and denying Olson's (D) motion to quash subpoenas, contending in part that those provisions were not violative of the Appointments Clause of the Constitution.

RULE OF LAW

The independent counsel provisions of the Ethics in Government Act are not violative of the Appointments Clause of the Constitution.

FACTS: Sections 591–599 of the Ethics in Government Act (the Act) allow for the appointment of an "independent counsel" to investigate and prosecute appropriate certain high-ranking government officials for violations of criminal laws. The Attorney General conducts an initial investigation, and only if the Attorney General applies to the Special Division, created by the Act, for appointment of independent counsel, is independent counsel appointed. The Special Division appoints independent counsel and defines his prosecutorial jurisdiction. Within this jurisdiction, the independent counsel is granted full power and independent authority to exercise all powers of the Department of Justice. The Attorney General and the Department of Justice are required to suspend all proceedings regarding matters within independent counsel's jurisdiction. Independent counsel's tenure is governed by two provisions. The first provision allows the Attorney General, on his own personal action, to remove independent counsel for good cause. Independent counsel can seek judicial review of this decision. The other provision allows termination of independent counsel's office when he informs the Attorney General he has substantially completed his investigations or prosecutions undertaken under the Act, or when the Special Division so determines. Finally, the Act provides for congressional oversight of independent counsel's activities. In 1984, the House Judiciary Committee began an investigation into the Justice Department's role in an EPA document production controversy. The chairman requested that the Attorney General seek the appointment of an independent counsel to investigate the role of Olson (D), Schmults (D), and Dinkins (D). The Attorney General applied for appointment of independent counsel with respect to Olson (D) only. McKay (D) was appointed independent counsel, and Morrison (D) succeeded him. After unsuccessfully attempting to have the Committee's allegations against Schmults (D) and Dinkins (D) reviewed, Morrison (D) subpoenaed them and Olson (D) pursuant to the Olson (D) investigation. All three moved to quash the subpoenas, claiming the independent counsel provisions were unconstitutional, and that therefore Morrison (D) had no authority to proceed. The district court disagreed and denied the motions to quash. The court of appeals reversed, and from that decision, Morrison (P) appealed, contending in part that the independent counsel provisions of the Act were not violative of the Appointments Clause of the Constitution.

ISSUE: Are the independent counsel provisions of the Ethics in Government Act violative of the Appointments Clause of the Constitution?

HOLDING AND DECISION: (Rehnquist, C.J.) No. The independent counsel provisions of the Ethics in Government Act are not violative of the Appointments Clause of the Constitution. Since Morrison (P) is subject to removal by a higher executive branch official, and since her office is restricted in jurisdiction, tenure, and authorized duties, it is clear she is an inferior officer, and not a principal officer as the court of appeals concluded. Secondly, the Appointments Clause does not on its face provide for any limitation on interbranch appointments; rather, it seems to grant Congress considerable discretion as to where to vest the power to appoint inferior officials. While congressional power to provide for interbranch appointments is not unlimited, it is not impermissible in this case for Congress to vest the power to appoint independent counsel in a specially created federal court (the Special Division). There is no actual incongruity in a court appointing prosecutorial officers where, as here, Special Division officers cannot participate in any matters handled by the appointed independent counsel. (The Court went on to conclude that these provisions did not violate Article III of the Constitution dealing with the separation of powers.) Reversed.

DISSENT: (Scalia, J.) The separation of powers principle vests all the "executive power" in the President. Even though the independent counsel exercises executive powers, and the statute deprives the President of the exclusive exercise of that power, the Court avoids the inevitable conclusion that the independent counsel provisions are unconstitutional.

Continued on next page.

ANALYSIS

Other cases have upheld the federal court's power to appoint private attorneys to prosecute contempt of court orders, justifying the decision in part on the need for the Judiciary to have the power to independently vindicate its own authority. Justice Scalia, the author of the dissent, concurred in this judgment. See *Young v. United States ex rel. Vuitton et Fils S.A.*, 107 S. Ct. 2124 (1987).

Quicknotes

APPOINTMENTS CLAUSE Article II, § 2, cl. 2 of the United States Constitution conferring power upon the President to appoint ambassadors, public ministers and consuls, judges of the United States Supreme Court, and all other officers of the United States with the advice and consent of the Senate.

ETHICS IN GOVERNMENT ACT Allows for the appointment of special independent counsel to investigate high-ranking government officials.

INFERIOR OFFICERS Members of the executive branch having less power or authority in relation to others.

SEPARATION OF POWERS The system of checks and balances preventing one branch of government from infringing upon exercising the powers of another branch of government.

Edmond v. United States

Citizen (P) v. Government (D)

520 U.S. 651 (1997)

NATURE OF CASE: Review of selection of military appellate judges.

FACT SUMMARY: Edmond (P) challenged the appointment of civilian members of the Coast Guard Court of Criminal Appeals.

RULE OF LAW

Congress may vest appointment of inferior officers in the President alone, in the courts, or in the heads of departments.

FACTS: Judges of the Court of Criminal Appeals were appointed by the Secretary of Transportation pursuant to 49 U.S.C. § 323(a). Edmond (P) challenged the appointments as unconstitutional. The United States Supreme Court granted certiorari.

ISSUE: May Congress vest appointment of inferior officers in the President alone, in the courts, or in the heads of departments?

HOLDING AND DECISION: (Scalia, J.) Yes. Congress may vest appointment of inferior officers in the President alone, in the courts, or in the heads of departments. The Appointments Clause of the Constitution includes civilian military appellate judges since they are "inferior Officers" within the meaning of that provision. The Appointments Clause of Article II of the Constitution vests the President with the exclusive power to select the principal (noninferior) officers of the United States with the advice and consent of the Senate. Inferior officers are officers whose work is directed and supervised by others who were appointed by presidential nomination. The Secretary of Transportation is authorized by Congress to appoint judges of the Coast Guard Court of Criminal Appeals. The judicial appointments were therefore valid. Affirmed.

CONCURRENCE: (Souter, J.) Having a superior officer is necessary for inferior officer status, but not sufficient to establish it. The duties, jurisdiction, and tenure associated with the office must also be examined before concluding an officer is an inferior, rather than a principal, officer.

ANALYSIS

The President has the power to appoint judges with the approval of the Senate. Presidential appointments are subject to Senate confirmation. In this action, it was found that the judges of the Coast Guard Court of Criminal Appeals were supervised by the General Counsel of the Department of Transportation in his capacity as Judge Advocate General.

Quicknotes

APPOINTMENTS CLAUSE Article II, § 2, cl. 2 of the United States Constitution conferring power upon the President to appoint ambassadors, public ministers and consuls, judges of the United States Supreme Court, and all other officers of the United States with the advice and consent of the Senate.

INFERIOR OFFICERS Members of the executive branch having less power or authority in relation to others.

United States v. Arthrex, Inc.

Federal government (P) v. Patent holder (D)

141 S. Ct. 1970 (2021)

NATURE OF CASE: Appeal in action challenging the review structure of the Patent Trial and Appeal Board as unconstitutional under the Appointments Clause. [The procedural posture of the case is not presented in the casebook excerpt.]

FACT SUMMARY: Arthrex, Inc. (D), a patent holder, contended that permitting administrative patent judges (APJs), who were appointed as inferior officers to the Patent Trial and Appeal Board (PTAB), to render final decisions without further review in inter partes review proceedings, violated the Appointments Clause.

RULE OF LAW

(1) The unreviewable authority held by administrative patent judges (APJs) during inter partes review proceedings of the Patent Trial and Appeal Board (PTAB) is incompatible, under the Appointments Clause, with their appointment by the Secretary of Commerce to an inferior office.

(2) For a system of review in the Patent and Trademark Office (PTO) to be constitutional under the Appointments Clause, the PTO director must be statutorily authorized to review final Patent Trial and Appeal Board (PTAB) decisions rendered by administrative patent judges (APJs) and, upon review, issue decisions on behalf of the PTAB.

FACTS: Administrative patent judges (APJs) conduct adversarial proceedings for challenging the validity of an existing patent before the Patent Trial and Appeal Board (PTAB). Such proceedings are known as "inter partes review." During such proceedings, the PTAB sits in panels of at least three of its members, who are predominantly APJs. The Secretary of Commerce appoints the APJs. Congress provided that APJs would be appointed as inferior officers. The PTAB is part of the Patent and Trademark Office (PTO), which is headed by a director appointed by the President with the advice and consent of the Senate. The director fixes the rate of pay for APJs, controls the decision whether to institute inter partes review, and selects the APJs to reconsider the validity of the patent. The director also promulgates regulations governing inter partes review, issues prospective guidance on patentability issues, and designates past PTAB decisions as "precedential" for future panels. The director is thus "the boss," except when it comes to reviewing APJ decisions. The PTAB's panels have the final say as to the validity of a challenged patent, and billions of dollars can turn on a single PTAB decision. When a patent held by Arthrex, Inc. (D) was held invalid by the PTAB as part of inter partes review filed by Arthrex's (D) competitor, Smith & Nephew, Inc. (P), Arthrex (D) challenged the constitutionality under the Appointments Clause of permitting APJs to bind the executive branch with no further review, arguing that, based on APJs' responsibilities and lack of review of their decisions, APJs were, in fact, principal officers who had to be appointed by the President with the Senate's advice and consent. The Appointments Clause provides that only the President, with the advice and consent of the Senate, can appoint principal officers. With respect to inferior officers, the Clause permits Congress to vest appointment power in the President alone, in the courts, or in department heads. The United States Supreme Court granted certiorari. [The procedural posture of the case is not presented in the casebook excerpt.]

ISSUE:

(1) Is the unreviewable authority held by administrative patent judges (APJs) during inter partes review proceedings of the Patent Trial and Appeal Board (PTAB) incompatible, under the Appointments Clause, with their appointment by the Secretary of Commerce to an inferior office?

(2) For a system of review in the Patent and Trademark Office (PTO) to be constitutional under the Appointments Clause, must the PTO director be statutorily authorized to review final Patent Trial and Appeal Board (PTAB) decisions rendered by administrative patent judges (APJs) and, upon review, issue decisions on behalf of the PTAB?

HOLDING AND DECISION: (Roberts, C.J.)

(1) Yes. The unreviewable authority held by administrative patent judges (APJs) during inter partes review proceedings of the Patent Trial and Appeal Board (PTAB) is incompatible, under the Appointments Clause, with their appointment by the Secretary of Commerce to an inferior office. To determine whether the nature of the APJs' responsibilities is inconsistent with their method of appointment, the Court looks to *Edmond v. United States,* 520 U.S. 651 (1997), where the Court held that whether one is an inferior officer depends on whether one has a superior other than the President. In other words, an inferior officer must be directed and supervised

Continued on next page.

at some level by others who were appointed by presidential nomination with the advice and consent of the Senate. Although the PTO director possesses powers of administrative oversight, the director lacks statutory authority to review the APJs' decisions. Thus, there is no principal officer at any level within the executive branch who directs and supervises the APJs' most important power—to render decisions as to patentability. This "diffusion of power carries with it a diffusion of accountability." The United States (P) and Smith & Nephew (P) contend that the director has various ways to indirectly influence the course of inter partes review. The director, for example, could designate APJs predisposed to decide a case in the director's preferred manner, or stack a rehearing panel, but such machinations are not the solution; they reflect the problem. To force such maneuvering blurs the lines of accountability demanded by the Appointments Clause and leave the parties with neither an impartial decision by a panel of experts nor a transparent decision for which a politically accountable officer must take responsibility. Given the insulation of PTAB decisions from any executive review, the President can neither oversee the PTAB directly nor attribute the PTAB's failings to those whom the President can oversee. APJs accordingly exercise power that conflicts with the design of the Appointments Clause to preserve political accountability. Accordingly, the statutory review system currently in place is unconstitutional.

(2) Yes. For a system of review in the Patent and Trademark Office (PTO) to be constitutional under the Appointments Clause, the PTO director must be statutorily authorized to review final Patent Trial and Appeal Board (PTAB) decisions rendered by administrative patent judges (APJs) and, upon review, issue decisions on behalf of the PTAB. The appropriate remedy in this case is to remand to the director for the director to decide whether to rehear the petition filed by Smith & Nephew (P). A limited remand provides an adequate opportunity for review by a principal officer. Because the source of the constitutional violation is the restraint on the review authority of the director, rather than the appointment of APJs by the Secretary, Arthrex (D) is not entitled to a hearing before a new panel of APJs.

CONCURRENCE AND DISSENT: (Gorsuch, J.) The plurality is correct that the statutory review system is unconstitutional. However, it errs as to the appropriate remedy. It is not the Court's place to repair the unconstitutional statutory review system. The majority should not speculate as to what Congress might have done or would do. Such raw speculation is beyond a court's authority. Instead, the Court should have limited itself to identifying the constitutional violation, explain its reasoning, and set aside the PTAB decision in the case at bar.

CONCURRENCE AND DISSENT: (Breyer, J.) The plurality's remedy is sensible, but the plurality errs in holding that the statutory review system is unconstitutional. Instead, the Court should interpret the Appointments Clause as granting Congress a degree of leeway to establish and empower federal offices. Neither that Clause nor anything else in the Constitution describes the degree of control that a superior officer must exercise over the decisions of an inferior officer. To the contrary, the Constitution says only that "Congress may by Law vest the Appointment of such inferior Officers, as they think proper, . . . in the Heads of Departments." Art. II, § 2, cl. 2. The words "by Law . . . as they think proper" strongly suggest that Congress has considerable freedom to determine the nature of an inferior officer's job, and that courts ought to respect that judgment. The Court's precedents merely require that an inferior officer be "supervised" not "controlled." Congress had good reason for not wanting the director to directly rehear and decide individual cases; it wanted independent PTAB determinations in such cases. The Court should have conducted a functional examination of the offices and duties in question, rather than a formalistic, judicial-rules-based approach, that accounted for why Congress enacted the statutory limitations involved and that considered the practical consequences of Congress's chosen scheme. Viewed through such a functional approach, Congress's scheme is constitutionally justified. Given the technical nature of patents, the need for expertise, and the importance of avoiding political interference, Congress chose to grant the APJs a degree of independence and to restrict the director's authority. Also, there is no reason to believe this scheme will prevent the director from exercising policy control over the APJs or will break the chain of accountability that is needed to hold the President responsible for bad nominations. The nature of the PTAB calls for technically correct adjudicatory decisions, which in turn calls for greater, not less, independence from those potentially influenced by political factors. The Court's decision unfortunately prevents Congress from establishing a patent review scheme consistent with those legislative objectives. Going beyond the patent arena, the Court should adopt a functional approach to its jurisprudence. First, the executive branch has many constituent bodies, and appreciating the great variety in their administration is especially important in the context of administrative adjudication, which typically demands decisionmaking that is free of political influence. The President and Congress should not be denied the ability to create independent adjudicators through judicial insistence upon certain mechanisms for removal or review. Second, the Constitution is a document of broad strokes, and for good reason: the nation's desires and needs change, sometimes over long

Continued on next page.

periods of time. The Founders intended the Constitution to be flexible enough to respond to such changes, while protecting certain core principles—a principle that prevents Congress from affording inferior-level adjudicators some decisionmaking independence was not among them. Finally, the executive branch and Congress are more likely than are judges to understand how to implement the tasks that Congress has written into legislation. That understanding encompasses the nature of different mechanisms of bureaucratic control that may apply to the many thousands of administrators who will carry out those tasks. It also includes an awareness of the reasonable limits that can be placed on supervisors to ensure that those working under them enjoy a degree of freedom sufficient to carry out their responsibilities. Unelected judges, as a group, have little, if any, experience related to this kind of a problem. Although that does not mean that Congress has free rein, in this area of the law a functional approach is more likely to prevent inappropriate judicial interference.

DISSENT: (Thomas, J.) There cannot be serious dispute that APJs in fact are inferior officers under the Constitution. They are lower in rank by two levels to the director and to the Secretary. Further, the director already has the ability to influence individual proceedings, by deciding in the first instance whether to institute review, and then, if review is instituted, by either selecting the APJs that will hear the review, or, in the alternative, designating himself or herself and other higher-ups in the PTO hierarchy to review the case. In addition, the director decides which of the thousands of decisions issued each year bind other panels as precedent, and no statute bars the director from taking an active role to ensure the PTAB's decisions conform to his or her policy direction. Moreover, if the administrative patent judges reach a result the director does not like, the director can add more members to the panel—including himself or herself—and order the case reheard. The plurality boils down "inferior-officer" status to the way Congress structured a particular agency's process for reviewing decisions, but there is no precedent for such an approach. In doing so, the Court seems to be creating a new form of intrabranch separation of powers law. Because the plurality indicates that the appointment of the APJs by the Secretary of Commerce is not the constitutional problem, then that means APJs must be inferior officers under the Constitution—and that should be enough to resolve the issue. Instead, the Court's new Appointments Clause doctrine looks at the dispersion of executive power among officers, and that approach is doubly flawed because the Constitution nowhere mentions, or distinguishes between, "inferior-officer power" or "principal-officer power." Also, history shows that under early patent review schemes, nonprincipal officers could and did render final decisions in patent appeals. A bigger problem is that interpreting the Appointments Clause to bar any nonprincipal officer from taking "final" action poses serious line-drawing problems that could lead to courts having to sort through lists of each officer's duties and categorize each one as principal or inferior. Although it does not do so directly, the plurality seems to suggest that the real issue is that the scheme at issue violates the Vesting Clause because the PTAB's review process inverts the executive "chain of command" by allowing APJs to wield "unchecked" executive power and to dictate what the director must do. However, even if the chain of command were broken, Senate confirmation of APJs would not be a constitutionally workable remedy, since the Senate's role in appointments is an exception to the vesting of executive power in the President; the solution cannot be to strip more power away from the President. In any event, historical practice establishes that the vesting of executive power in the President did not require that every patent decision be appealable to a principal officer.

ANALYSIS

Justice Gorsuch emphasizes that the remedy chosen by the plurality—to strip away statutory constraints from the director's review powers—is at odds with Congress's intent. Justice Gorsuch points out that the plurality believes that Congress would have wanted to render PTAB decisions reviewable by the director, since that regime is consistent with the "standard federal model" for agency adjudication. However, as he observes, it is clear that Congress rejected this familiar approach when it came to PTAB proceedings, apparently to ensure that APJs enjoy independence from superior executive officers and, therefore, are more impartial. In fact, the Court in prior cases noted that there was a possibility that permitting politically motivated executive officials to "cancel" patents might raise due process concerns, especially since for two centuries only courts could do so. Accordingly, Justice Gorsuch bemoans that allowing executive officials to assume an historic judicial function was always destined to invite familiar due process problems—like decisions favoring those with political clout, the powerful and the popular, given that those with power can amass armies of lobbyists and lawyers to influence (and even capture) politically accountable bureaucracies. To illustrate his point, Justice Gorsuch relates the tale of a "supposedly" independent APJ, who had formerly been a patent attorney at one of the world's largest technology companies and left the company to become an APJ. He then presided over dozens of inter partes reviews (IPRs) brought by his former company, in which the company prevailed in its efforts to cancel patents damaging to its private economic interests 96% of the time, and after six years

Continued on next page.

of work, he resigned his position of APJ and returned to the technology company. "Without a hint of irony, that company has filed an *amicus* brief in this case to inform us, as a self-described 'frequent user of the IPR process,' about 'the benefits of the system.'" Accordingly, Justice Gorsuch is grateful that at least the Court's decision avoided "investing the power to revoke an individual's property rights in some unaccountable fourth branch controlled by powerful companies seeking a competitive advantage."

Quicknotes

***AMICUS* BRIEF** A brief submitted by a third party, not a party to the action, that contains information for the court's consideration in conformity with its position.

APPOINTMENTS CLAUSE Article II, section 2, clause 2 of the United States Constitution conferring power upon the President to appoint ambassadors, public ministers and consuls, judges of the Supreme Court, and all other officers of the United States with the advice and consent of the Senate.

INTER PARTES Between the parties. May refer to contracts, conveyances, or other transactions having legal significance.

Seila Law LLC v. Consumer Financial Protection Bureau

Subject of agency investigation (D) v. Agency (P)

140 S. Ct. 2183 (2020)

NATURE OF CASE: Appeal in action challenging the structure of an independent agency as violating the Constitution's separation of powers. [The procedural posture of the case is not presented in the casebook excerpt.]

FACT SUMMARY: Seila Law LLC (D) contended that the structure of the Consumer Financial Protection Bureau (P), an independent agency headed by a single Director appointed by the President and removable from office only for "inefficiency, neglect of duty, or malfeasance in office," violated the Constitution's separation of powers.

RULE OF LAW

(1) An independent agency's structure violates the Constitution's separation of powers where the agency is vested with significant executive power and is led by a single individual removable from office only for inefficiency, neglect, or malfeasance in office.

(2) Where Congress has violated the Constitution's separation of powers by creating an independent agency that is headed by a single individual leader who can be removed only for inefficiency, neglect, or malfeasance in office, the appropriate remedy is to sever those provisions of the act creating the agency that prevent the President from removing the agency head at will.

FACTS: In response to the Great Recession financial crisis, Congress in the Dodd-Frank Act (the Act) created the Consumer Financial Protection Bureau (CFPB) (P) as an independent financial regulatory agency within the Federal Reserve System tasked with ensuring that consumer debt products are fair, safe, competitive, and transparent. Congress gave the CFPB (P) extensive rulemaking, enforcement, and adjudicatory powers, including the authority to conduct investigations, issue subpoenas and civil investigative demands, initiate administrative adjudications, prosecute civil actions in federal court, and issue binding decisions in administrative proceedings. The CFPB (P) may seek restitution, disgorgement, injunctive relief, and significant civil penalties for violations of the 19 federal statutes under its purview. Unlike traditional independent agencies headed by multimember boards or commissions, the CFPB (P) is led by a single Director who is appointed by the President with the advice and consent of the Senate for a five-year term, during which the President may remove the Director only for "inefficiency, neglect of duty, or malfeasance in office." Seila Law LLC (D), which was being investigated by the CFPB (P), refused to comply with an investigation order to produce documents issued by the CFPB (P), contending that the CFPB's (P) structure violated the Constitution's separation of powers. The United States Supreme Court granted certiorari in the case. [The procedural posture of the case is not presented in the casebook excerpt.]

ISSUE:

(1) Does an independent agency's structure violate the Constitution's separation of powers where the agency is vested with significant executive power and is led by a single individual removable from office only for inefficiency, neglect, or malfeasance in office?

(2) Where Congress has violated the Constitution's separation of powers by creating an independent agency that is headed by a single individual leader who can be removed only for inefficiency, neglect, or malfeasance in office, is the appropriate remedy to sever those provisions of the act creating the agency that prevent the President from removing the agency head at will?

HOLDING AND DECISION: (Roberts, C.J.)

(1) Yes. An independent agency's structure violates the Constitution's separation of powers where the agency is vested with significant executive power and is led by a single individual removable from office only for inefficiency, neglect, or malfeasance in office. Article II vests the entire executive power in the President alone, but the Constitution presumes that lesser executive officers will assist the President in discharging executive duties. The President's executive power generally includes the power to supervise—and, if necessary, remove—those who exercise the President's authority on the President's behalf. The President's removal power has long been confirmed by history and precedent. It was recognized by the First Congress in 1789, confirmed by the Court in *Myers v. United States,* 272 U.S. 52 (1926), and reiterated in *Free Enterprise Fund v. Public Company Accounting Oversight Bd.,* 561 U.S. 477 (2010), in which the Court left in place only two exceptions to the President's unrestricted removal power. First, *Humphrey's Executor v. United States* 295 U.S. 602 (1935), permitted Congress to give for-cause removal protection to the Commissioners of the Federal Trade Commission (FTC), a multimember body of experts who were balanced along

Continued on next page.

partisan lines, appointed to staggered terms, performed only "quasi-legislative" and "quasi-judicial functions," and were said not to exercise any executive power. Second, *Morrison v. Olson*, 487 U.S. 654 (1988), approved good-cause tenure protection for an inferior officer—the independent counsel—who had limited duties and no policymaking or administrative authority. Neither *Humphrey's Executor* nor *Morrison* resolves whether the CFPB (P) Director's insulation from removal is constitutional. The New Deal-era FTC upheld in *Humphrey's Executor* bears little resemblance to the Consumer Financial Protection Bureau (CFPB) (P). Unlike the multiple Commissioners of the FTC, who were balanced along partisan lines and served staggered terms to ensure the accumulation of institutional knowledge, the CFPB (P) Director serves a five-year term that guarantees abrupt shifts in leadership and the loss of agency expertise. In addition, the Director cannot be dismissed as a mere legislative or judicial aid. Rather, the Director possesses significant administrative and enforcement authority, including the power to seek daunting monetary penalties against private parties in federal court—a quintessentially executive power not considered in *Humphrey's Executor.* The logic of *Morrison* also does not apply. The independent counsel approved in *Morrison* was an inferior officer who lacked policymaking or administrative authority and exercised narrow authority to initiate criminal investigations and prosecutions of governmental actors identified by others. By contrast, the CFPB (P) Director is a principal officer whose duties are far from limited. The Director promulgates binding rules fleshing out 19 consumer-protection statutes that cover everything from credit cards and car payments to mortgages and student loans. Moreover, the Director brings the coercive power of the state to bear on millions of private citizens and businesses, imposing potentially billion-dollar penalties through administrative adjudications and civil actions. The question, therefore, is whether to extend the *Humphrey's Executor* and *Morrison* exceptions to a "new situation." Because the CFPB's (P) structure has no foothold in history or tradition, and is incompatible with the Constitution's power structure, the Court declines to extend those precedents to the CFPB (P). First, an agency with a structure like that of the CFPB (P) is almost wholly unprecedented. Congress has provided removal protection to principal officers who alone wield power in only four isolated instances: the Comptroller of the Currency (for a one-year period during the Civil War), the Office of Special Counsel, the Administrator of the Social Security Administration (SSA), and the Director of the Federal Housing Finance Agency (FHFA). Aside from the one-year blip for the Comptroller of the Currency, these examples are modern and contested; and they do not involve regulatory or enforcement authority comparable to that exercised by the CFPB (P). As compared to these other agencies, the CFPB (P) is in an entirely different league. It acts as a mini legislature, prosecutor, and court, responsible for creating substantive rules for a wide swath of industries, prosecuting violations, and levying weighty penalties against private citizens, not to mention that it is the only agency of its kind run by a single Director. Second, the CFPB's (P) single-Director configuration is also incompatible with the structure of the Constitution, which—with the sole exception of the presidency—scrupulously avoids concentrating power in the hands of any single individual. The Framers' constitutional strategy is straightforward: divide power everywhere except for the presidency, and render the President directly accountable to the people through regular elections. In that scheme, individual executive officials may wield significant authority, but that authority remains subject to the ongoing supervision and control of the elected President. The CFPB's (P) single-Director structure contravenes this carefully calibrated system by vesting significant governmental power in the hands of a single individual who is neither elected by the people nor meaningfully controlled (through the threat of removal) by someone who is. The Director may unilaterally, without meaningful supervision, issue final regulations, oversee adjudications, set enforcement priorities, initiate prosecutions, and determine what penalties to impose on private parties. Additionally, the Director may do so without even having to rely on Congress for appropriations. Although the CFPB's (P) independent, single-Director structure is sufficient to render the agency unconstitutional, the Director's five-year term and receipt of funds outside the appropriations process heighten the concern that the agency will "slip from the executive's control, and thus from that of the people." *Amicus* raises several arguments in the agency's defense. First, *amicus* challenges the textual basis for the President's removal power and highlights statements from individual Framers expressing divergent views on the subject. Although it is true that there is no "removal clause" in the Constitution, neither is there a "separation of powers clause" or a "federalism clause." These foundational doctrines are instead evident from the Constitution's vesting of certain powers in certain bodies. In similar fashion, the Court's precedents make clear that the President's removal power derives from the "executive Power" vested exclusively in the President by Article II. Second, *amicus* claims that *Humphrey's Executor* and *Morrison* establish a general rule that Congress may freely constrain the

Continued on next page.

President's removal power, but the Constitution's text, core constitutional principles, the First Congress's decision in 1789, *Myers*, and *Free Enterprise Fund* all establish that the President's removal power is the rule, not the exception. Finally, *amicus* submits that the Court can cure any constitutional defect in the CFPB's (P) structure by interpreting the language "inefficiency, neglect of duty, or malfeasance in office," to reserve substantial discretion to the President. However, it is clear that with the CFPB (P) Congress intended to impose meaningful restrictions on the President's removal authority, and the Court cannot rewrite the statute Congress promulgated. For these reasons, the CFPB's (P) leadership by a single independent Director violates the separation of powers.

(2) Yes. Where Congress has violated the Constitution's separation of powers by creating an independent agency that is headed by a single individual leader who can be removed only for inefficiency, neglect, or malfeasance in office, the appropriate remedy is to sever those provisions of the act creating the agency that prevent the President from removing the agency head at will. The only constitutional defect in the CFPB's (P) structure is the Director's insulation from removal. If the director were removable at will by the President, the constitutional violation would disappear. The Dodd-Frank Act (the Act) contains a severability clause, and severing from the Act the provisions that insulate the Director from removal will not affect the remaining provisions relating to the CFPB's (P) structure and duties, which will remain fully operative. Additionally, there is no indication in the legislative history or the Act's text that Congress would have preferred no CFPB (P) to one where the President can remove the Director at will. Therefore, the appropriate remedy is to sever and remove the Director tenure restrictions from the Act.

CONCURRENCE AND DISSENT: (Thomas, J.) Given that *Humphrey's Executor* is erroneous, it should be repudiated completely. Nonetheless, the Court correctly decides the removability issue in this case. *Humphrey's Executor's* tolerance for independent agencies, which are a de facto fourth branch of government with no accountability to the President or to the people, threatens the constitutional order and the peoples' liberty. Those agencies increasingly encroach on the executive's power, contrary to constitutional design. If *Humphrey's Executor* had not created the notions of "quasi-legislative" and "quasi-judicial" power, which are nowhere to be found in the Constitution, Congress would not have been able to constitutionally create agencies that straddle multiple branches of government and that violate the discrete classifications set forth in the Constitution. The existence of independent agencies, which are unconstitutional, subverts political accountability and the liberty that comes with it. Although the Court correctly resolved the merits of the question before it, the Court did not need to resort to severability to decide this case. The Court should have simply denied the CFPB's (P) petition to enforce its investigative demand.

CONCURRENCE AND DISSENT: (Kagan, J.) Until now, the Court has left most decisions about how to structure administrative agencies to the legislative and executive branches and has on numerous occasions upheld removal restrictions identical to those it now invalidates. The Court also should have left intact the CFPB's (P) structure, and the Director removal restrictions, as a matter of historical practice and the Constitution's text. The Constitution grants to Congress the authority to organize all the institutions of American governance, provided only that those arrangements allow the President to perform the duties the Constitution assigns to the President, and, throughout the nation's history, Congress has created spheres of administration detached from direct presidential control, confident it could do so under the Constitution. The Court's differentiation of the CFPB (P) structure from the structure of agencies that the Court previously approved rests on flawed premises and distinctions. The Court's distinction between multimember bodies and single directors does not at all respond to the constitutional values at stake. The issue should have been framed exclusively as whether the agency's structure so deprives the President of control over an official that it impedes the President's functions, and, regardless of whether there is for-cause removal provision, the President has at least as much control over an individual as over a commission, and possibly more. The Court's decision not only rewrites the Constitution and repudiates centuries of experience, it also condemns the nation to a static version of governance that is incapable of responding to new conditions and challenges in times and situations when independence from political pressure is needed. The Constitution does not expressly mention separation of powers or the President's removal authority, and the Founders intended separation of powers to be flexible, not rigid as the majority seems to believe. The branches of government are interconnected, and must be, for government to work. The Constitution reflects that vision of adaptability and flexibility by giving Congress broad authority to establish and organize the executive branch. Article II presumes the existence of "Officer[s]" in "executive Departments." § 2, cl. 1. However, contrary to the majority's insinuation, it does not give the President authority to decide what kinds of officers—in what departments, with what responsibilities—the executive branch requires. Instead, Article I's Necessary and Proper Clause puts those decisions in Congress's hands. Similarly, the Appointments Clause reflects Congress's central role

Continued on next page.

in structuring the executive branch. To construct the executive branch, the President must work his will through the legislative process. The majority rests its decision on the Vesting Clause, which says only that "[t]he executive Power shall be vested in a President." However, the general and open-ended language of the Vesting Clause cannot establish a constitutional violation when Congress has constrained the way the executive power is implemented, since that is exactly the power the Necessary and Proper Clause gives to Congress. Only "a specific historical understanding" can bar Congress from enacting a given constraint, and there is no such historical understanding that broadly prevents Congress from limiting the President's removal power. The Take Care Clause also does not support the majority's position, since that Clause, which says "he shall take Care that the Laws be faithfully executed," addresses duty, not power. The majority's position fares no better when viewed through an accurate historical perspective. The Founders were deeply divided about the President's removal power, and eventually settled on wide latitude for Congress to create spheres of administrative independence. The First Congress gave officials handling financial affairs—as compared to diplomatic and military ones—some independence from the President. Thus, even as the founding era closed without any agreement that Congress lacked the power to curb the President's removal authority, Congress took the first steps of distinguishing between certain kinds of regulators and officials, and these first steps evolved into a tradition. As Congress began addressing the new nation's finances, it started to use its powers under the Necessary and Proper Clause to design effective administrative institutions, and it took steps to insulate certain officers from political influence. This pattern was repeated over decades and centuries to provide pockets of independence with the federal bureaucracy so the nation could address new economic, technological, and social conditions. The Second Bank of the United States, created in 1816, was the nation's first truly independent agency and wielded enormous financial power mostly outside the President's control. More such agencies followed. In 1887, for example, the growing power of the railroads over the American economy led Congress to create the Interstate Commerce Commission. Under that legislation, the President could remove the five Commissioners only "for inefficiency, neglect of duty, or malfeasance in office"—the same standard Congress applied to the CFPB (P) Director. Many more independent agencies followed as administrative needs became greater and more complex; they now are "everywhere." Until now, however, the Court accepted the role of independent agencies in government and repeatedly upheld provisions that prevent the President from firing regulatory officials except for such matters as neglect or malfeasance. Nowhere do the Court's precedents suggest what the majority announces in its decision: that the President has an "unrestricted removal power" subject to two bounded exceptions. Instead, the majority relies on *Myers*, ignoring the way the Court subsequently cabined that decision and limited it to its specific facts. The majority says *Myers* found an unrestrained removal power "essential to the [President's] execution of the laws." but the majority fails to acknowledge that within a decade the Court unanimously abandoned that view in *Humphrey's Executor*. What *Myers* decided as a matter of stare decisis is that the President could remove a postmaster of the first class without the advice and consent of the Senate, and that Congress cannot reserve to itself the power to remove executive officers. What *Humphrey's* decided was that a statute identical to the one here, providing that the President could remove FTC Commissioners for "inefficiency, neglect of duty, or malfeasance in office," was constitutional. That decision did not turn on the agency's organizational structure, but rather on the type of work the commissioner performed. Although the majority is correct that the contemporary understanding is that all activities of administrative agencies comprise executive power, what the majority fails to account for is that those activities may take "legislative" and "judicial" forms. Recently, the Court held a removal provision invalid, but did so within this framework. It said that it did not take issue with for-cause limitations in general, but instead held that two layers of insulation from the President were unconstitutional. The Court's remedy was merely to strike one level of insulation, leaving in place the first level whereby the President could remove agency officials for malfeasance or neglect, but not for policy disagreements. For almost a century, the Court has made clear that Congress has broad discretion to enact for-cause protections in pursuit of good governance, and this deferential approach has given Congress the flexibility it needs to craft administrative agencies. Sometimes presidential engagement and a high degree of control is needed, whereas at other times, insulation from political pressure helps ensure impartial adjudications and leaves technical issues in the hands of those most capable of addressing them. Such flexibility promotes continuity and prevents short-term electoral interests from distorting policy. Precisely because the right balance between these levels of presidential control and independence is often uncertain, contested, and value-laden, striking that balance should be left up to the political branches, not the judiciary. At the time the CFPB (P) was created—out of a financial crisis that wiped out over $10 trillion in American household wealth, and cost millions of Americans their jobs, their retirements and homes—there was no doubt the CFPB (P) should be independent, and that the CFPB (P) Director could not be removed for policy differences. The CFPB (P) Director exercises the same powers, and receives the same removal protections, as the heads of other,

Continued on next page.

constitutionally permissible independent agencies. Why, then, is the majority treating this case differently? The majority says it is because the CFPB (P) Director is singular, not plural. However, there is no precedential support for this position. There is no support for the proposition that the number of people at the apex of an agency matters to the constitutional issue. Neither is there support for the position that novelty is a constitutional test for structuring agencies. In deciding what this moment demanded, Congress had no obligation to make a carbon copy of a design from a bygone era. If, as the majority says, the problem is that an official has slipped away from presidential control and supervision, its distinction between singular and plural cuts in favor of a single agency head, because it is more difficult to control, and to hold accountable, multiple heads of an agency or commission. In short, the majority gets the matter backward. There is no separation of powers problem in the CFPB's (P) structure. The majority is effectively legislating, since nothing in the Constitution or historical practice requires the outcome it mandates. The Court in this instance has no business in overriding Congress, acting with the President's approval, in creating an agency based on a far greater understanding of political control mechanisms and agency design than any Court Justice has. In deciding for itself what is "proper," the Court goes beyond its own proper bounds.

ANALYSIS

Following the Court's decision in this case, the Court in *Collins v. Yellen,* 141 S. Ct. 1761 (2021), invalidated as an unconstitutional violation of separation of powers the structure of the Federal Housing Finance Agency (FHFA), "an independent agency" tasked with regulating Fannie Mae and Freddie Mac, two of the nation's leading sources of mortgage financing. The FHFA, like the CFPB (P), was created in response to the financial crisis known as the Great Recession, and, as with the CFPB (P), was an agency led by a single Director, and the President's power to remove the FHFA head was restricted. The Court relied on its decision in *Seila Law,* saying that a straightforward application of *Seila Law*'s reasoning dictated the result. The Court rejected distinctions drawn between the FHFA and the CFPB (P) as insufficient to justify a different result. The Court rejected the argument that Congress should have greater leeway to restrict the President's power to remove the FHFA Director because the FHFA's authority is more limited than that of the CFPB (P), saying that the nature and breadth of an agency's authority is not dispositive in determining whether Congress may limit the President's power to remove its head. The Court also rejected this distinction on the grounds that Courts are not well-suited to weigh the relative importance of the regulatory and enforcement authority of disparate agencies. The Court likewise rejected the assertion that the FHFA's structure did not violate the separation of powers because the entities it regulated were government-sponsored enterprises that had federal charters, served public objectives, and received special privileges. This argument failed, the Court said, because the President's removal power serves important purposes regardless of whether the agency in question affects ordinary Americans by directly regulating them or by taking actions that have a profound but indirect effect on their lives. Finally, the Court rejected the contention that there was no constitutional problem because the FHFA's head was given only "modest" tenure protection, saying that the Constitution prohibits even "modest restrictions" on the President's power to remove the head of an agency with a single top officer.

Quicknotes

APPOINTMENTS CLAUSE Article II, Section 2, clause 2 of the United States Constitution conferring power upon the President to appoint ambassadors, public ministers and consuls, judges of the Supreme Court, and all other officers of the United States with the advice and consent of the Senate.

NECESSARY AND PROPER CLAUSE Article I, § 8 of the Constitution; it enables Congress to make all laws that may be "necessary and proper" to execute its other, enumerated powers.

SEPARATION OF POWERS The system of checks and balances preventing one branch of government from infringing upon exercising the powers of another branch of government.

STARE DECISIS Doctrine whereby courts follow legal precedent unless there is good cause for departure.

TAKE CARE CLAUSE Language found in Article II, § 3 of the Constitution, stating the President "shall take Care that the Laws be faithfully executed." This clause is also referred to as the "Faithful Execution Clause."

National Labor Relations Board v. Noel Canning

Federal agency (P) v. Employer (D)

572 U.S. 513 (2014)

NATURE OF CASE: Appeal in action challenging the validity of orders of the National Labor Relations Board on the grounds the President's appointment of a majority of the board that rendered the orders was itself invalid. [The procedural posture of the case is not presented in the casebook extract.]

FACT SUMMARY: Noel Canning (D), an employer that the National Labor Relations Board (the NLRB *or* the Board) (P) determined had violated the National Labor Relations Act, challenged the NLRB's (P) orders as void on the grounds that the appointment of a majority of the NLRB (P) members by the President was invalid, so that the Board (P) lacked a quorum to conduct business.

RULE OF LAW

The Recess Appointments Clause empowers the President to fill any existing vacancy during any recess—intra-session or inter-session—of sufficient length.

FACTS: The National Labor Relations Board (the NLRB *or* the Board) (P) has five members who are appointed by the President. The Board (P) must have a quorum to conduct business and issue orders. Ordinarily, the President must obtain Senate approval of appointments of officers. However, the Recess Appointments Clause gives the President the power "to fill up all Vacancies that may happen during the Recess of the Senate," art. II, § 2, cl. 3. Invoking this clause, President Obama appointed three members to the NLRB (P) on January 4, 2012, during a three-day pro forma session of the Senate. At that time the Senate was in recess pursuant to a December 17, 2011, resolution providing for a series of brief recesses punctuated by such pro forma sessions with no business transacted every Tuesday and Friday through January 20, 2012. Shortly thereafter, the NLRB (P) found that a Pepsi-Cola distributor, Noel Canning (D), had violated the National Labor Relations Act by refusing to execute a collective-bargaining agreement with a labor union. Noel Canning (D) challenged the NLRB's (P) orders, contending they were void because the three new Board (P) members had been invalidly appointed, so that the Board (P) lacked a quorum for conducting business. Specifically, Noel Canning (D) argued that the Recess Appointments Clause did not authorize those appointments because the Clause's words "the recess of the Senate" do not include recesses that occur within a formal session of Congress, i.e., intra-session recesses. Rather, Noel Canning (D) claimed that those words apply only to recesses between those formal sessions, i.e., inter-session recesses. Since the second session of the 112th Congress began on January 3, 2012, the day before the President's appointments, those appointments occurred during an intra-session recess, and the appointments consequently fell outside the scope of the Clause. Noel Canning (D) also argued that the phrase "vacancies that may happen during the recess" applies only to vacancies that come into existence during a recess. Because the vacancies that were filled had arisen before the beginning of the recess during which they were appointed, Noel Canning (D) contended that for this reason, too, the President's appointments were invalid. Noel Canning's (D) third argument was that the Senate was not in recess because of the pro forma sessions, while the Solicitor General argued that they were a sham and that the President could disregard them because the Senate conducted no business until January 20th. The United States Supreme Court granted certiorari in the case. [The procedural posture of the case is not presented in the casebook extract.]

ISSUE: Does the Recess Appointments Clause empower the President to fill any existing vacancy during any recess—intra-session or inter-session—of sufficient length?

HOLDING AND DECISION: (Breyer, J.) Yes. The Recess Appointments Clause empowers the President to fill any existing vacancy during any recess—intra-session or inter-session—of sufficient length. The constitutional text is ambiguous. Founding-era usages show that the phrase "the recess" can encompass intra-session breaks. And this broader interpretation is demanded by the purpose of the Clause, which is to allow the President to make appointments to ensure the continued functioning of the government while the Senate is away. The Senate is equally away and unavailable to participate in the appointments process during both an inter-session and an intra-session recess. History offers further support for this interpretation. From the founding until the Great Depression, every time the Senate took a substantial, non-holiday intra-session recess, the President made recess appointments. Since 1929, and particularly since the end of World War II, Congress has shortened its inter-session breaks and taken longer and more frequent intra-session breaks; Presidents accordingly have made more intra-session recess appointments. Meanwhile, the Senate has never taken any formal action to deny the validity of intra-session recess appointments. The next question is whether intra-session breaks of any length

Continued on next page.

come within the Clause. The Clause itself does not specify how long a recess must be to fall within the Clause, but even the Solicitor General concedes that a three-day recess would be too short. The Adjournments Clause, art. I, § 5, cl. 4, reflects the fact that a three-day break is not a significant interruption of legislative business. A Senate recess that is so short that it does not require the consent of the House under that Clause is not long enough to trigger the President's recess-appointment power. Moreover, the Court has not found a single example of a recess appointment made during an intra-session recess that was shorter than 10 days. There are a few examples of inter-session recess appointments made during recesses of less than 10 days, but these are anomalies. In light of historical practice, a recess of more than three days but less than 10 days is presumptively too short to fall within the Clause. The word "presumptively" leaves open the possibility that a very unusual circumstance, e.g., a national catastrophe, could demand the exercise of the recess-appointment power during a shorter break. Accordingly, the President's recess-appointment powers were not triggered and the NLRB (P) members were not validly appointed. Additionally, Noel Canning's (D) argument that a vacancy must arise during a recess is rejected. Again, the text is ambiguous. It may mean "vacancies that may happen to be" or "may happen to fall" during a recess. The broader reading is more consonant with the reason and spirit of the Clause, which is to permit the President, who is always acting to execute the law, to obtain the assistance of subordinate officers while the Senate, which acts only in intervals, is unavailable to confirm them. If a vacancy arises too late in the session for the President and Senate to have an opportunity to select a replacement, the narrower reading could paralyze important functions of the federal government, particularly at the time of the founding. History overwhelmingly supports such a broad interpretation. The tradition of applying the Clause to pre-recess vacancies dates at least to President Madison. Nearly every Attorney General to consider the question has approved the practice, and every President since James Buchanan has made recess appointments to pre-existing vacancies. Although the Senate did early on take the narrower view, it has not countered this practice for nearly three-quarters of a century, perhaps longer. Accordingly, this traditional practice should not be changed where doing so would seriously shrink the authority that Presidents have believed existed and have exercised for so long. Thus, the phrase "vacancies that may happen during the recess of the Senate," applies both to vacancies that first come into existence during a recess and to vacancies that initially occur before a recess but continue to exist during the recess. Finally, for purposes of the Recess Appointments Clause, the Senate is in session when it says that it is, provided that, under its own rules, it retains the capacity to transact Senate business. This standard is consistent with the Constitution's broad delegation of authority to the Senate to determine how and when to conduct its business, as recognized by this Court's precedents. Although the Senate's own determination of when it is and is not in session should be given great weight, the Court's deference cannot be absolute. When the Senate is without the capacity to act, under its own rules, it is not in session even if it so declares. Applying these principles to the case at bar, the Senate was in session during the pro forma sessions at issue, during which it actually passed legislation. Judgment for Noel Canning (D). [The disposition of the case is not presented in the casebook extract.]

CONCURRENCE: (Scalia, J.) Although the Court reaches the correct result in this case it errs as to several points. First, contrary to the majority's conclusion, the Clause's text is unambiguous and applies only to inter-session recesses, and then only to vacancies that have arisen between sessions. Also contrary to the majority's conclusion, there has not been executive branch consensus, or Senate acquiescence, as to the correct interpretation of the Clause. Further, given that the text is unambiguous, the Court should not defer to intra-branch conventions to reach its decision. When questions involving the Constitution's government-structuring provisions are presented to the Court, the Court must say what the law is. The Court's role is in no way "lessened" because it might be said that the other two political branches are adjusting their own powers between themselves. Since the separation of powers exists for the protection of individual liberty, the vitality of the governmental structure set forth in the Constitution does not depend on whether an encroached-upon branch approves the encroachment. To the contrary, policing the enduring structure of constitutional government when the political branches fail to do so is one of the Court's most vital functions. Thus, it is wrong for the majority to rely primarily on the entrenched, self-aggrandizing practice adopted for decades by the executive branch without further detailed constitutional analysis.

ANALYSIS

One effect of this decision is that the Court has legitimated the strategy of using pro forma Senate sessions to prevent recess appointments. Thus, if the party opposing the President controls the Senate, it can effectively prevent all recess appointments by refusing to adjourn through use of such pro forma sessions.

Quicknotes

AMBIGUOUS Vague; unclear; capable of being understood to have more than one meaning.

Immigration and Naturalization Service v. Chadha

Federal agency (D) v. Alien (P)

462 U.S. 919 (1983)

NATURE OF CASE: Consolidated actions challenging the constitutionality of a federal statute.

FACT SUMMARY: Chadha (P) and others challenged the constitutionality of a federal statute that purported to authorize one House of Congress, by resolution, to invalidate the decision of the Attorney General (made under authority delegated by Congress) to allow a particular deportable alien to remain in the United States.

RULE OF LAW

Because it constitutes an exercise of legislative power and is thus subject to the bicameralism and presentment requirements of Article I of the Constitution, the federal statute purporting to authorize a one-house veto of the Attorney General's decision to allow a particular deportable alien to remain in the United States is unconstitutional.

FACTS: Three cases consolidated on appeal all presented the question of the constitutionality of a federal statute that authorized either House of Congress, by resolution, to invalidate the decision of the Attorney General (made pursuant to authority delegated by Congress) to allow a particular deportable alien to remain in the United States. After such a one-house veto effectively overturned the Attorney General's decision to let Chadha (P) and certain other individuals remain in the United States, each instituted action challenging the constitutionality of the aforesaid statute. Chadha (P) filed a petition for a review of his deportation order, with the Immigration and Naturalization Service (INS) (D) actually agreeing with his contention that the statute was unconstitutional. The court of appeals held that the statute violated the doctrine of separation of powers.

ISSUE: Is it constitutional for Congress to statutorily authorize a one-house veto of a decision the Attorney General makes, under authority delegated to him by Congress, to allow a particular deportable alien to remain in the United States?

HOLDING AND DECISION: (Burger, C.J.) No. The Constitution does not permit Congress to statutorily authorize a one-house veto of a decision the Attorney General makes, pursuant to authority delegated to him by Congress, to allow a particular deportable alien to remain in the United States. Such an action is clearly an exercise of legislative power, which makes it subject to the bicameralism and presentment requirements of Article I of the Constitution unless one of the express constitutional exceptions authorizing one House to act alone applies. None of them apply. Thus, to accomplish what has been attempted by one House of Congress in this case requires action in conformity with the express procedures of the Constitution's prescription for legislative action, passage by majority of both Houses, and presentment to the President (for his signing or his veto). Such requirements were built into the Constitution to act as enduring checks on each branch and to protect the people from the improvident exercise of power by mandating certain prescribed steps. In attempting to bypass those steps, Congress has acted unconstitutionally.

CONCURRENCE: (Powell, J.) This case should be decided on the narrower ground that Congress assumes a judicial function in violation of the principle of separation of powers when it finds that a particular person does not satisfy the statutory criteria for permanent residence in this country. The Court's broader decision will apparently invalidate every use of the legislative veto, which is a procedure that has been much used by Congress and one it clearly views as essential to controlling the delegation of power to administrative agencies. While one may reasonably disagree with Congress's assessment of the veto's utility, the respect due its judgment as a coordinate branch of government cautions that our holding should be no more extensive than necessary to decide this case.

DISSENT: (White, J.) Today's decision sounds the death knell for nearly two hundred statutory provisions in which Congress has reserved a "legislative veto," which has become a central means by which Congress secures the accountability of executive and independent agencies. Without this particular tool Congress faces a Hobson's choice: either to refrain from delegating the necessary authority, leaving itself with a hopeless task of writing laws with the requisite specificity to cover endless special circumstances across the entire policy landscape, or, in the alternative, to abdicate its lawmaking function to the executive branch and independent agencies. Thus, the apparent sweep of the Court's decision today, which appears to invalidate all legislative vetoes irrespective of form or subject, is regrettable. Furthermore, the Court's decision fails to recognize that the legislative veto is not the type of action subject to the bicameralism and presentment requirements of Article I. Only bills and their equivalent are subject to such requirements. The initial legislation delegating to the Attorney General the power to make a decision on the deportation of a particular

Continued on next page.

alien complied with the Article I requirements. Congress's power to exercise a legislative veto over that decision cannot be viewed, then, as the power to write new law without bicameral approval or presidential consideration. If Congress can delegate lawmaking power to executive agencies, it is most difficult to understand Article I as forbidding Congress from simply reserving a check on legislative power for itself. Without the veto, agencies to whom power has been delegated may issue regulations having the force of law without bicameral approval and without the President's signature. It is thus not apparent why the reservation of a veto over the exercise of that legislative power must be subject to a more exacting test. In both cases, it is enough that the initial statutory authorizations comply with the Article I requirements.

DISSENT: (Rehnquist, J.) Congress did not intend the one-house veto provision to be severable from the rest of the statute; it never intended to permit suspensions of deportation unless it could retain some sort of veto. The judgment of the court of appeals should be reversed.

ANALYSIS

It is only within the last 50 years that the legislative veto has come into widespread use. When the federal government began its massive growth in response to the Depression, the legislative veto was "invented" as one means of keeping a check on the sprawling new structure. While many commentators, upon the Court's announcement of this decision, opined that the result was a major shift of power from the legislative branch to the executive branch, Congress through more restrictive draftsmanship should actually see minimal diminishment of its control of those areas over which it desires to retain control.

Quicknotes

BICAMERALISM The necessity for approval by a majority of both houses of Congress when ratifying legislation or approving other legislative action.

LEGISLATIVE VETO A statutory provision that contemplates the congressional ability to require the President or another part of the executive branch to act or refrain from taking action.

PRESENTMENT The act of bringing a congressional decision before the President for his approval or veto.

SEPARATION OF POWERS The system of checks and balances preventing one branch of government from infringing upon exercising the powers of another branch of government.

Youngstown Sheet & Tube Co. v. Sawyer

Steel companies (P) v. Federal government (D)

343 U.S. 579 (1952)

NATURE OF CASE: Suit for declaratory and injunctive relief from a presidential order.

FACT SUMMARY: Faced with an imminent steel strike during the Korean War, the President ordered governmental seizure of the steel companies to prevent the strike. The companies challenged his power to take such action as being without constitutional authority or prior congressional approval.

RULE OF LAW

The President, as leader of the executive branch, is bound to enforce the laws within the limits of the authority expressly granted to him by the Constitution, and he cannot usurp the lawmaking power of Congress by an assertion of an unspecified aggregation of his specified powers.

FACTS: As a result of long but unsuccessful negotiations with various steel companies, the United Steelworkers of America served notice of intent to strike in April 1952. Through the last months of the negotiations the President had utilized every available administrative remedy to affect a settlement and avert a strike. Congress had engaged in extensive debate on solutions but had passed no legislation on the issue. By order of the President, the Secretary of Commerce seized the steel companies so that steel production would not be interrupted during the Korean War. The steel companies sued in federal district court to have the seizure order declared invalid and to enjoin its enforcement. The government asserted that the President had "inherent power" to make the order and that it was "supported by the Constitution, historical precedent and court decisions." The district court granted a preliminary injunction that was stayed the same day by the court of appeals. The United States Supreme Court granted certiorari and ordered immediate argument.

ISSUE: May the President, relying on a concept of inherent powers, and in his capacity as Commander-in-Chief, make an order that usurps the lawmaking authority of Congress on the basis of compelling need to protect the national security?

HOLDING AND DECISION: (Black, J.) No. There is, admittedly, no express congressional authority for these seizures, and so, if any authority for the President's act can be found, it must come from the Constitution. In the absence of express authority for the President's act, it is argued that the power can be implied from the aggregate of his express powers granted by the Constitution. This order cannot be justified by reliance on the President's role as Commander-in-Chief. Even though the term "theater of war" has enjoyed an expanding definition, it cannot embrace the taking of private property to prevent a strike. The President's powers in the area of legislation are limited to proposing new laws to Congress or vetoing laws that the President deems inadvisable. This order is not executive implementation of a congressional action but a legislative act performed by the President. Only Congress may do what the President has attempted here. The Constitution is specific in vesting the lawmaking powers in Congress, and we, therefore, affirm the district court's decision to enjoin the enforcement of this order.

CONCURRENCE: (Frankfurter, J.) This decision does not attempt to define the limits of presidential authority. The President cannot act in contravention of an express congressional act, nor may he act where Congress has done nothing. Were this a case of a long history of congressional acquiescence to presidential practice our decision might be different, but no such showing has been made.

CONCURRENCE: (Douglas, J.) The only branch of government that may authorize seizures is the branch that must authorize compensation, i.e., the Congress.

CONCURRENCE: (Jackson, J.) The power of the President to act can be viewed as three separate categories of circumstances. First, the President's power is at its maximum when he acts pursuant to express or implied congressional authority. Second, in the absence of a congressional grant of power, the President acts solely on the basis of his powers as specified in the Constitution. Third, when the President acts in contravention of congressional action, he may do so only where it can be shown that Congress has exceeded its constitutional powers and the President is acting in his own sphere of authority. It is in this last area where presidential acts are subject to the closest scrutiny. This order is clearly not in the first category. His act cannot be justified in the second category since Congress has limited seizure powers to specific instances not embracing this order. The constitutional grant of powers to the President is in specific terms that do not permit any loose aggregation to create powers not specified. There is little question that Congress could have authorized those seizures and this very power denies the same authority to the President. Finally, the President's act is justified by arguing it is the result of powers accruing

Continued on next page.

to his office by custom and practice of previous administrations. Present unconstitutional acts cannot be justified by the prior unconstitutional acts of others. Presidential power may, in fact, enlarge due to congressional inaction, but the courts will not assist or approve this process.

CONCURRENCE: (Burton, J.) The President's order invaded Congress's jurisdiction and violated the use of separation of powers. The injunction should be sustained.

CONCURRENCE: (Clark, J.) Congress has prescribed the measures necessary to meet the emergencies of this nature, and I cannot find any justification to sanction deviation from those measures.

DISSENT: (Vinson, C.J.) The majority's opinion has left the President powerless to act at the very time the need for his independent and immediate action is greatest. From Washington to Roosevelt, history is replete with examples of needed presidential action in the face of congressional inaction. Jefferson's Louisiana Purchase, Lincoln's Emancipation Proclamation, Wilson's War Labor Board with accompanying industrial seizures, and Roosevelt's seizure of an aircraft plant to avert a strike are but a few examples of presidential action that received subsequent, not prior, congressional or judicial authorization. The President's seizure in this case is in accord with congressional intent to support the resistance of aggression in the world and is in furtherance of his duty to execute the laws of this nation. The executive is the only branch of government that may, by design, act swiftly to meet national emergencies. This decision emasculates that necessary power.

ANALYSIS

Justice Black's broad language was criticized by many scholars as being overly expansive for the case presented. However, other authorities pointed out that the broad arguments advanced by the government required a broad response. During oral argument before the court, the government counsel stated that while the Constitution imposed limits on congressional and judicial powers, no such limits were imposed on the presidency. While supplemental briefs were filed modifying this position, the damage may already have been done. The Court was faced with a paucity of judicial precedents. The President and Congress have traditionally preferred political rather than judicial solutions to their conflicts. This practice avoids the limitations imposed on future actions by binding judicial precedents. And, as can be seen by the cases of *Marbury v. Madison*, 5 U.S. (1 Cranch) 137 (1803), and *United States v. Nixon*, 418 U.S. 683 (1974), the executive branch has not fared well when it has submitted to judicial jurisdiction.

Quicknotes

EXECUTIVE ORDER An order issued by the President, or another executive of government, which has the force of law.

PRELIMINARY INJUNCTION A judicial mandate issued to require or restrain a party from certain conduct; used to preserve a trial's subject matter or to prevent threatened injury.

SEPARATION OF POWERS The system of checks and balances preventing one branch of government from infringing upon exercising the powers of another branch of government.

Hamdi v. Rumsfeld

Alleged enemy combatant (P) v. Secretary of Defense (D)

542 U.S. 507 (2004)

NATURE OF CASE: Appeal from the denial of right to challenge enemy-combatant status.

FACT SUMMARY: Hamdi (P), an American citizen designated as an enemy-combatant, argued that he was entitled to contest such designation in court.

RULE OF LAW

Due process requires that a citizen held in the United States as an enemy combatant be given a meaningful opportunity to contest the factual basis for that detention before a neutral decision maker.

FACTS: Hamdi (P), an American citizen, was designated by the Government (D) an "enemy combatant" and placed into indefinite detainment. The federal court of appeals held the detention to be legally authorized and that Hamdi (P) was entitled to no further opportunity to challenge his enemy-combatant label. Hamdi (P) appealed to the United States Supreme Court.

ISSUE: Does due process require that a citizen held in the United States as an enemy combatant be given a meaningful opportunity to contest the factual basis for that detention before a neutral decision maker?

HOLDING AND DECISION: (O'Connor, J.) Yes. Due process requires that a citizen held in the United States as an enemy combatant be given a meaningful opportunity to contest the factual basis for that detention before a neutral decision maker. It is vital not to give short shrift to the values that this country holds dear or to the privilege that is American citizenship. At the same time, the exigencies of the circumstances may demand that, as here, aside from certain core elements, enemy combatant proceedings may be tailored to alleviate their uncommon potential to burden the executive branch at a time of ongoing military conflict. Hearsay, for example, may need to be accepted as the most reliable available evidence from the government in such a proceeding. Furthermore, even a burden-shifting scheme in which credible government evidence is presumed true would not offend the Constitution so long as such presumption remains a rebuttable one and fair opportunity for rebuttal is provided. The parties agree that initial captures on the battlefield need not receive the full range of constitutional guarantees. While the Court accords the greatest respect and consideration to the judgments of military authorities in matters relating to the actual prosecution of a war and recognizes the scope of that discretion is necessarily wide, it does not infringe on the core role of the military for the courts to exercise their own time-honored and constitutionally mandated roles of reviewing and resolving claims such as those present here. A state of war is not a blank check for the President when it comes to the rights of the nation's citizens. Vacated and remanded.

CONCURRENCE AND DISSENT: (Souter, J.) The Government (D) has failed to demonstrate that the Force Resolution authorizes the detention complained of here, even on the facts the Government (D) claims. If the government (D) raises nothing further than the record now shows, the Non-Detention Act entitles Hamdi (P) to be released. The branch of government asked to counter a serious threat is not the branch on which to rest the Nation's entire reliance in striking the balance between the will to win and "the cost in liberty on the way to victory."

DISSENT: (Scalia, J.) If civil rights are to be curtailed during wartime, it must be done openly and democratically, as the Constitution requires, rather than by silent erosion through an opinion of the Court. Whatever the merits of the view that war silences law or modulates its voice, such view has no place in the interpretation and application of a Constitution designed precisely to confront war and, in a manner that accords with democratic principles, to accommodate it.

DISSENT: (Thomas, J.) The executive branch, acting pursuant to powers vested in the President by the Constitution and by explicit congressional approval, has determined that Hamdi (P) is an enemy combatant and should be detained. This detention falls squarely within the war powers of the federal government, and the Court lacks the expertise and capacity to second-guess such decision. Accordingly, Hamdi's (P) habeas challenge should fail, and there is no reason to remand the case.

ANALYSIS

As made clear in the *Hamdi* decision, in cases of this type the Court must balance two vital yet competing interests: on the one hand, respect for separation of powers and the fundamental importance of the nation to be able to protect itself during time of war; on the other hand, the critical and deep-seated individual constitutional interests at stake.

Continued on next page.

Quicknotes

DUE PROCESS CLAUSE Language found in the Fifth and Fourteenth Amendments to the United States Constitution providing that no person shall be deprived of "life, liberty, or property without due process of law."

SEPARATION OF POWERS The system of checks and balances preventing one branch of government from infringing upon exercising the powers of another branch of government.

Boumediene v. Bush

Guantanamo detainees (P) v. Federal government (D)

553 U.S. 723 (2008)

NATURE OF CASE: Appeal from judgment denying habeas corpus rights to enemy combatants held abroad.

FACT SUMMARY: [Boumediene (P) and other detainees (P) held at Guantanamo Bay, Cuba, petitioned the court for a writ of habeas corpus. The federal appeals court ruled in favor of the U.S. government (D).]

RULE OF LAW

(1) The Military Commissions Act of 2006 strips federal courts of jurisdiction over habeas petitions filed by foreign citizens detained at Guantanamo Bay.
(2) Detainees are not barred from seeking habeas or invoking the Suspension Clause simply because they had been designated as enemy combatants or held at Guantanamo Bay.
(3) The Military Commissions Act of 2006 is a violation of the Suspension Clause of the Constitution.

FACTS: [Bosnian police captured Boumediene (P) and five other Algerian natives after U.S. intelligence officers suspected them of plotting to attack the U.S. embassy there. The U.S. government (D) classified the men as enemy combatants in the war on terror and held them at the Guantanamo Bay. Boumediene (P) filed a petition for a writ of habeas corpus, claiming that the U.S. government (D) violated the Due Process Clause of the U.S. Constitution, various statutes and treaties, the common law, and international law. A district court judge granted the U.S. government's (D) motion to have all of the claims dismissed on the ground that Boumediene (P), as an alien held at an overseas military base, had no right to a habeas petition. The Court of Appeals for the D.C. Circuit affirmed, but the United States Supreme Court reversed in *Rasul v. Bush*, 542 U.S. 466, 473 (2004), holding that the habeas statute extends to noncitizen detainees at Guantanamo. In 2006, Congress passed the Military Commissions Act of 2006 (the MCA), which withdrew the jurisdiction of federal courts to hear habeas applications from detainees classified as enemy combatants under the Detainee Treatment Act of 2005 (DTA). The case was appealed to the D.C. Circuit for the second time, and this time the detainees (P) argued that the MCA did not apply to their petitions, and that if it did, it was unconstitutional under the Suspension Clause. The D.C. Circuit ruled in favor of the U.S. government (D) on both points, holding that the MCA applied to "all cases, without exception," that pertain to aspects of detention. One of the purposes of the MCA, according to the court, was to overrule the Supreme Court's opinion in *Hamdan v. Rumsfeld*, 548 U.S. 557 (2006), which had allowed petitions like Boumediene's (P) to go forward. The D.C. Circuit held that the Suspension Clause protects only the writ of habeas corpus as it existed in 1789, and that the writ would not have been understood in 1789 to apply to an overseas military base leased from a foreign government. Constitutional rights do not apply to aliens outside of the United States, the court held, and the leased military base in Cuba does not qualify as inside the geographic borders of the United States. The United States Supreme Court granted certiorari after initially denying review, three months earlier.]

ISSUE:

(1) Does the Military Commissions Act of 2006 strip federal courts of jurisdiction over habeas petitions filed by foreign citizens detained at Guantanamo Bay?
(2) Are detainees barred from seeking habeas or invoking the Suspension Clause simply because they had been designated as enemy combatants or held at Guantanamo Bay?
(3) Is the Military Commissions Act of 2006 a violation of the Suspension Clause of the Constitution?

HOLDING AND DECISION: (Kennedy, J.)

(1) Yes. The Military Commissions Act of 2006 (the MCA) strips federal courts of jurisdiction over habeas petitions filed by foreign citizens detained at Guantanamo Bay. If the MCA is considered valid, its legislative history requires that the detainees' cases be dismissed.
(2) No. Detainees are not barred from seeking habeas or invoking the Suspension Clause simply because they had been designated as enemy combatants or held at Guantanamo Bay. The Suspension Clause provides that the "Privilege of the Writ of Habeas Corpus shall not be suspended, unless when in Cases of Rebellion or Invasion the public Safety may require it." The Framers thought the writ was an essential mechanism in the separation of powers scheme. Moreover, the Suspension Clause applies to Guantanamo, despite the fact the United States (D) does not claim sovereignty over the place of detention. Even when the United States (D) acts outside its borders, its powers are subject to the Constitution.

Continued on next page.

(3) Yes. The Military Commissions Act of 2006 (the MCA) is a violation of the Suspension Clause of the Constitution. Because the procedures laid out in the Detainee Treatment Act are not adequate substitutes for the habeas writ, the MCA operates as an unconstitutional suspension of that writ. Reversed.

DISSENT: (Roberts, C.J.) The procedural protections offered aliens who are detained by this country as enemy combatants were already generous under the Detainee Treatment Act (DTA). Although the majority grants even greater procedural protections to such combatants for the first time in the nation's history, the detainees now face the prospect of greatly increased and protracted litigation, as compared to what they would have faced to vindicate their rights under the DTA.

DISSENT: (Scalia, J.) The Court's grant of a constitutional right to habeas corpus to alien enemies detained abroad by military forces occurs for the first time in the nation's history, and in course of an ongoing war. This grant will result in more American lives being lost.

ANALYSIS

President Bush agreed to honor the ruling. At a June 2008 town hall meeting, then-Republican presidential nominee John McCain said the ruling was "one of the worst decisions in the history of this country." He said that "[t]hese are people who are not citizens. They do not and never have been given the rights that citizens in this country have." Then-Democratic presidential nominee Barack Obama described the ruling as "a rejection of the Bush administration's attempt to create a legal black hole at Guantanamo" and "an important step toward re-establishing our credibility as a nation committed to the rule of law."

Quicknotes

DUE PROCESS The constitutional mandate requiring the courts to protect and enforce individuals' rights and liberties consistent with prevailing principles of fairness and justice and prohibiting the federal and state governments from such activities that deprive its citizens of life, liberty, or property interest.

DUE PROCESS CLAUSE Language found in the Fifth and Fourteenth Amendments to the U.S. Constitution providing that no person shall be deprived of "life, liberty, or property without due process of law."

HABEAS CORPUS A proceeding in which a defendant brings a writ to compel a judicial determination of whether he is lawfully being held in custody.

SUSPENSION CLAUSE A clause found in Article I of the U.S. Constitution that protects against arbitrary suspensions of the writ of habeas corpus.

Zivotofsky v. Kerry (Zivotofsky II)

Minor child born to U.S. citizens abroad (P) v. United States Secretary of State (D)

135 S. Ct. 2076 (2015)

NATURE OF CASE: Action involving the issue of whether the Foreign Relations Authorization Act may override the President's recognition powers.

FACT SUMMARY: The President had never recognized Israel as sovereign over Jerusalem, but, in 2002, Congress passed the Foreign Relations Authorization Act, Fiscal Year 2003 (the FRAA) allowing citizens born in Jerusalem to list their place of birth on documents such as passports as "Israel." Zivotofsky (P), a minor child born to U.S. citizens in Jerusalem, invoking the FRAA, challenged the State Department's refusal to record "Israel" as his place of birth on his passport, which raised the issue of whether Congress could constitutionally override the President's position on the matter.

RULE OF LAW

The President has the exclusive power to grant formal recognition to a foreign sovereign.

FACTS: Although the President has recognized Israel as a nation, no President has ever recognized any country's sovereignty over Jerusalem, which Israel considers to be its capital. The President's position on Jerusalem is reflected in State Department policy regarding passports and consular reports of birth abroad. Understanding that passports will be construed as reflections of U.S. policy, the State Department's Foreign Affairs Manual (the FAM) instructs its employees, in general, to record the place of birth on a passport as the "country [having] present sovereignty over the actual area of birth." Because the President has not recognized any country as having sovereignty over Jerusalem, the FAM instructs employees to record the place of birth of citizens born there as "Jerusalem." Congress passed the Foreign Relations Authorization Act, Fiscal Year 2003 (the FRAA), seeking, in section 214(d) of the Act, to override the FAM by allowing citizens born in Jerusalem to list their place of birth as "Israel." Zivotofsky (P), a minor child born to U.S. citizens in Jerusalem, invoking the FRAA, challenged the State Department's refusal to record "Israel" as his place of birth on his passport, which raised the issue of whether Congress could constitutionally override the President's position on the matter. The United States Supreme Court granted certiorari in the case.

ISSUE: Does the President have the exclusive power to grant formal recognition to a foreign sovereign?

HOLDING AND DECISION: (Kennedy, J.) Yes. The President has the exclusive power to grant formal recognition to a foreign sovereign. Recognition is a "formal acknowledgement" that a particular entity possesses the qualifications for statehood or that a particular regime is the effective government of a state. The Constitution's text and structure grant the President the power to recognize foreign nations and governments. The Reception Clause directs that the President "shall receive Ambassadors and other public Ministers," art. II, § 3. At the time of the founding, receiving an ambassador was considered tantamount to recognizing the sending state's sovereignty. It is thus logical and proper to infer that the Reception Clause would be understood to acknowledge the President's power to recognize other nations. This inference is further supported by the President's additional Article II powers: to negotiate treaties and to nominate the nation's ambassadors and dispatch other diplomatic agents. Though ratifying a treaty and confirming an ambassador require congressional approval, Congress lacks authority to initiate the actions without the President's involvement. The President, unlike Congress, also has the power to open diplomatic channels simply by engaging in direct diplomacy with foreign heads of state and their ministers. The Constitution thus assigns the President, not Congress, means to effect recognition on his own initiative. Functional considerations also suggest that the President's recognition power is exclusive. The nation must "speak . . . with one voice" regarding which governments are legitimate in the eyes of the United States and which are not, and only the Executive has the characteristic of unity at all times. Unlike Congress, the President is also capable of engaging in the delicate and often secret diplomatic contacts that may lead to a recognition decision, and is better positioned to take the decisive, unequivocal action necessary to recognize other states at international law. The President has also exercised unilateral recognition power since the founding, a practice endorsed by the Court. Nevertheless, Congress, which has the central role in making laws, has substantial authority regarding many policy determinations that precede and follow an act of recognition. The President's recognition determination is thus only one part of the political process. The President alone may not determine the whole content of the nation's foreign policy and is not free from the ordinary controls and checks of Congress merely because foreign affairs are at issue. Because the power to recognize foreign states resides in the President alone, § 214(d) infringes on the Executive's consistent decision to withhold recognition with respect to Jerusalem. If the recognition power is to mean anything, it must mean that the President not

Continued on next page.

only makes the initial, formal recognition determination but also may maintain that determination in his and his agent's statements. Otherwise, Congress could command the President to state a recognition position inconsistent with his own, and, thus, override the President's recognition determination. Although Congress may express its disagreement with the President in many ways, as, for example, by enacting an embargo or declining to confirm an ambassador, it may not force the President to contradict his earlier statement of recognition.

CONCURRENCE: (Breyer, J.) This case presents a political question and should not be resolved judicially.

CONCURRENCE AND DISSENT: (Thomas, J.) The Vesting Clause of Article II of the Constitution vests all powers in the President originally understood as falling within the executive power, not just those powers expressly identified in the Constitution. Such power at founding included the foreign affairs powers, and this was understood to encompass all foreign affairs powers other than those otherwise allocated by the Constitution. One of those powers was the issuing and control of passports under his residual foreign affairs power, and this portion of § 214(d) does not fall within any of Congress's enumerated powers. By contrast, § 214(d) poses no such problem insofar as it regulates consular reports of birth abroad. Unlike passports, these reports were developed to effectuate the naturalization laws, and they continue to serve the role of identifying persons who need not be naturalized to obtain U.S. citizenship. The regulation of these reports does not fall within the President's foreign affairs powers, but within Congress's enumerated powers under the Naturalization and Necessary and Proper Clauses.

DISSENT: (Roberts, C.J.) The majority errs on the fundamental question of separation of powers presented by the case, as it has been stressed that the President's power is at its lowest when he contravenes the express will of Congress. The Reception Clause is framed as an obligation rather than as an authorization, and it appears alongside the duties imposed on the President, not the powers granted to him. Additionally, the President's powers to make treaties and appoint ambassadors are shared with Congress. Therefore, the majority's textual bases for its decision are tenuous, and do not support the inference that the recognition power is exclusive. Historically, too, some Presidents have claimed an exclusive recognition power, but others have expressed uncertainty about whether such preclusive authority exists. Congress has also asserted the recognition power at various points throughout history. Thus, contrary to the majority's assertion, it cannot be said that Congress has accepted the President's exclusive recognition power, and, in any event, congressional acquiescence has been held to be pertinent only when the President acts in the absence of express congressional authorization. Even assuming the President does have exclusive recognition power, he still cannot prevail in this case, because the statute at issue does not implicate recognition. Congress has not disputed the Executive's assurances that § 214(d) does not alter the longstanding United States position on Jerusalem, and diplomatic history offers no examples of official recognition accomplished via an optional passport designation. Ultimately, the only power that could support the President's position is the one the majority purports to reject: the "exclusive authority to conduct diplomatic relations." Yet, even this power is not one that permits the Executive to contravene a statute, but rather may be exercised pursuant to a legislative delegation.

DISSENT: (Scalia, J.) The Constitution rejected the notion that foreign affairs would be vested exclusively in the Executive, as they had been in England's King, and, instead contemplated shared power in this area between the President and Congress. Congress has the power to grant American citizenship to someone born abroad under its naturalization power, art. I, § 8, cl. 4, and this power enables Congress to furnish those citizens with papers, such as passports, that verify their citizenship. It follows that Congress may require what is placed on those documents as the citizen's place of birth. The birthplace specification promotes the document's citizenship-authenticating function and promotes other objectives. Although recording Zivotofsky's (P) birthplace as "Jerusalem" rather than "Israel" would fulfill these objectives, when faced with alternative ways to carry its powers into execution, Congress has the discretion to choose the one it deems most beneficial to the people. Therefore, for example, Congress has the right to decide that recording birthplaces as "Israel" makes for better foreign policy. Additionally, § 214(d) has nothing to do with recognition. That provision does not require the Secretary of State (Secretary) (D) to make a formal declaration about Israel's sovereignty over Jerusalem, and nobody suggests that international custom infers acceptance of sovereignty from the birthplace designation on a passport or birth report, as it does from bilateral treaties or exchanges of ambassadors. Instead, the provision addresses what the Government says about its citizens' identities. The best indication that § 214(d) does not concern recognition comes from the State Department's policies concerning Taiwan. The State Department has for a long time recorded the birthplace of a citizen born in Taiwan as "China." It indeed insisted on doing so until Congress passed a law (on which § 214(d) was modeled) giving citizens the option to have their birthplaces recorded as "Taiwan." The designation "China" "involves a geographic description, not an assertion that Taiwan is part of sovereign China. Section 214(d) likewise calls for

Continued on next page.

nothing beyond a "geographic description;" it does not require the President even to assert, never mind formally recognize, that Jerusalem is a part of sovereign Israel. Since birthplace specifications in citizenship documents are matters within Congress's control, Congress may treat Jerusalem as a part of Israel when regulating the recording of birthplaces, even if the President does not do so when extending recognition. Even if the Constitution gives the President sole power to extend recognition, it does not give him sole power to make all decisions relating to foreign disputes over sovereignty. To the contrary, a fair reading of Article I allows Congress to decide for itself how its laws should handle such controversies. Recognition is a type of legal act, not a statement, so it is a large and illogical leap to go from exclusive authority over making legal commitments regarding sovereignty to exclusive authority over making statements or issuing documents regarding national borders. Moreover, history does not even support an exclusive presidential power to make what the majority calls "formal statements" about the legitimacy of a state or government and its territorial bounds. Regardless of whether Congress has the recognition power under the Constitution, § 214(d) does not make (or require the President to make) a commitment accepting Israel's sovereignty over Jerusalem. To the extent doubts linger about whether the United States recognizes Israel's sovereignty over Jerusalem, § 214(d) leaves the President free to dispel them by issuing a disclaimer of intent to recognize; such a disclaimer always suffices to prevent an act from effecting recognition, and nothing stops the President from making such a disclaimer here.

ANALYSIS

In *Zivotofsky*, the Court rejected the Secretary's (D) reliance on *United States v. Curtiss-Wright Export Corp.*, 299 U.S. 304 (1936) for the proposition that the President is "the sole organ of the federal government in the field of international relations." The Court rejected such unbounded power in the President, noting that this description of the President's powers was not necessary to the holding in *Curtiss-Wright*, and that the case dealt with congressionally authorized action, rather than a unilateral presidential determination. Thus, although the Court held that Congress has no power to make recognition determinations contrary to those of the President, it did not question Congress's substantial powers over foreign affairs in general or passports in particular.

Quicknotes

SEPARATION OF POWERS The system of checks and balances preventing one branch of government from infringing upon exercising the powers of another branch of government.

CHAPTER 7

Race and the Equal Protection Clause

Quick Reference Rules of Law

CHAPTER 7

28. *Trump v. Hawaii.* (1) A President has authority under the Immigration and Nationality Act, 8 U.S.C. § 1182(f), to suspend the entry of aliens from specific countries where the President finds that their entry would be detrimental to United States interests. (2) Where a presidential proclamation is neutral on its face toward religion and putatively furthers national security interests, but disproportionately impacts a religious group toward which the President publicly has expressed great animus, the proclamation survives an attack on Establishment Clause grounds under rational basis review. *219*

Brown v. Board of Education of Topeka, Kansas (Brown I)

Students (P) v. School board (D)

347 U.S. 483 (1954)

NATURE OF CASE: Black minors sought the court's aid in obtaining admission to the public schools of their community on a nonsegregated basis.

FACT SUMMARY: Black children were denied admission to public schools attended by White children.

RULE OF LAW

The "separate but equal" doctrine has no application in the field of education, and the segregation of children in public schools based solely on their race violates the Equal Protection Clause.

FACTS: Black children had been denied admission to public schools attended by White children under laws requiring or permitting segregation according to race. It was found that the Black children's schools and the White children's schools had been or were being equalized with respect to buildings, curricula, qualifications, and salaries of teachers.

ISSUE: Does segregation of children in public schools solely on the basis of race, even though the physical facilities are equal, deprive the children of the minority group of equal protection of the law?

HOLDING AND DECISION: (Warren, C.J.) Yes. The "separate but equal" doctrine has no application in the field of education, and the segregation of children in public schools based solely on their race violates the Equal Protection Clause. First, intangible as well as tangible factors may be considered. Hence, the fact that the facilities and other tangible factors in the schools have been equalized is not controlling. Segregation of White and Black children in public schools has a detrimental effect on the Black children because the policy of separating the races is usually interpreted as denoting the inferiority of the Black children. A sense of inferiority affects children's motivation to learn. Segregation tends to deprive Black children of some of the benefits they would receive in an integrated school. Any language in *Plessy v. Ferguson*, 163 U.S. 537 (1896), contrary to this is rejected. The "separate but equal" doctrine has no place in the field of education. Separate facilities are inherently unequal. Such facilities deprive Black children of their right to equal protection of the laws.

ANALYSIS

In *Plessy* the court sustained a Louisiana statute requiring "equal, but separate accommodations" for Black and White railway passengers. The separate but equal doctrine was born and under it a long line of statutes providing separate but equal facilities were upheld. Justice Harlan was the only dissenter in *Plessy.* He stated, "The arbitrary separation of citizens, on the basis of race, while they are on a public highway . . . cannot be justified upon any legal grounds. The thin disguise of equal accommodations for passengers in railway cars will not mislead anyone, nor atone for the wrong done this day." After the 1954 decision in *Brown,* the court found segregation unconstitutional in other public facilities as well. Despite the emphasis on the school context in *Brown,* the later cases resulted in per curiam orders simply citing *Brown.* Facilities that were desegregated included beaches, buses, golf courses, and parks.

Quicknotes

EQUAL PROTECTION CLAUSE A constitutional provision that each person be guaranteed the same protection of the laws enjoyed by other persons in like circumstances.

Bolling v. Sharpe

[Parties not identified.]

347 U.S. 497 (1954)

NATURE OF CASE: Constitutional challenge to school segregation in the District of Columbia (D).

FACT SUMMARY: The District of Columbia's (D) school segregation policy was challenged by Black students (P).

RULE OF LAW

Separate school facilities are so fundamentally unfair and discriminatory as to violate the Due Process Clause of the Fifth Amendment.

FACTS: Black students (P) challenged the validity of the District of Columbia's (D) practice of segregating schools by race. The District (D) argued that separate but equal facilities have long been recognized in the District (D) and have been allowed by the courts. The students (P) contended that this was a badge of servitude and inferiority.

ISSUE: Is the enforced separation of the races so fundamentally unfair as to violate the Fifth Amendment Due Process Clause?

HOLDING AND DECISION: (Warren, C.J.) Yes. There is no Equal Protection Clause in the federal Constitution, and the Fourteenth Amendment is only applicable to the states. However, where discrimination is so fundamentally unfair as to offend the American ideal of fairness and justice then it violates the Due Process Clause of the Fifth Amendment. Racial classifications are fundamentally suspect and must be scrutinized with care. Where racial classifications conflict with the individual's right to freedom, they can only be justified by the most compelling governmental interests. Segregation in the schools is not related to any proper governmental objective. Such an unreasonable classification constitutes an arbitrary deprivation of individual liberty and violates the Due Process Clause. In view of our decision in *Brown v. Board of Education*, 347 U.S. 483 (1954), we hold that the federal government has the same duty to desegregate as do the states.

ANALYSIS

The decisions in *Brown* and *Bolling* were applied to many other previously segregated areas. Examples include segregated transportation, entertainment, restaurants, public restrooms, etc. Where state action, as such, was not present, Congress sought to regulate private discrimination under its Commerce Clause powers.

Quicknotes

COMMERCE CLAUSE Article I, § 8, cl. 3 of the United States Constitution, granting Congress the power to regulate commerce with foreign countries and between the states.

DUE PROCESS CLAUSE Language in the Fifth and Fourteenth Amendments to the United States Constitution providing that no person shall be deprived of "life, liberty, or property without due process of law."

EQUAL PROTECTION CLAUSE A constitutional guarantee that no person should be denied the same protection of the laws enjoyed by other persons in like circumstances.

FIFTH AMENDMENT Provides that no person shall be compelled to serve as a witness against oneself, be subject to trial for the same offense twice, or be deprived of life, liberty, or property without due process of law.

SUSPECT CLASSIFICATION A class of persons that have historically been subject to discriminatory treatment; statutes drawing a distinction between persons based on a suspect classification, i.e., race, nationality, or alienage, are subject to a strict scrutiny standard of review.

Brown v. Board of Education (Brown II)

African American minor (P) v. School board (D)

349 U.S. 294 (1955)

NATURE OF CASE: Decision setting forth the manner in which relief from unconstitutional public school segregation was to be rendered.

FACT SUMMARY: On May 17, 1954, the United States Supreme Court decided in *Brown v. Board of Education*, 347 U.S. 483 (1954) (*Brown I*) that racial discrimination in public education is unconstitutional. The Court requested further arguments on the question of how best to end racial segregation in public schools.

RULE OF LAW

School authorities have the primary responsibility for assessing and solving the problem of achieving racial integration in the public schools, and the district courts must ensure school authorities carry out these responsibilities promptly and in keeping with constitutional principles.

FACTS: On May 17, 1954, the United States Supreme Court decided unanimously in *Brown v. Board of Education*, 347 U.S. 483 (1954) (*Brown I*) that racial discrimination in public education is unconstitutional. That landmark case was a consolidation of several cases from several states that challenged public school segregation. *Brown I*, however, did not resolve how to effect desegregation, and the Court requested further arguments on the question of how best to implement relief to end racial segregation. A unanimous Court again rendered its decision on how to create a system of public education freed of racial discrimination.

ISSUE: Do school authorities have the primary responsibility for assessing and solving the problem of achieving racial integration in the public schools, and must the district courts ensure school authorities carry out these responsibilities promptly and in keeping with constitutional principles?

HOLDING AND DECISION: (Warren, C.J.) Yes. School authorities have the primary responsibility for assessing and solving the problem of achieving racial integration in the public schools, and the district courts must ensure school authorities carry out these responsibilities promptly and in keeping with constitutional principles. Whereas school authorities have the primary responsibility for achieving racial integration in the public schools, the district courts will have to consider whether the school authorities' actions are good faith implementation of the governing constitutional principles. Because of their proximity to local conditions and the possible need for further hearings, the courts that originally heard these cases can best perform this judicial appraisal. In doing so, the courts will be guided by the equitable principles of practical flexibility in shaping remedies and the facility for adjusting and reconciling public and private needs. The courts will require that the defendants make a prompt and reasonable start toward full racial integration in the public schools. Once such a start is made, the courts may determine that additional time is required to carry out the May 1954 ruling. However, the burden rests upon the school boards to determine that such time is necessary and consistent with good faith compliance with the Constitution. The courts may consider problems related to administration, the facilities, school transportation systems, and revision of school districts and local laws. They will also consider the adequacy of any plans proposed by the school boards and will retain jurisdiction during the transition period. The cases are remanded to the lower courts to enter orders consistent with this opinion as necessary to ensure that the children-plaintiffs in these cases are admitted to public schools on a racially nondiscriminatory basis with all deliberate speed. Judgments reversed and all cases remanded.

ANALYSIS

After its promulgation of general guidelines in *Brown II* in 1955, the Court maintained silence about implementation for several years. Enforcement of the desegregation requirement was left largely to lower court litigation. The Court broke its silence in *Cooper v. Aaron*, 358 U.S. 1 (1958), where it reaffirmed the *Brown* principles in the face of official resistance in Little Rock, Arkansas. It was not until the early 1960s, however, that the Court began to consider the details of desegregation plans. During the late 1960s, Court rulings on implementation came with greater frequency, specificity, and urgency. Finally, in *Alexander v. Holmes County Board of Education*, 369 U.S. 19 (1969), the Court called for an immediate end to dual school systems.

Quicknotes

DESEGRATION A judicial order prohibiting a person's race to be used as a basis for disqualification in attending the school of his or her choice, or to work at a place of his or her choice.

Continued on next page.

STRICT SCRUTINY The method by which courts determine the constitutionality of a law, when a law affects a fundamental right. Under the test, the legislature must have a compelling interest to enact the law, and measures prescribed by the law must be the least restrictive means possible to accomplish its goal.

SUSPECT CLASSIFICATION A class of persons that have historically been subject to discriminatory treatment; statutes drawing a distinction between persons based on a suspect classification, i.e., race, nationality, or alienage, are subject to a strict scrutiny standard of review.

Missouri v. Jenkins (Jenkins II)

State (D) v. African American student (P)

515 U.S. 70 (1995)

NATURE OF CASE: Appeal in action challenging segregation remedial orders. [The complete procedural posture of the case is not presented in the casebook extract.]

FACT SUMMARY: Missouri (D) challenged a district court's segregation remedial orders requiring the state (1) to fund salary increases for teachers and staff within the Kansas City Metropolitan School District (KCMSD), and (2) to continue to fund remedial magnet programs as long as student achievement levels remained at or below national norms. Missouri (D) argued that these orders exceeded the district court's remedial powers.

RULE OF LAW

A district court's intra-district desegregation powers do not include crafting a remedial plan that has as one of its purposes the goal of attracting nonminority students into the district.

FACTS: After many years of desegregation litigation, in 1985, a district court ordered the state to fund and implement within the Kansas City Metropolitan School District (KCMSD) a comprehensive magnet school and capital improvements plan. The primary goals of this plan were to attract nonminority students into the district and to provide minority students an educational experience of the quality they would have received absent the effects of segregation. To this end the district court ordered the state (1) to fund salary increases for teachers and staff within the Kansas City Metropolitan School District (KCMSD), and (2) to continue to fund remedial magnet programs as long as student achievement levels remained at or below national norms. Missouri (D) argued that these orders exceeded the district court's remedial powers. The United States Supreme Court granted certiorari in the case. [The complete procedural posture of the case is not presented in the casebook extract.]

ISSUE: Do a district court's intra-district desegregation powers include crafting a remedial plan that has as one of its purposes the goal of attracting nonminority students into the district?

HOLDING AND DECISION: (Rehnquist, C.J.) No. A district court's intra-district desegregation powers do not include crafting a remedial plan that has as one of its purposes the goal of attracting nonminority students into the district. [The decision and disposition are not presented in the casebook extract.]

CONCURRENCE: (Thomas, J.) Desegregation requires only an end to intentional segregation, but it does not require that minority and nonminority students attend the same schools. Implied in the district court's plan, based on the assumption that Black students suffer an unspecified psychological harm from segregation that retards their mental and educational development, is that Blacks are inferior to non-Blacks, and that Blacks cannot succeed absent the company of Whites. Merely because a school is predominantly Black does not necessarily mean that the state has intentionally engaged in unconstitutional segregation. Such a situation may reflect private choices, as where families choose to live. The district as a whole is over two-thirds Black, so it is not surprising that some of its schools, too, are overwhelmingly Black. This de facto—as opposed to de jure—segregation alone does not constitute a constitutional violation. Simply put, the government cannot discriminate among its citizens on basis of race. Regardless of whether racially isolated schools inflict psychological harm or benefit, the only question that the court may address is whether state actors have engaged in intentional discrimination. The courts are competent to resolve this only relevant question by making independent determinations concerning the existence of state action without the unnecessary and misleading assistance of the social sciences. The Constitution does not prevent individuals from choosing to live together, to work together, or to send their children to school together, so long as the state does not interfere with their choices on basis of race; the courts should follow the Constitution's lead. There is no reason to think that Black students cannot learn as well when surrounded by members of their own race as when they are in an integrated environment. To think that integration is the only way that Blacks can receive a proper education is to believe there must be something inferior about Blacks. To the contrary, however, it is very possible that all-Black schools will instill pride in Black students and their communities and will enable them to succeed just as well as nonminority students.

ANALYSIS

Justice Souter in a dissent asserted that the majority's consideration of the magnet school remedy and its limitation on the district court's remedial authority was contrary to controlling precedent, e.g., *Milliken v. Bradley,*

Continued on next page.

418 U.S. 717 (1974), *(Milliken I)*. Similarly, some commentators have argued that this case represented an end to court-ordered desegregation of schools, achieved through the Court's reliance on relatively narrow, case-specific grounds, without articulation of legal justifications for its departure from precedent.

Quicknotes

CERTIORARI A discretionary writ issued by a superior court to an inferior court to review the lower court's decisions; the United States Supreme Court's writ ordering such review.

Korematsu v. United States

Japanese American (D) v. Federal government (P)

323 U.S. 214 (1944)

NATURE OF CASE: Appeal from a conviction for violation of exclusion order No. 34.

FACT SUMMARY: Korematsu (D), an American citizen of Japanese ancestry, was convicted of violating exclusion order No. 34, a World War II decree that ordered all persons of Japanese ancestry to leave the military area of the Western United States.

RULE OF LAW

Apprehension by the proper military authorities of the gravest imminent danger to the public safety can justify the curtailment of the civil rights of a single racial group.

FACTS: Korematsu (D), an American citizen of Japanese ancestry, was convicted in federal district court for remaining in San Leandro, California, a "military area," contrary to civilian exclusion order No. 34 of the commanding general of the western command. The order directed that after May 9, 1942, all persons of Japanese ancestry should be excluded from the area to protect against acts of sabotage and espionage during World War II. Those of Japanese ancestry were to report to and temporarily remain in an assembly center and go under military control to a relocation center for an indeterminate period. Korematsu (D) appealed on grounds that the order denied equal protection.

ISSUE: Can apprehension by the proper military authorities of the gravest imminent danger to the public safety justify the curtailment of the civil rights of a single racial group?

HOLDING AND DECISION: (Black, J.) Yes. Apprehension by the proper military authorities of the gravest imminent danger to the public safety can justify the curtailment of the civil rights of a single racial group. While such a classification is immediately suspect and subject to the most rigid scrutiny, pressing public necessity can sometimes justify such exclusions. When under conditions of modern-warfare the country is threatened, "the power to protect must be commensurate with the threatened danger." Korematsu (D) was excluded because the United States was at war with the Empire of Japan, because the proper military authorities feared invasion of the West Coast and believed security required exclusion, and because Congress, placing its confidence in the military, determined that the military should have that power. Affirmed.

CONCURRENCE: (Frankfurter, J.) This decision says only that the Constitution was not violated, and not that the Court approved of the methods used.

DISSENT: (Murphy, J.) It cannot be reasonably assumed that all persons of Japanese ancestry may have a dangerous tendency to commit enemy acts.

DISSENT: (Jackson, J.) A civil court should not be made to enforce an order that violates constitutional limitations even if it is a reasonable exercise of military authority.

ANALYSIS

This case has received severe and growing criticism over the years. However, Chief Justice Warren expressed the view that in some circumstances the Court will simply not be in position to reject descriptions by the executive branch of the degree of military necessity. Where time is of the essence, the Court could only reject the necessity not on grounds of factual unassailability, but for insufficiency. Justice Douglas, 30 years later, wrote, "the decisions were extreme and went to the verge of wartime power . . . It is easy in retrospect to denounce what was done, as there actually was no attempted Japanese invasion of our country . . . but those making plans for the defense of the nation had no such knowledge and were planning for the worst." *De Funis v. Odegaard*, 416 U.S. 312 (1974).

Quicknotes

EQUAL PROTECTION CLAUSE A constitutional guarantee that no person should be denied the same protection of the laws enjoyed by other persons in like circumstances.

Oyama v. California

Japanese citizen (D) v. State (P)

332 U.S. 633 (1948)

NATURE OF CASE: Appeal in action by state to sell land bought by individual ineligible to become a United States citizen as a gift for minor child born in the U.S. [The procedural posture of the case is not presented in the casebook summary.]

FACT SUMMARY: Kajiro Oyama (D), a Japanese citizen purchased land as a gift for his minor son, Fred (D), who was born in the United States. The Oyamas (D) contended that California's (P) attempt to sell the land on the ground that the gift was in fact an attempt to evade the state's Alien Land Laws, which prohibited ownership of agricultural land by persons ineligible to become U.S. citizens, violated Fred's (D) rights under the Equal Protection Clause because California (P) treated similar purchases by non-Japanese parents for their minor children differently.

RULE OF LAW

Discrimination on the basis of racial descent between a minor American citizen, whose parents are ineligible for naturalization, and other minor citizens, whose parents are either citizens or eligible for naturalization, violates the Equal Protection Clause.

FACTS: California's (P) Alien Land Laws prohibited ownership of agricultural land by persons ineligible to become U.S. citizens. Kajiro Oyama (D), a Japanese citizen, purchased land as a gift for his minor son, Fred (D), who was born in the United States, and, therefore was a U.S. citizen. When the family was sent to an internment camp during World War II, California (P) attempted to sell the land, claiming that Kajiro's (D) purchases were not gifts but in fact were an attempt to circumvent the Alien Land Laws. California (P) had treated similar purchases by non-Japanese parents for their children differently. Accordingly, the Oyamas (D) argued that California (P) violated Fred's (D) equal protection rights. The United States Supreme Court granted certiorari. [The procedural posture of the case is not presented in the casebook summary.]

ISSUE: Does discrimination on the basis of racial descent between a minor American citizen, whose parents are ineligible for naturalization, and other minor citizens, whose parents are either citizens or eligible for naturalization, violate the Equal Protection Clause?

HOLDING AND DECISION: (Vinson, C.J.) Yes. Discrimination on the basis of racial descent between a minor American citizen, whose parents are ineligible for naturalization, and other minor citizens, whose parents are either citizens or eligible for naturalization, violates the Equal Protection Clause. However, the Court does not reach the question of whether the Alien Land Laws are unconstitutional.

CONCURRENCE: (Black, J.) The California Alien Land Laws violate the equal protection clause of the Fourteenth Amendment because they are designed to discriminate against aliens of Japanese ancestry. The Fourteenth Amendment was intended to bar the states from denying to some groups, on account of their race or color, any rights, privileges, and opportunities accorded to other groups. Therefore, California's (P) Alien Land Laws, and similar laws of other states, should be held unconstitutional and invalidated.

CONCURRENCE: (Murphy, J.) The Alien Land Laws were designed to effectuate a purely racial discrimination, to prohibit a Japanese alien from owning or using agricultural land solely because he or she is a Japanese alien. It is rooted deeply in racial, economic, and social antagonisms, and violates the Fourteenth Amendment's Equal Protection Clause.

DISSENT: (Reed, J.) There has been no violation by California (P) of Fred Oyama's (D) equal protection rights here.

ANALYSIS

Oyama is considered a landmark decision. It saved many Japanese Americans from impoverishment, as California (P) ceased escheat proceedings against them after the *Oyama* decision was handed down, and four years later in 1952, the Alien Land Acts were struck down by the California Supreme Court in *Fujii v. California*, 38 Cal.2nd 718, 242 P.2d 617 (1952), and *Masaoka v. People*, 39 Cal.2d 883 (1952), signaling the end of California's (P) historic legal discrimination against Japanese aliens. Shortly after the California Supreme Court decisions, which found the Alien Land Laws violated the Fourteenth Amendment, Congress passed the McCarran-Walter Immigration Act, which eliminated the category of "immigrant ineligible to citizenship." The *Oyama* decision also is credited with establishing the Supreme Court's doctrine of "strict scrutiny," according to which judges have the duty to presume that any laws that make facial racial classifications are unconstitutional unless they are narrowly

Continued on next page.

tailored to meet compelling state interests, and to examine those laws' provisions closely to determine whether they do so.

Quicknotes

EQUAL PROTECTION CLAUSE A constitutional provision that each person be guaranteed the same protection of the laws enjoyed by other persons in like circumstances.

ESCHEAT The transfer of property to the state because the owner of the property died with no one legally entitled to claim it.

FOURTEENTH AMENDMENT Declares that no state shall make or enforce any law that shall abridge the privileges and immunities of citizens of the United States. No state shall deny to any person within its jurisdiction the equal protection of the laws.

Loving v. Virginia

White husband (D) v. State (P)

388 U.S. 1 (1967)

NATURE OF CASE: Appeal after conviction for violation of state law barring interracial marriage.

FACT SUMMARY: Loving (D), a White man, and Jeter (D), a Black woman, both Virginia residents, were married in the District of Columbia. When they returned to Virginia, they were indicted for violating the state's ban on interracial marriage.

RULE OF LAW

A state law restricting the freedom to marry solely because of racial classification violates the Equal Protection Clause.

FACTS: In June 1958, Loving (D), a White man, and Jeter (D), a Black woman, both Virginia residents, were married in the District of Columbia, pursuant to its laws. Shortly after their marriage, the Lovings (D) returned to Virginia and were indicted for violating the state's law barring interracial marriage. They pleaded guilty and were sentenced to one year in jail. The trial judge suspended the sentence for 25 years on the condition that the Lovings (D) leave the state and not return for 25 years. In 1963, they filed a motion to have the judgment vacated and set aside.

ISSUE: Does a state law, which prevents marriages between persons solely on the basis of racial classifications, violate the Equal Protection Clause?

HOLDING AND DECISION: (Warren, C.J.) Yes. A state law that prevents marriages between persons solely on basis of racial classifications violates the Equal Protection Clause. At the very least, the Equal Protection Clause demands that racial classifications, especially suspect in criminal statutes, be subjected to the most rigid scrutiny. If they are ever to be upheld, they must be shown to be necessary to the accomplishment of some legitimate state objective. Here, there is no question that Virginia's miscegenation statutes rest solely upon distinctions drawn according to race. The statutes proscribe generally accepted conduct if engaged in by members of different races. The fact that the statute prohibits only interracial marriages involving White persons indicates that its aim is to maintain White supremacy. There is patently no legitimate overriding purpose independent of invidious discrimination that justifies the classification. A statute restricting marriage solely because of race violates the Equal Protection Clause. These statutes also deprive the Lovings (D) of liberty without due process. Since marriage is a basic human civil right, to deny this freedom on so insupportable a basis as racial classifications deprives all the state's citizens of liberty without due process of the law.

CONCURRENCE: (Stewart, J.) It is simply not possible for a state law to be valid under the Constitution that makes the criminality of an act depend upon the race of the actor.

ANALYSIS

In *McLaughlin v. Florida*, 379 U.S. 184 (1964), a state law banning habitual nighttime cohabitation between Whites and Blacks not married to each other was held to violate the Equal Protection Clause, since other unmarried couples were not subject to prosecution for the same acts. Ordinances establishing ghettos in which Blacks must reside were found to violate the clause [*Buchanan v. Warley*, 245 U.S. 60 (1917)], as was judicial enforcement of covenants restricting ownership of land to Whites [*Shelley v. Kramer*, 334 U.S. 1 (1948)]. Racial discrimination in the selection of jurors [*Patton v. Mississippi*, 332 U.S. 463 (1947)], hiring Blacks for certain occupations, and establishing racial qualifications for public offices [*Anderson v. Martin*, 375 U.S. 399 (1964)] have all been held to violate equal protection.

Quicknotes

DUE PROCESS CLAUSE Language found in the Fifth and Fourteenth Amendments to the United States Constitution providing that no person shall be deprived of "life, liberty, or property without due process of law."

EQUAL PROTECTION A constitutional guarantee that no person shall be denied the same protection of the laws enjoyed by other persons in like circumstances.

MISCEGENATION Marriage between two persons of different races.

SUSPECT CLASSIFICATION A class of persons that have historically been subject to discriminatory treatment; statutes drawing a distinction between persons based on a suspect classification, i.e., race, nationality, or alienage, are subject to a strict scrutiny standard of review.

Johnson v. California

Prisoner (P) v. Prison system (D)

543 U.S. 499 (2005)

NATURE OF CASE: Review of federal court judgment.

FACT SUMMARY: California prisoner Garrison Johnson (P) alleged in federal district court that the California Department of Corrections (D) used race to assign temporary cell mates for new prisoners, a practice Johnson (P) said violated the United States Constitution's Equal Protection Clause.

RULE OF LAW

Strict scrutiny is the proper standard of review for an equal protection challenge to a department of corrections unwritten policy of racially segregating prisoners in double cells in reception centers for up to 60 days each time they enter a new correctional facility.

FACTS: California prisoner Garrison Johnson (P) alleged in federal district court that the California Department of Corrections (D) used race to assign temporary cellmates for new prisoners, a practice Johnson (P) said violated the United States Constitution's Equal Protection Clause. New inmates are held in reception centers for up to 60 days upon their arrival, and during that time are evaluated by prison officials to determine ultimate placement. The rest of the prison facilities, including permanent cells, are fully integrated. The prison's (D) rationale for the policy is that it is necessary to prevent violence caused by racial gangs.

ISSUE: Is strict scrutiny the proper standard of review for an equal protection challenge to a department of corrections unwritten policy of racially segregating prisoners in double cells in reception centers for up to 60 days each time they enter a new correctional facility?

HOLDING AND DECISION: (O'Connor, J.) Yes. Strict scrutiny is the proper standard of review for an equal protection challenge to a department of corrections unwritten policy of racially segregating prisoners in double cells in reception centers for up to 60 days each time they enter a new correctional facility. The fact that the policy was neutral in the sense that all prisoners were equally segregated does not allow the policy to escape strict scrutiny. Racial classifications must receive strict scrutiny even when they may be said to affect the races equally. In addition, the fact that the policy applies only in the prison context does not entitle it to a deferential standard of review.

CONCURRENCE: (Ginsburg, J.) The same standard of review need not control judicial inspection of every official race classification. State actions taken in the prison context, where prisoners have long been denied the full panoply of rights accorded full citizens, are significantly different from actions taken to undo the effects of invidious discrimination. Here, there was no pretense that the actions taken were of the latter kind.

DISSENT: (Stevens, J.) The state policy of segregation in prisons violates the Equal Protection Clause of the Fourteenth Amendment. The prison system (D) has failed to justify its policy under strict scrutiny or a more deferential standard. Segregation is inherently wrong, and the system (D) failed to explain why it could not rely on individual assessment of the prisoners' risk of violence as an alternative to automatic segregation.

DISSENT: (Thomas, J.) This case requires the reconciliation of two conflicting lines of precedent. On the one hand *Gratz v. Bollinger*, 539 U.S. 244 (2003), holds that all racial classifications reviewable under the Equal Protection Clause must be strictly scrutinized. But the Court also held in *Turner v. Safley*, 482 U.S. 78 (1987), that the relaxed standard of review applies to all circumstances in which the needs of prison administration affect constitutional rights. The majority followed the former line of cases to its conclusion that strict scrutiny was appropriate. But the Constitution demands less inside prison walls. The deferential standard set forth in *Turner* is more appropriate.

ANALYSIS

The *Johnson* case stands in contrast with a long line of cases, beginning with *Brown v. Board of Education*, 347 U.S. 483 (1954), that hold that because racial segregation is inherently unequal, it violates of the Fourteenth Amendment. *Johnson* holds that racial segregation is now to be treated like any other racial classification, and the court does not limit its decision to the prison context.

Quicknotes

EQUAL PROTECTION CLAUSE A constitutional provision that each person be guaranteed the same protection of the laws enjoyed by other persons in like circumstances.

Continued on next page.

FOURTEENTH AMENDMENT Declares that no state shall make or enforce any law that shall abridge the privileges or immunities of citizens of the United States. No state shall deny to any person within its jurisdiction the equal protection of the laws.

STRICT SCRUTINY A method by which courts determine the constitutionality of a law, when a law affects a fundamental right. Under the test, the legislature must have had a compelling interest to enact the law, and measures prescribed by the law must be the least restrictive means possible to accomplish its goal.

Yick Wo v. Hopkins

Laundry operator (D) v. City (P)

118 U.S. 356, (1886)

NATURE OF CASE: Appeal from conviction of violating a city health and safety ordinance.

FACT SUMMARY: Only Chinese aliens were prosecuted under an ordinance requiring laundries to be constructed out of brick.

RULE OF LAW

A valid law unevenly and discriminatorily administered violates the Equal Protection Clause of the Constitution.

FACTS: A San Francisco ordinance made it unlawful to operate a laundry without consent of the board of supervisors unless the laundry was constructed of either stone or brick. Under the ordinance, the supervisors denied permission to Chinese aliens but granted it to Whites. Yick Wo (D) was arrested for violating the ordinance. He appealed his conviction on the basis that the law was being administered in a discriminatory fashion.

ISSUE: Can a valid law be declared unconstitutional because it is being arbitrarily and discriminatorily applied?

HOLDING AND DECISION: (Matthews, J.) Yes. When, as here, it can be objectively demonstrated that a law is being discriminatorily applied, a court may declare the law unconstitutional. We can decide this case without ever reaching the question of the ordinance's validity (which is seriously in question). Even if valid, the San Francisco Supervisors (P) applied it in a highly discriminatory and systematic fashion to exclude those of Chinese origin from practicing the laundry business. Such discriminatory treatment violates both the spirit and letter of the Equal Protection Clause and Yick Wo's (D) conviction must be discharged. Reversed and remanded.

ANALYSIS

Other examples in this area include the systematic exclusion of Black people from jury panels through use of the prosecutor's preemptory challenge power or by excluding them from jury rolls. Also, in *Mayor of Philadelphia v. Educational Equality League*, 415 U.S. 605 (1974), the Mayor was charged with discrimination in his appointment of a selection committee for school board members. However, in this case, the proof of discrimination was insufficient to establish a prima facie case and the charges were dismissed. The Court held that mere statistical data concerning population mixtures was insufficient to prove discrimination as a matter of law.

Quicknotes

EQUAL PROTECTION CLAUSE A constitutional guarantee that no person should be denied the same protection of the laws enjoyed by other persons in like circumstances.

PEREMPTORY CHALLENGE The exclusion by a party to a lawsuit of a prospective juror without the need to specify a particular reason.

Ho Ah Kow v. Nunan

Male Chinese national (P) v. Municipal official (D)

12 F. Cas. 252 (No. 6546) (C.C.D. Cal. 1879)

NATURE OF CASE: Action for damages arising from the enforcement of allegedly unconstitutional class legislation.

FACT SUMMARY: Ho Ah Kow (P), a male Chinese national, contended that a law requiring the shaving of a male prisoner's hair to within an inch of the scalp was unconstitutional class legislation, since it was demonstrably targeted at Chinese men, who, at the time, wore their hair in queues (a form of waist-length pigtail) and who believed that the deprivation of the queue was a disgrace and resulted in future suffering.

RULE OF LAW

A law is unconstitutional where, although on its face it is generally applicable, in fact it is targeted at a class of persons, thereby denying that class equal protection of the laws.

FACTS: A San Francisco ordinance required that every male imprisoned in the county jail have his hair "cut or clipped to a uniform length of one inch from the scalp thereof." Ho Ah Kow (P), who had been imprisoned in San Francisco for a misdemeanor, along with many other Chinese nationals, brought suit in federal court against San Francisco's sheriff, Nunan (D), claiming that the ordinance was unconstitutionally targeted at Chinese males, who, at the time, wore their hair in queues (a form of waist-length pigtail) and who believed that the deprivation of the queue was a disgrace and resulted in future suffering. The ordinance was justified as promoting discipline and sanitary conditions. However, the ordinance was enforced only against Chinese men, and it was widely known in the community as the "Queue Ordinance." Another justification for the law was that Chinese men would pay their fines only upon fear of losing their queues, in addition to their imprisonment. Ho Ah Kow (P), whose queue had been shaved off, asserted that the ordinance not only violated equal protection of the law as class legislation, but also constituted cruel and unusual punishment.

ISSUE: Is a law unconstitutional where, although on its face it is generally applicable, in fact it is targeted at a class of persons, thereby denying that class equal protection of the laws?

HOLDING AND DECISION: (Field, J.) Yes. A law is unconstitutional where, although on its face it is generally applicable, in fact it is targeted at a class of persons, thereby denying that class equal protection of the laws. The ordinance is special legislation on the part of San Francisco against a class of persons who, under the Constitution and laws of the United States, are entitled to the equal protection of the laws. The ordinance was intended only for the Chinese in San Francisco, and this was acknowledged by the city supervisors who passed the ordinance, and it was so understood by everyone in the community. It cannot be justified as a law promoting discipline, because it does not serve that purpose, nor can it be justified as a sanitary regulation. Had the ordinance contemplated a mere sanitary regulation, it would have been made applicable to females as well as to males, and to persons awaiting trial as well as to convicted persons. Notwithstanding that the ordinance is expressed in general terms, the court need not take it at face value, when it is clear from its legislative history and broad understanding in the community that it was targeted at, and only enforced against, a specific class. Otherwise, constitutional protections could be evaded by couching ordinances in general terms when they in fact are directed at only a specific class of persons. Here, it is clear the ordinance acts with special severity upon Chinese prisoners, inflicting upon them suffering altogether disproportionate to what would be endured by other prisoners if enforced against them. Upon the Chinese prisoners, its enforcement operates as a cruel and unusual punishment. An ordinance would, similarly, be unconstitutional if it required all prisoners to be fed pork, as a general matter, but it was clearly hostile only to Jews, whose observance of their religious kashrut laws would prohibit them from eating that particular kind of meat. The San Francisco ordinance is unconstitutional. [Judgment for Ho Ah Kow (P).]

ANALYSIS

As this case illustrates, class legislation did not have to formally express a classification for it to be found unconstitutional. Instead, the key issue—as in this case—was whether the legislation unjustifiably had the effect of singling out a single group for special burdens. Thus, the courts held early on that laws that do not overtly classify on basis of race may nonetheless violate the Fourteenth Amendment if they are administered in a race-dependent manner.

Continued on next page.

Quicknotes

CRUEL AND UNUSUAL PUNISHMENT Punishment that is excessive or disproportionate to the offense committed and which is prohibited by the Eighth Amendment to the U.S. Constitution.

FOURTEENTH AMENDMENT Declares that no state shall make or enforce any law that shall abridge the privileges and immunities of citizens of the United States. No state shall deny to any person within its jurisdiction the equal protection of the laws.

Griggs v. Duke Power Co.

African American employee (P) v. Employer (D)

401 U.S. 424 (1971)

NATURE OF CASE: Appeal from affirmance of judgment that an employer's practices that do not intend to discriminate against African Americans, but operate to exclude them from employment, do not violate Title VII of the Civil Rights Act of 1964.

FACT SUMMARY: Griggs (P), an African American employee of Duke Power Co. (D), contended that Duke Power's (D) requirement for certain jobs of a high school diploma and scoring at a certain level on an intelligence test violated Title VII of the Civil Rights Act of 1964 because these requirements had a negative disparate impact on African Americans, and because the requirements were unrelated to successful job performance.

RULE OF LAW

Under Title VII of the Civil Rights Act of 1964, an employer may not use employment requirements that discriminate against minorities where such requirements are not demonstrably related to successful job performance, notwithstanding a lack of discriminatory intent.

FACTS: Duke Power Co. (D) required that a job applicant for certain jobs have a high school diploma and score at a certain level on an intelligence test. These requirements had a negative disparate impact on African American employees. Griggs (P), an African American employee, contended that Duke Power's (D) job requirements violated Title VII of the Civil Rights Act of 1964 because of their discriminatory effect and because the requirements were unrelated to successful job performance. In fact, employees hired before the requirements were put in place, and who did not have high school diplomas or pass the intelligence test, continued to perform satisfactorily and make progress in departments for which the high school and test criteria were now used. Both the district court and court of appeals, finding no discriminatory intent, concluded that Title VII was not violated. The United States Supreme Court granted certiorari.

ISSUE: Under Title VII of the Civil Rights Act of 1964, may employer use employment requirements that discriminate against minorities where such requirements are not demonstrably related to successful job performance, notwithstanding a lack of discriminatory intent?

HOLDING AND DECISION: (Burger, C.J.) No. Under Title VII of the Civil Rights Act of 1964, an employer may not use employment requirements that discriminate against minorities where such requirements are not demonstrably related to successful job performance, notwithstanding a lack of discriminatory intent. The Act requires the elimination of artificial, arbitrary, and unnecessary barriers to employment that operate invidiously to discriminate on basis of race, and, if, as here, an employment practice that operates to exclude African Americans cannot be shown to be related to job performance, it is prohibited, notwithstanding the employer's lack of discriminatory intent. Although the Act's goal is that the status quo of past discrimination be eradicated, it does not intend to guarantee a job to every person regardless of qualifications. Job qualifications that have a discriminatory effect, but no relation to job performance, are prohibited. Here, neither the high school completion requirement nor the general intelligence test has been shown to bear a demonstrable relationship to successful performance of the jobs for which it was used. The evidence showed, to the contrary, that employees who had not completed high school or taken the intelligence tests had continued to perform satisfactorily and make progress in departments for which the high school and test criteria were now being used. Accordingly, these requirements are prohibited by Title VII, regardless of the lack of discriminatory intent, since they are unrelated to measuring job capability. Reversed.

ANALYSIS

In *Griggs*, the Court also held that an employer has the burden of showing that any given requirement has a manifest relationship to the employment in question. Before *Griggs*, employees or job applicants who accused employers of racial discrimination had to prove discriminatory intent, but after *Griggs*, they had to prove only discriminatory effects of hiring or advancement practices to be successful in their Title VII litigation. The Civil Rights Act of 1991 codified the *Griggs* standard.

Quicknotes

DISCRIMINATION Unequal treatment of a class of persons.

TITLE VII Prohibits unlawful discrimination against individuals based on race or sex.

Washington v. Davis

State (D) v. Police applicants (P)

426 U.S. 229 (1976)

NATURE OF CASE: Action for a declaratory judgment.

FACT SUMMARY: A qualifying test for positions as police officers in the District of Columbia was failed by a disproportionate high number of Black applicants (P).

RULE OF LAW

A law or official governmental practice must have a "discriminatory purpose," not merely a disproportionate effect on one race, to constitute "invidious discrimination" under the Fifth Amendment Due Process Clause or the Fourteenth Amendment Equal Protection Clause.

FACTS: To be accepted in the District of Columbia Metropolitan Police Department, all applicants must receive a grade of at least 40 on "Test 21." This test was developed by the Civil Service Commission for use throughout the federal service to test "verbal ability, vocabulary, reading and comprehension." After failing this test, several Black applicants (P) brought an action against the Commissioners of the United States Civil Service Commission (Commissioners) (D) for a declaratory judgment that "Test 21" was unconstitutional. In this action, the Black applicants (P) claimed that "Test 21" was unlawfully discriminatory against Blacks, and, therefore, was in violation of the Fifth Amendment Due Process Clause. After the test was invalidated by the court of appeals, the Commissioners (D) appealed to this court.

ISSUE: Does a law or official governmental practice constitute "invidious discrimination" merely because it affects a greater proportion of one race than another?

HOLDING AND DECISION: (White, J.) No. A law or official governmental practice must have a "discriminatory purpose," not merely a disproportionate effect on one race, to constitute "invidious discrimination" under the Fifth Amendment Due Process Clause or the Fourteenth Amendment Equal Protection Clause. Of course, a disproportionate impact may be relevant as "evidence" of a "discriminatory purpose." However, such impact "is not the sole touchstone of invidious racial discrimination forbidden by the Constitution," and, standing alone, "it does not trigger the rule that racial classifications are to be subjected to the strictest scrutiny." Here, "Test 21" is racially "neutral" on its face (i.e., it is designed to disqualify anyone who cannot meet the requirements of the police training program). As such, it is valid even though it has a disproportionate effect on Blacks. Reversed.

CONCURRENCE: (Stevens, J.) There is no "purposeful discrimination" here, since "Test 21" serves "the neutral and legitimate purpose of requiring all applicants to meet a uniform minimum standard of literacy."

ANALYSIS

Generally, classifications based upon race are considered "suspect" and, therefore, are subjected to "strict scrutiny" under the Equal Protection Clause or the Due Process Clause (i.e., such classifications must be justified by a "compelling state interest"). However, as this case illustrates, such "strict scrutiny" is applied only when there is "purposeful discrimination." As such, the Court (as here) can avoid applying "strict scrutiny" by finding that any discriminatory impact is merely incidental. Note that here the Court also avoided applying the strict standard in Title VII of the Civil Rights Act of 1964 (by saying that only the constitutional issue was raised). Under Title VII, whenever hiring and promotion practices disqualify disproportionate numbers of Black people, the disqualifications must be justified by more than a rational basis, i.e., they must be validated in terms of job performance, even if no discriminatory purpose is shown.

Quicknotes

DUE PROCESS CLAUSE Language found in the Fifth and Fourteenth Amendments to the United States Constitution providing that no person shall be deprived of "life, liberty, or property without due process of law."

EQUAL PROTECTION CLAUSE A constitutional guarantee that no person should be denied the same protection of the laws enjoyed by other persons in like circumstances.

INVIDIOUS DISCRIMINATION Unequal treatment of a class of persons that is particularly malicious or hostile.

STRICT SCRUTINY The method by which courts determine the constitutionality of a law, when a law affects a fundamental right. Under the test, the legislature must have a compelling interest to enact the law, and measures prescribed by the law must be the least restrictive means possible to accomplish its goal.

SUSPECT CLASSIFICATION A class of persons that have historically been subject to discriminatory treatment; statutes drawing a distinction between persons based on a suspect classification, i.e., race, nationality, or alienage, are subject to a strict scrutiny standard of review.

Village of Arlington Heights v. Metropolitan Housing Development Corp.

Municipality (D) v. Real estate developer (P)

429 U.S. 252 (1977)

NATURE OF CASE: Appeal from judgment that a municipality's denial of rezoning was unconstitutional because it had a discriminatory effect. [The complete procedural posture of the case is not presented in the casebook extract.]

FACT SUMMARY: The Village of Arlington Heights (the Village) (D) contended that its denial of rezoning to the Metropolitan Housing Development Corp. (MHDC) (P), which sought to develop low-income housing in the Village (D), was not unconstitutional, despite having a discriminatory effect, because the denial was not motivated by a discriminatory purpose.

RULE OF LAW

Government action that has a racially discriminatory effect, but that is not motivated by a racially discriminatory purpose, does not violate the Fourteenth Amendment.

FACTS: The Metropolitan Housing Development Corp. (MHDC) (P) sought to develop low-income housing in The Village of Arlington Heights (the Village) (D). The development was conditioned on obtaining necessary rezoning, which the Village (D) denied. The denial was motivated by factors typically relied on by the Village (D) in making rezoning decisions. The effect of the denial arguably bore more heavily on racial minorities. Thus, MHDC (P) brought suit alleging the denial was unconstitutional because it had a discriminatory impact, notwithstanding that the denial was not motivated by a discriminatory purpose. The court of appeals ruled that the denial was unconstitutional because it found that the denial had an ultimate racially discriminatory effect. The United States Supreme Court granted certiorari. [The complete procedural posture of the case is not presented in the casebook extract.]

ISSUE: Does government action that has a racially discriminatory effect, but that is not motivated by a racially discriminatory purpose, violate the Fourteenth Amendment?

HOLDING AND DECISION: (Powell, J.) No. Government action that has a racially discriminatory effect, but that is not motivated by a racially discriminatory purpose, does not violate the Fourteenth Amendment. Proof of a racially discriminatory intent or purpose is required, and MHDC (P) failed to carry the burden of proving that such an intent or purpose was a motivating factor in the Village's (D) rezoning decision. A racially discriminatory intent may be evidenced by such factors as disproportionate impact, the historical background of the challenged decision, the specific antecedent events, departures from normal procedures, and contemporary statements of the decision makers. Here, the Village's (D) decision progressed according to usual procedures, and the decision was based on zoning factors typically used in making rezoning decisions. Reversed.

ANALYSIS

Justice Powell noted that even proof that the decision by the Village (D) was motivated in part by a racially discriminatory purpose would not necessarily have required invalidation of the challenged decision. He explained that such proof would, however, have shifted to the Village (D) the burden of establishing that the same decision would have resulted even had the impermissible purpose not been considered. If this were established, the complaining party in a case of this kind no longer fairly could attribute the injury complained of to improper consideration of a discriminatory purpose. In such circumstances, there would be no justification for judicial interference with the challenged decision.

Quicknotes

DISCRIMINATORY IMPACT The effect of an action that affects one group of persons more significantly than another; insufficient to prove discriminatory intent on its own.

DISCRIMINATORY PURPOSE Intent to discriminate; must be shown to establish an Equal Protection violation.

Personnel Administrator of Massachusetts v. Feeney

State (D) v. Job applicant (P)

442 U.S. 256 (1979)

NATURE OF CASE: Appeal in action asserting that a state veterans' civil service preference statute violated the Equal Protection Clause. [The procedural posture of the case is not presented in the casebook extract.]

FACT SUMMARY: Feeney (P) challenged a Massachusetts (D) statute that gave absolute preference to veterans, male and female, who had served in the armed forces, as violative of the Equal Protection Clause, since the statute's effect was to discriminate against women and the state legislature could have easily foreseen this effect when it enacted the statute, and more narrowly tailored the statute to eliminate such discrimination.

RULE OF LAW

A state statute granting an absolute lifetime preference to veterans in public employment opportunities does not violate the Equal Protection Clause of the Fourteenth Amendment merely because the state legislature could easily have foreseen that it would discriminate against women.

FACTS: A Massachusetts (D) statute gave an absolute lifetime civil service preference to all veterans, male and female. Because the great majority of individuals serving in the armed forces were male (only 1.8 percent of Massachusetts (D) veterans were women), the statute worked to their advantage in filling the state civil service positions. Feeney (P) brought suit alleging that the preference excluded women from consideration for the best state civil service jobs and thus discriminated against women in violation of the Equal Protection Clause of the Fourteenth Amendment. She also contended that the Massachusetts (D) legislature could easily have foreseen this effect, given that federal law excluded most women from military service during the relevant period. The United States Supreme Court granted certiorari in the case. [The procedural posture of the case is not presented in the casebook extract.]

ISSUE: Does a state statute granting an absolute lifetime preference to veterans in public employment opportunities violate the Equal Protection Clause of the Fourteenth Amendment merely because the state legislature could easily have foreseen that it would discriminate against women?

HOLDING AND DECISION: (Stewart, J.) No. A state statute granting an absolute lifetime preference to veterans in public employment opportunities does not violate the Equal Protection Clause of the Fourteenth Amendment merely because the state legislature could easily have foreseen that it would discriminate against women. When a basic classification is rationally based, uneven effects upon particular groups within a class are ordinarily not unconstitutional. While the decision to grant a preference to veterans was intentional, discriminatory purpose implies more than intent as volition or intent as awareness of consequences; it implies that the decision maker selected or reaffirmed a particular course of action at least in part "because of," not merely "in spite of," its adverse effects upon an identifiable group. When the totality of legislative actions establishing and extending the Massachusetts (D) veterans' preference are considered, the law remains a preference for veterans of either sex over nonveterans of either sex, not for men over women.

ANALYSIS

The Court explains that certain classifications in themselves supply a reason to infer antipathy. A racial classification, for example, regardless of purported motivation, is presumptively invalid and can be upheld only upon an extraordinary justification. This rule applies as well to a classification that is ostensibly neutral but is an obvious pretext for racial discrimination. But, as was made clear in *Washington v. Davis*, 426 U.S. 229 (1976), and *Arlington Heights v. Metropolitan Housing Dev. Corp.*, 429 U.S. 252 (1977), even if a neutral law has a disproportionately adverse effect upon a racial minority, it is unconstitutional under the Equal Protection Clause only if that impact can be traced to a discriminatory purpose.

Quicknotes

DISCRIMINATORY IMPACT The effect of an action that affects one group of persons more significantly than another; insufficient to prove discriminatory intent on its own.

EQUAL PROTECTION CLAUSE A constitutional provision that each person be guaranteed the same protection of the laws enjoyed by other persons in like circumstances.

Ricci v. DeStefano

Firefighter (P) v. City official (D)

557 U.S. 557 (2009)

NATURE OF CASE: Appeal from affirmance of summary judgment for defendants in action alleging disparate treatment on basis of race in violation of Title VII of the Civil Rights Act of 1964.

FACT SUMMARY: White and Hispanic firefighters who passed New Haven, Connecticut's (the City's) examinations to identify those firefighters best qualified for promotion, contended that the City (D) violated Title VII of the Civil Rights Act of 1964 by failing to certify the results of the exams, which had the effect of denying promotions to African American firefighters.

RULE OF LAW

A municipality violates Title VII of the Civil Rights Act of 1964 when it rejects results from an otherwise valid civil service exam when the results unintentionally prevent the promotion of minority candidates.

FACTS: Title VII of the Civil Rights Act of 1964 prohibits intentional acts of employment discrimination based on race, color, religion, sex, and national origin (disparate treatment), as well as policies or practices that are not intended to discriminate but in fact have a disproportionately adverse effect on minorities (disparate impact). Once a plaintiff has established a prima facie case of disparate impact, the employer may defend by demonstrating that its policy or practice is job related for the position in question and consistent with business necessity. If the employer meets that burden, the plaintiff may still succeed by showing that the employer refuses to adopt an available alternative practice that has less disparate impact and serves the employer's legitimate needs. New Haven, Connecticut (the City) (D) used objective examinations to identify those firefighters best qualified for promotion. The exams were 60 percent written and 40 percent oral. When the results of such an exam to fill vacant lieutenant and captain positions showed that White candidates had outperformed minority candidates, a rancorous public debate ensued. Confronted with arguments both for and against certifying the test results—and threats of a lawsuit either way—the City (D) threw out the results based on the statistical racial disparity. White and Hispanic firefighters who passed the exams but were denied a chance at promotions by the City's (D) refusal to certify the test results, sued the City (D) and its officials (D), alleging that discarding the test results discriminated against them based on their race in violation of Title VII of the Civil Rights Act of 1964. The defendants responded that had they certified the test results, they could have faced Title VII liability for adopting a practice having a disparate impact on minority firefighters. The district court granted summary judgment for the defendants, and the court of appeals affirmed. The United States Supreme Court granted certiorari.

ISSUE: Does a municipality violate Title VII of the Civil Rights Act of 1964 when it rejects results from an otherwise valid civil service exam when the results unintentionally prevent the promotion of minority candidates?

HOLDING AND DECISION: (Kennedy, J.) Yes. A municipality violates Title VII of the Civil Rights Act of 1964 when it rejects results from an otherwise valid civil service exam when the results unintentionally prevent the promotion of minority candidates. The City's (D) actions would violate Title VII's disparate-treatment prohibition absent some valid defense. Here, all the evidence demonstrates that the City (D) rejected the test results because the higher scoring candidates were White. Without some other justification, this express, race-based decisionmaking is prohibited. The question, therefore, is whether the purpose to avoid disparate-impact liability excuses what otherwise would be prohibited disparate-treatment discrimination. In Equal Protection Clause cases, the Court has previously held that certain government actions to remedy past racial discrimination—actions that are themselves based on race—are constitutional only where there is a "strong basis in evidence" that the remedial actions were necessary. The same interests are at work in the interplay between Title VII's disparate-treatment and disparate-impact provisions. In this context, a strict approach, whereby an employer in fact must be in violation of the disparate-impact provision before it can use compliance as a defense in a disparate-treatment suit, is overly simplistic and too restrictive of Title VII's purpose. Congress intended compliance to be voluntary, and forbidding employers to act unless they know, with certainty, that a practice violates the disparate-impact provision would bring compliance efforts to a near standstill. On the other hand, an employer's mere good-faith belief that its actions are necessary to comply with Title VII's disparate-impact provision is also insufficient by itself to justify race-conscious conduct. A middle ground is needed, so that voluntary employer compliance is encouraged, and that employer design of employment tests provides a fair opportunity for all individuals, regardless of their race. The "strong basis in evidence" standard meets that objective. Applying that standard to the City's (D) actions, it

Continued on next page.

is clear those actions fail to meet the strong basis in evidence test. Reversed.

DISSENT: (Ginsburg, J.) The majority is wrong to characterize the City's (D) actions as done "because of race." Title VII's disparate-treatment and disparate-impact proscriptions must be read as complementary, rather than reading them, as does the majority, as in conflict. Congress has declared that selection criteria operating to the disadvantage of minority group members can be retained only if justified by business necessity. Thus, in keeping with Congress's mandate, employers who reject such criteria due to reasonable doubts about their reliability can hardly be held to have engaged in discrimination "because of" race. Instead, it should be held that an employer who discards a selection device when its disproportionate racial impact becomes apparent does not violate Title VII's disparate-treatment bar automatically or at all, unless the employer has good reason to believe the device is justified by business necessity. Here, the City (D) had cause to be concerned that its exams would not pass muster, since the 60/40 ratio for written and oral parts of the exam was not necessary to effective job performance, especially since the oral portion addressed the sort of "real-life scenarios" fire officers encounter on the job. In any event, the standard announced by the majority will make voluntary compliance more difficult, will promote litigation, and will, in effect, require employers to establish that they have violated the law. As to Justice Alito's argument that the City's (D) actions were impermissibly politically motivated, such motivation is (contrary to Justice Alito) permissible if it is not discriminatory. The City (D) was not motivated to exclude White firefighters from promotion; rather, it was motivated in avoiding a disparate-impact lawsuit. Accordingly, the City (D) did not commit a disparate-treatment violation.

CONCURRENCE: (Scalia, J.) An issue that the majority decision fails to address, but that must be faced, is whether Title VII's disparate-impact liability is consistent with the Equal Protection Clause, since Title VII affirmatively requires remedial race-based actions when a disparate-impact violation would otherwise result. Under the Constitution, the federal government is prohibited from discriminating on basis of race; a fortiori, it is prohibited from passing statutes—like Title VII—that mandate other parties, such as states or private employers, to do so. Just because Title VII does not require racial quotas does not save it, since employers can achieve quota-like results through their hiring practices. Either way, intentional discrimination is still happening at the federal government's mandate, and the constitutionality of such a mandate is not ensured by whatever good intentions motivate it. Further, the disparate-impact provisions sweep too broadly to be fairly characterized as merely an evidentiary tool used to identify genuine, intentional discrimination, especially since they fail to provide an affirmative defense for good-faith conduct, i.e., they do not permit an employer to prove that its motives were pure and its actions reasonable.

CONCURRENCE: (Alito, J.) Here there was evidence that the City's (D) conduct was motivated by the illegitimate reason of placating African Americans in the City (D), who were an important constituency for the mayor. Thus, regardless of which test is applied, such conduct was a pretext for intentional discrimination, and, therefore, prohibited.

ANALYSIS

Arguably, *Ricci* makes it harder for employers to discard tests that adversely affect protected groups such as women and minorities. To prevent lawsuits, employers will now have to consider the impact a test may have on protected groups as it is being developed rather than after it has been administered—which may not always be apparent before the fact.

Quicknotes

DISPARATE TREATMENT Unequal treatment of employees or of applicants for employment without justification.

TITLE VII Prohibits unlawful discrimination against individuals based on race or sex.

United States v. Clary

Federal government (P) v. Convicted possessor of crack cocaine (D)

4 F.3d 709 (8th Cir. 1994)

NATURE OF CASE: Appeal from sentence for possession with intent to distribute crack cocaine.

FACT SUMMARY: The United States (P) contended that Clary (D), who had been convicted of possession with intent to distribute crack cocaine, should not have received a reduced sentence on grounds that the 100 to 1 ratio for crack cocaine to powder cocaine in the federal sentencing guidelines violated equal protection by discriminating against African Americans.

RULE OF LAW

A significant penalty differential for possessing crack cocaine versus powder cocaine does not violate equal protection where, although the differential disproportionately impacts African Americans, there is insufficient evidence that Congress acted with discriminatory intent in enacting the differential.

FACTS: The federal sentencing guidelines provided for a ten-year minimum sentence for persons found possessing 50 grams or more of cocaine base (crack cocaine), whereas they provided a similar penalty for those possessing over 5,000 grams of powder cocaine. Clary (D), who had been convicted of possession with intent to distribute crack cocaine, contended in the district court that this 100 to 1 ratio discriminated against African Americans. The district court, which agreed with Clary (D), departed from the sentencing guidelines and gave him a reduced sentence. In doing so, the district court relied on evidence that in passing the crack statute, Congress relied significantly on media reports that portrayed crack dealers as unemployed, gang-affiliated, gun-toting, young Black males. The district court also pointed to procedural irregularities, such as a dearth of congressional hearings on the matter, and the fact that the ratio, originally set at 50 to 1, was arbitrarily doubled. The district court also noted that nationally 92.6 percent of those convicted of crack cocaine charges were African American, as opposed to 4.7 percent who were White. With respect to powder cocaine, the percentages were largely reversed. The district court found that this statistical evidence demonstrated both the disparate impact of the 100 to 1 ratio and the probability that the subliminal influence of unconscious racism had permeated federal prosecution throughout the nation. The district court also discounted evidence that Congress believed that crack cocaine was more potent and addictive than powder cocaine, given that there was testimony that there is no reliable medical evidence that crack cocaine is more addictive than powder cocaine. Accordingly, the district court concluded that the 100 to 1 ratio was irrational. However, Congress had been presented with evidence that inhaling crack vapors was significantly more dangerous than sniffing cocaine powder, and that crack was, at least initially, more affordable. Finally, there was also evidence that Congress's motivation for the legislation was a perception that crack cocaine posed a unique and unprecedented problem for American narcotics enforcement, rather than any racial animus. The court of appeals granted review.

ISSUE: Does a significant penalty differential for possessing crack cocaine versus powder cocaine violate equal protection where, although the differential disproportionately impacts African Americans, there is insufficient evidence that Congress acted with discriminatory intent in enacting the differential?

HOLDING AND DECISION: (Gibson, J.) No. A significant penalty differential for possessing crack cocaine versus powder cocaine does not violate equal protection where, although the differential disproportionately impacts African Americans, there is insufficient evidence that Congress acted with discriminatory intent in enacting the differential. Congress had rational motives for creating the distinction between crack and powder cocaine. Among these were the potency of the drug, the ease with which drug dealers can carry and conceal it, the highly addictive nature of the drug, and the violence that often accompanies trade in it. Even assuming crack cocaine sentences disparately impact on African Americans (previously it was held they do not), such sentences are unconstitutional only if they were enacted with a discriminatory purpose. Here, there was no evidence that Congress or the Sentencing Commission had a racially discriminatory motive when it crafted the sentencing guidelines with extended sentences for crack cocaine felonies. Further, the district court's reliance on "unconscious racism" simply does not address the question whether Congress acted with a discriminatory purpose. Similarly, the district court's pointing to media reports as a source of congressional prejudice and stereotyping is a far leap. While such information may have affected at least some legislators, these articles hardly demonstrate that the stereotypical images "undoubtedly" influenced the legislators' racial perceptions so that they enacted the crack statute because of its adverse effect on African American males, instead of the stated purpose of responding to the serious impact of a rapidly developing and particularly-dangerous form of drug use. Similarly,

Continued on next page.

the evidence of the haste with which Congress acted and the action it took is as easily explained by the seriousness of the perceived problem as by racial animus. Moreover, there was other evidence presented that Congress was motivated by the problem crack posed for law enforcement, and, even though the scientific evidence regarding the differences between crack and powder cocaine is contradictory, scientific disagreement with testimony in congressional hearings, offered at later time and after additional research, simply does not establish discriminatory purpose. Reversed and remanded.

ANALYSIS

In 2010, President Obama signed into law the Fair Sentencing Act of 2010 (Public Law 111-220), which reduced the ratio for crack cocaine versus powder cocaine from 100 to 1 to 18 to 1. While it is generally believed that this Act will improve the fairness of the justice system, some believe that the disparity should be eliminated in its entirety, and that the impact of the reduced ratio on racial disparities will be limited, especially given that the Act does not achieve full parity, and that it does not address the enforcement prerogatives of federal criminal justice agencies, which seems to still be racially biased against African Americans. For example, some statistics show that African American defendants account for roughly 80 percent of those arrested for crack-related offenses, notwithstanding that public health data shows that two-thirds of crack cocaine users are White or Hispanic.

Quicknotes

DISCRIMINATORY PURPOSE Intent to discriminate; must be shown to establish an Equal Protection violation.

McCleskey v. Kemp

Inmate (D) v. State (P)

481 U.S. 279 (1987)

NATURE OF CASE: Appeal from denial of writ of habeas corpus.

FACT SUMMARY: McCleskey (D) contended he was denied equal protection when sentenced to death because Blacks were statistically more likely to be so sentenced, and such was racially-based.

RULE OF LAW

Capital cases require an evaluation of the motivations of individual jurors in sentencing; thus, raw abstract statistical data are not dispositive of a lack of equal protection.

FACTS: McCleskey (D), an African American, was sentenced to death for killing a White police officer. He petitioned for a writ of habeas corpus presenting a statistical study indicating Blacks were more likely to be sentenced to death, and that such was racially motivated. The district court and the court of appeals rejected the statistical data as irrelevant to the disposition, and the Supreme Court granted certiorari.

ISSUE: May statistical data be used in a capital case to determine an absence of equal protection?

HOLDING AND DECISION: (Powell, J.) No. Capital cases require an evaluation of the motivations of individual jurors in sentencing; thus, raw abstract statistical studies are irrelevant and not dispositive of a lack of equal protection. Each jury is unique in its composition, rendering statistical studies useless. Each case must be evaluated on its own merits. Thus, these data were properly excluded. Affirmed.

DISSENT: (Brennan, J.) The facts and statistics show that there was a high risk that McCleskey's (D) death-penalty sentence was influenced by racial considerations. His evidence should not be evaluated solely on the numbers; in addition, the numbers should be evaluated against history and human experience. The Court itself has recognized the persistent danger that racial attitudes may affect all stages of criminal proceedings. This danger has not been eradicated and should not be ignored or denied.

DISSENT: (Blackmun, J.) Where racial discrimination in the administration of the criminal justice system is established, it has been settled law that the conviction must be set aside. In this case, the effect of racial discrimination is especially strong with regard to the office of the prosecutor's decision to seek the death penalty and the point at which it proceeded to the penalty phase following conviction. The majority ignored such effect. To establish purposeful discrimination for an equal-protection claim, McCleskey (D) must meet a three-factor standard. First, he must establish that he is a member of a group "that is a recognizable, distinct class, singled out for different treatment." Second, he must make a showing of a substantial degree of differential treatment. Third, he must establish that the allegedly discriminatory procedure is susceptible to abuse or is not racially neutral. Here, McCleskey (D) has clearly satisfied the first prong, because in Georgia, Blacks are a distinct group singled out for different treatment in the capital-sentencing system. The Baldus study shows that systemic and substantial disparities existed in the penalties imposed upon homicide defendants in Georgia based on race of the homicide victim, that the disparities existed at a less substantial rate in death sentencing based on race of defendants, and that the factors of race of the victim and defendant were at work in Fulton County the county in which McCleskey (D) was tried. The question remaining, therefore, is at what point disparity becomes constitutionally unacceptable. McCleskey (D) established that because he was charged with killing a White person, he was 4.3 times as likely to be sentenced to death as he would have been had he been charged with killing a Black person. The most persuasive evidence of the constitutionally significant effect of racial factors in the Georgia capital sentencing system is McCleskey's (D) proof that the race of the victim is more important in explaining the imposition of a death sentence than is the factor whether the defendant was a prime mover in the homicide. While the state may not use race as an aggravating factor in its statutes, the state's capital-sentencing and criminal justice system effectively does so. "What we have held to be unconstitutional if included in the language of the statute surely cannot be constitutional because it is a de facto characteristic of the system." McCleskey (D) established that the race of the victim is an especially significant factor at the point where the defendant has been convicted of murder and the prosecutor must choose whether to proceed to the penalty phase of the trial and create the possibility that a death sentence may be imposed or to accept the imposition of a sentence of life imprisonment. McCleskey (D) demonstrated this effect throughout the state. McCleskey (D) also demonstrated that the entire capital sentencing process was susceptible to abuse, both through the prosecutor's discretion and based on the history of prior discrimination. His showing is of sufficient magnitude that, absent evidence to the contrary,

Continued on next page.

one must conclude racial factors entered into the decisionmaking process that yielded McCleskey's (D) death sentence. Therefore, the state should be required to show that racially neutral criteria and procedures yielded this racially skewed result. The majority's explanations for its failure to apply this well-established equal protection analysis are unpersuasive. Finally, and very disturbing, is the majority's statement that granting McCleskey (D) relief could lead to further constitutional challenges. That, of course, is no reason to deny McCleskey (D) his rights under the Equal Protection Clause. If a grant of relief to him were to lead to a closer examination of the effects of racial considerations throughout the criminal justice system, the system, and hence society, might benefit.

ANALYSIS

The Court appeared reluctant to rely upon statistical data in overturning a jury verdict. The statistical manipulations and fact-gathering methodology in such studies may give a false conclusion regarding the result. Extrapolation and mathematical interpretation was felt to unreasonably impact upon the ultimate conclusion. Any individual jury, after voir dire, can be as independent as necessary, according to the Court, and thus such statistics merely cloud the issue.

Quicknotes

EQUAL PROTECTION A constitutional provision that each person be guaranteed the same protection of the laws enjoyed by other persons in life circumstances.

WRIT OF HABEAS CORPUS A proceeding in which a defendant brings a writ to compel a judicial determination of whether he is lawfully being held in custody.

Brown v. City of Oneonta

African American residents (P) v. Municipality (D)

221 F.3d 329 (2d Cir. 1999)

NATURE OF CASE: Appeal from summary judgment in action alleging that the polices' stopping and questioning of a city's Black residents constituted racial profiling that violated the Equal Protection Clause. [The procedural posture of the case is not presented in the casebook extract.]

FACT SUMMARY: After a crime victim reported to the police that she believed her assailant was a Black male, Black residents (P) of the City of Oneonta (City) (D) who had been stopped and questioned by the police brought suit contending the police "sweep" was based on impermissible racial profiling in violation of the Equal Protection Clause.

RULE OF LAW

Police stopping and questioning members of a minority group on basis of a physical description given by the victim of a crime does not constitute impermissible racial profiling in violation of the Equal Protection Clause.

FACTS: A 77-year-old woman informed the City of Oneonta (City) (D) police that someone had broken into her house and attacked her with a knife. Although she could not identify the assailant's face, the woman told the police that he was a Black man, based on her view of his hand and forearm, and that he was young, because of the speed with which he crossed her room. She also told the police that, as they struggled, the suspect had cut himself on the hand with the knife. A police canine unit tracked the assailant's scent from the scene of the crime toward the State University of New York College at Oneonta (SUCO) campus but lost the trail after several hundred yards. Fewer than 300 Blacks lived in the city, and only two percent of SUCO students were Black. The police immediately contacted SUCO and requested a list of its Black male students, which was provided. The police attempted to locate and question every Black male student at SUCO. This endeavor produced no suspects. Then, over the next several days, the police conducted a "sweep" of Oneonta, stopping and questioning non-White persons on the streets and inspecting their hands for cuts. More than 200 persons were questioned during that period, but no suspect was apprehended. Those Black residents (P) whose names appeared on the SUCO list and those who were approached and questioned by the police, believing that they had been unlawfully singled out because of their race, sued, alleging the police had engaged in impermissible racial profiling that violated the Equal Protection Clause. The case was resolved on summary judgment, and the court of appeals granted review. [The procedural posture of the case is not presented in the casebook extract.]

ISSUE: Does police stopping and questioning members of a minority group on basis of a physical description given by the victim of a crime constitute impermissible racial profiling in violation of the Equal Protection Clause?

HOLDING AND DECISION: [Judge not identified in the casebook extract.] No. Police stopping and questioning members of a minority group on basis of a physical description given by the victim of a crime does not constitute impermissible racial profiling in violation of the Equal Protection Clause. The Blacks (P) were not stopped and questioned solely on basis of their race, but the basis of the physical description given by the victim of a crime. The City's (D) policy was race-neutral on its face, i.e., to investigate crimes by interviewing the victim, getting a description of the assailant, and seeking out persons who matched that description. Here, the description contained not only race but also gender and age, as well as the possibility of a cut on the hand. By acting on the victim's description, which included race as only one element, the City (D) did not engage in a suspect racial classification that would draw strict scrutiny. The description, which originated not with the state but with the victim, was a legitimate classification within which potential suspects might be found. In a municipality such as the City (D), where there are relatively few Blacks, and few of them fit a victim's description, it might be more useful for the police to use race to find a Black suspect than a White one. It may also be practicable for law enforcement to attempt to contact every Black person who fits certain characteristics of a victim's description, but not practicable to contact every such White person. If a community were primarily Black with very few Whites and the search were, for example, for a young White male, the impact would be reversed. Absent discriminatory intent, governmental action that has a disparate impact on a minority group does not violate the Equal Protection Clause. That is the case here, as there is insufficient evidence to show that the police investigation was motivated by discriminatory animus. Judgment for the City (D).

Continued on next page.

ANALYSIS

There are several ways for a plaintiff to plead intentional discrimination that violates the Equal Protection Clause. A plaintiff could point to a law or policy that expressly classifies persons on basis of race, or, a plaintiff could identify a facially neutral law or policy that has been applied in an intentionally discriminatory manner. A plaintiff could also allege that a facially neutral statute or policy has an adverse effect and that it was motivated by discriminatory animus. Here the court concluded that the plaintiffs failed to plead any of these, or any other manner of intentional discrimination, and held that, therefore, strict scrutiny of the governmental action was unnecessary.

Quicknotes

DISCRIMINATION Unequal treatment of a class of persons.

EQUAL PROTECTION CLAUSE A constitutional provision that each person be guaranteed the same protection of the laws enjoyed by other persons in like circumstances.

Regents of the University of California v. Bakke

University (D) v. Applicant (P)

438 U.S. 265 (1978)

NATURE OF CASE: Action under state and federal Equal Protection Clauses.

FACT SUMMARY: Bakke (P) challenged the constitutionality of the University of California, Davis's (UC) (D) minority admissions policy to its medical school.

RULE OF LAW

The Equal Protection Clause's guarantees are equally applicable to both minorities and the White majority, and preference of one group over another solely because of race is facially invalid.

FACTS: University of California, Davis (UC) (D) had a minorities' admissions quota requiring that at least 16 out of every 100 students admitted to its medical school were from certain specified minority groups. Bakke (P), a Caucasian, alleged that his applications for admission were denied in 1973 and 1974 while less qualified minority applicants were accepted. Bakke (P) brought an action under Title VI of the C.R.A. of 1964 and the state and federal Equal Protection Clauses. The racial classifications were subjected to strict scrutiny. While the state goal of increasing professionals among minorities was deemed a compelling state interest, the California Supreme Court found that there were less intrusive methods available. The court held that the Equal Protection Clause of the Fourteenth Amendment prohibited rejection of better-qualified applicants in favor of less-qualified applicants on basis of race. Bakke (P) was ordered admitted to the medical school since UC (D) could not meet its burden of proof that he would not have been admitted if the special minority admissions program had not been in effect.

ISSUE: Does the Equal Protection Clause prohibit even benign discrimination?

HOLDING AND DECISION: (Powell, J.) Yes. The Equal Protection Clause prohibits discrimination regardless of race. It protects both minorities and the White majority. Benign discrimination to aid minorities at the expense of the White majority is facially invalid where race is the sole criterion or justification. Where race is the basis of a classification, strict judicial scrutiny is required. To justify the use of a suspect classification, it must be established that the state's purpose is both constitutionally permissible and substantial and that the classification is necessary to the accomplishment of its purpose or a safeguarding of its interests. Since the classification herein denies White applicants the right to compete for 100 seats while it grants minorities the opportunity to compete for the full number of seats based solely on their race, the classification is inherently suspect. The state justifications, i.e., remedial efforts to correct general societal discrimination, ethnic parity, aid to underserved communities, etc., are not sufficient to justify its use of racially based admissions. The use of racial quotas to achieve a proper racial mix/balance is facially invalid. UC (D) has no history of racial discrimination, so our rulings in cases involving remedial programs are not applicable. Innocent third parties should not be penalized for general societal discrimination. Neither the UC's (D) special admissions program nor any of the requirements under it are related to supplying medical aid to underserviced areas. Hence, the admissions program may not be justified on this basis. While ethnic diversity is a proper goal, it is not substantial enough alone to justify the admissions policy and other less intrusive methods are available if that is the UC's (D) goal. As the only criterion, race is an improper basis for achieving such diversity. We find that the use of an explicit racial classification upon which admissions are based is a violation of the Equal Protection Clause of the Fourteenth Amendment. A properly devised admissions policy may consider race as one of the elements in its selection of students and the injunction against ever considering race must be reversed as overbroad. Affirmed in part and reversed in part.

DISSENT: (Brennan, J.) Government may only take race into account where it does not demean or insult any racial group and is to remedy past acts of discrimination. We agree that Title VI, as found by the majority, goes no further than the Fourteenth Amendment in prohibiting racial discrimination. Only impermissible use of racial standards violates Title VI. Because of the significant risk that ostensibly benign racial classifications may be misused, an articulated and important purpose must be established. However, while we should strictly scrutinize all racially based classifications for impermissible discriminatory effects, we should be more lenient in finding a substantial and important governmental purpose where the discrimination is "benign." Some preferential treatment may be afforded those minorities that have a history of being socially disadvantaged to redress past societal discrimination. UC's (D) policy of aiding previously disadvantaged minorities is justified. There is no stigmatization of races associated with the UC's (D) admissions policy. Its purpose is to bring the races together and the "quota" is based on population percentages. Since race

Continued on next page.

was the reason for the original disadvantaged position, it is reasonable to use race as a ground for remedying this situation. Each applicant is judged on his or her individual abilities and only when less than 16 minority applicants have been admitted on this basis does the quota system become applicable.

DISSENT: (Marshall, J.) UC's (D) admissions program does not violate the constitution. The Fourteenth Amendment was adopted to protect racial minorities and should not be a bar to aiding such minorities to overcome the effects of past discrimination.

DISSENT: (Blackmun, J.) The judiciary is poorly equipped to consider the validity of academic admission policies. I feel it should be left to them, but I find it encouraging that the majority finds race a proper consideration.

CONCURRENCE AND DISSENT: (Stevens, J.) The settled practice of this Court is to avoid decisions on constitutional grounds if a statutory ground exists. Title VI (The Civil Rights Act of 1964, § 601) stands for the proposition that no person may be excluded from participation in a federally funded program on the ground of race, color, or national origin.

ANALYSIS

Bakke lacks focus based on the diversity of opinions expressed by the Justices. Racial quotas conceivably could be validly included in admissions programs if the university sets it up properly, i.e., race is only one of the criteria referred to in the program and admissions are on a case-by-case basis. Informal benign discrimination can easily be justified on the basis of achieving a homogenous student body. Therefore, *Bakke* should have a very limited effect on those who wish to aid minorities.

Quicknotes

BENIGN DISCRIMINATION A government action that favors particular minorities and is subject to a strict scrutiny standard.

EQUAL PROTECTION CLAUSE A constitutional guarantee that no person should be denied the same protection of the laws enjoyed by other persons in like circumstances.

QUOTA A goal or limited number.

STRICT SCRUTINY The method by which courts determine the constitutionality of a law, when a law affects a fundamental right. Under the test, the legislature must have a compelling interest to enact the law, and measures prescribed by the law must be the least restrictive means possible to accomplish its goal.

SUSPECT CLASSIFICATION A class of persons that have historically been subject to discriminatory treatment; statutes drawing a distinction between persons based on a suspect classification, i.e., race, nationality, or alienage, are subject to a strict scrutiny standard of review.

City of Richmond v. J.A. Croson Co.

City (D) v. Contractor (P)

488 U.S. 469 (1989)

NATURE OF CASE: Appeal from decision invalidating a set-aside program.

FACT SUMMARY: After the City of Richmond (D) adopted a plan requiring prime contractors to whom it awarded construction contracts to subcontract at least 30 percent of the dollar amount of the contract, to one or more minority business enterprises, J.A. Croson Co. (P) filed suit to challenge the set-aside.

RULE OF LAW

When establishing a quota or set-aside program apportioning public contracting opportunities on basis of race, the city must demonstrate a compelling interest narrowly tailored to remedy the effects of prior discrimination.

FACTS: To remedy past discrimination against minorities in the construction industry, the City of Richmond (Richmond) (D) adopted a plan requiring prime contractors to whom it awarded construction contracts to subcontract at least 30 percent of the dollar amount of the contract to one or more minority business enterprises (MBEs). A qualified MBE from anywhere in the United States could avail itself of the 30 percent set-aside. There was no direct evidence of race discrimination on the part of Richmond (D) in letting contracts or any evidence that the city's prime contractors had discriminated against minority-owned subcontractors. J.A. Croson Co. (Croson) (P) challenged the ordinance after his request for a waiver of the MBE requirement had been denied. The first time the case reached the Supreme Court, it was remanded for further consideration in light of *Wygant v. Jackson Board of Education*, 476 U.S. 267 (1986). On remand, the court of appeals struck down the Richmond (D) set-aside program.

ISSUE: When establishing a quota or set-aside program apportioning public contracting opportunities on basis of race, must the city demonstrate a compelling interest narrowly tailored to remedy the effects of prior discrimination?

HOLDING AND DECISION: (O'Connor, J.) Yes. When establishing a quota or set-aside program apportioning public contracting opportunities on basis of race, the city must demonstrate a compelling interest narrowly tailored to remedy the effects of prior discrimination. The rights created by the first § of the Fourteenth Amendment are personal rights guaranteed to the individual. The Richmond (D) plan denies certain citizens the opportunity to compete for a fixed percentage of public contracts based solely upon their race. To whatever racial group these citizens belong, their "personal rights" to be treated with equal dignity and respect are implicated by a rigid rule erecting race as the sole criterion in an aspect of decisionmaking. The guarantee of equal protection cannot mean one thing when applied to one individual and something else when applied to a person of another color. In this case, Blacks comprise approximately 50 percent of the population of Richmond (D) and hold five of the nine seats on the City Council. Under Richmond's (D) scheme, a successful minority entrepreneur from anywhere in the country enjoys an absolute preference over other citizens based solely on race. It is thus obvious that such a program is not narrowly tailored to remedy the effects of prior discrimination. Because Richmond (D) has failed to identify the need for remedial action in the awarding of its public construction contracts, its treatment of its citizens on a racial basis violates the dictates of the Equal Protection Clause. Affirmed.

CONCURRENCE: (Scalia, J.) The difficulty of overcoming the effects of past discrimination is nothing compared with the difficulty of eradicating from our society the tendency to classify and judge men and women on basis of their country of origin or the color of their skin. Since Blacks have been disproportionately disadvantaged by racial discrimination, any race-neutral remedial program aimed at the disadvantaged as such will have a disproportionately beneficial impact on Blacks. Only such a program is in accord with the letter and the spirit of our Constitution.

DISSENT: (Marshall, J.) Today, for the first time, a majority of this Court has adopted strict scrutiny as its standard of Equal Protection Clause review of race-conscious, government-enacted remedial measures. In concluding that remedial classifications warrant no different standard of review under the Constitution than the most brute and repugnant forms of state-sponsored racism, a majority of this Court signals that it regards racial discrimination as largely a phenomenon of the past, and that government bodies need no longer preoccupy themselves with rectifying racial injustice. This nation is not anywhere close to eradicating racial discrimination or its vestiges.

Continued on next page.

ANALYSIS

Relying on *Wygant v. Jackson Board of Education*, 476 U.S. 267 (1986), Croson (P) argued that the city must limit any race-based remedial efforts to eradicating the effects of its own prior discrimination. Richmond (D), however, argued that *Fullilove v. Klutznick*, 448 U.S. 448 (1980), was controlling, and thus Richmond (D) enjoys sweeping legislative power to define and attack the effects of prior discrimination in its local construction industry. *Fullilove* approved a 10 percent federal set-aside where Congress had carefully examined and rejected race-neutral alternatives before enacting the MBE set-aside, which also included a waiver procedure. Unlike the program upheld in *Fullilove*, Richmond's (D) waiver system focused solely on the availability of MBEs, with no inquiry into whether the particular minority business enterprise seeking a racial preference suffered from the effects of past discrimination by the city or prime contractors.

Quicknotes

EQUAL PROTECTION CLAUSE A constitutional guarantee that no person should be denied the same protection of the laws enjoyed by other persons in like circumstances.

QUOTA A goal or limited number.

STRICT SCRUTINY Method by which courts determine the constitutionality of a law, when a law affects a fundamental right. Under the test, the legislature must have a compelling interest to enact the law, and measures prescribed by the law must be the least restrictive means possible to accomplish its goal.

Adarand Constructors v. Pena

Subcontractor (P) v. Federal government (D)

515 U.S. 200 (1995)

NATURE OF CASE: Challenges to federal program of encouraging the awarding of federal contracts to minority-owned businesses.

FACT SUMMARY: A federal program giving preferences in federal contracting to minority-owned businesses was challenged as unconstitutional.

RULE OF LAW

Federal contracting set-asides for minorities are unconstitutional unless they are narrowly tailored to remedy demonstrable past discrimination.

FACTS: The U.S. Department of Transportation awarded a construction contract. The contractor solicited subcontracts. Adarand Constructors, Inc. (Adarand) (P) submitted the low bid, but because of federal incentives favoring minority contracts, Adarand (P) was rejected in favor of a minority-owned business. Adarand (P) brought an action, contending that the incentive program was a violation of equal protection. The Ninth Circuit rejected the challenge, and the United States Supreme Court granted review.

ISSUE: Are federal contracting set-asides for minorities unconstitutional if they are not narrowly tailored to remedy demonstrable past discrimination?

HOLDING AND DECISION: (O'Connor, J.) Yes. Federal contracting set-asides for minorities are unconstitutional unless they are narrowly tailored to remedy demonstrable past discrimination. There is no equal protection provision in the Fifth Amendment, such as is found in the Fourteenth. However, it is clear the federal government's due process obligations under the Due Process Clause require it to treat similarly situated individuals in a similar fashion, much as states must do. While there is some prior authority for the proposition that "benign" racial discrimination by Congress is subject to less rigorous scrutiny than traditional discrimination, these decisions were in error. Racial classification of any sort is subject to the highest level of judicial review: the classification must be narrowly tailored to serve a compelling state interest. The eradication of racism in contracting is such an interest, but the means to achieve it must be carefully drawn. It is not sufficient that a general history of discrimination be shown. Rather, specific patterns of discrimination must be shown, as well as a remedy that was chosen to be narrowly tailored to address the problem. This was not done in the present case. Reversed.

CONCURRENCE: (Scalia, J.) Government can never "make up" for past discrimination by present discrimination. In our constitutional system, there can never be a debtor race or a creditor race. The Constitution protects persons, not races.

CONCURRENCE: (Thomas, J.) There is no racial paternalism exception to the principle of equal protection.

DISSENT: (Stevens, J.) Congress has greater leeway in remedying past discrimination than do the states.

ANALYSIS

In 1989, the Court decided *Richmond v. J.A. Croson Co.*, 488 U.S. 469 (1989). In that case the Court applied strict scrutiny to a municipal preference scheme. The Court left open the question of whether this would also be the case with respect to congressional action. This question was answered by the present opinion.

Quicknotes

BENIGN DISCRIMINATION Government action that favors particular minorities and is subject to a strict scrutiny standard.

DUE PROCESS CLAUSE Language found in the Fifth and Fourteenth Amendments to the United States Constitution providing that no person shall be deprived of "life, liberty, or property without due process of law."

STRICT SCRUTINY The method by which courts determine the constitutionality of a law, when a law affects a fundamental right. Under the test, the legislature must have a compelling interest to enact the law, and measures prescribed by the law must be the least restrictive means possible to accomplish its goal.

Grutter v. Bollinger

Law school applicant (P) v. Law school (D)

539 U.S. 306 (2003)

NATURE OF CASE: Appeal in racial discrimination case.

FACT SUMMARY: When Grutter (P), a White Michigan resident, was denied admission to the University of Michigan Law School (the Law School) (D), she sued the latter in federal district court, alleging racial discrimination against her in violation of the Equal Protection Clause on basis of the Law School's (D) express consideration of race as a factor in the admissions process.

RULE OF LAW

Student body diversity is a compelling state interest that can justify the use of race in university admissions.

FACTS: To attempt to achieve student body diversity, the University of Michigan Law School (the Law School) (D) admissions committee required admissions officials to evaluate each applicant based on all the information in the file, including a personal statement, letters of recommendation, a student's essay, GPA score, LSAT score, as well as so-called "soft variables." The admissions policy, furthermore, specifically stressed the Law School's (D) long-standing commitment to racial and ethnic diversity. When Grutter (P), a White Michigan resident, applied for admission but was denied, she sued the Law School (D) in federal district court, alleging racial discrimination against her in violation of the Equal Protection Clause. [The district court upheld Grutter's (P) claim. The court of appeals reversed, and Grutter (P) appealed.]

ISSUE: Is student body diversity a compelling state interest that can justify the use of race in university admissions?

HOLDING AND DECISION: (O'Connor, J.) Yes. Student body diversity is a compelling state interest that can justify the use of race in university admissions. Here, the Law School's (D) admissions program bears the hallmarks of a narrowly tailored plan. Truly individualized consideration demands that race be used in a flexible, nonmechanical way. It follows from this mandate that universities cannot establish quotas for members of certain racial groups or put members of those groups on separate admissions tracks. Nor can universities insulate applicants who belong to certain racial or ethnic groups from the competition for admission. Universities can, however, as was done here, consider race or ethnicity more flexibly as a plus factor in the context of individualized consideration of each and every applicant. The Law School's (D) goal of attaining a critical mass of underrepresented minority students does not transform its program into a quota. The evidence indicated that the Law School (D) engaged in a highly individualized, holistic review of each applicant's file, giving serious consideration to all the ways an applicant might contribute to a "diverse educational environment." Furthermore, evidence showed that the Law School (D) gives substantial weight to diversity factors besides race by frequently accepting nonminority applicants with grades and test scores lower than underrepresented minority applicants. There was no Law School (D) policy, either de facto or de jure, of automatic acceptance or rejection based on any single "soft" variable. Narrow tailoring does not require exhaustion of every conceivable race-neutral alternative. Nor does it require a university to choose between maintaining a reputation for excellence nor fulfilling a commitment to provide educational opportunities to members of all racial groups. Affirmed.

DISSENT: (Rehnquist, C.J.) Although the Law School (D) claims it must take the steps it does to achieve "critical mass" of underrepresented minority students, its actual program bears no relation to this asserted goal. Stripped of its "critical mass" veil, the Law School's (D) program is revealed as a naked effort to achieve racial balancing.

DISSENT: (Kennedy, J.) Refusal of the Court to apply strict scrutiny that is meaningful will lead to serious consequences. By deferring to the law school's choice of minority admissions programs, courts will lose the talents and resources of the faculties and administrators in devising new and fairer ways to ensure individual consideration.

CONCURRENCE AND DISSENT: (Scalia, J.) Unlike a clear constitutional holding that racial preferences in state educational institutions are impermissible, or even a clear anticonstitutional holding, today's decision seems perversely designed to prolong the controversy and the litigation. The Constitution proscribes government discrimination on the basis of race, and state-provided education is no exception.

CONCURRENCE AND DISSENT: (Thomas, J.) Blacks can achieve in every avenue of American life without the meddling of university administrators, and racial discrimination is not a permissible solution to the self-inflicted wounds of an elitist admissions policy. The majority upholds this racial discrimination not by interpreting

Continued on next page.

the Constitution, but by responding to a faddish slogan of the cognoscenti. The majority is correct, however, to the extent that it holds that further use of racial discrimination in higher education admissions is unlawful. The Law School's (D) use of race constitutes an Equal Protection Clause violation. The government's discrimination based on race should be permissible only in the direst of circumstances, such as national security; otherwise, such discrimination demeans everyone. The Law School's (D) interest in a diverse student body is no more than a forbidden interest in racial balancing—which the majority expressly rejects. The Law School's (D) failure to entertain changing its current admissions policies is tantamount to its reluctance to sacrifice its exclusivity and elite status. First, there is no pressing public necessity in maintaining a public school at all—and certainly not an elite public law school. Likewise, marginal improvements in legal education do not qualify as a compelling state interest. Because a very high percentage of its graduates leave the state, the Law School (D) as an elite institution does little to advance the welfare of the state's people or any cognizable interest of the state. The Law School (D) should, therefore, be forced to choose between its "classroom aesthetic and its exclusionary admissions system—it cannot have it both ways." With the adoption of different admissions methods, such as accepting all students who meet minimum qualifications, the Law School (D) could achieve its vision of the racially aesthetic student body without the use of racial discrimination. The majority also ignores studies that show heterogeneity may actually impair learning among Black students, and simply accepts the Law School's (D) assessment that diversity will yield educational benefits. In other states where preferential admissions based on race are prohibited, public law schools have enrolled Black and minority students at increasing rates, and those schools have satisfied their sense of mission without resorting to prohibited racial discrimination. The majority blindly ignores this reality. In addition, that admissions are made only on the basis of merit is a myth. Elite institutions use a so-called "legacy" preference to give the children of alumni an advantage in admissions. This, and other, exceptions to a "true" meritocracy give the lie to protestations that merit admissions are in fact the order of the day at the Nation's universities. The Equal Protection Clause does not, however, prohibit the use of unseemly legacy preferences or many other kinds of arbitrary admissions procedures. What the Equal Protection Clause does prohibit are classifications made on basis of race. So while legacy preferences can stand under the Constitution, racial discrimination cannot. In any event, there is nothing ancient, honorable, or constitutionally protected about "selective" admissions. Since its inception, selective admissions have been the vehicle for racial, ethnic, and religious tinkering and experimentation by university administrators. Additionally, no modern law school can claim ignorance of the poor performance of Blacks, relatively speaking, on the Law School Admissions Test (LSAT). Having decided to use the LSAT, the Law School (D) must accept the constitutional burdens that come with this decision. The Law School (D) may freely continue to employ the LSAT and other allegedly merit-based standards in whatever fashion it likes. What the Equal Protection Clause forbids, but the Court today allows, is the use of these standards hand-in-hand with racial discrimination. An infinite variety of admissions methods are available to the Law School (D). Considering all the radical thinking that has historically occurred at this country's universities, the Law School's (D) intractable approach toward admissions is striking. The majority does not even attempt to force the Law School (D) to try other methods, but instead gives it a 25-year license to practice racial discrimination. Given that there are no legal principles that provide support for the majority's opinion, it might be that its decision is based on the notion that one can tell when racial discrimination benefits minority groups, and that such discrimination is necessary to remedy general societal ills. Such a notion is flawed. Racial classifications are per se harmful and almost no amount of benefit in the eye of the beholder can justify such classifications. The unprepared students admitted on basis of their race only find that they cannot succeed in the cauldron of competition. While these students may graduate with law degrees, there is no evidence that they have received a qualitatively better legal education (or become better lawyers) than if they had gone to a less "elite" law school for which they were better prepared. However, no social science has disproved the notion that this discrimination engenders attitudes of superiority or, alternatively, provokes resentment among those who believe that they have been wronged by the government's use of race. When Blacks take positions in the highest places of government, industry, or academia, it is an open question today whether their skin color played a part in their advancement. The question itself is the stigma.

ANALYSIS

As seen in *Grutter* and predecessor Supreme Court decisions, not every decision influenced by race is equally objectionable, and "strict scrutiny" is designed to provide a framework for carefully examining the importance and the sincerity of the reasons advanced by the governmental decision maker for the use of race in any given context.

Quicknotes

EQUAL PROTECTION CLAUSE A constitutional provision that each person be guaranteed the same protection of the laws enjoyed by other persons in like circumstances.

Gratz v. Bollinger

College applicants (P) v. University (D)

539 U.S. 244 (2003)

NATURE OF CASE: Certiorari review of constitutionality of admissions policy.

FACT SUMMARY: Gratz (P) and other "qualified" White students who were denied admission as undergraduates to the University of Michigan (D) sued the University (D), arguing the admission policy of automatically distributing one-fifth of the points needed to guarantee admission to every single "underrepresented minority" solely because of race constituted prohibited racial discrimination.

RULE OF LAW

A university admissions policy that automatically distributes one-fifth of the points needed to guarantee admission to every single "underrepresented minority" solely because of race is not narrowly tailored to achieve the interest in educational diversity so as to avoid violation of the Equal Protection Clause of the Fourteenth Amendment.

FACTS: Gratz (P) and other White students, who were denied admission as undergraduates to the University of Michigan (D), although they were deemed "qualified" by the college admissions committee, brought suit against the University (D), arguing that its applicant selection method violated the Equal Protection Clause of the Fourteenth Amendment on the grounds that the University (D) automatically distributes one-fifth of the points needed to guarantee admission to every single "underrepresented minority" solely because of race. [The procedural posture of the case is not set forth in the textbook excerpt.]

ISSUE: Is a university admissions policy that automatically distributes one-fifth of the points needed to guarantee admission to every single "underrepresented minority" solely because of race narrowly tailored to achieve the interest in educational diversity so as to avoid violation of the Equal Protection Clause of the Fourteenth Amendment?

HOLDING AND DECISION: (Rehnquist, C.J.) No. A university admissions policy that automatically distributes one-fifth of the points needed to guarantee admission to every single "underrepresented minority" solely because of race is not narrowly tailored to achieve the interest in educational diversity to avoid violation of the Equal Protection Clause of the Fourteenth Amendment. This Court emphasizes the importance of considering each particular applicant as an individual, assessing all of the qualities that an individual possesses, and in turn, evaluating that individual's ability to contribute to the unique setting of higher education. In this regard, the Court does not contemplate that any single characteristic automatically ensures a specific and identifiable contribution to a university's diversity. Here, the University's (D) admission policy does not provide such individualized consideration; to the contrary, it automatically distributes 20 points to "underrepresented minority" groups, the only consideration being whether the applicant is a member of one of these minority groups. Even if an applicant's extraordinary artistic talent rivaled that of Monet or Picasso, the applicant would receive, at most, five points under the University's (D) admissions system. Clearly, such a system does not offer applicants an individualized selection process. Nor does the fact that the implementation of a program capable of providing individualized consideration might present administrative challenges render constitutional an otherwise problematic system. The admissions policy violates the Equal Protection Clause of the Fourteenth Amendment.

CONCURRENCE: (O'Connor, J.) The selection index, by setting up automatic, predetermined point allocations for the soft variables, ensures that the diversity contributions of applicants cannot be individually assessed. This is in sharp contrast to the law school's admission plan, which enables admissions officers to make nuanced judgments as to the contributions each applicant is likely to make.

CONCURRENCE: (Thomas, J.) A state's use of racial discrimination in higher education admissions is categorically prohibited by the Equal Protection Clause.

DISSENT: (Stevens, J.) The plaintiffs lack standing because they had already enrolled at other schools before they filed their class-action complaint in the case.

DISSENT: (Souter, J.) On its face, the assignment of specific points does not set race apart from all other weighted considerations. Since college admission is not left entirely to inarticulate intuition, it is hard to see what is inappropriate in assigning some stated value to a relevant characteristic, whether it be reasoning ability, writing style, running speed, or minority race.

DISSENT: (Ginsburg, J.) The stain of generations of racial oppression is still visible in our society, and the determination to hasten its removal remains vital. Here, there has been no demonstration that the University (D)

Continued on next page.

unduly constricts admissions opportunities for students who do not receive special consideration based on race.

ANALYSIS

As made clear by the Supreme Court in its *Gratz* and *Grutter*, 539 U.S. 306 (2003), decisions, achieving diversity in higher education, whether it be at college level or graduate school, remains a compelling state interest sufficient to justify some degree of racial preferences without violating the Equal Protection Clause of the Fourteenth Amendment.

Quicknotes

EQUAL PROTECTION CLAUSE A constitutional guarantee that no person should be denied the same protection of the laws enjoyed by other persons in like circumstances.

Parents Involved in Community Schools v. Seattle School District No. 1

Parents of unadmitted students (P) v. Public school district (D)

551 U.S. 701 (2007)

NATURE OF CASE: Suits challenging school-assignment plans under the Equal Protection Clause.

FACT SUMMARY: Two metropolitan school districts sought to assign students to schools to achieve racial balance.

RULE OF LAW

Racial balance between local high school districts is not a compelling government interest under the Equal Protection Clause.

FACTS: The Seattle School District (Seattle) (D) implemented a student assignment plan designed to achieve numerically defined racial balance between Seattle's (D) ten public high schools. Seattle (D), however, had never been found to run racially segregated schools. The Jefferson County Public Schools in Louisville, Kentucky (Louisville), was under a desegregation order from 1975 to 2000; the order was dissolved in 2001 when a federal court ruled that Louisville (D) had reached unitary status by largely eliminating the district's earlier racial segregation. After the decree was dissolved, Louisville (D) voluntarily adopted a student-assignment plan that required specific minimum and maximum enrollment percentages for Black students. Parents (P) of students who were denied admission in each school district sued their respective district, alleging, in part, violations of the Equal Protection Clause. After the intermediate appellate courts in both cases upheld the assignment plans, the parents (P) petitioned the United States Supreme Court for further review.

ISSUE: Is racial balance between local high-school districts a compelling government interest under the Equal Protection Clause?

HOLDING AND DECISION: (Roberts, C.J.) No. Racial balance between local high-school districts is not a compelling government interest under the Equal Protection Clause. Because both school districts (D) have apportioned government benefits on basis of race, the applicable standard of review in these cases is strict scrutiny: Seattle (D) and Louisville (D) must show that their race-based discrimination (1) advances a compelling government interest through (2) means that are narrowly tailored to achieve the intended purpose. The asserted interests in both Seattle (D) and Louisville (D) reduce to nothing more than the goal of numerical racial balance between each district's (D) schools. This Court has consistently found such a purpose illegitimate. *Grutter v. Bollinger*, 539 U.S. 306 (2003), does not control here because *Grutter* involved the specific interests of higher education; it is also instructive, though, that *Grutter* upheld the law-school admission policy there because racial diversity was only one of a mix of admissions criteria. Here, on the other hand, pure numerical racial balance, by itself, is the government interest, and that interest has never been recognized as valid. The plans at issue here also fail because the school districts (D) have failed to show that they seriously considered other means besides explicit racial classifications. Reversed.

CONCURRENCE: (Thomas, J.) Racial imbalance and racial segregation are not synonymous; it is possible to have racial imbalance through no conscious decision to segregate. Further, forced racial mixing of students may or may not provide educational benefits in general or higher achievement for Black students particularly. The color-blind Constitution, then, requires that these student assignment plans be struck down.

CONCURRENCE: (Kennedy, J.) Contrary to the Chief Justice's plurality opinion, race can be considered as one among several factors in examining school enrollments. General, indirect solutions to problems of racial composition of schools are much better than the crude plans in these cases as ways to address those problems. The United States has special obligations to ensure equal opportunity for all children, and government should be permitted to consider race in its attempts to fulfill that mission. As the plurality correctly notes, though, government may not classify students based solely on race without first making a showing that such a step is necessary.

DISSENT: (Stevens, J.) In his demand of strict equality under the Constitution, the Chief Justice forgets that, before *Brown*, 347 U.S. 483 (1954), only Black students were told where they could and could not go to school. Today's plurality decision rewrites the history of our landmark school-desegregation decision.

DISSENT: (Breyer, J.) These voluntary plans bear striking resemblances to plans that this Court has long required, permitted, and encouraged local school districts to formulate and use. Every branch of government has acknowledged that government may voluntarily use race-conscious plans to address race-based problems even when such plans are not constitutionally obligatory. The plurality overlooks the fact that no case has ever decided that all racial classifications should receive precisely the same scrutiny. Actually, our decisions have

Continued on next page.

applied different standards to assess racial classifications depending on whether the government's purpose was to exclude persons from, or to include persons in, government programs. The plurality's interpretation of strict scrutiny, however, would automatically invalidate all race-conscious government action. The school districts' (D) interest here serves remedial, educational, and democratic purposes; such a multiplicity of concerns means that *Grutter's* rationale controls here and requires upholding these assignment plans. Even under the strictest scrutiny, though, the plans here pass muster under the Equal Protection Clause because they are more narrowly tailored than the plan approved in *Grutter.* Accordingly, these plans are consistent with equal protection of the laws.

ANALYSIS

Chief Justice Roberts's plurality opinion in *Parents Involved* focuses on the firm percentages used by Seattle (D) and Louisville (D) in making student-assignment decisions. Despite Justice Breyer's objections in dissent, it is difficult to see how such an overtly numerical approach differs from the quota-based systems that the Court consistently has struck down under the Equal Protection Clause. See, e.g., *Regents of the University of California v. Bakke,* 438 U.S. 265, 307 (1978): "If [the University's] purpose is to assure within its student body some specified percentage of a particular group merely because of its race or ethnic origin, such a preferential purpose must be rejected not as insubstantial but as facially invalid."

Quicknotes

EQUAL PROTECTION CLAUSE A constitutional provision that each person be guaranteed the same protection of the laws enjoyed by other persons in like circumstances.

STRICT SCRUTINY A method by which courts determine the constitutionality of a law, when a law affects a fundamental right. Under the test, the legislature must have had a compelling interest to enact the law and measures prescribed by the law must be the least restrictive means possible to accomplish its goal.

Fisher v. University of Texas at Austin (Fisher II)

University applicant (P) v. State university (D)

136 S. Ct. 2198 (2016)

NATURE OF CASE: Appeal from judgment upholding a state university's race-conscious admissions program as constitutional under the Equal Protection Clause.

FACT SUMMARY: Fisher (P), a Caucasian who had been denied admission to the University of Texas at Austin (the University *or* UT) (D), contended that the University's (D) race-conscious admissions program did not meet the requirements for being constitutional under the Equal Protection Clause.

RULE OF LAW

A state university's race-conscious admissions program is lawful under the Equal Protection Clause where it satisfies strict scrutiny and is narrowly tailored to achieve the university's permissible goals.

FACTS: The University of Texas at Austin (the University *or* UT) (D) used an undergraduate admissions system containing two components. First, as required by the state's Top Ten Percent Law, it offered admission to any students who graduate from a Texas high school in the top 10 percent of their class. It then filled the remainder of its incoming freshman class, some 25 percent, by combining an applicant's Academic Achievement Index—the student's test score and high school academic performance—with the applicant's Personal Achievement Index (PAI), a holistic review containing numerous factors, including race. The University (D) adopted its admissions process after a year-long study of its admissions process led it to conclude that its prior race-neutral system did not reach its goal of providing the educational benefits of diversity to its undergraduate students. Fisher (P), who was not in the top 10 percent of her high school class, was denied admission to the University's (D) 2008 freshman class, after her application was reviewed through the University's (D) holistic review process. She filed suit, alleging that the University's (D) consideration of race as part of this process disadvantaged her and other Caucasian applicants, in violation of the Equal Protection Clause. In that case, *Fisher v. University of Texas at Austin*, 133 S. Ct. 2411 (2013) (*Fisher I*), the Supreme Court set forth three controlling principles relevant to assessing the constitutionality of a public university's affirmative action program. First, a university may not consider race unless the admissions process can withstand strict scrutiny, i.e., it must show that its purpose or interest is both constitutionally permissible and substantial and that its use of the classification is necessary to accomplish that purpose. Second, the decision to pursue the educational benefits that flow from student body diversity is, in substantial measure, an academic judgment to which some, but not complete, judicial deference is proper. Third, when determining whether the use of race is narrowly tailored to achieve the university's permissible goals, the school bears the burden of demonstrating that available and workable race-neutral alternatives do not suffice. Under these principles, a state university has a continuing obligation to satisfy the strict scrutiny burden: by periodically reassessing the admission program's constitutionality, and efficacy, in light of the school's experience and the data it has gathered since adopting its admissions plan, and by tailoring its approach to ensure that race plays no greater role than is necessary to meet its compelling interests. The court of appeals upheld the plan in light of these principles, and Fisher (P) appealed. The Supreme Court again granted certiorari in the case.

ISSUE: Is a state university's race-conscious admissions program lawful under the Equal Protection Clause where it satisfies strict scrutiny and is narrowly tailored to achieve the university's permissible goals?

HOLDING AND DECISION: (Kennedy, J.) Yes. A state university's race-conscious admissions program is lawful under the Equal Protection Clause where it satisfies strict scrutiny and is narrowly tailored to achieve the university's permissible goals. Here, Fisher (P) contends that the University (D) has not articulated its compelling interest with sufficient clarity because it has failed to state more precisely what level of minority enrollment would constitute a "critical mass." However, the compelling interest that justifies consideration of race in college admissions is not an interest in enrolling a certain number of minority students, but an interest in obtaining the educational benefits that flow from student body diversity. Since the University (D) is prohibited from seeking a particular-number or quota of minority students, it cannot be faulted for failing to specify the particular-level of minority enrollment at which it believes the educational benefits of diversity will be obtained. On the other hand, asserting an interest in the educational benefits of diversity writ large is insufficient. A university's goals cannot be elusory or amorphous—they must be sufficiently measurable to permit judicial scrutiny of the policies adopted to reach them. The University (D) not only articulated concrete and precise goals, but it also gave a reasoned,

Continued on next page.

principled explanation for its decision in a 39-page proposal written after a year-long study revealed that its race-neutral policies and programs did not meet its goals. For these reasons, Fisher's (P) argument that the University's (D) goal was insufficiently concrete is rejected. Second, Fisher (P) claims that the University (D) need not consider race because it had already achieved critical mass by 2003 under the Top Ten Percent Plan and race-neutral holistic review. The record, however, reveals that the University (D) studied and deliberated for months, concluding that race-neutral programs had not achieved its diversity goals, a conclusion supported by significant statistical and anecdotal evidence. Third, Fisher (P) claims that it was unnecessary to consider race because such consideration had only a minor impact on the number of minority students the school admitted. However, the record shows that the consideration of race has had a meaningful, if still limited, effect on freshman class diversity. That race consciousness played a role in only a small portion of admissions decisions should be a hallmark of narrow tailoring, not evidence of unconstitutionality. Finally, Fisher (P) argues that there were numerous other race-neutral means to achieve the University's (D) goals. However, as the record reveals, none of those alternatives was a workable means of attaining the University's educational goals as of the time of Fisher's (P) application, and her argument ignores precedent making clear that the Equal Protection Clause does not force universities to choose between a diverse student body and a reputation for academic excellence. Further, Fisher's (P) proposal to uncap the Top Ten Percent Plan overlooks the fact that the Top Ten Percent Plan, though facially neutral, cannot be understood apart from its basic purpose, which is to boost minority enrollment. Even if, as a matter of raw numbers, minority enrollment would increase under such a regime, there is little support for the proposition that college admissions would be improved if they were a function of class rank alone, since this approach would sacrifice all other aspects of diversity in pursuit of enrolling a higher number of minority students. Accordingly, the University (D) has met its burden of demonstrating that its admissions program was narrowly tailored when it rejected Fisher's (P) application. [Affirmed.]

DISSENT: (Thomas, J.) A state's use of race in higher education admissions decisions is categorically prohibited by the Equal Protection Clause because every time the government places citizens on racial registers and makes race relevant to the provision of burdens or benefits, it demeans us all.

DISSENT: (Alito, J.) *Fisher I* required UT (D) to identify the interests justifying its plan with enough specificity to permit a reviewing court to determine whether the requirements of strict scrutiny were met, and to show that those requirements were in fact satisfied. UT (D) failed to do meet these obligations. *Fisher I* rejected the argument that the courts should defer to the University (D) as to these matters, and by invoking "the educational benefits of diversity," UT (D) fails to identify any metric that would allow a court to determine whether its plan is needed to serve, or is actually serving, those interests. This amounts to nothing less than the plea for deference that was emphatically rejected in *Fisher I.* The University (D) has never shown that its race-conscious plan actually ameliorates the concerns it claims the plan addresses. It has never adduced specific evidence to show that the plan actually supports its stated goals. Thus, UT (D) has failed to meet its burden of showing that its race-conscious plan was narrowly tailored to serve compelling interests. By accepting UT's (D) rationales as sufficient to meet its burden, the majority licenses UT's (D) perverse assumptions about different groups of minority students—the precise assumptions strict scrutiny is supposed to stamp out. UT (D) has failed to define its interest in using racial preferences with clarity. As a result, the narrow tailoring inquiry is impossible, and UT (D) cannot satisfy strict scrutiny. UT (D) indicated it failed to achieve a critical mass of underrepresented minorities, but it has never explained, except in the vaguest of terms, what it means by "critical mass." The effect of this imprecision is to insulate UT's (D) program from meaningful judicial review. Even assuming UT (D) need only cite a generic interest in the educational benefits of diversity, its plan still fails strict scrutiny because it is not narrowly tailored. Narrow tailoring requires a careful judicial inquiry into whether a university could achieve sufficient diversity without using racial classifications. Here, there is no evidence that race-blind, holistic review would not achieve UT's (D) goals at least about as well as UT's (D) race-based policy. UT (D) could have adopted other approaches to further its goals. Whereas a university may adopt an admissions plan that results in a student body with a broad representation of students from all racial and ethnic groups, it may not justify systematic racial discrimination simply by asserting that such discrimination is necessary to achieve "the educational benefits of diversity," without explaining—much less proving—why the discrimination is needed or how the discriminatory plan is well crafted to serve its objectives. Here, the majority incorrectly concludes that UT (D) has met its heavy burden by using precisely such a justification.

ANALYSIS

Supporters of this decision hailed it as a landmark decision that will promote racial diversity and educational inclusion. Its detractors claimed that it permitted the University (D) to benefit advantaged students over impoverished ones, and even Justice Alito was reported

Continued on next page.

to have told his colleagues that it was "affirmative action gone berserk." Because many colleges and universities base all their admissions decisions on academic achievement as well as factors such as race and ethnicity, this decision lets stand such admissions programs all over the nation, and, importantly, recognizes that there are many ways to achieve diversity, and that some deference to an institution's particular formula for obtaining a diverse student population is necessary. The decision also emphasizes that schools will need to continually assess their admissions programs to determine whether race-conscious policies are needed in light of changing demographics and the impacts their affirmative action programs have had.

Quicknotes

AFFIRMATIVE ACTION A form of benign discrimination designed to remedy existing discrimination by favoring one group over another.

STRICT SCRUTINY Method by which courts determine the constitutionality of a law, when a law affects a fundamental right. Under the test, the legislature must have had a compelling interest to enact the law, and measures prescribed by the law must be the least restrictive means possible to accomplish its goal.

Graham v. Richardson

State (D) v. Welfare applicant (P)

403 U.S. 365 (1971)

NATURE OF CASE: Appeal from decision that invalidated state requirements for receipt of welfare benefits.

FACT SUMMARY: Richardson's (P) application for welfare benefits was denied due to an Arizona statute conditioning receipt of such benefits on citizenship or residence in the United States for 15 years.

RULE OF LAW

A state statute that denies welfare benefits to resident aliens, or to aliens who have not resided in the United States for a specified number of years, violates the Equal Protection Clause.

FACTS: Richardson (P) had lived in Arizona since coming to the United States from Mexico in 1956. She applied for welfare benefits because she was "permanently and totally disabled." Her application was denied, however, due to an Arizona statute conditioning receipt of welfare benefits either on citizenship or residence in the United States for 15 years. At the time she applied for benefits, Richardson (P) was neither a citizen nor a person who had lived in the United States for the required length of time. The court of appeals ruled that Richardson (P) was entitled to receive welfare benefits. On appeal, the Court combined this case with one under a Pennsylvania statute limiting welfare only to citizens.

ISSUE: Does a state statute that denies welfare benefits to resident aliens, or to aliens who have not resided in the United States for a specified number of years violate the Equal Protection Clause?

HOLDING AND DECISION: (Blackmun, J.) Yes. A state statute that denies welfare benefits to resident aliens, or to aliens who have not resided in the United States for a specified number of years, violates the Equal Protection Clause. The Fourteenth Amendment term "person" encompasses lawfully admitted resident aliens as well as citizens of the United States and entitles both citizens and aliens to the equal protection of the laws of the state in which they reside. Classifications based on alienage, like those based on nationality or race, are inherently suspect and subject to close judicial scrutiny. Arizona and Pennsylvania seek to justify their restrictions on the eligibility of aliens for public assistance solely on the basis of a state's "special public interest" in favoring its own citizens over aliens in the distribution of limited resources such as welfare benefits. However, Congress has broadly declared as federal policy that lawfully admitted resident aliens who become public charges for causes arising after their entry are not subject to deportation, and that as long as they are here they are entitled to the full and equal benefit of all state laws for the security of persons and property. Thus, state laws that restrict the eligibility of aliens for welfare benefits merely because of their alienage conflict with overriding national policies in an area constitutionally entrusted to the federal government. Since such laws encroach upon exclusive federal power, they are constitutionally impermissible. Affirmed.

ANALYSIS

In his treatise on American Constitutional Law, Professor Laurence Tribe notes that the Court's unanimous opinion in the instant case constituted the high-water mark of judicial protection of aliens. Thereafter, the margin for applying strict scrutiny to all alienage classifications narrowed steadily. The tide finally turned against alienage as a suspect classification in *Foley v. Connelie*, 435 U.S. 291 (1978), where six Justices voted to uphold a New York law requiring police officers to be American citizens. The previous dissenters in *Nyquist v. Mauclet*, 432 U.S. 1 (1977), Chief Justice Burger and Justices Stewart, Powell, and Rehnquist, were joined by Justice White to make the new majority, with Justice Blackmun concurring in the result.

Quicknotes

EQUAL PROTECTION CLAUSE A constitutional guarantee that no person should be denied the same protection of the laws enjoyed by other persons in like circumstances.

RESIDENT ALIEN An alien who resides in this country with the intent to remain.

STRICT SCRUTINY The method by which courts determine the constitutionality of a law, when a law affects a fundamental right. Under the test, the legislature must have a compelling interest to enact the law, and measures prescribed by the law must be the least restrictive means possible to accomplish its goal.

Bernal v. Fainter

Resident alien (P) v. State (D)

467 U.S. 216 (1984)

NATURE OF CASE: Appeal from decision upholding state statute denying aliens the opportunity to become notaries public.

FACT SUMMARY: Bernal (P), a resident alien living and working in Texas, challenged the state statute under which his application for a notary public license was denied.

RULE OF LAW

When a state denies a resident alien the opportunity to become a public officer whose duties are essentially clerical and ministerial, strict scrutiny is the applicable standard of review.

FACTS: Bernal (P), a Mexican citizen living and working in Texas, applied for a notary public license in 1978. Fainter (D), the Texas Secretary of State, denied Bernal's (P) application because a state statute required that a notary public be a citizen of the United States. The court of appeals upheld the citizenship requirement of the state statute. On appeal, Texas argued that because the duties of Texas notaries entailed the performance of functions sufficiently consequential to be deemed "political," the political function exception to the general rule applied, thus lowering the standard of review.

ISSUE: When a state denies a resident alien the opportunity to become a public officer whose duties are essentially clerical and ministerial, is strict scrutiny the applicable standard of review?

HOLDING AND DECISION: (Marshall, J.) Yes. When a state denies a resident alien the opportunity to become a public officer whose duties are essentially clerical and ministerial, strict scrutiny is the applicable standard of review. As a general matter, a state law that discriminates on basis of alienage can be sustained only if it can withstand strict judicial scrutiny. A narrow exception to the rule has been developed allowing aliens to be excluded from positions intimately related to the process of democratic self-governance. A notary's duties, important as they are, hardly implicate responsibilities that go to the heart of representative government. Rather, these duties are essentially clerical and ministerial. What distinguishes such personnel from those to whom the political-function exception is properly applied is that the latter are invested either with policy-making responsibility or broad discretion in the execution of public policy that requires the routine exercise of authority over individuals. Neither of these characteristics pertains to the functions performed by Texas notaries. Thus, the state's asserted interest lacks the weight required of interests properly denominated as compelling. Reversed.

DISSENT: (Rehnquist, J.) The Court holds an alien is not really different from a citizen, and any legislative classification on the basis of alienage is "inherently suspect." But there is no language used in the Fourteenth Amendment that would suggest to the slightest degree that it was intended to render alienage a "suspect" classification, or that it would in any way justify the result reached by the Court.

ANALYSIS

Eight members of the Court joined in applying the strict scrutiny standard to this category, with only then-Justice Rehnquist dissenting. The Court was not swayed by the fact that the Texas Constitution designated notaries as public officers. Indeed, the Court declared it had never deemed the source of a position as the dispositive factor in determining whether a state may entrust that position only to citizens. Rather, the Court declared it has always looked to the actual function of the position as the dispositive factor in determining whether a position exercised power of the sort that a self-governing community could properly entrust only to full-fledged members of that community.

Quicknotes

RESIDENT ALIEN An alien who resides in this country with the intent to remain.

STRICT SCRUTINY The method by which courts determine the constitutionality of a law, when a law affects a fundamental right. Under the test, the legislature must have a compelling interest to enact the law, and measures prescribed by the law must be the least restrictive means possible to accomplish its goal.

Trump v. Hawaii

President (D) v. State (P)

138 S. Ct. 2392 (2018)

NATURE OF CASE: Appeal from preliminary injunction enjoining President's entry ban on aliens from certain countries, granted on grounds that the ban exceeds the President's authority and violates the Establishment Clause.

FACT SUMMARY: A district court preliminarily enjoined President Trump's (D) ban on entry of aliens from certain nations, on grounds that the ban exceeded President Trump's (D) authority and violated the Establishment Clause. President Trump (D) contended that these grounds were unsupported.

RULE OF LAW

(1) A President has authority under the Immigration and Nationality Act, 8 U.S.C. § 1182(f), to suspend the entry of aliens from specific countries where the President finds that their entry would be detrimental to United States interests.

(2) Where a presidential proclamation is neutral on its face toward religion and putatively furthers national security interests, but disproportionately impacts a religious group toward which the President publicly has expressed great animus, the proclamation survives an attack on Establishment Clause grounds under rational basis review.

FACTS: Under the Immigration and Nationality Act (the INA *or* the Act), foreign nationals seeking entry into the United States undergo a vetting process to ensure that they satisfy the numerous requirements for admission. The Act also vests the President with authority to restrict the entry of aliens whenever he finds that their entry "would be detrimental to the interests of the United States." 8 U.S.C. § 1182(f). In September 2017, President Trump (D) issued Proclamation No. 9645, Enhancing Vetting Capabilities and Processes for Detecting Attempted Entry Into the United States by Terrorists or Other Public-Safety Threats ("the Proclamation"), seeking to improve vetting procedures for foreign nationals traveling to the United States by identifying ongoing deficiencies in the information needed to assess whether nationals of particular countries present a security threat. The Proclamation placed entry restrictions on the nationals of eight foreign states whose systems for managing and sharing information about their nationals that President Trump (D) deemed inadequate. Foreign states were selected for inclusion based on a review undertaken pursuant to one of President Trump's (D) executive orders. As part of that review, the Department of Homeland Security (DHS), in consultation with the State Department and intelligence agencies, developed an information and risk assessment "baseline." DHS then collected and evaluated data for all foreign governments, identifying those having deficient information-sharing practices and presenting national security concerns, as well as other countries "at risk" of failing to meet the baseline. After a 50-day period during which the State Department made diplomatic efforts to encourage foreign governments to improve their practices, the Acting Secretary of Homeland Security concluded that eight countries—Chad, Iran, Iraq, Libya, North Korea, Syria, Venezuela, and Yemen—remained deficient. She recommended entry restrictions for certain nationals from all those countries but Iraq, which had a close cooperative relationship with the United States. She also recommended including Somalia, which met the information-sharing component of the baseline standards but had other special risk factors, such as a significant terrorist presence. After consulting with multiple Cabinet members, President Trump (D) adopted the recommendations and issued the Proclamation. Invoking his authority under 8 U.S.C. §§ 1182(f) and 1185(a), he determined that certain restrictions were necessary to "prevent the entry of those foreign nationals about whom the United States Government lacks sufficient information" and to "elicit improved identity-management and information-sharing protocols and practices from foreign governments." The Proclamation imposes a range of entry restrictions that vary based on the "distinct circumstances" in each of the eight countries. It exempts lawful permanent residents and provides case-by-case waivers under certain circumstances. It also directs DHS to assess on a continuing basis whether the restrictions should be modified or continued, and to report to President Trump (D) every 180 days. At the completion of the first such review period, President Trump (D) determined that Chad had sufficiently improved its practices, and he accordingly lifted restrictions on its nationals. Proclamation No. 9645 was challenged by various plaintiffs, including the State of Hawaii (collectively "the plaintiffs") (P), on the grounds that President Trump (D) lacked authority to issue the Proclamation, and that even if he did, the Proclamation violated the First Amendment's Establishment Clause because, allegedly, its true purpose was to exclude Muslims from entering the country. The latter claim was based in large part on statements made by President Trump (D) and

Continued on next page.

his advisers when he was a candidate for office, as well as after he became President, that showed extreme animus toward Muslims, and because the countries affected by the Proclamation largely were Muslim-majority nations. The district court granted a preliminary injunction barring enforcement of the Proclamation, the Ninth Circuit affirmed, and the Supreme Court granted certiorari.

ISSUE:

(1) Does a President have authority under the Immigration and Nationality Act, 8 U.S.C. § 1182(f), to suspend the entry of aliens from specific countries where the President finds that their entry would be detrimental to United States interests?

(2) Where a presidential proclamation is neutral on its face toward religion and putatively furthers national security interests, but disproportionately impacts a religious group towards which the President publicly has expressed great animus, does the proclamation survive an attack on Establishment Clause grounds under rational basis review?

HOLDING AND DECISION: (Roberts, C.J.)

(1) Yes. A President has authority under the Immigration and Nationality Act (the INA), 8 U.S.C. § 1182(f), to suspend the entry of aliens from specific countries where the President finds that their entry would be detrimental to United States interests. By its terms, § 1182(f) exudes deference to the President in every clause. It entrusts to the President the decisions whether and when to suspend entry, whose entry to suspend, for how long, and on what conditions. It thus vests the President with "ample power" to impose entry restrictions in addition to those elsewhere enumerated in the INA. Proclamation No. 9645, Enhancing Vetting Capabilities and Processes for Detecting Attempted Entry into the United States by Terrorists or Other Public-Safety Threats ("the Proclamation"), falls well within this comprehensive delegation. The sole prerequisite set forth in § 1182(f) is that the President "find[]" that the entry of the covered aliens "would be detrimental to the interests of the United States." President Trump (D) has undoubtedly fulfilled that requirement here. The plaintiffs (P) also argue that President Trump's (D) entry suspension violates § 1152(a)(1)(A). This argument ignores the basic distinction between admissibility determinations and visa issuance that runs throughout the INA. Section 1182 defines the universe of aliens who are admissible into the United States (and therefore eligible to receive a visa). Once § 1182 sets the boundaries of admissibility, § 1152(a)(1)(A) prohibits discrimination in the allocation of immigrant visas based on nationality and other traits. Had Congress intended in § 1152(a)(1)(A) to constrain the President's power to determine who may enter the country, it could have chosen language directed to that end. Common sense and historical practice confirm that § 1152(a)(1)(A) does not limit the President's delegated authority under § 1182(f). Presidents have repeatedly exercised their authority to suspend entry on the basis of nationality.

(2) Yes. Where a presidential proclamation is neutral on its face toward religion and putatively furthers national security interests, but disproportionately impacts a religious group towards which the President publicly has expressed great animus, the proclamation survives an attack on Establishment Clause grounds under rational basis review. The plaintiffs (P) allege that the primary purpose of the Proclamation was religious animus and that President Trump's (D) stated concerns about vetting protocols and national security were but pretexts for discriminating against Muslims. At the heart of their case is a series of statements by President Trump (D) and his advisers both during the campaign and since President Trump (D) assumed office. The issue, however, is not whether to denounce President Trump's (D) statements, but the significance of those statements in reviewing a presidential directive, neutral on its face, addressing a matter within the core of executive responsibility. In doing so, the Court must consider not only the statements of a particular President but also the authority of the presidency itself. The admission and exclusion of foreign nationals is a fundamental sovereign attribute exercised by the government's political departments largely immune from judicial control. Although foreign nationals seeking admission have no constitutional right to entry, this Court has engaged in a circumscribed judicial inquiry when the denial of a visa allegedly burdens the constitutional rights of a U.S. citizen. The Court must tread very lightly in this area, since judicial inquiry into the national-security realm raises concerns for the separation of powers by intruding on the President's constitutional responsibilities in the area of foreign affairs, and since, as to collecting evidence and drawing inferences on questions of national security, the lack of competence on the part of the judiciary is marked. Hence, judicial review is limited to whether the executive gives a facially legitimate and bona fide reason for its action, but the Court need not define the precise contours of that narrow inquiry in this case. The Court assumes in this case that it may look behind the face of the Proclamation to the extent of applying rational basis review, i.e., whether the entry policy is plausibly related to the government's stated objective to protect the country and improve vetting processes. The plaintiffs' (P) extrinsic evidence may be considered,

Continued on next page.

but the policy will be upheld so long as it can reasonably be understood to result from a justification independent of unconstitutional grounds. On the few occasions where the Court has struck down a policy as illegitimate under rational basis scrutiny, a common thread has been that the laws at issue were divorced from any factual context from which the Court could discern a relationship to legitimate state interests, or could be explained only by animus. The Proclamation does not fit that pattern. It is expressly premised on legitimate purposes and says nothing about religion. The entry restrictions on Muslim-majority nations are limited to countries that were previously designated by Congress or prior administrations as posing national security risks and cover just 8 percent of the world's Muslims. Moreover, the Proclamation reflects the results of a worldwide review process undertaken by multiple Cabinet officials and their agencies. Plaintiffs (P) challenge the entry suspension based on their perception of its effectiveness and wisdom, but the Court cannot substitute its own assessment for the executive's predictive judgments on such matters. [Reversed and remanded.]

CONCURRENCE: (Kennedy, J.) Although there are numerous instances in which the statements and actions of government officials are not subject to judicial scrutiny or intervention, that does not mean those officials are free to disregard the Constitution and the rights it proclaims and protects. To the contrary, it is imperative such officials adhere to the Constitution and to its meaning and its promise. This is equally true in the realm of foreign affairs, so that an anxious world knows our government remains committed always to the liberties the Constitution seeks to preserve and protect, so that freedom extends outward and lasts.

DISSENT: (Breyer, J.) The Court is divided principally as to the factual question of whether Proclamation No. 9645, Enhancing Vetting Capabilities and Processes for Detecting Attempted Entry into the United States by Terrorists or Other Public-Safety Threats ("the Proclamation") was, in fact, motivated primarily by religious animus. That system provides for case-by-case consideration of persons who may qualify for visas despite the Proclamation's general ban. Those persons include lawful permanent residents, asylum seekers, refugees, students, children, and numerous others. There are likely many such persons, perhaps in the thousands. It is appropriate to take account of their Proclamation-granted status when considering the Proclamation's lawfulness: if the government is in fact applying the exemption and waiver provisions as written, then its argument for the Proclamation's lawfulness is strengthened, especially since the case-by-case exemptions and waivers apply without regard to an individual's religion, and application of that system would help make clear that the Proclamation does not deny visas to numerous Muslim individuals who do not pose a security threat. If, on the other hand, the government is not applying the provisions as written, its argument for the Proclamation's lawfulness becomes significantly weaker, since it cannot successfully claim that the Proclamation rests on security needs if it is excluding Muslims who satisfy the Proclamation's own terms. Unfortunately, there is evidence the government is not applying the Proclamation as written, and that supports the theory that it is, in application, a "Muslim ban." However, such evidence, which is composed of declarations, anecdotal evidence, facts, and numbers taken from amicus briefs, does not constitute judicial factfinding. The government has not had an opportunity to respond, and a court has not had an opportunity to decide. However, given the need for assurance the Proclamation does not rest upon a "Muslim ban" and the assistance in deciding the issue that answers to the "exemption and waiver" questions may provide, the district court's injunction should remain in effect while the matter is litigated.

DISSENT: (Sotomayor, J.) The Proclamation, which was advertised openly and unequivocally as a "total and complete shutdown of Muslims entering the United States," must be set aside as violative of the Establishment Clause. In determining whether plaintiffs have proved an Establishment Clause violation, the Court asks whether a reasonable observer would view the government action as taken for the purpose of disfavoring a religion. In answering that question, the Court has generally considered the text of the government policy, its operation, and any available evidence regarding the historical background of the decision under challenge, the specific series of events leading to the enactment or official policy in question, and the legislative or administrative history, including contemporaneous statements made by the decisionmaker. The majority opinion is deceptively thin on Trump's (D) unrelenting animus toward Muslims, both as a candidate for the presidency and once he took office. As to his first ban, EO-1, which he signed a week after taking office, he explained to the media that, under EO-1, Christians would be given priority for entry as refugees into the United States. While litigation over his second executive order attempting to ban Muslims from entering the U.S. (EO-2) was ongoing, President Trump (D) repeatedly made statements alluding to a desire to keep Muslims out of the country. The list of such statements, made to the media and in tweets, goes on and on. As the majority correctly notes, the issue before the Court is not whether to denounce these offensive statements. Rather, the dispositive and narrow question here is whether a reasonable observer, presented with

Continued on next page.

all "openly available data," the text and "historical context" of Proclamation No. 9645, Enhancing Vetting Capabilities and Processes for Detecting Attempted Entry into the United States by Terrorists or Other Public-Safety Threats ("the Proclamation"), and the "specific sequence of events" leading to it, would conclude that the primary purpose of the Proclamation is to disfavor Islam and its adherents by excluding them from the country. The answer is unquestionably "yes." Taking all the relevant evidence together, a reasonable observer would conclude that the Proclamation was driven primarily by anti-Muslim animus rather than by the government's asserted national-security justifications. Moreover, despite several opportunities to do so, President Trump (D) has never disavowed any of his prior statements about Islam. Instead, he has continued to make remarks that a reasonable observer would view as an unrelenting attack on the Muslim religion and its followers. Ultimately, what began as a policy explicitly calling for a total and complete shutdown of Muslims entering the United States has since morphed into a "Proclamation" putatively based on national-security concerns. However, this new window dressing cannot conceal an unassailable fact: the words of the President and his advisers create the strong perception that the Proclamation is contaminated by impermissible discriminatory animus against Islam and its followers. None of the features of the Proclamation highlighted by the majority supports the government's claim that the Proclamation is genuinely and primarily rooted in a legitimate national-security interest. Thus, even under rational basis review, the Proclamation must fall because the Proclamation is divorced from any factual context from which a relationship to legitimate state interests can be discerned, and because its sheer breadth is so discontinuous with the reasons offered for it that the policy is inexplicable by anything but animus. In holding that the First Amendment gives way to an executive policy that a reasonable observer would view as motivated by animus against Muslims, the majority opinion upends the Court's precedent, repeats tragic mistakes of the past, and denies countless individuals the fundamental right of religious liberty. The majority completely sets aside Trump's (D) charged statements about Muslims as irrelevant, and by so doing, erodes the foundational principles of religious tolerance the Court elsewhere has so emphatically protected. The majority's decision is "gravely wrong."

ANALYSIS

One of the few principles the majority and dissent agreed on is that the Court's decision in *Korematsu v. United States,* 323 U.S. 214 (1944), which upheld, pursuant to executive decree, the forcible relocation of Japanese U.S. citizens to concentration camps solely and explicitly on the basis of race, was wrong, and that such an order was "objectively unlawful and outside the scope of presidential authority." Chief Justice Roberts expressly abrogated *Korematsu,* stating that *Korematsu* "was gravely wrong the day it was decided, has been overruled in the court of history, and—to be clear—'has no place in law under the Constitution.' 323 U.S., at 248 (Jackson, J., dissenting)." In her dissent, Justice Sotomayor lauds this formal repudiation of a "shameful" precedent that is "long overdue," but adds that "[b]y blindly accepting the government's misguided invitation to sanction a discriminatory policy motivated by animosity toward a disfavored group, all in the name of a superficial claim of national security, the Court redeploys the same dangerous logic underlying *Korematsu* and merely replaces one 'gravely wrong' decision with another." Chief Justice Roberts rejects the comparison, saying that it is wholly inapt to liken the morally repugnant order in *Korematsu* to the order of Proclamation No. 9645, Enhancing Vetting Capabilities and Processes for Detecting Attempted Entry into the United States by Terrorists or Other Public-Safety Threat, the facially neutral policy of denying certain foreign nationals the privilege of admission.

Quicknotes

ESTABLISHMENT CLAUSE The constitutional provision prohibiting the government from favoring any one religion over others or engaging in religious activities or advocacy.

EXTRINSIC EVIDENCE Evidence that is not contained within the text of a document or contract, but which is derived from the parties' statements or the circumstances under which the agreement was made.

JUDICIAL REVIEW The authority of the courts to review decisions, actions, or omissions committed by another agency or branch of government.

PRELIMINARY INJUNCTION A judicial mandate issued to require or restrain a party from certain conduct; used to preserve a trial's subject matter or to prevent threatened injury.

RATIONAL BASIS REVIEW A test employed by the court to determine the validity of a statute in equal protection actions, whereby the court determines whether the challenged statute is rationally related to the achievement of a legitimate state interest.

CHAPTER 8

Sex Equality

Quick Reference Rules of Law

Frontiero v. Richardson

Servicewoman (P) v. Court (D)

411 U.S. 677 (1973)

NATURE OF CASE: Suit challenging the constitutionality of a statute.

FACT SUMMARY: A statute provides that servicemen's wives are automatically eligible for benefits as dependents while servicewomen must demonstrate that their husbands are dependent on them before they are eligible for the benefits.

RULE OF LAW

Statutes providing stricter requirements for servicewomen's husbands claiming dependency benefits than for servicemen's wives claiming such benefits are unconstitutionally discriminatory.

FACTS: A servicewoman's request for increased benefits for her dependent husband was denied because she failed to affirmatively demonstrate that her husband was dependent on her for over one-half of his support. The controlling statute provided that a serviceman may claim his wife as a dependent without regard to whether she is actually dependent on him. A servicewoman can claim her husband as a dependent only if she demonstrates he is actually dependent on her for over one-half of his support.

ISSUE: Are statutes providing stricter requirements for servicewomen's husbands claiming dependency benefits than for servicemen's wives claiming such benefits unconstitutionally discriminatory?

HOLDING AND DECISION: (Brennan, J.) Yes. Classifications based upon sex, like those based upon race, alienage, or national origin, are inherently suspect and must be subjected to strict scrutiny. The United States has had a long and unfortunate history of sex discrimination. During the nineteenth century, the position of women was in many ways similar to that of Blacks before the Civil War. Neither could hold office, serve on juries, or bring suit, and although Black men were given the right to vote in 1870, women did not gain suffrage until 50 years later. Women (like Blacks) still face pervasive, although at times more subtle discrimination in education, employment, and especially in politics. Sex, like race, is an immutable characteristic, determined solely by birth and bears no relation to the ability to perform in society. Hence, statutory distinctions between the sexes often have the effect of invidiously regulating an entire class to an inferior legal status. Hence, a compelling state interest must be demonstrated if such distinctions are to be upheld. Here, it is argued that Congress might have reasonably concluded that it would be cheaper and easier to presume that wives were dependent on their husbands while presuming that husbands are not dependent on their wives. However, to withstand scrutiny, it must be shown that this practice is actually cheaper, which was not done here. In fact, there was evidence that many servicemen's wives are not dependent on their husbands for over one-half of their support. Insofar as the statute requires female members to prove their husband's dependency while not so requiring male members, it violates the Due Process Clause of the Fifth Amendment. Reversed.

CONCURRENCE: (Powell, J.) Another reason exists for the Court's not declaring sex to be a suspect classification. As the Equal Rights Amendment is before the states for ratification, it should be left to the people to make this decision. The Court should not interfere in this democratic process.

ANALYSIS

Despite the holding of the plurality opinion, the majority has consistently failed to adopt the view that sex classifications are inherently suspect. This has led to widely varying results when challenges to statutes on basis of sex discrimination are brought before the Court. The Court has sustained an attack on the Social Security System, which provided survivor's benefits to a minor child and widow but not to a widower, because it discriminated against women wage earners by affording them less protection for their survivors. A Utah court's finding—that support payments ended at 18 for a daughter and 21 for a son—was struck down as discriminatory. But in a California case, the Court upheld a provision in the state's disability insurance program that excluded coverage for a woman undergoing a normal pregnancy. Also upheld was a Florida statute that provided property tax exemptions for widows but not for widowers. And a naval regulation allowing women officers a longer tenure before discharge due to lack of promotion was approved. The proposed Twenty-Seventh Amendment to the Constitution provides that "equality of rights under the law shall not be denied or abridged by the United States or by any state on basis of sex."

Continued on next page.

Quicknotes

PROCEDURAL DUE PROCESS The constitutional mandate that if the state or federal government acts so as to deny a citizen of a life, liberty, or property interest the individual is first entitled to notice and the right to be heard.

SUSPECT CLASSIFICATION A class of persons that have historically been subject to discriminatory treatment; statutes drawing a distinction between persons based on a suspect classification, i.e., race, nationality, or alienage, are subject to a strict scrutiny standard of review.

United States v. Virginia (The VMI Case)

Federal government (P) v. State (D)

518 U.S. 515 (1996)

NATURE OF CASE: Petition to allow females into an all-male school.

FACT SUMMARY: The Virginia Military Institute (VMI) refused to let women enter. A female high school student seeking admission to VMI brought suit under equal protection grounds.

RULE OF LAW

The Constitution's equal protection principle is not satisfied if there is not substantial equality in the remedial measure.

FACTS: The Virginia Military Institute (VMI) is an all-male military college. A female student filed a complaint seeking admission to VMI. The court of appeals found a violation of the Equal Protection Clause of the Fourteenth Amendment. The state of Virginia (D) proposed a remedial plan, under which a parallel program for women would be created and called Virginia Women's Institute for Leadership (VWIL). VWIL would be located at Mary Baldwin College, a private liberal arts school for women.

ISSUE: Is the Constitution's equal protection principle satisfied if there is not substantial equality in the remedial measure?

HOLDING AND DECISION: (Ginsburg, J.) No. The Constitution's equal protection principle is not satisfied if there is not substantial equality in the remedial measure. Although VMI and VWIL share the same mission, the VWIL program would differ from VMI in academic offerings, methods of education, and financial resources. The average combined SAT score of entrants to Mary Baldwin College is about 100 points lower than that for VMI freshmen. Mary Baldwin College offered only Bachelor of Arts degrees, while VMI offers degrees in liberal arts, the sciences, and engineering. Instead of VMI's adversative method, VWIL would offer a cooperative method that reinforces self-esteem. VMI also had a much larger endowment, better faculty, larger course offerings, and better facilities than VWIL. Since there is no substantial equality in the separate educational opportunities at VMI and VWIL, Virginia's (D) solution violates the Equal Protection Clause of the Fourteenth Amendment.

CONCURRENCE: (Rehnquist, C.J.) An adequate remedy would be a demonstration by Virginia (D) that its interest in educating men in a single-sex environment is matched by its interest in educating women in a single-sex institution. It would be sufficient if the two offered the same quality of education and were of the same overall caliber.

DISSENT: (Scalia, J.) The majority criticizes our ancestors' regard to providing women educational opportunities, but this Court now has embarked on a course of proscribing its own elite opinions on society. Virginia (D) has an important interest in providing education, and single-sex instruction is an approach substantially related to this goal. The proposed VWIL was designed for women and not designed to be exactly equal to VMI.

ANALYSIS

Justice Scalia's dissent carries a tone of disgust for the majority opinion. As he did in *Romer v. Evans*, 116 S. Ct. 1620 (1996), Scalia states that the majority seeks to satisfy some unidentified group of antimajoritarian elites. This attitude is unusual for a member of the Supreme Court since dissents are usually restricted to attacks on the majority's legal reasoning.

Quicknotes

EQUAL PROTECTION CLAUSE A constitutional provision that each person be guaranteed the same protection of the laws enjoyed by other persons in like circumstances.

Tuan Anh Nguyen v. INS

Child born abroad to American father (D) v. Federal agency (P)

533 U.S. 53 (2001)

NATURE OF CASE: Appeal in deportation proceedings.

FACT SUMMARY: Nguyen (D) argued that 8 U.S.C. § 1409(a), which, for a child born out of wedlock outside the United States or its possessions to one citizen parent and one alien parent, imposes different requirements for acquiring United States citizenship depending on the citizen parent's gender, violated the equal protection guarantee of the Fifth Amendment's Due Process Clause.

RULE OF LAW

The gender-based classification in 8 U.S.C. § 1409(a), which, for a child born out of wedlock outside the United States or its possessions to one citizen parent and one alien parent, imposes different requirements for acquiring United States citizenship depending on the citizen parent's gender, does not violate the equal protection guarantee of the Fifth Amendment's Due Process Clause.

FACTS: 8 U.S.C. § 1409(a), which, for a child born out of wedlock outside the United States or its possessions, automatically grants U.S. citizenship upon birth to the child if the mother is a U.S. citizen, but denies citizenship in the same circumstances if the only U.S. parent is the father, unless a paternity decree is entered before the child turns 18. Nguyen (D) was born in Vietnam to an American father and a Vietnamese mother and came to the United States when he was six. When he was 22, Nguyen (D) pleaded guilty to sexual assault on a minor. The Immigration and Naturalization Service (INS) initiated deportation proceedings against him. Nguyen (D) defended on the grounds he was a U.S. citizen, his father established paternity when Nguyen (D) was 28, and § 1409 violated equal protection by providing different citizenship rules for children born abroad and out of wedlock depending on whether the citizen parent is the mother or the father. The United States Supreme Court granted review.

ISSUE: Does the gender-based classification in 8 U.S.C. § 1409(a), which, for a child born out of wedlock outside the United States or its possessions to one citizen parent and one alien parent, imposes different requirements for acquiring United States citizenship depending on the citizen parent's gender, violate the equal protection guarantee of the Fifth Amendment's Due Process Clause?

HOLDING AND DECISION: (Kennedy, J.) No. The gender-based classification in 8 U.S.C. § 1409(a), which, for a child born out of wedlock outside the United States or its possessions to one citizen parent and one alien parent, imposes different requirements for acquiring United States citizenship depending on the citizen parent's gender, does not violate the equal protection guarantee of the Fifth Amendment's Due Process Clause. Section 1409(a) imposes a set of requirements on the children of citizen fathers born abroad and out of wedlock to a noncitizen mother that are not imposed under like circumstances when the citizen parent is the mother. The issue here is whether § 1409(a)(4), relating to a citizen father's acknowledgment of a child while the child is under 18, is unconstitutional. For a gender-based classification to withstand equal protection scrutiny, it must be established that the challenged classification serves "important governmental objectives" that are "substantially related to the achievement of those objectives." Section 1409(a)(4) requires one of three affirmative steps to be taken if the citizen parent is the father, but not if the citizen parent is the mother: legitimation; a declaration of paternity under oath by the father; or a court order of paternity. Congress's decision is based on the significant difference between their respective relationships to the potential citizen at the time of birth and is justified by two important governmental objectives. The first such interest is the importance of assuring that a biological parent-child relationship exists. The mother's relation is verifiable from the birth itself and is documented by the birth certificate or hospital records and the witnesses to the birth. However, a father need not be present at the birth, and his presence is not incontrovertible proof of fatherhood. Nguyen (D) argues that § 1409(a)(1)'s requirement that a father provide clear and convincing evidence of parentage is sufficient to achieve the end of establishing paternity, given the sophistication of modern DNA tests. However, that section does not mandate DNA testing. With respect to DNA testing, the expense, reliability, and availability of such testing in various parts of the world may have been of particular concern to Congress. Moreover, the Constitution does not require that Congress elect one particular mechanism from among many possible methods of establishing paternity. Finally, even a facially neutral rule would sometimes require fathers to take additional affirmative steps that would not be required of mothers, whose names will be on the birth certificate as result of their presence at the birth, and who will have the benefit of witnesses to the birth to call upon. The second governmental interest

Continued on next page.

furthered by § 1409(a)(4) is the determination to ensure that the child and citizen parent have some demonstrated opportunity to develop a relationship that consists of real, everyday ties providing a connection between child and citizen parent and, in turn, the United States. Such an opportunity inheres in the event of birth in the case of a citizen mother and her child but does not result as a matter of biological inevitability in the case of an unwed father. He may not know that a child was conceived, and a mother may be unsure of the father's identity. One concern in this context has always been with young men on duty with the Armed Forces in foreign countries. Today, the ease of travel and willingness of Americans to visit foreign countries have resulted in numbers of trips abroad that must be of real concern when contemplating the prospect of mandating, contrary to Congress's wishes, citizenship by male parentage subject to no condition other than the father's residence in this country. Equal protection principles do not require Congress to ignore this reality. Section 1409 takes the unremarkable step of ensuring that the opportunity inherent in the event of birth as to the mother-child relationship exists between father and child before citizenship is conferred upon the latter. Congress is well within its authority in refusing, absent proof of an opportunity for a relationship to develop, to commit this country to embracing a child as a citizen. Contrary to Nguyen's (D) argument, § 1409 does not embody a gender-based stereotype. There is nothing irrational or improper in recognizing that at the moment of birth—a critical event in the statutory scheme and tradition of citizenship law—the mother's knowledge of the child and the fact of parenthood have been established in a way not guaranteed to the unwed father. The means Congress chose substantially relates to its interest in facilitating a parent-child relationship. First, various statutory provisions, in addition to § 1409(a), require that some act linking a child to the United States occur before the child turns 18. Even if one conceives of Congress's real interest as the establishment of a meaningful relationship, it is almost axiomatic that a policy seeking to foster the opportunity for meaningful parent-child bonds to develop has a close and substantial bearing on the governmental interest in that bond's formation. Mechanistic classification of all our differences as stereotypes would operate to obscure those misconceptions and prejudices that are real. The distinction embodied in the statutory scheme here at issue is not marked by misconception and prejudice, nor does it show disrespect for either class. The difference between men and women in relation to the birth process is a real one, and the principle of equal protection does not forbid Congress to address the problem at hand in a manner specific to each gender. Affirmed.

CONCURRENCE: (Scalia, J.) The Court lacks power to confer citizenship on a basis other than that prescribed by Congress.

DISSENT: (O'Connor, J.) Sex-based statutes, even when accurately reflecting the way most men or women behave, deny individuals opportunity, and the existence of comparable or superior sex-neutral alternatives is a powerful reason to reject a sex-based classification. Here, the idea that a mother's presence at birth supplies adequate assurance of an opportunity to develop a relationship while a father's presence at birth does not would appear to rest only on an overbroad sex-based generalization. A mother may not have an opportunity for a relationship if the child is removed from the child's mother on account of alleged abuse or neglect, or if the child and mother are separated by tragedy, such as disaster or war, of the sort apparently present in this case. There is no reason, other than stereotype, to say that fathers who are present at birth lack an opportunity for a relationship on similar terms. If Congress wished to advance this end, it could easily do so by employing a sex-neutral classification that would be a more germane basis of classification than sex; for example, it could require some degree of regular contact between the child and the citizen parent over a period of time. The claim that § 1409(a)(4) substantially relates to the achievement of the goal of a "real, practical relationship" finds support not in biological differences but instead in a stereotype—the generalization that mothers are significantly more likely than fathers to develop caring relationships with their children. Such a claim relies on "the very stereotype the law condemns," "lends credibility" to the generalization, and helps to convert that "assumption" into "a self-fulfilling prophecy." In fact, in this case, the father raised Nguyen (D), who did not have a relationship with his mother. The majority asserts that a "stereotype" is "defined as a frame of mind resulting from irrational or uncritical analysis." This Court has long recognized, however, that an impermissible stereotype may enjoy empirical support and thus be in a sense "rational." The hallmark of a stereotypical sex-based classification under this Court's precedents is not whether the classification is insulting, but whether it "relies upon the simplistic, outdated assumption that gender could be used as a 'proxy for other, more germane bases of classification.'" *Mississippi Univ. for Women v. Hogan*, 458 U.S. 718, 726 (1982). Section 1409(a)(4) is paradigmatic of a historic regime that left women with responsibility, and freed men from responsibility, for nonmarital children. States' child custody and support laws no longer assume that mothers alone are "bound" to serve as "natural guardians" of nonmarital children. The majority, however, rather than confronting the stereotypical notion that mothers must care for such children and fathers may ignore them, condones the "very stereotype the law condemns."

Continued on next page.

ANALYSIS

In dissent, Justice O'Connor argues that Congress could have used a sex-neutral classification to further the purported objective of § 1409(a)(4). Although the majority raised the possibility of the use of sex-neutral means, it dismissed such a possibility as irrelevant. The majority admitted that "Congress could excuse compliance with the formal requirements when an actual father-child relationship is proved," but also speculated that Congress did not do so "perhaps because of the subjectivity, intrusiveness, and difficulties of proof that might attend an inquiry into any particular bond or tie." Interestingly, the majority does not speculate about why Congress might not have required women to similarly prove a bond or tie to their children—but just assumed it. However, as Justice O'Connor observes, the Court has repeatedly rejected efforts to justify sex-based classifications on the ground of administrative convenience, and posits that there is no reason to think that this is a case where administrative convenience concerns are so powerful that they would justify sex-based discrimination, "especially where the use of sex as a proxy is so ill fit to the purported ends as it is here." Justice O'Connor adds that to the extent Congress might seek simply to ensure an "opportunity" for a relationship, little administrative inconvenience would seem to accompany a sex-neutral requirement of presence at birth, knowledge of birth, or contact between parent and child prior to a certain age. Additionally, § 1409 imposes a financial obligation on men who wish to obtain citizenship for their children born out of wedlock outside the United States that the statute does not impose on women. Arguably, this requirement benefits fathers, who may avoid such a financial burden by dissociating from their nonmarital children. At the same time, the law implicitly burdens mothers with the full responsibility of child raising. Historically, such a maternal obligation developed in coverture and citizenship law to protect fathers from claims for property or support by nonmarital children.

Quicknotes

COVERTURE The former common law rule precluding a married woman from possessing property not subject to her husband's control.

DUE PROCESS CLAUSE Language found in the Fifth and Fourteenth Amendments to the United States Constitution providing that no person shall be deprived of "life, liberty, or property without due process of law."

Sessions v. Morales-Santana

U.S. Attorney General (P) v. Individual born abroad asserting derivative U.S. citizenship (D)

137 S. Ct. 1678 (2017)

NATURE OF CASE: Appeal in action challenging gender-based duration-of-residence distinctions in The Immigration and Nationality Act as violating equal protection. [The procedural posture of the case is not presented in the casebook extract.]

FACT SUMMARY: Morales-Santana (D), who was born outside the United States to a U.S.-citizen unwed father and a non-U.S.-citizen unwed mother, claimed that gender-based duration-of-residence distinctions between unwed U.S.-citizen mothers and unwed U.S.-citizen fathers in the Immigration and Nationality Act violated equal protection when those distinctions were used as a basis for determining the U.S. citizenship of their children born abroad.

RULE OF LAW

(1) Gender-based duration-of-residence distinctions between unwed U.S.-citizen mothers and unwed U.S.-citizen fathers do not survive heightened scrutiny for equal protection purposes when those distinctions are used as a basis for determining the U.S. citizenship of their children born abroad.

(2) Congress's intent, as revealed in a statute that violates equal protection, governs the choice between the two remedial alternatives for such a violation: either extending favorable treatment to the excluded class or withdrawing favorable treatment from the favored class.

FACTS: The Immigration and Nationality Act (the Act), in 8 U.S.C. § 1401(a)(7) (1958 ed.), provided that where a child was born abroad to unwed parents, one of whom was a U.S. citizen father, the other an alien mother, that child could obtain U.S. citizenship through the citizen father, but only if the father had ten years' physical presence in the United States prior to the child's birth, at least five of which were after attaining age 14. However, § 1409(c) of the Act created an exception for an unwed U.S.-citizen mother, whose citizenship could be transmitted to a child born abroad if she had lived continuously in the United States for just one year prior to the child's birth. Morales-Santana (D) was born outside the United States. His biological father, Morales, a U.S. citizen, moved to the Dominican Republic 20 days short of his 19th birthday, therefore failing to satisfy § 1401(a)(7)'s requirement of five years' physical presence after age 14. Morales lived with the Dominican woman who gave birth to Morales-Santana (D), and Morales accepted parental responsibility and included Morales-Santana in his household. Morales-Santana (D) then moved to the United States when he was 13 and lived there since. Years after moving to the United States, Morales-Santana (D) was threatened with deportation on the basis of criminal convictions, and because he was seen as an alien rather than a U.S. citizen, since Morales failed to meet § 1401(a)(7)'s requirement of five years' physical presence after age 14, Morales-Santana (D) contended that § 1401(a)(7) unconstitutionally discriminated on the basis of sex and that he should be considered a U.S. citizen (arguing that the exception for unwed citizen mothers should apply to unwed citizen fathers, thus enabling him to get citizenship derivatively through Morales). The United States Supreme Court granted certiorari in the case. [The procedural posture of the case is not presented in the casebook extract.]

ISSUE:

(1) Do gender-based duration-of-residence distinctions between unwed U.S.-citizen mothers and unwed U.S.-citizen fathers survive heightened scrutiny for equal protection purposes when those distinctions are used as a basis for determining the U.S. citizenship of their children born abroad?

(2) Does Congress's intent, as revealed in a statute that violates equal protection, govern the choice between the two remedial alternatives for such a violation: either extending favorable treatment to the excluded class or withdrawing favorable treatment from the favored class?

HOLDING AND DECISION: (Ginsburg, J.)

(1) No. Gender-based duration-of-residence distinctions between unwed U.S.-citizen mothers and unwed U.S.-citizen fathers do not survive heightened scrutiny for equal protection purposes when those distinctions are used as a basis for determining the U.S. citizenship of their children born abroad. The Government (P) asserts that Congress sought to ensure that a child born abroad has a strong connection to the United States. The statute, the Government (P) suggests, bracketed an unwed U.S.-citizen mother with a married couple in which both parents are U.S. citizens because she is the only legally recognized parent at birth; and aligned an unwed U.S.-citizen father with a married couple, one spouse a citizen, the other, an alien, because of the competing national influence of the alien mother. The underlying assumption for this

Continued on next page.

rationale is the long-held view that unwed fathers care little about their children. Lump characterization of that kind, however, no longer passes equal protection inspection. The gender-based distinctions in the statute scarcely serve the suggested congressional interest. Citizenship may be transmitted to children who have no tie to the United States so long as their U.S.-citizen mother was continuously present in the United States for one year at any point in her life prior to the child's birth; but it may not be transmitted by an unwed U.S.-citizen father who falls a few days short of meeting § 1401(a)(7)'s longer physical-presence requirements, even if he acknowledges paternity on the day the child is born and raises the child in the United States. This driven-by-gender scheme thus fails to meet the close means-end fit required to survive heightened scrutiny. Also rejected is the claim that the exception for unwed mothers will reduce the risk that a foreign-born child of a U.S. citizen will be born stateless, since expert studies show that this risk is actually higher for children of unwed U.S.-citizen fathers. In sum, the gender-based distinctions at issue cannot withstand inspection under a Constitution that requires the Government (P) to respect the equal dignity and stature of its male and female citizens. [Judgment for Morales-Santana (D) as to this issue.]

(2) Yes. Congress's intent, as revealed in a statute that violates equal protection, governs the choice between the two remedial alternatives for such a violation: either extending favorable treatment to the excluded class or withdrawing favorable treatment from the favored class. Ordinarily, the preferred rule is to extend favorable treatment. Here, however, extension to fathers of § 1409(c)'s favorable treatment for mothers would displace Congress's general rule, the longer physical-presence requirements of §§ 1401(a)(7) and 1409 applicable to unwed U.S.-citizen fathers and U.S.-citizen parents, male as well as female, married to the child's alien parent. Thus, Congress's commitment to this policy and the degree of potential disruption of the statutory scheme that would occur by extension as opposed to abrogation, indicate that Congress would likely have abrogated § 1409(c)'s special exception, preferring to preserve the importance of residence in this country as the talisman of dedicated attachment to the country and its values. Congress may address the issue and settle on a uniform prescription that neither favors nor disadvantages any person on basis of gender. In the interim, § 1401(a)(7)'s now-five-year requirement should apply, prospectively, to children born to unwed U.S.-citizen mothers. [Judgment for the Government (P) as to this issue.]

DISSENT: (Thomas, J.) Because Morales-Santana (D) cannot obtain relief in any event, it is unnecessary for the Court to decide whether § 1401(a)(7) is constitutional.

ANALYSIS

In this case, for the first time, the Supreme Court ruled that distinctions between fathers and mothers for purposes of determining their children's U.S. citizenship were unjustifiably discriminatory. In *Fiallo v. Bell,* 430 U.S. 787 (1977), the Court gave special immigration preferences to alien children of citizen (or lawful-permanent-resident) mothers, and to alien unwed mothers of citizen (or lawful-permanent-resident) children. In *Nguyen v. INS,* 533 U.S. 53 (2001), the Court upheld a provision requiring unwed U.S.-citizen fathers, but not mothers, to formally acknowledge parenthood of their foreign-born children in order to transmit their U.S. citizenship to those children. As Justice Ginsburg notes in her decision, these distinctions were historically motivated by assumptions about differences between women and men that increasingly are suspect. In particular, the Court has come to recognize that if a statutory objective is to exclude or protect members of one gender in reliance on fixed notions concerning that gender's roles and abilities, the objective itself is illegitimate. The Court's decision in Morales-Santana reflects this contemporary understanding of unconstitutional sex discrimination.

Quicknotes

HEIGHTENED SCRUTINY A purposefully vague judicial description of all levels of scrutiny more exacting than minimal scrutiny.

Personnel Administrator of Massachusetts v. Feeney

State (D) v. Job applicant (P)

442 U.S. 256 (1979)

NATURE OF CASE: Appeal from judgment that a state veterans' civil service preference statute violated the Equal Protection Clause on grounds that it overwhelmingly discriminated against women.

FACT SUMMARY: After she had lost several attempts for promotion to a better civil service position to male veterans who had lower test scores, Feeney (P) challenged the Massachusetts (D) statute, which gave absolute preference points to veterans, male and female, who had served in the armed forces, on the grounds that statute's effect was to discriminate against women and the state legislature could have easily foreseen this effect when it enacted the statute and could have narrowly tailored the statute to eliminate such discrimination.

RULE OF LAW

Where a state statute that grants an absolute lifetime preference to veterans in public employment opportunities is enacted without discriminatory intent but overwhelmingly discriminates against women, and the legislature could have foreseen such discriminatory effect, the statute does not violate the Equal Protection Clause.

FACTS: A Massachusetts (D) statute gave an absolute lifetime civil service preference to all veterans, men and women, who were honorably discharged after at least 90 days of active service, with at least one day occurring during "wartime." Because the great majority of individuals serving in the armed forces were male, the statute worked to their advantage in filling the state civil service positions. During her 12 years as a state employee, Feeney (P) had taken and passed a number of civil service examinations for better jobs, but each time she was ranked below male veterans who had lower test scores. Feeney (P) brought suit in federal district court, alleging that the absolute preference excluded women from consideration for the best state civil service jobs and thus discriminated against women in violation of the Equal Protection Clause of the Fourteenth Amendment. The three-judge district court declared the statute unconstitutional and enjoined its operation, ruling that while the statute did not have a discriminatory purpose, its discriminatory impact was so severe that other methods were required to achieve the state's goals. The United States Supreme Court granted review.

ISSUE: Where a state statute that grants an absolute lifetime preference to veterans in public employment opportunities is enacted without discriminatory intent but overwhelmingly discriminates against women, and the legislature could have foreseen such discriminatory effect, does the statute violate the Equal Protection Clause?

HOLDING AND DECISION: (Stewart, J.) No. Where a state statute that grants an absolute lifetime preference to veterans in public employment opportunities is enacted without discriminatory intent but overwhelmingly discriminates against women, and the legislature could have foreseen such discriminatory effect, the statute does not violate the Equal Protection Clause. Many classifications that have a rational basis and affect different groups unequally, with being motivated by antipathy towards those groups, are constitutional. Some classifications, like those based on race, are automatically suspect and are examined under strict scrutiny. Because classifications based on gender have traditionally been the touchstone for pervasive and subtle discrimination, they must bear a close and substantial relationship to important governmental objectives. When a statute gender-neutral on its face is challenged on the ground its effects upon women are disproportionably adverse, a twofold inquiry is appropriate. The first question is whether the statutory classification is indeed neutral in the sense that it is not gender-based. If the classification itself, covert or overt, is not based upon gender, the second question is whether the adverse effect reflects invidious gender-based discrimination. Feeney (P) conceded that the statute is neutral on its face and acknowledged that state hiring preferences for veterans are not per se invalid. Apart from the facts that the definition of "veterans" in the statute has always been neutral as to gender and that Massachusetts (D) has consistently defined veteran status in a way that has been inclusive of women who have served in the military, this is not a law that can plausibly, or even rationally, be explained only as a gender-based classification. Significant numbers of nonveterans are men, and all nonveterans—male as well as female—are placed at a disadvantage. The distinction made by the statute is, as it seems to be, quite simply between veterans and nonveterans, not between men and women. Since the distinction between veterans and nonveterans drawn by the statute is not a pretext for gender discrimination, the dispositive question is whether the veterans' preference legislation has a gender-based discriminatory purpose. Feeney's (P) contention that the veterans' preference is "inherently nonneutral" or "gender-biased" in the sense that it favors a

Continued on next page.

status reserved under federal military policy primarily to men is wholly at odds with the lower court's central finding that Massachusetts (D) has not offered a preference to veterans for purpose of discriminating against women. Feeney (P) and the district court also assumed that a more limited hiring preference for veterans could be sustained, but the degree of the preference makes no constitutional difference for purpose of discriminatory intent, which is not subject to calibration: either there is intent or there isn't. There is no evidence that the Massachusetts (D) legislature had intent to exclude women from significant public jobs. To claim that there was such intent, by describing the preference as "inherently nonneutral" or "gender-biased," is merely to restate the fact of impact, not to answer the question of intent. While the decision to grant a preference to veterans was intentional, discriminatory purpose implies that the decisionmaker selected or reaffirmed a particular course of action at least in part because of its adverse effects upon an identifiable group. When the totality of legislative actions establishing and extending the Massachusetts (D) veterans' preference are considered, the law remains a preference for veterans of either sex over nonveterans of either sex, not for men over women. Reversed.

CONCURRENCE: (Stevens, J.) However the question is phrased the answer is largely provided by the fact that the number of males disadvantaged by veterans' preference at issue is sufficiently large and sufficiently close to the number of disadvantaged females to refute the claim that the rule was intended to benefit males as a class over females as a class.

DISSENT: (Marshall, J.) Massachusetts's (D) choice of an absolute veterans' preference system evinces purposeful gender-based discrimination. And because the statutory scheme bears no substantial relationship to a legitimate governmental objective, it cannot withstand scrutiny under the Equal Protection Clause. Merely because a legislature intends to advantage one group does not mean that it does not also intend to disadvantage another group. Where discrimination has been one of several factors in the legislature's decision, judicial deference is not warranted. Such discriminatory intent can be inferred from objective factors. It is undisputed that the statute impacts disproportionately on women and the legislature could have foreseen such effect. Where the foreseeable impact of a facially neutral policy is so disproportionate, the burden should rest on the state to prove that sex-based considerations played no part in the choice of the particular legislative scheme. The legislative history shows that Massachusetts (D) cannot sustain that burden here. The statute and implementing civil service regulations exempted from operation of the preference any job requisitions "especially calling for women." In practice, this exemption, coupled with the absolute preference for veterans, has created a gender-based civil service hierarchy, with women occupying low-grade clerical and secretarial jobs and men holding more responsible and remunerative positions. The statute thus exacts a substantial price from a discrete group of individuals who have long been subject to employment discrimination, and who, because of circumstances beyond their control, have had little if any chance of becoming members of the preferred class. The statutory scheme both reflects and perpetuates precisely the kind of archaic assumptions about women's roles that have previously been held invalid. Moreover, the statute—which clearly is gender-based—does not promote important state interests. It is claimed that the statute (1) assists veterans in their readjustment to civilian life; (2) encourages military enlistment; and (3) rewards those who have served their country. While these are legitimate state interests, the statutory scheme adopted is not substantially related to those objectives. First, the statute is overinclusive insofar as it confers a permanent preference, thus enabling veterans to invoke their advantage repeatedly, without regard to their date of discharge. As to encouraging enlistment, the statute is also overinclusive because it applies to both veterans who were drafted as well as those who voluntarily enlisted. Finally, the statute could have been more narrowly tailored and still rewarded veterans through significantly less discriminatory means. For example, Massachusetts (D) could have adopted a point system used by many states and the federal government, or it could have adopted an absolute preference for a limited duration. The state can, and does, provide other benefits exclusively to veterans, and the cost of such benefits is borne by the state's taxpayers. Here, the only ones paying the price for the program are women.

ANALYSIS

The Court explains that certain classifications in themselves supply a reason to infer antipathy. A racial classification, for example, regardless of purported motivation, is presumptively invalid and can be upheld only upon an extraordinary justification. This rule applies as well to a classification that is ostensibly neutral but is an obvious pretext for racial discrimination. But, as was made clear in *Washington v. Davis*, 426 U.S. 229 (1976), and *Arlington Heights v. Metropolitan Housing Dev. Corp.*, 429 U.S. 252 (1977), even if a neutral law has a disproportionately adverse effect upon a racial minority, it is unconstitutional under the Equal Protection Clause only if that impact can be traced to a discriminatory purpose.

Continued on next page.

Quicknotes

DISCRIMINATORY IMPACT The effect of an action that affects one group of persons more significantly than another; insufficient to prove discriminatory intent on its own.

EQUAL PROTECTION CLAUSE A constitutional provision that each person be guaranteed the same protection of the laws enjoyed by other persons in like circumstances.

Nevada Department of Human Resources v. Hibbs

State agency (D) v. FMLA claimant (P)

538 U.S. 721 (2003)

NATURE OF CASE: Appeal from the reversal of a summary judgment in a suit under the family-care provision of the Family and Medical Leave Act of 1993.

FACT SUMMARY: When Hibbs's (P) employment was terminated by the Nevada Department of Human Resources (D) when he failed to report to work because of caring for his ailing wife, he brought suit against the latter for money damages, arguing denial of his rights under the family-care provision of the Family and Medical Leave Act of 1993.

RULE OF LAW

Eligible employees may recover money damages against an employer (including a state employer) who interferes with, restrains, or denies the exercise of rights under the family-care provision of the Family and Medical Leave Act of 1993.

FACTS: Hibbs (P), an employee of the Nevada Department of Welfare (D), sought leave under the Family and Medical Leave Act of 1993 (FMLA) to care for his ailing wife. The Department (D) granted the request for the full 12 weeks of FMLA leave. When Hibbs (P) had exhausted his FMLA leave, he failed to report to work and was terminated. When Hibbs (P) sued the Department (D) in federal court, seeking damages, injunction, and declaratory relief for violations of FMLA, the district judge granted the Department's (D) motion for summary judgment on the grounds the FMLA claim was barred by the Eleventh Amendment and that Hibbs's (P) Fourteenth Amendment rights had not been violated. The federal court of appeals reversed, and the Department (D) appealed.

ISSUE: May eligible employees recover money damages against an employer (including a state employer) who interferes with, restrains, or denies the exercise of rights under the family-care provision of the Family and Medical Leave Act of 1993?

HOLDING AND DECISION: (Rehnquist, C.J.) Yes. Eligible employees may recover money damages against an employer (including a state employer) who interferes with, restrains, or denies the exercise of rights under the family-care provision of the Family and Medical Leave Act of 1993 (FMLA). According to evidence that was before Congress when it enacted the FMLA, states continue to rely on invalid gender stereotypes in the employment context, specifically in the administration of leave benefits. Reliance on such stereotypes cannot justify the states' gender discrimination in this area. The long and extensive history of sex discrimination prompts us to hold that measures that differentiate on basis of gender warrant heightened scrutiny. Here, the persistence of such unconstitutional discrimination by the states justifies Congress's passage of prophylactic remedial legislation. Furthermore, Congress had evidence that, even when state laws and policies were not facially discriminatory, they were applied in discriminatory ways. It was only since federal family-leave legislation was first introduced that the states had even begun to consider family-leave initiatives. The states' record of unconstitutional participation in, and fostering of, gender-based discrimination in the administration of benefits is weighty enough to justify the enactment of the instant remedial legislation. The FMLA is congruent and proportional to its remedial object, and can be understood as responsive to, or designed to prevent, unconstitutional behavior. Affirmed.

ANALYSIS

As the *Hibbs* case points out, in light of the evidence before Congress, a statute mirroring Title VII, that simply mandated gender equality in the administration of leave benefits, would not have achieved Congress's remedial object.

Quicknotes

DECLARATORY RELIEF A judgment of the court establishing the rights of the parties.

FAMILY AND MEDICAL LEAVE ACT OF 1993 Requires that employers of 50 or more employees must permit eligible workers to take up to 12 weeks of unpaid leave in any 12-month period for child care or for the worker's own serious health condition. 29 U.S.C. §§ 2601-2654.

INJUNCTION A remedy imposed by the court ordering a party to cease the conduct of a specific activity.

SUMMARY JUDGMENT Judgment rendered by a court in response to a motion by one of the parties, claiming that the lack of a question of material fact in respect to an issue warrants disposition of the issue without consideration by the jury.

City of Cleburne, Texas v. Cleburne Living Center

Municipality (D) v. Zoning permit applicant (P)

473 U.S. 432 (1985)

NATURE OF CASE: Appeal of order voiding municipal special use permit ordinance.

FACT SUMMARY: Cleburne Living Center, Inc. (P) contended that laws impacting the mentally retarded should be given heightened constitutional scrutiny.

RULE OF LAW

Laws impacting the mentally retarded are not to be given heightened constitutional scrutiny.

FACTS: The City of Cleburne, Texas, (D) had zoned multiple-residence dwellings as R-3. Most R-3 structures required no permit; however, any proposed home for the mentally retarded did. The Cleburne Living Center, Inc. (P) applied for such a permit. Responding to objections from nearby residents, the city council refused the application. The Center (P) challenged the ordinance as a denial of equal protection. The Fifth Circuit Court of Appeals, applying an intermediate level of scrutiny toward the mentally retarded, voided the ordinance. The United States Supreme Court granted review.

ISSUE: Are laws impacting the mentally retarded to be given heightened constitutional scrutiny?

HOLDING AND DECISION: (White, J.) No. Laws impacting the mentally retarded are not to be given heightened scrutiny. This Court has defined certain characteristics to be so irrelevant to a person's potential contribution to society that, when combined with their political minority status, the conclusion follows that they are entitled to special protection under the Equal Protection Clause. Examples include race, alienage, and religious belief. Mental retardation does not fit this profile. The retarded person's status does relate to his ability to contribute to society. Second, there is ample evidence that lawmakers are responsive to retarded people's plights, showing that they are not politically powerless. Finally, if a large and amorphous class such as the mentally retarded were to be given special Fourteenth Amendment protection, it is hard to see where the process would stop. For these reasons, the Court concludes that the mentally retarded are not entitled to heightened scrutiny. [The Court went on to hold that, even under low-level scrutiny, the ordinance failed to pass constitutional scrutiny.] Affirmed.

CONCURRENCE: (Stevens, J.) Equal protection review involves a continuum of responses, rather than stratified tiers of review, and rationality review requires that a classification be based on criteria that are neutral and legitimate. Accordingly, racial classifications are usually invalidated, and economic classifications are usually upheld, not because of an application of an "intermediate standard of review" but because the characteristics of the groups involved are sometimes relevant and sometimes irrelevant to the public purpose that the challenged classification purports to serve. Thus, every law that places the mentally retarded in a special class is not presumptively irrational, as with laws that provide special funding for the education of the mentally retarded or that provide for special supervision of the mentally retarded in special situations. Here, however, requiring an annual special permit before an apartment house could be used as a group home for mildly retarded persons was irrational and was based on the fears of neighboring property owners rather than on an effort to protect the mentally retarded.

CONCURRENCE AND DISSENT: (Marshall, J.) In equal protection review, the "substantiality of the state interest to be served" and "the reasonableness of the means, by which the State has sought to advance its interests" are critical factors to be considered. Differences in the application of this test are a function of the constitutional importance of the interests at stake and the invidiousness of the particular classification. When the mentally retarded are subject to laws that discriminate on their face against them, such discrimination is based on irrational prejudices. Heightened scrutiny should be applied where the classifications in such laws are based on irrational hostility or thoughtlessness. By applying heightened scrutiny, the Court recognizes that a group may well be the target of the kind of prejudiced, thoughtless, or stereotypical action that offends the Fourteenth Amendment's principles of equality. Applying heightened scrutiny here, the ordinance should be struck down because it sweeps too broadly to "dispel the suspicion that it rests on a bare desire to treat the retarded as . . . pariahs. . . ." The majority is wrong to merely invalidate the ordinance as applied to the group here; the ordinance, based on irrational prejudice, should not be allowed to stand at all. The issue here is whether the city must enact a new ordinance carefully tailored to the exclusion of some well-defined subgroup of retarded people in circumstances in which such exclusion could further legitimate city purposes. When a statute is overbroad, it must be invalidated on its face and not treated on an as-applied basis.

Continued on next page.

ANALYSIS

The Court's Equal Protection Clause analysis continues to evolve. As of the time of this case, three levels of scrutiny existed: rational basis, heightened, and strict. In years past, strict scrutiny automatically led to invalidation, rational basis to approval. As this case shows, this is no longer true.

Quicknotes

EQUAL PROTECTION A constitutional guarantee that no person shall be denied the same protection of the laws enjoyed by other persons in like circumstances.

HEIGHTENED SCRUTINY A purposefully vague judicial description of all levels of scrutiny more exacting than minimal scrutiny.

QUASI-SUSPECT CLASS A specific class of persons subjected to unequal treatment but deserving less than strict scrutiny.

CHAPTER 9

Liberty, Equality, and Fundamental Rights: The Constitution, the Family, and the Body

Quick Reference Rules of Law

Griswold v. Connecticut

Contraception advisors (D) v. State (P)

381 U.S. 479 (1965)

NATURE OF CASE: Appeal from conviction for violating state laws prohibiting the counseling of married persons to take contraceptives.

FACT SUMMARY: Doctor (D) and layman (D) were prosecuted for advising married persons on the means of preventing conception.

RULE OF LAW

The right to marital privacy, although not explicitly stated in the Bill of Rights, is a penumbra formed by certain other explicit guarantees. As such, it is protected against state regulation that sweeps unnecessarily broad.

FACTS: Griswold (D), the Executive Director of the Planned Parenthood League of Connecticut, and Dr. Burton (D) were convicted under a Connecticut law that made counseling of married persons to take contraceptives a criminal offense.

ISSUE: Is the right to marital privacy, although not explicitly stated in the Bill of Rights, a penumbra formed by certain other explicit guarantees? As such, is it protected against state regulation that sweeps unnecessarily broad.

HOLDING AND DECISION: (Douglas, J.) Yes. The right to marital privacy, although not explicitly stated in the Bill of Rights, is a penumbra formed by certain other explicit guarantees. As such, it is protected against state regulation that sweeps unnecessarily broad. The various guarantees that create penumbras, or zones, of privacy include the First Amendment's right of association, the Third Amendment's prohibition against the peacetime quartering of soldiers, the Fourth Amendment's prohibition against unreasonable searches and seizures, the Fifth Amendment's self-incrimination clause, and the Ninth Amendment's reservation to the people of unenumerated rights. The Connecticut law by forbidding the use of contraceptives, rather than regulating their manner of sale, seeks to achieve its goals by means having a maximum destructive impact upon that relationship. Reversed.

CONCURRENCE: (Goldberg, J.) The Ninth Amendment, while not constituting an independent source of rights, suggests that the list of rights in the first eight amendments is not exhaustive. This right is a "fundamental" one that cannot be infringed on the state's slender justification in protecting marital fidelity.

CONCURRENCE: (Harlan, J.) The Court, instead of focusing on "specific provisions" of the Bill of Rights, should have instead relied on the Due Process Clause in finding this law violative of basic values "implicit in the concept of ordered liberty."

DISSENT: [in *Poe v. Ullman*, 367 U.S. 497 (1961)] (Harlan, J.) Due process is not merely a procedural safeguard but is the bulwark against arbitrary legislation. It is not the particular enumeration of rights in the first eight Amendments that spell out the reach of Fourteenth Amendment due process. Instead, it is those concepts that embrace those rights that are considered "fundamental." Due process is not reducible to a formula, or by referring to a particular statute. The best way to describe it is as the balance between our Nation's respect for the individual's liberty and the demands of organized society. Thus, when interpreting the Constitution, this Court discerns a particular provision's meaning in the context of this country's history and purpose. Therefore, liberty is viewed as a rational continuum, which, broadly speaking, includes freedom from all substantial arbitrary impositions and purposeless restraints. Here, the state is asserting the right to enforce its moral judgment by intruding upon the most intimate details of the marital relation with the full power of the criminal law. Potentially, this could allow the deployment of all the incidental machinery of the criminal law, arrests, searches and seizures; inevitably, it must mean at the very least the lodging of criminal charges, a public trial, and testimony. Nor could any imaginable elaboration of presumptions, testimonial privileges, or other safeguards, alleviate the necessity for testimony as to the mode and manner of the married couples' sexual relations, or at least the opportunity for the accused to make denial of the charges. Thus, the statute allows the state to inquire into, prove, and punish married people for the private use of their marital intimacy. The statute, therefore, involves a most fundamental aspect of liberty: the privacy of the home in its most basic sense. This Court has held in the strongest terms that the concept of "privacy" embodied in the Fourth Amendment is part of the "ordered liberty" assured against state action by the Fourteenth Amendment. The statute here does not invade the privacy of the home in the usual sense, since the invasion involved here may, and doubtless usually would, be accomplished without any physical intrusion whatever into the home. What the statute undertakes to do, however, is to create a crime that is grossly offensive to this privacy. A literal reading of the Constitution would find no protection from this kind of invasion of privacy.

Continued on next page.

However, such a reading is justifiable only if due process is limited to what is explicitly provided in the Constitution, divorced from the rational purposes, historical roots, and subsequent developments of the relevant provisions. "It would surely be an extreme instance of sacrificing substance to form were it to be held that the Constitutional principle of privacy against arbitrary official intrusion comprehends only physical invasions by the police." If the physical aspects of the home are protected, it is because of solicitude to protect the privacies of the life within; the safeguarding of the home does not follow merely from the sanctity of property rights, but because it is the seat of family life. And, of all of family life, there is nothing more private than the intimacy of husband and wife. Accordingly, because the statute constitutes an abridgment of fundamental liberties, protected by the Fourth Amendment, it must be strictly scrutinized.

CONCURRENCE: (White, J.) The law at issue here deprives a married couple of liberty without due process of law.

DISSENT: (Black, J.) While the law is offensive, neither the Ninth Amendment nor the Due Process Clause invalidates it. Both lead the Court into imposing its own notions as to what are wise or unwise laws. What constitutes "fundamental" values this court is incapable of determining. Keeping the Constitution "in tune with the times" is accomplished only through the amendment process. Similarly, the Due Process Clause is too imprecise and lends itself to subjective interpretation.

DISSENT: (Stewart, J.) The Due Process Clause is not the "guide" because there was no claim here that the statute is unconstitutionally vague, or that the defendants were denied any of the elements of procedural due process at their trial. The Ninth Amendment simply restricts the federal government to a government of express and limited powers. Finally, the Constitution is silent on the "right to privacy."

ANALYSIS

Although the theory of "substantive due process" has declined as means to review state economic regulation—at least since 1937—the Court, as here, has freely applied strict scrutiny to state laws affecting social areas.

Quicknotes

DUE PROCESS CLAUSE Language found in the Fifth and Fourteenth Amendments to the United States Constitution providing that no person shall be deprived of "life, liberty, or property without due process of law."

PENUMBRA A doctrine whereby authority of the federal government is implied pursuant to the Necessary and Proper Clause; one implied power may be inferred from the conferring of another implied power.

RIGHT TO PRIVACY Those personal liberties or relationships that are protected against unwarranted governmental interference.

STRICT SCRUTINY The method by which courts determine the constitutionality of a law, when a law affects a fundamental right. Under the test, the legislature must have a compelling interest to enact the law, and measures prescribed by the law must be the least restrictive means possible to accomplish its goal.

SUBSTANTIVE DUE PROCESS A constitutional safeguard limiting the power of the state, irrespective of how fair its procedures may be; substantive limits placed on the power of the state.

Eisenstadt v. Baird

Sheriff (P) v. Abortion clinic director (D)

405 U.S. 438 (1972)

NATURE OF CASE: Appeal from vacatur of a dismissal of a writ of habeas corpus petition for conviction under a state statute making it a crime to give contraceptives to an unmarried person.

FACT SUMMARY: Massachusetts made it a crime to give contraceptives to an unmarried person. Baird (D) gave a contraceptive to a single person and was convicted under the Massachusetts law. Baird (D) challenged his conviction under the Equal Protection Clause.

RULE OF LAW

A state law that makes it a crime to give contraceptives to an unmarried person violates the Equal Protection Clause.

FACTS: At the end of his lecture on birth control, Baird (D), who was neither a physician nor a pharmacist, gave a single woman a package of vaginal foam. He was convicted under a Massachusetts statute that made it a crime to give contraceptives to an unmarried person. The statute permitted only physicians and pharmacists to dispense contraceptives, and then only to married persons. The state courts upheld the conviction, the district court dismissed his petition for a writ of habeas corpus, and the court of appeals vacated the dismissal. The United States Supreme Court granted review.

ISSUE: Does a state law that makes it a crime to give contraceptives to an unmarried person violate the Equal Protection Clause?

HOLDING AND DECISION: (Brennan, J.) Yes. A state law that makes it a crime to give contraceptives to an unmarried person violates the Equal Protection Clause. There is no rational basis for treating married persons and unmarried persons differently. Even if the state's goal is to limit fornication, the ban on distributing contraceptives to unmarried persons has a tenuous relation to achieving that goal—it is unreasonable to think that pregnancy and childbirth are the punishment the state wants to inflict on those who fornicate. Therefore, the law cannot be upheld as either a health measure or as a deterrent to fornication. Regardless of what the law's purpose is, the rights of access to contraceptives must be the same for the unmarried as they are for the married. "If the right of privacy means anything, it is the right of the individual, married or single, to be free from unwarranted governmental intrusion into matters so fundamentally affecting a person as the decision whether to bear or beget a child."

DISSENT: (Burger, C.J.) Baird (D) was properly convicted for dispensing medicine without a license. Nothing in the Constitution requires that contraceptives be available to everyone. Here, limiting the class of distributors of contraceptives will not impair the right—affirmed in *Griswold v. Connecticut*, 381 U.S. 479 (1965)—to use contraceptives.

ANALYSIS

Eisenstadt recognized the right to control reproduction as a fundamental right of both single and married persons, as well as the right to distribute and use contraceptives. In doing so, the Court continued its revival of the use of substantive due process that it had started in *Griswold,* 381 U.S. 479 (1965). Justice Brennan's dictum ("[i]f the right of privacy means anything, it is the right of the individual, married or single, to be free from unwarranted governmental intrusion into matters so fundamentally affecting a person as the decision whether to bear or beget a child") was influential in subsequent cases in this area.

Quicknotes

DUE PROCESS CLAUSE Language found in the Fifth and Fourteenth Amendments to the United States Constitution providing that no person shall be deprived of "life, liberty, or property without due process of law."

EQUAL PROTECTION CLAUSE A constitutional provision that each person be guaranteed the same protection of the laws enjoyed by other persons in like circumstances.

FUNDAMENTAL RIGHT A liberty that is either expressly or impliedly provided for in the United States Constitution, the deprivation or burdening of which is subject to a heightened standard of review.

Roe v. Wade

Single pregnant woman (P) v. State (D)

410 U.S. 113 (1973)

NATURE OF CASE: Challenge to state laws making it a crime to procure an abortion except by medical advice to save the life of the mother.

FACT SUMMARY: Roe (P), a single woman, wished to have her pregnancy terminated by an abortion.

RULE OF LAW

The right of privacy found in the Fourteenth Amendment's concept of personal liberty and restrictions upon state action is broad enough to encompass a woman's decision whether or not to terminate her pregnancy.

FACTS: The Texas abortion laws challenged here were typical of those adopted by most states. The challengers were Roe (P), a single pregnant woman, a childless couple with the wife not pregnant (J and M Doe), and a licensed physician with two criminal charges pending (Halford). Only Roe (P) was found to be entitled to maintain the action. Although her 1970 pregnancy had been terminated, her case was not found moot since pregnancy "truly could be capable of repetition, yet evading review."

ISSUE: Is the right of privacy found in the Fourteenth Amendment's concept of personal liberty and restrictions upon state action broad enough to encompass a woman's decision whether or not to terminate her pregnancy?

HOLDING AND DECISION: (Blackmun, J.) Yes. The right of privacy found in the Fourteenth Amendment's concept of personal liberty and restrictions upon state action is broad enough to encompass a woman's decision whether or not to terminate her pregnancy. While the Constitution does not explicitly mention any right of privacy, such a right has been recognized. This right of privacy, whether founded in the Fourteenth Amendment's concept of personal liberty and restrictions upon state action, as this court feels it is, or in the Ninth Amendment's reservation of rights to the people, is broad enough to encompass a woman's decision to terminate her pregnancy. A statute regulating a fundamental right, such as the right to privacy, may be justified only by a compelling state interest and such statutes must be narrowly drawn. Here, Texas (D) argued that the fetus is a person within the meaning of the Fourteenth Amendment whose right to life is guaranteed by that Amendment. However, there are no decisions indicating such a definition for "fetus." The unborn have never been recognized in the law as persons in the whole sense. Texas (D) may not, by adopting one theory of life, override the rights of the pregnant woman that are at stake. However, neither are the woman's rights to privacy absolute. The state does have a legitimate interest in preserving the health of the pregnant woman and in protecting the potentiality of life. Each of these interests grows in substantiality as the woman approaches term, and, at a point, each becomes compelling. During the first trimester, mortality in abortion is less than mortality in childbirth. After that point, in promoting its interest in the mother's health, the state may regulate the abortion procedure in ways related to maternal health (i.e., licensing of physicians, facilities, etc.). Prior to viability, the physician, in consultation with the pregnant woman, is free to decide that a pregnancy should be terminated without interference by the state. Subsequent to viability, the state, in promoting its interest in the potentiality of life, may regulate, and even prescribe abortion, except where necessary to save the mother's life. Because the Texas (D) statute makes no distinction between abortions performed in early pregnancy and those performed later, it sweeps too broadly and is, therefore, invalid.

DISSENT: (Rehnquist, J.) The test to be applied is whether the abortion law has a rational relation to a valid state objective. Here, the court applies the compelling state interest test. The application of this test requires the court to examine the legislative policies and pass on the wisdom of those policies, tasks better left to the legislature.

DISSENT: (White, J.) This issue, for the most part, should be left with the people. There is nothing in the language or history of the Constitution to support the court's opinion. The Texas statute is not constitutionally infirm because it denies abortions to those who seek to serve only their own convenience rather than to protect their life or health.

ANALYSIS

Doe v. Bolton, 410 U.S. 179 (1973), was the companion case to *Roe v. Wade*. The Georgia laws attacked in *Doe* were more modern than the Texas laws. They allowed a physician to perform an abortion when the mother's life was in danger or the fetus would likely be born with birth defects or the pregnancy had resulted from rape. The court held that a physician could consider all attendant circumstances in deciding whether an abortion should be performed. No longer could only the three situations specified be considered. The court also struck down the requirements of prior approval for

Continued on next page.

an abortion by the hospital staff committee and of confirmation by two physicians. They concluded that the attending physician's judgment was sufficient. Lastly, the court struck down the requirement that the woman be a Georgia resident.

Quicknotes

FOURTEENTH AMENDMENT Declares that no state shall make or enforce any law that shall abridge the privileges and immunities of citizens of the United States.

MOOTNESS Judgment on the particular issue would not resolve the controversy.

Doe v. Bolton

Woman denied abortion (P) v. State official (D)

410 U.S. 179 (1973)

NATURE OF CASE: Appeal in action challenging the constitutionality of a state's abortion reform statute. [The procedural posture of the case is not presented in the casebook extract.]

FACT SUMMARY: Doe (P), who had been denied an abortion, challenged as unconstitutional, inter alia, various procedural provisions of Georgia's (D) abortion reform statute.

RULE OF LAW

(1) A state abortion statute violates the Fourteenth Amendment where it requires that all abortions, even in the earliest phases of pregnancy, be performed in hospitals as opposed to less expensive abortion clinics.
(2) A state abortion statute violates the Fourteenth Amendment where it requires that hospitals that perform abortions have special accreditation not required for hospitals not specifically connected to abortion practice and not required for hospitals performing any other kind of surgery.
(3) A state abortion statute violates the Fourteenth Amendment where it requires that a special hospital staff committee give permission prior to an abortion, a restriction not required for any other surgical procedures.
(4) A state abortion statute violates the Fourteenth Amendment where it requires that two physicians other than the patient's physician independently examine the patient and acquiesce in the abortion, a restriction not required for any other surgical procedures.
(5) A state abortion statute violates the Privileges and Immunities Clause where it limits abortions to state residents.

FACTS: Doe (P), who had been denied an abortion, challenged as unconstitutional, inter alia, various procedural provisions of Georgia's (D) abortion reform statute. These procedural requirements included: (1) all abortions, even in the earliest phases of pregnancy, had to be performed in hospitals as opposed to less expensive abortion clinics; (2) hospitals that performed abortions had to have special accreditation requirements separate from those for hospitals not specifically connected to abortion practice and not required for hospitals performing any other kind of surgery; (3) a special hospital staff committee had to give permission prior to the abortion (this was not required for any other surgical procedures); (4) two physicians other than the patient's physician had to independently examine the patient and acquiesce in the abortion (this was not required for any other surgical procedures); and (5) only state residents could receive abortions. The United States Supreme Court granted review in the case. [The procedural posture of the case is not presented in the casebook extract.]

ISSUE:

(1) Does a state abortion statute violate the Fourteenth Amendment where it requires that all abortions, even in the earliest phases of pregnancy, be performed in hospitals as opposed to less expensive abortion clinics?
(2) Does a state abortion statute violate the Fourteenth Amendment where it requires that hospitals that perform abortions have special accreditation not required for hospitals not specifically connected to abortion practice and not required for hospitals performing any other kind of surgery?
(3) Does a state abortion statute violate the Fourteenth Amendment where it requires that a special hospital staff committee give permission prior to an abortion, a restriction not required for any other surgical procedures?
(4) Does a state abortion statute violate the Fourteenth Amendment where it requires that two physicians other than the patient's physician independently examine the patient and acquiesce in the abortion, a restriction not required for any other surgical procedures?
(5) Does a state abortion statute violate the Privileges and Immunities Clause where it limits abortions to state residents?

HOLDING AND DECISION: (Blackmun, J.)

(1) Yes. A state abortion statute violates the Fourteenth Amendment where it requires that all abortions, even in the earliest phases of pregnancy, be performed in hospitals as opposed to less expensive abortion clinics. This provision is invalid insofar as it covers abortions performed in the first trimester of pregnancy.
(2) Yes. A state abortion statute violates the Fourteenth Amendment where it requires that hospitals that perform abortions have special accreditation not required for hospitals not specifically connected to abortion practice and not required for hospitals performing any other kind of surgery. Georgia (D) must show more than it has in order to prove that only the

Continued on next page.

full resources of a specially accredited hospital, rather than those of some other appropriately licensed institution, satisfy the health interests it seeks to promote.

(3) Yes. A state abortion statute violates the Fourteenth Amendment where it requires that a special hospital staff committee give permission prior to an abortion, a restriction not required for any other surgical procedures. The interposition of a hospital committee on abortion, a procedure not applicable as a matter of state law to other surgical situations, is unduly restrictive of the patient's rights, which are already safeguarded by her personal physician.

(4) Yes. A state abortion statute violates the Fourteenth Amendment when it requires that two physicians other than the patient's physician independently examine the patient and acquiesce in the abortion, a restriction not required for any other surgical procedures. If the patient's physician is licensed by the state, she is recognized by the state as capable of exercising acceptable clinical judgment. Thus, required acquiescence by two co-practitioners has no rational connection with a patient's needs and unduly infringes on her physician's right to practice.

(5) Yes. A state abortion statute violates the Privileges and Immunities Clause where it limits abortions to state residents. The Clause protects persons who enter Georgia (D) to obtain medical services there. To hold otherwise would mean that a state could limit to its own residents the general medical care available within its borders.

[The disposition of the case is not presented in the casebook extract.]

ANALYSIS

Doe was the companion case to *Roe v. Wade,* 410 U.S. 113 (1973), both of which challenged criminal abortion laws. The laws challenged in *Roe*, which were similar to those of many states, had at the time been in effect for around a century. The Georgia (D) statute in *Doe*, however, was a more modern statute that, as Justice Blackmun noted, "reflects the influences of recent attitudinal change, of advancing medical knowledge and techniques, and of new thinking about an old issue." The Court invalidated much of the Georgia (D) statute in *Doe*, notwithstanding that it was a more modern statute. *Doe* and *Roe* were meant to be read together.

Quicknotes

FOURTEENTH AMENDMENT Declares that no state shall make or enforce any law that shall abridge the privileges and immunities of citizens of the United States. No state shall deny to any person within its jurisdiction the equal protection of the laws.

PRIVILEGES AND IMMUNITIES CLAUSE Article IV, section 2, clause 1 of the U.S. Constitution, which states that a state cannot favor its own citizens by discriminating against other states' citizens who may come within its borders.

Planned Parenthood of Southeastern Pennsylvania v. Casey

Abortion facility (P) v. State (D)

505 U.S. 833 (1992)

NATURE OF CASE: Appeal of order upholding abortion statutes, except a husband-notification provision.

FACT SUMMARY: Planned Parenthood (P) facially challenged the constitutionality of Pennsylvania's (D) abortion law.

RULE OF LAW

A law is unconstitutional as an undue burden on a woman's right to an abortion before fetal viability, if the law places a substantial obstacle in the path of a woman seeking to exercise her right.

FACTS: The Pennsylvania Abortion Control Act required (a) a doctor to provide a woman seeking an abortion with information designed to persuade her against abortion and imposed a waiting period of at least 24 hours between provision of the information and the abortion; (b) a minor to obtain consent of one parent or a judge's order before having an abortion; (c) a married woman to sign a statement averring that either her husband had been notified, her husband was not the father, her husband forcibly had impregnated her, or that she would be physically harmed if she notified her husband; and (d) a public report on every abortion, detailing information on the facility, physician, patient, and steps taken to comply with the Act. The name of the patient was confidential. It provided the first three provisions would not apply in a "medical emergency," i.e., a condition a doctor determines to require immediate abortion to avert death or serious risk of substantial, irreversible impairment of a major bodily function. Five clinics (P), including Planned Parenthood (P), and five doctors (P) sued Pennsylvania (D), including Governor Casey (D), claiming the Act was unconstitutional on its face. The district court held the entire Act invalid under *Roe v. Wade*, 410 U.S. 113 (1973). The court of appeals reversed, upholding the entire Act except the husband-notification requirement. Planned Parenthood et al. (P) appealed.

ISSUE: Is a law unconstitutional as an undue burden on a woman's right to an abortion before fetal viability, if the law places a substantial obstacle in the path of a woman's exercise of her right?

HOLDING AND DECISION: (O'Connor, J.) Yes. A law is unconstitutional as an undue burden on a woman's right to an abortion before fetal viability when it places a substantial obstacle in the path of a woman seeking to exercise her right. For two decades people have organized lives relying on the availability of abortion. The Court rarely resolves a controversy as intensely divisive as in *Roe*. Such a decision only should be overturned if it proves unworkable or if new information arises which renders the decision unjustified in the present. *Roe* is neither unworkable nor based on outdated assumptions. Medical technology has altered the age of viability, but that does not affect the validity of viability as a dividing line. Viability is the point at which a fetus can be said to be an independent life, so that the state's interest in protecting it then outweighs the mother's decisionmaking interest. The Court and the nation would be seriously damaged if the Court were to overturn *Roe* simply on basis of a philosophical disagreement with the 1973 Court, or as a surrender to political pressure. The liberty rights of women and the personal, intimate nature of child bearing sharply limit state power to insist a woman carry a child to term or accept the state's vision of her role in society. Thus, the integrity of the Court, stare decisis, and substantive due process require the central principle of *Roe* to be reaffirmed: a state may not prevent a woman from making the ultimate decision to terminate her pregnancy before viability. *Roe* also recognized the state interest in maternal health and in protecting potential life. Application of the rigid trimester framework often ignored state interests, leading to a striking down of abortion regulations that in no real sense deprived women of the ultimate decision. Therefore, the trimester framework must be rejected with undue burden analysis put in its place. Here, the information requirement is not an undue burden. Truthful, nonmisleading information on the nature of abortion procedure, health risks, and consequences to the fetus is reasonable to ensure informed choice, one which might cause a woman to choose childbirth. The 24-hour waiting period does not create a health risk and reasonably furthers the state interest in protecting the unborn. Requiring a period of reflection to make an informed decision is reasonable. A waiting period may increase cost and risk of delay, but on a facial challenge it cannot be called a substantial obstacle. Prior cases establish that a state may require parental consent before abortions by minors, provided there is a judicial bypass procedure. On its face, the statute's definition of "medical emergency" is not too narrow. The reporting requirement is reasonably directed to the preservation of maternal health, providing a vital element of medical research, and the statute protects patient confidentiality. The husband-notification requirement imposes an undue burden on abortion rights of the abused women

Continued on next page.

who fear for their safety and the safety of their children and are likely to be deterred from procuring an abortion as surely as if the state outlawed abortion. A husband has a strong interest in his wife's pregnancy, but before birth it is a biological fact that regulation of the fetus has a far greater impact on the woman. The husband-notification requirement is unconstitutional, and the rest of the statute is valid. Affirmed.

CONCURRENCE AND DISSENT: (Stevens, J.) A burden is "undue" if it is too severe or lacks legitimate justification. The information, waiting period, and parental consent requirements, as well as the husband-notification requirement, are invalid. The Court's opinion implicitly reaffirms its holding that a fetus is not a "person" within the meaning of the Fourteenth Amendment. The state interest in protecting potential life is legitimate but not grounded in the Constitution. A woman has constitutional liberty rights to bodily integrity and to decide personal and private matters. So, the state may promote a preference for childbirth, but decisional autonomy must limit the state's power to interject into a woman's most personal deliberations its own views of what is best. Pennsylvania's law goes too far by requiring a doctor to provide information designed to persuade a woman to opt against abortion, just as she is weighing her personal choice. In contrast, the requirement of informing a woman of the nature and risks of abortion and childbirth enhances decisionmaking. The 24-hour waiting period illegitimately rests on assumptions that a decision to terminate pregnancy is wrong, and that a woman is unable to make decisions. There is no legitimate reason to require a woman who has agonized over her decision to leave the hospital and return another day.

CONCURRENCE AND DISSENT: (Blackmun, J.) The Court correctly reaffirms a woman's right to abortion. However, that right should remain fundamental, and any state-imposed burden upon it should be subjected to the strictest judicial scrutiny. Categorizing a woman's right to abortion as merely a "liberty interest" is not sufficient. In striking down the husband-notification requirement, the Court sets up a framework for evaluating abortion regulations in the social context of women facing issues of reproductive choice. The Court failed to strike down the information, waiting period, parental consent, and reporting requirements on their face, but the Court's standard at least allows future courts to hold that in practice such regulations are undue burdens. The reporting requirement does not further maternal health. Fearing harassment, many doctors will stop performing abortions if their names appear on public reports. However, none of these requirements would survive under the strict-scrutiny standard of review. The trimester framework should be maintained. No other approach better protects a woman's fundamental right while accommodating legitimate state interests. The Court's cases do not create a list of personal liberties: they are a principled account of how these rights are grounded in a general right of privacy.

CONCURRENCE AND DISSENT: (Rehnquist, C.J.) *Roe* was wrongly decided, has led to a confusing body of law, and should be overturned. The Court's decision, replacing *Roe*'s strict scrutiny standard and trimester framework with a new, unworkable undue burden test, cannot be justified by stare decisis. Authentic principles of stare decisis do not require erroneous decisions to be maintained. The Court's integrity is enhanced when it repudiates wrong decisions. Americans have grown accustomed to *Roe*, but that should not prevent the Court from correcting a wrong decision. The Fourteenth Amendment concept of liberty does not incorporate any all-encompassing right of privacy. Unlike marriage, procreation, and contraception, abortion terminates potential life and must be analyzed differently. Historic traditions of the American people, critical to an understanding of fundamental rights, do not support a right to abortion. A woman's interest in having an abortion is liberty protected by due process, but states may regulate abortion in ways rationally related to a legitimate state interest. All provisions of the Pennsylvania law do so and are constitutional. The husband-notification requirement is reasonably related to promoting state interests in protecting the husband's interests, potential life, and the integrity of marriage.

CONCURRENCE AND DISSENT: (Scalia, J.) The limits on abortion should be decided democratically. The Constitution is silent on abortion, and American traditions have allowed it to be proscribed. Applying the rational basis test, the Pennsylvania law should be upheld in its entirety. *Roe* was wrongly decided. It begged the question by assuming a fetus is merely potential human life. The whole argument of abortion opponents is that the state seeks to protect human life. *Roe* also failed to produce a settled body of law. *Roe* did not resolve the deeply divisive issue of abortion. It made compromise impossible and elevated the issue to a national level where it has proven infinitely more difficult to resolve. Here, the Court claims to rely on stare decisis but throws out *Roe*'s trimester framework. The new undue burden standard is meaningless in application, giving a district judge freedom to strike down almost any abortion restriction he does not like. The Court's suggestion that public opposition to an erroneous decision mitigates against overturning it is appalling.

ANALYSIS

The Court also affirmed *Roe*'s holding that after viability the state may regulate, or even proscribe, abortion, except where it is necessary to preserve the life

Continued on next page.

or health of the mother. This is only the second time in modern Supreme Court jurisprudence that an opinion has been jointly authored. Justice Kennedy's portion of the opinion addresses the importance of public faith in and acceptance of the Court's work by opening with the statement: "Liberty finds no refuge in a jurisprudence of doubt." Justice O'Connor expounds on the essential nature of a woman's right to an abortion, while Justice Souter performs the stare decisis analysis, concluding that there is no reason to reverse the essential holding of *Roe*. It appears that the instant case marks the first time the Court has downgraded a fundamental right to a protected liberty and by so doing removed from the usual strict scrutiny standard of review.

Quicknotes

RIGHT TO PRIVACY Those personal liberties or relationships that are protected against unwarranted governmental interference.

STARE DECISIS Doctrine whereby courts follow legal precedent unless there is good cause for departure.

STRICT SCRUTINY The method by which courts determine the constitutionality of a law, when a law affects a fundamental right. Under the test, the legislature must have a compelling interest to enact the law, and measures prescribed by the law must be the least restrictive means possible to accomplish its goal.

SUBSTANTIVE DUE PROCESS A constitutional safeguard limiting the power of the state, irrespective of how fair its procedures may be; substantive limits placed on the power of the state.

Gonzales v. Carhart (Carhart II)

Attorney General (D) v. Abortion doctor (P)

550 U.S. 124 (2007)

NATURE OF CASE: Facial due-process challenge to the federal Partial-Birth Abortion Ban Act.

FACT SUMMARY: Congress passed a statute that criminalized doctors' performance of partial-birth abortions.

RULE OF LAW

The Partial-Birth Abortion Ban Act does not place a substantial obstacle to late-term, but pre-viability, abortions.

FACTS: In 2003, Congress enacted the Partial-Birth Abortion Ban Act, which criminalized doctors' performance of partial-birth abortions. The Act explicitly and precisely defined "partial-birth abortion," in part as an abortion following the "deliver[y] [of] a living fetus." [Carhart (P), a doctor who performed partial-birth abortions, filed suit for injunctive relief to prohibit the Act from being applied against him. The trial court granted the injunction, and the intermediate appellate court affirmed.] The Government (D) sought further review in the United States Supreme Court.

ISSUE: Does the Partial-Birth Abortion Ban Act place a substantial obstacle to late-term, but previability, abortions?

HOLDING AND DECISION: (Kennedy, J.) No. The Partial-Birth Abortion Ban Act (the Act) does not place a substantial obstacle to late-term, but previability, abortions. The Act can be construed as not prohibiting the standard form of partial-birth abortion invalidated in *Stenberg v. Carhart*, 530 U.S. 914 (2000), and the Act therefore is not facially invalid on that basis. Further, instead of placing a substantial obstacle to a partial-birth abortion, the Act simply respects human life—an objective that lies within the legislative power. The Act advances that objective by ensuring that women will be fully informed about the methods of abortion to which they consent. Moreover, Congress can legitimately legislate even in the face of the medical uncertainty whether such a prohibition on one form of abortion subjects women "to significant health risks." Such uncertainty does not support a facial challenge to the Act. The proper way to attack the Act would be through an as-applied challenge that would permit review of a more precise factual scenario. [Reversed.]

CONCURRENCE: (Thomas, J.) The Court correctly applies existing law, but the Constitution provides no basis at all for the Court's abortion jurisprudence.

DISSENT: (Ginsburg, J.) This decision mocks *Planned Parenthood of Southeastern Pennsylvania v. Casey*, 505 U.S. 833 (1992), and *Stenberg v. Carhart*, 530 U.S. 914 (2000), and it flies in the face of medical approval of abortion procedures. The Partial-Birth Abortion Ban (the Act) does subject women to significant health risks by forcing them to choose less safe methods of abortion, and, in the process, the statute does not save even one fetus because the Act merely criminalizes a method of abortion, not abortion itself. As the Court suggests, the real basis for today's decision is "moral concerns" for what the majority sees as emotionally fragile women. This rationale circumvents the concerns for stare decisis that have supported our prior decisions in this area. Today's decision is actually only a veiled attempt to undermine, in a piecemeal fashion, a woman's established right to an abortion.

ANALYSIS

The right to an abortion announced in *Roe v. Wade*, 410 U.S. 113 (1973), remains intact after *Gonzales v. Carhart*, 505 U.S. 833 (1992). That right is now more difficult to exercise, though, and, as Justice Ginsburg suggests in dissent, the federal statute's omission of safeguards for women's health is at best problematic under the Court's prior abortion decisions.

Quicknotes

DUE PROCESS The constitutional mandate requiring the courts to protect and enforce individuals' rights and liberties consistent with prevailing principles of fairness and justice and prohibiting the federal and state governments from such activities that deprive its citizens of life, liberty, or property interest.

INJUNCTION A court order requiring a person to do, or prohibiting that person from doing, a specific act.

INJUNCTIVE RELIEF A court order issued as a remedy, requiring a person to do, or prohibiting that person from doing, a specific act.

STARE DECISIS Doctrine whereby courts follow legal precedent unless there is good cause for departure.

Whole Woman's Health v. Hellerstedt

Abortion providers (P) v. State official (D)

136 S. Ct. 2292 (2016)

NATURE OF CASE: Appeal from reversal of judgment that enjoined the enforcement of abortion regulations on the grounds the regulations unconstitutionally imposed an undue burden on the right to an abortion.

FACT SUMMARY: Abortion providers (P) challenged as unconstitutional two abortion regulations as unduly burdensome on the right to an abortion: (1) an "admitting-privileges requirement" that provided that a physician performing or inducing an abortion had to have admitting privileges at a hospital located not further than 30 miles from the abortion facility, and (2) a "surgical-center requirement" that required an abortion facility to meet the minimum standards for ambulatory surgical centers under state law.

RULE OF LAW

Where evidence in the record and a weighing of benefits against burdens demonstrates that an abortion regulation has the purpose or effect of presenting a substantial obstacle to a woman seeking an abortion and imposes an undue burden on the right to have a previability abortion, the regulation is unconstitutional.

FACTS: Texas (D) enacted House Bill 2, which contained two abortion regulations: (1) an "admitting-privileges requirement" that provided that a physician performing or inducing an abortion had to have admitting privileges at a hospital located not further than 30 miles from the abortion facility, and (2), a "surgical-center requirement" that required an abortion facility to meet the minimum standards for ambulatory surgical centers (ASCs) under state law. Abortion providers (P) challenged and sought to enjoin these requirements as unconstitutional, claiming that they had the purpose or effect of presenting a substantial obstacle to a woman seeking an abortion, and imposed an undue burden on the right to have a previability abortion. The district court made extensive findings, including, but not limited to: as the admitting-privileges requirement began to be enforced, the number of facilities providing abortions dropped in half, from about 40 to about 20; this decrease in geographical distribution means that the number of women of reproductive age living more than 50 miles from a clinic has doubled, the number living more than 100 miles away has increased by 150 percent, the number living more than 150 miles away by more than 350 percent, and the number living more than 200 miles away by about 2,800 percent; the number of facilities would drop to seven or eight if the surgical-center provision took effect, and those remaining facilities would see a significant increase in patient traffic; facilities would remain only in five metropolitan areas; before the passage of House Bill 2, abortion was an extremely safe procedure with very low rates of complications and virtually no deaths; it was also safer than many more common procedures not subject to the same level of regulation; and the cost of compliance with the surgical-center requirement would most likely exceed $1.5 million to $3 million per clinic. The district court enjoined enforcement of the provisions, holding that the surgical-center requirement imposed an undue burden on the right of women in Texas (D) to seek previability abortions; that, together with that requirement, the admitting-privileges requirement imposed an undue burden in the Rio Grande Valley, El Paso, and West Texas; and that the provisions together created an "impermissible obstacle as applied to all women seeking a previability abortion." The court of appeals reversed, stating that a law is constitutional if (1) it does not have the purpose or effect of placing a substantial obstacle in the path of a woman seeking an abortion of a nonviable fetus and (2) it is reasonably related to a legitimate state interest. The court of appeals concluded that both requirements were rationally related to a compelling state interest in protecting women's health. The court of appeals also held that the district court erred by substituting its own judgment for that of the legislature when it conducted its undue burden inquiry, in part because medical uncertainty underlying a statute is for resolution by legislatures, not the courts. The United States Supreme Court granted certiorari.

ISSUE: Where evidence in the record and a weighing of benefits against burdens demonstrates that an abortion regulation has the purpose or effect of presenting a substantial obstacle to a woman seeking an abortion, and imposes an undue burden on the right to have a previability abortion, is the regulation unconstitutional?

HOLDING AND DECISION: (Breyer, J.) Yes. Where evidence in the record and a weighing of benefits against burdens demonstrates that an abortion regulation has the purpose or effect of presenting a substantial obstacle to a woman seeking an abortion and imposes an undue burden on the right to have a previability abortion, the regulation is unconstitutional. The court of appeals's standard of review may be read to imply that a district court should not consider the existence or nonexistence of medical benefits when deciding the undue burden

Continued on next page.

question, but precedent requires courts to consider the burdens a law imposes on abortion access together with the benefits those laws confer. The court of appeals's test also mistakenly equates the judicial review applicable to the regulation of a constitutionally protected personal liberty with the less strict review applicable to, e.g., economic legislation. Additionally, the court of appeals's requirement that legislatures resolve questions of medical uncertainty is inconsistent with this Court's case law, which has placed considerable weight upon evidence and argument presented in judicial proceedings when determining the constitutionality of laws regulating abortion procedures. Contrary to the court of appeals's conclusion, the district court applied the correct standard, and correctly considered the evidence in the record—including expert evidence—and then weighed the asserted benefits against the burdens. The record contained adequate legal and factual support for the district court's conclusion that the admitting-privileges requirement imposed an "undue burden" on a woman's right to choose. The requirement's purpose was to help ensure that women had easy access to a hospital should complications arise during an abortion procedure, but the district court, relying on evidence showing extremely low rates of serious complications before the passage of House Bill 2, found no significant health-related problem for the new law to cure. Texas's (D) record evidence, in contrast, did not show how the new law advanced its legitimate interest in protecting women's health when compared to the prior law. At the same time, the record evidence indicated that the requirement placed a "substantial obstacle" in a woman's path to abortion because it led to a dramatic drop in the number of clinics, which meant fewer doctors, longer waiting times, and increased crowding. The surgical-center requirement also provides few, if any, health benefits for women, poses a substantial obstacle to women seeking abortions, and constitutes an "undue burden" on their constitutional right to do so. Before this requirement was enacted, Texas (D) law required abortion facilities to meet a host of health and safety requirements. There was considerable evidence in the record supporting the district court's findings indicating that the statutory provision requiring all abortion facilities to meet all surgical-center standards did not benefit patients and was not necessary. This evidence, along with the absence of any contrary evidence, supported the district court's conclusions, including its ultimate legal conclusion that the requirement was not necessary. At the same time, the record provided adequate evidentiary support for the district court's conclusion that the requirement placed a substantial obstacle in the path of women seeking an abortion. The district court found that it "strained credulity" to think that the seven or eight abortion facilities remaining in the state would be able to meet the demand for abortions. In sum, the challenged provisions had the effect of closing most of the abortion facilities in Texas (D) and placed added stress on those facilities able to remain open. They vastly increased the obstacles confronting women seeking abortions in Texas (D) without providing any benefit to women's health capable of withstanding any meaningful scrutiny. Thus, the provisions are unconstitutional on their face. Reversed and remanded.

CONCURRENCE: (Ginsburg, J.) The truth is that complications from an abortion are both rare and rarely dangerous. Many medical procedures, including childbirth, are far more dangerous to patients, yet are not subject to ambulatory-surgical-center or hospital admitting-privileges requirements. Thus, the claimed benefits of the regulations in House Bill 2 are in reality nothing more than impediments to abortion that do little or nothing for health. Accordingly, such regulations cannot withstand judicial scrutiny, and are unconstitutional.

DISSENT: (Thomas, J.) The Court's abortion jurisprudence is untenable. However, even accepting the Court's precedents in this area, the majority rewrites the undue-burden test. First, the majority requires courts to consider the burdens a law imposes on abortion access together with the benefits those laws confer. Second, the majority tells the courts that, when the law's justifications are medically uncertain, they need not defer to the legislature, and must instead assess medical justifications for abortion restrictions by scrutinizing the record themselves. Finally, even if a law imposes no "substantial obstacle" to women's access to abortions, the law now must have more than a reasonable relation to a legitimate state interest. These precepts are nowhere to be found in the Court's precedents, and they transform the undue-burden test into a test more akin to strict scrutiny. The majority also fails to acknowledge the premise of prior precedent that holds "that the government has a legitimate and substantial interest in preserving and promoting fetal life" from conception, not just in regulating medical procedures. Moreover, the majority appoints the Court as a de facto medical board that can decide what constitutes medical quality of care, and its undue burden test seriously burdens states, which now must guess at how much more compelling their interests must be to pass muster and what "commonsense inferences" of an undue burden this Court will identify next.

DISSENT: (Alito, J.) The abortion providers (P) failed to show that H.B. 2 would have an unconstitutional impact on a large fraction of Texas (D) women of reproductive age. Although they pointed to large number of abortion clinics that closed after enactment of this legislation, they failed to directly link those closures to the legislation. They also failed to provide any direct evidence of the actual capacity of the ambulatory surgical centers (ASCs)

Continued on next page.

that would be available to perform abortions in compliance with the new law, and instead relied on inference to posit that the lower number of abortions performed at ASCs as compared to all abortions performed in the state meant that ASC-compliant clinics could not meet the demands of women in Texas (D). H.B. 2 was intended to shut down unsafe clinics performing abortions, so it follows that some clinics closed. The lack of specific evidence explaining the closures, however, does not show whether the closures were in fact related to H.B. 2, and, therefore, it cannot be shown whether H.B. 2 affected women's access to abortions clinics. Even if immaterial closures had been factored out, however, scant evidence was presented on the capacity of the clinics that were able to comply with the admitting privileges and ASC requirements, or on those clinics' geographic distribution. Thus, reviewing the evidence in the record, it is far from clear that there has been a material impact on access to abortion. More evidence on this factor might have shown that ASCs would have been able, without prohibitively great expense, to accommodate increased demand for abortions.

ANALYSIS

In this landmark abortion rights decision, the Supreme Court vindicated the use of record evidence to determine the real-world effects of a challenged statute, rather than deferring to a legislature's characterization of what the statute would achieve. In relying extensively on the district court's assessment of the substantial evidence in the case, the majority essentially found that the Texas (D) legislature's characterization of House Bill 2 as promoting health was, in fact, a pretext for impeding women's access to legal abortion.

Quicknotes

UNDUE BURDEN A burden that is unlawfully oppressive or troublesome.

June Medical Services L.L.C. v. Russo

Abortion provider (P) v. State official (D)

140 S. Ct. 2103 (2020)

NATURE OF CASE: Appeal in action challenging as unconstitutional a state law requiring every doctor who performed abortions to have active hospital admitting privileges at a hospital within 30 miles of where abortions were performed or induced. [The procedural posture of the case is not presented in the casebook excerpt.]

FACT SUMMARY: Abortion providers challenged as unconstitutional a state law requiring every doctor who performed abortions to have active hospital admitting privileges at a hospital within 30 miles of where abortions were performed or induced.

RULE OF LAW

A law that requires every doctor who performs abortions to have active hospital admitting privileges at a hospital within 30 miles of where abortions are performed or induced imposes an undue burden on a woman's constitutional right to choose to have an abortion.

FACTS: Louisiana (D) passed a law requiring every doctor who performed abortions to have active hospital admitting privileges at a hospital within 30 miles of where abortions were performed or induced. This law was almost identical to a similar Texas law that the Court struck down in *Whole Woman's Health v. Hellerstedt*, 579 U. S. 582 (2016), because it impermissibly imposed a substantial obstacle to women seeking to exercise their constitutional right to choose to have an abortion. The federal district court in Louisiana (D) determined that the Louisiana (D) law likewise imposed such an obstacle. Abortion providers (P) challenged the law. The United States Supreme Court granted certiorari in the case. [The procedural posture of the case is not presented in the casebook excerpt.]

ISSUE: Does a law that requires every doctor who performs abortions to have active hospital admitting privileges at a hospital within 30 miles of where abortions are performed or induced impose an undue burden on a woman's constitutional right to choose to have an abortion?

HOLDING AND DECISION: (Breyer, J.) Yes. A law that requires every doctor who performs abortions to have active hospital admitting privileges at a hospital within 30 miles of where abortions are performed or induced imposes an undue burden on a woman's constitutional right to choose to have an abortion. The Louisiana (D) law is practically identical to a similar Texas law that the Court held unconstitutional in *Whole Woman's Health* v. *Hellerstedt*, 579 U. S. 582 (2016), on the grounds that the law impermissibly imposed a substantial obstacle to women seeking to exercise their constitutional right to choose to have an abortion. Because the district court determined that the Louisiana (D) law would impose a substantial obstacle to women seeking abortions, the doctrine of stare decisis requires holding the law unconstitutional.

CONCURRENCE: (Roberts, C.J.) The doctrine of stare decisis requires courts to treat like cases alike, absent special circumstances. As no such circumstances are presented here, and because the law at issue is almost identical to the Texas law the Court struck down in *Whole Woman's Health* and imposes a burden on abortion access just as severe as that imposed by the Texas law, the Louisiana law cannot stand under the Court's precedents. However, the Court should not use the balancing test adopted in *Whole Woman's Health*, whereby a law's asserted benefits are weighed against the burdens it imposes on abortion access. In the abortion context, such a balancing test would ask courts to balance a state's interest in protecting the potentiality of human life and the health of women on the one hand, against a woman's liberty interest in defining her own concept of existence, of meaning, of the universe, and of the mystery of human life on the other. There is no plausible sense in which anyone, let alone a court, could objectively assign weight to such imponderable values and no meaningful way to compare them if there were. If a court attempted to do so, it would be acting legislatively, not judicially. Accordingly, the only question courts should address in the abortion context is whether a given law imposes a substantial obstacle to a constitutional right, once it has been shown that a state has a legitimate purpose for enacting the law, and the law is reasonably related to that purpose.

DISSENT: (Thomas, J.) Abortion providers should not have standing to raise the constitutional claims of pregnant women who want abortions.

DISSENT: (Alito, J.) Not only should abortion providers not have standing to raise the constitutional claims of pregnant women who want abortions, since such providers cannot fairly represent the interests of such women, but also there is insufficient evidence that the Louisiana (D) law creates a substantial obstacle to women seeking abortions.

Continued on next page.

ANALYSIS

The regulation of abortion is a highly politicized and contentious arena. The Court itself has indicated that the judicial responsibility to avoid standardless decisionmaking is at its apex when faced with the most heated partisan issues. *Rucho v. Common Cause,* 139 S. Ct. 2484 (2019). However, it is arguable that in this case the legal standard the plurality applies when it comes to admitting privileges for abortion clinics turns out to be exactly the sort of all-things-considered balancing of benefits and burdens the Court has long rejected. In fact, the Court has described this sort of decisionmaking as "inherently, and therefore permanently, unpredictable." *Crawford v. Washington,* 541 U.S. 36 (2004). Under the Court's rule, whether a burden is deemed undue will depend heavily on which factors a judge considers and how much weight the judge accords each of them. Arguably, the Court does not provide lower court judges an administrable, neutral legal rule that is outside themselves to guide their decision. As Justice Gorsuch remarks, "When judges take it upon themselves to assess the raw costs and benefits of a new law or regulation, it can come as no surprise that '[s]ome courts wind up attaching the same significance to opposite facts,' and even attaching the opposite significance to the same facts. [*Crawford.*] It can come as no surprise, either, that judges retreat to their underlying assumptions or moral intuitions when deciding whether a burden is undue."

Quicknotes

STARE DECISIS Doctrine whereby courts follow legal precedent unless there is good cause for departure.

Bowers v. Hardwick

State officials (D) v. Homosexual man (P)

478 U.S. 186 (1986)

NATURE OF CASE: Appeal from decision finding state sodomy statute unconstitutional.

FACT SUMMARY: Bowers (D) and other state officials appealed from a court of appeals decision finding the Georgia sodomy statute unconstitutional in that it violated Hardwick's (P) fundamental rights, since it applied to consensual, homosexual sodomy.

RULE OF LAW

The Constitution does not grant a fundamental right to engage in consensual homosexual sodomy.

FACTS: Hardwick (P), a gay man, was charged with violating a state law criminalizing sodomy. After a preliminary hearing, the district attorney decided not to present the matter to the grand jury unless further evidence developed. Hardwick (P) brought suit, challenging the constitutionality of the statute in that it criminalized consensual sodomy. He claimed the law as administered by the state placed him in imminent danger of arrest and was unconstitutional on a number of grounds. The district court dismissed the action for failing to state a claim, relying heavily on the United States Supreme Court decision in *Doe v. Commonwealth's Attorney for the City of Richmond*, 425 U.S. 901 (1976), which summarily affirmed a case involving a similar Virginia sodomy statute. The court of appeals reversed, finding that the statute violated Hardwick's (P) fundamental rights because the homosexual activity was a private and intimate association beyond the reach of state regulation. From this decision, Bowers (D) and other state officials appealed.

ISSUE: Does the Constitution grant a fundamental right to engage in consensual homosexual sodomy?

HOLDING AND DECISION: (White, J.) No. The Constitution does not grant a fundamental right to engage in consensual homosexual sodomy. None of the fundamental rights announced in previous cases bears any resemblance to the claimed constitutional right to engage in sodomy asserted in the present case. Fundamental liberties identified by this Court, and deserving of heightened judicial scrutiny, have either been liberties implicit in the concept of ordered liberty or liberties deeply rooted in this nation's history and traditions. Neither of these formulations would extend the liberty sought in the present case. Great restraint should be used when expanding the contours of constitutional due process. The fact that the conduct in question occurred in the privacy of the home does not necessarily shield it from regulation, as can be seen in statutes punishing a number of other victimless and/or sex crimes. The conduct at issue is not a fundamental right, and the state has provided a rational basis for the statute. Reversed.

CONCURRENCE: (Burger, C.J.) This is a question not of personal preference but of the legislative authority of the state, and nothing in the Constitution forbids the state statute at issue.

CONCURRENCE: (Powell, J.) Hardwick (P) may be protected under the Eighth Amendment, but he has not been tried, sentenced, or convicted, and has not raised any Eighth Amendment issues.

DISSENT: (Blackmun, J.) The state in the present case is legislating particular forms of private, consensual sexual conduct. The Court's obsession with homosexual activity is difficult to justify, since the statute's language encompasses nonhomosexual conduct. The Court fails to comprehend the magnitude of the liberty interest at stake in this case.

DISSENT: (Stevens, J.) The essential liberty to choose how to conduct private sexual conduct surely encompasses the right to engage in nonreproductive, sexual conduct that others may find offensive or immoral. The state cannot justify the selective application of the statute in question, given the conceded unconstitutionality of the statute as applied to nonhomosexual conduct. Hardwick (P) at this state of the litigation has stated a constitutional claim sufficient to withstand a motion to dismiss.

ANALYSIS

Plaintiffs in the original action were a "*Doe*" couple, who had alleged that they wished to engage in the proscribed activity and were chilled and deterred by the existence of the statute and Hardwick's (P) arrest. The district court dismissed their claim for lack of standing, as the selective enforcement of the law left them in no immediate danger, and this judgment was upheld by the court of appeals. The "*Does*" did not challenge this holding in the present case.

Quicknotes

FUNDAMENTAL RIGHT A liberty that is either expressly or impliedly provided for in the United States Constitution,

Continued on next page.

the deprivation or burdening of which is subject to a heightened standard of review.

GRAND JURY A group summoned to investigate, inform, and accuse persons of crimes when sufficient evidence exists to do so.

Romer v. Evans

Municipality (P) v. State (D)

517 U.S. 620 (1996)

NATURE OF CASE: Review of order striking down state constitutional amendment.

FACT SUMMARY: A Colorado law that preempted local ordinances prohibiting discrimination against homosexuals was challenged as unconstitutional.

RULE OF LAW

States may not enact laws prohibiting localities from proscribing discrimination against a class of persons.

FACTS: In 1992, a statewide initiative was adopted by Colorado voters. The law, known as Amendment 2, preempted local ordinances from prohibiting discrimination on basis of sexual preference. The Colorado Supreme Court struck down the law as contrary to equal protection. The United States Supreme Court granted review.

ISSUE: May states enact laws prohibiting localities from proscribing discrimination against a class of persons?

HOLDING AND DECISION: (Kennedy, J.) No. States may not enact laws prohibiting localities from proscribing discrimination against a class of persons. Amendment 2 has the peculiar property of imposing a broad and undifferentiated disability on a single named group, as it places a particular burden in terms of access to the political process. Groups not affected by this law have greater access to this process. This clearly implicates the Equal Protection Clause of the Fourteenth Amendment. Such a law must bear a rational relationship to a legitimate government purpose. Amendment 2 is a status-based law undertaken for its own sake without serving any legitimate interest. Therefore, it is unconstitutional. Affirmed.

DISSENT: (Scalia, J.) Amendment 2 is a modest attempt against assaults on basic morals by a politically powerful interest group. States must be free to disfavor conduct its citizens find reprehensible.

ANALYSIS

Interestingly, the majority opinion here did not mention the last major case involving homosexuality, *Bowers v. Hardwick*, 478 U.S. 18 (1986). That case held it constitutional for a state to criminalize homosexual conduct. Assuming *Bowers* to still be good law, it seems that states can criminalize homosexual conduct, but cannot preempt local laws regarding homosexuals as a class.

Quicknotes

EQUAL PROTECTION A constitutional guarantee that no person shall be denied the same protection of the laws enjoyed by other persons in like circumstances.

RATIONAL BASIS REVIEW A test employed by the court to determine the validity of a statute in equal protection actions, whereby the court determines whether the challenged statute is rationally related to the achievement of a legitimate state interest.

SUSPECT CLASSIFICATION A class of persons that have historically been subject to discriminatory treatment; statutes drawing a distinction between persons based on a suspect classification, i.e., race, nationality, or alienage, are subject to a strict scrutiny standard of review.

Lawrence v. Texas

Sodomy convict (D) v. State (P)

539 U.S. 558 (2003)

NATURE OF CASE: Appeal from a criminal conviction.

FACT SUMMARY: When Lawrence (D) and his male partner, both adults, were prosecuted and convicted for consensual sodomy in their own private dwelling, they argued the unconstitutionality of the statute.

RULE OF LAW

Legislation that makes consensual sodomy between adults in their own dwelling criminal violates due process.

FACTS: Two Houston, Texas, police officers were dispatched to a private residence in response to a reported weapons disturbance. They entered an apartment where Lawrence (D) resided. The right of the police to enter was not an issue. The officers observed Lawrence (D) and another man engaging in sodomy. Both men were arrested, charged, and convicted before a justice of the peace of the statutory crime of "deviate sexual intercourse, namely anal sex, with a member of the same sex." Both men were adults at the time of the alleged offense. Their conduct was in private and consensual. Lawrence (D) and his partner appealed to the United States Supreme Court, arguing the Texas statute to be unconstitutional.

ISSUE: Does legislation that makes consensual sodomy between adults in their own dwelling criminal violate due process?

HOLDING AND DECISION: (Kennedy, J.) Yes. Legislation that makes consensual sodomy between adults in their own dwelling criminal violates due process. Liberty protects the person from unwarranted government intrusions into a dwelling or other private places. In our tradition, the state is not omnipresent in the home. Furthermore, freedom extends beyond spatial bounds. Liberty presumes freedom of thought, belief, expression, and certain intimate conduct. The penalties and purposes of the Texas statute in the instant case have far-reaching consequences, touching upon the most private human conduct, sexual behavior, and in the most private of places, the home. The statute seeks to control a personal relationship that, whether or not entitled to formal recognition in the law, is within the liberty of persons to choose without being punished as criminals. This Court acknowledges that adults may choose to enter private relationships in the confines of their own homes and their own private lives and still retain their dignity as free persons. When sexuality finds expression in intimate conduct with another person, the conduct can be but one element in a personal bond that is more enduring. The liberty protected by the Constitution allows homosexual persons the right to make this choice. Here, two adults who, with full and mutual consent from each other, engaged in sexual practices common to a homosexual lifestyle. They are entitled to respect in their private lives. The state cannot demean their existence or control their destiny by making their private sexual conduct a crime. Reversed and remanded.

CONCURRENCE: (O'Connor, J.) Rather than relying on the substantive component of the Fourteenth Amendment's Due Process Clause, as the Court does, I base my conclusion of unconstitutionality on the Fourteenth Amendment's Equal Protection Clause.

DISSENT: (Scalia, J.) Homosexual sodomy is not a right deeply rooted in our Nation's history and tradition. Constitutional entitlements do not spring into existence because some states choose to lessen or eliminate sanctions on criminal behavior. Today's opinion is the product of a Court that has largely signed on to the so-called homosexual agenda.

DISSENT: (Thomas, J.) Although finding the instant Texas statute to be "uncommonly silly" and would vote to repeal it if I were a member of the Texas Legislature, I nevertheless find no general constitutional right of privacy violated in this situation.

ANALYSIS

In *Lawrence*, the Supreme Court noted that of the 13 states with laws prohibiting sodomy, only four have enforced their legislation. In those states in which sodomy was still proscribed, whether for same-sex or heterosexual conduct, there was a pattern of nonenforcement with respect to consenting adults acting in private. Even Texas admitted in 1994, that as of that date it had not prosecuted anyone under those circumstances.

Quicknotes

DUE PROCESS CLAUSE Language found in the Fifth and Fourteenth Amendments to the United States Constitution providing that no person shall be deprived of "life, liberty, or property without due process of law."

FOURTEENTH AMENDMENT DUE PROCESS CLAUSE Provides that protections mandated by the United States Constitution and observed by the federal government are equally applicable, and therefore must be observed by the states.

United States v. Windsor

Federal government (D) v. Same-sex spouse (P)

570 U.S. 744 (2013)

NATURE OF CASE: Appeal from affirmance of judgment that § 3 of the Defense of Marriage Act, defining "marriage" and "spouse" to exclude same-sex partners, was unconstitutional.

FACT SUMMARY: The United States (D) contended that § 3 of the Defense of Marriage Act, which defined "marriage" and "spouse" to exclude same-sex partners, did not violate the Fifth Amendment's equal protection provisions.

RULE OF LAW

Section 3 of the Defense of Marriage Act (DOMA), which defines "marriage" and "spouse" to exclude same-sex partners, violates the Fifth Amendment's equal protection provisions.

FACTS: New York recognized the marriage of Windsor (P) and Spyer, a same-sex couple, who had wed in Canada. When Spyer died, she left her entire estate to Windsor (P). Windsor (P) sought to claim the federal estate tax exemption for surviving spouses but was barred from doing so by § 3 of the federal Defense of Marriage Act (DOMA), which amended the Dictionary Act—a law providing rules of construction for over 1,000 federal laws and the whole realm of federal regulations—to define "marriage" and "spouse" as excluding same-sex partners. Windsor (P) paid $363,053 in estate taxes and sought a refund, which the Internal Revenue Service (IRS) denied. Windsor (P) brought suit for a refund, contending that DOMA violates the principles of equal protection incorporated in the Fifth Amendment. While the suit was pending, the Attorney General notified the Speaker of the House of Representatives that the Department of Justice would no longer defend § 3's constitutionality. In response, the Bipartisan Legal Advisory Group (BLAG) of the House of Representatives voted to intervene in the litigation to defend § 3's constitutionality. The district court permitted the intervention, held § 3 unconstitutional, and ordered the IRS to refund Windsor's (P) tax with interest. The court of appeals affirmed, but the IRS refused to pay unless ordered to do so by the United States Supreme Court, which granted certiorari.

ISSUE: Does § 3 of the Defense of Marriage Act (DOMA), which defines "marriage" and "spouse" to exclude same-sex partners, violate the Fifth Amendment's equal protection provisions?

HOLDING AND DECISION: (Kennedy, J.) Yes. Section 3 of the Defense of Marriage Act (DOMA), which defines "marriage" and "spouse" to exclude same-sex partners, violates the Fifth Amendment's equal protection provisions. As a threshold jurisdictional matter, the United States (D) retains a stake sufficient to support jurisdiction based on the refund it was ordered to pay, notwithstanding that the Executive disagrees with § 3. Prudential considerations, however, require that there be concrete adverseness, which sharpens the presentation of issues upon which the court so largely depends for illumination of difficult constitutional questions. Here, the Bipartisan Legal Advisory Group's (BLAG's) substantial adversarial argument for § 3's constitutionality satisfies prudential concerns that otherwise might counsel against hearing an appeal from a decision with which the principal parties agree. This conclusion does not mean that it is appropriate for the Executive as a routine matter to challenge statutes in court instead of making the case to Congress for amendment or repeal. This case is not routine, however, and jurisdiction is established. By history and tradition, the definition and regulation of marriage has been treated as being within the authority and realm of the separate states. Nevertheless, Congress has enacted discrete statutes to regulate the meaning of marriage in order to further federal policy, but DOMA, with a directive applicable to over 1,000 federal statutes and the whole realm of federal regulations, has a far greater reach. Its operation is also directed to a class of persons that the laws of New York, and of several other jurisdictions, have sought to protect. Assessing the validity of that intervention requires discussing the historical and traditional extent of state power and authority over marriage. Subject to certain constitutional guarantees, regulation of domestic relations is an area that has long been regarded as a virtually exclusive province of the states. The significance of state responsibilities for the definition and regulation of marriage dates to the Nation's beginning, and when the Constitution was adopted, the common understanding was that the domestic relations of husband and wife and parent and child were matters reserved to the states. While marriage laws may vary from state to state, they are consistent within each state. DOMA rejects this long-established precept. The state's decision to give this class of persons the right to marry conferred upon them a dignity and status of immense import. But the federal government (D) uses the state-defined class for the opposite purpose—to impose restrictions and disabilities. The question is whether the resulting injury and indignity is a deprivation of an essential part of the liberty protected by the Fifth Amendment, since what New York treats as alike the federal law deems

Continued on next page.

unlike by a law designed to injure the same class the state seeks to protect. New York's actions were a proper exercise of its sovereign authority. They reflect both the community's considered perspective on the historical roots of the institution of marriage and its evolving understanding of the meaning of equality. By seeking to injure the very class New York seeks to protect, DOMA violates basic due process and equal protection principles applicable to the federal government (D). The Constitution's guarantee of equality must at the very least mean that a bare congressional desire to harm a politically unpopular group cannot justify disparate treatment of that group. DOMA cannot survive under these principles. Its unusual deviation from the tradition of recognizing and accepting state definitions of marriage operates to deprive same-sex couples of the benefits and responsibilities that come with federal recognition of their marriages. This is strong evidence of a law having the purpose and effect of disapproval of a class recognized and protected by state law. DOMA's avowed purpose and practical effect are to impose a disadvantage, a separate status, and so a stigma upon all who enter same-sex marriages made lawful by the unquestioned authority of the states. DOMA's history of enactment and its own text demonstrate that interference with the equal dignity of same-sex marriages, conferred by the states in the exercise of their sovereign power, was more than an incidental effect of the federal statute. It was its essence. BLAG's arguments are just as candid about the congressional purpose. DOMA's operation in practice confirms this purpose. It frustrates New York's objective of eliminating inequality by writing inequality into the entire United States Code. DOMA's principal effect is to identify and make unequal a subset of state-sanctioned marriages. It contrives to deprive some couples married under the laws of their state, but not others, of both rights and responsibilities, creating two contradictory marriage regimes within the same state. It also forces same-sex couples to live as married for purpose of state law but unmarried for purpose of federal law, thus diminishing the stability and predictability of basic personal relations the state has found it proper to acknowledge and protect. DOMA places same-sex couples in an unstable position of being in a second-tier marriage, thus demeaning the couple, whose moral and sexual choices the Constitution protects, and humiliating tens of thousands of children now being raised by same-sex couples. Under DOMA, same-sex married couples have their lives burdened, by reason of government decree, in visible and public ways, and for certain married couples, DOMA's unequal effects are even more serious and bring financial harm to children of same-sex couples. For these reasons, DOMA is unconstitutional as a deprivation of the liberty of the person protected by the Fifth Amendment—as to lawful same-sex marriages recognized by state law. Affirmed.

DISSENT: (Roberts, C.J.) First, the Court should have not reached the merits of this case, as it did not have the jurisdiction to do so. As to the merits, Congress did not act unconstitutionality in enacting DOMA. The majority makes an insufficient showing of malice on Congress's part, or an entire lack of a legitimate governmental purpose, in enacting DOMA. More importantly, it must be emphasized that the Court has not resolved the question of whether the states may continue to use the traditional definition of marriage. Instead, the majority's opinion is limited to resolving that the federal government may not intrude in this area of domestic relations, which is an area left to the states. The majority's opinion reaffirms state sovereignty in this area, as well as state diversity as to same-sex marriage. The majority's resolution of these issues may well come into play in the future if the Court is asked to resolve the question of whether a state's denial of same-sex marriage is unconstitutional.

DISSENT: (Scalia, J.) First, the Court had no power to hear this case, as is the correct outcome when the President and plaintiff agree that a statute is unconstitutional. The only reason the case reached the Court was because the President enforced the statute he believed to be unlawful, purely to give the plaintiff standing. Such executive contrivance should not be countenanced by the Court, so if the President expresses the view that a statute is unconstitutional, but enforces it nonetheless, the litigation should end in an order or a consent decree enjoining enforcement. In any event, the majority's decision on the merits is strikingly incorrect and inconsistent. The opinion fools its reader into believing it is about federalism, but then asserts that it is unnecessary to resolve the issue of whether the federal intrusion on state power is unconstitutional. Equally perplexing is the majority's treatment of equal protection doctrine. At one point the opinion seems to say that the Equal Protection Clause is not the basis of the decision, but at another point the majority cites equal protection cases to explain why DOMA is unconstitutional. Even if the decision is supposed to be an equal-protection opinion, it is a confusing one. The opinion does not resolve what had in the lower courts been the central question, namely whether laws restricting marriage to a man and a woman, are reviewed for more than mere rationality. The majority seems to indicate that rationality review is all that is necessary, but then does not apply that deferential standard. The majority avoids the tier of standards altogether by saying, effectively, that DOMA violates substantive due process, but it does not—nor could it—support this analysis with evidence that same-sex marriage is deeply rooted in the Nation's history and traditions—a necessary element of substantive due process doctrine. The upshot of the opinion, which is continually shifting in its justifications, is that DOMA is invalid because it is motivated to harm couples in same-sex marriages. As to that key

Continued on next page.

point, the Constitution does not forbid the government from enforcing traditional moral and sexual norm, nor does it require or prohibit society to approve of same-sex marriage. There are valid justifications, e.g., avoidance of complex choice-of-law questions—a classic purpose for a definitional provision—for DOMA. DOMA also preserves the intended effects of prior legislation against then-unforeseen changes in circumstance. Such justifications demonstrate legislative prudence rather than animus. To defend traditional marriage is not to demean, condemn, or humiliate those who would enter same-sex marriage. To accuse those who enacted DOMA of such animus is demeaning to the Court. It is one thing for society to elect change, but it is inappropriate for a court to effect such change by adjudging those who oppose it as seething with animus. The majority, with its self-righteous moral stance, is not to be believed when it says that its opinion is limited only to lawful same-sex marriages recognized by state law. Given the hodge-podge of rationales presented by the majority, it will not be difficult for lower courts to distinguish cases challenging states that prohibit same-sex marriages—and those lower courts should by all means distinguish the majority's opinion where appropriate. However, what is clear, despite the confusing majority opinion, is that its real rationale is that DOMA was motivated by hatred of gays, and that such a rationale will be applied to state legislation that prohibits same-sex marriage. The majority will hurtle the same accusations at state legislatures that it now throws at the Executive and Legislative branches that enacted DOMA. The majority will declare there is "no legitimate purpose" served by a law that prohibits same-sex marriage and will claim the traditional definition has the purpose and effect to disparage and to injure the "personhood and dignity" of same-sex couples. The result will be a judicial distortion of our society's debate over marriage, and that is not the democratic system our Founders envisioned. The Court should have let the People decide the issue, with resulting winners and losers in a democratic process. Instead, the Court has cheated both sides, robbing the winners of an honest victory, and the losers of the peace that comes from a fair defeat.

DISSENT: (Alito, J.) The Constitution does not enshrine a particular understanding of marriage, but leaves it to the people to decide, through their elected representatives, how marriage should be understood. Given that DOMA was the people's expression of their choice, DOMA is not unconstitutional. Same-sex marriage does not present a difficult question of constitutional law. Applying substantive due process to same-sex marriage is inappropriate, because such application protects only those fundamental rights and liberties that are, objectively, deeply rooted in this country's history and tradition. Same-sex marriage is not deeply rooted in this nation's—or any other nation's—history or tradition; it is a novel right. Windsor (P) seeks protection of this right not from elected officials but from the unelected judiciary. In the face of such innovation, the judiciary must tread very carefully, as it is not known—nor will it be for a long time to come—what the ramifications of this innovation will be, assuming same-sex marriage takes hold as an institution. The Court should stick to interpreting the Constitution, not making important changes to society's institutions; under the Constitution, that is left to the people. Windsor (P), couching her arguments in equal protection terms, contends that classifications based on sexual orientation should trigger a form of "heightened" scrutiny, and that § 3 cannot survive such scrutiny. While the majority does not directly adopt this argument, its decision also seems to ultimately rest on equal protection grounds. Such an approach is misguided and ill-suited for evaluating the constitutionality of laws based on the traditional understanding of marriage, which fundamentally turn on what marriage is. Classifications subject to strict scrutiny, which must be narrowly tailored to achieve a compelling government interest, are those that are so seldom relevant to the achievement of any legitimate state interest that laws grounded in such considerations are deemed to reflect prejudice and antipathy. On the other hand, characteristics subject to intermediate scrutiny, which must be substantially related to the achievement of important governmental objectives, are those that are sometimes relevant considerations to be taken into account by legislators, but generally provide no sensible ground for different treatment. Finally, under rational-basis review, where the classification at issue is not viewed as inherently suspect, the courts do not closely scrutinize legislative choices as to whether, how, and to what extent those interests should be pursued. By arguing that DOMA be subject to heightened scrutiny, Windsor (P) is asking that the Court to rule that the presence of two members of the opposite sex is rationally related to marriage. Doing so, however, "would cast all those who cling to traditional beliefs about the nature of marriage in the role of bigots or superstitious fools." The Court should not resolve the debate between two competing views of marriage. The "traditional" or "conjugal" view of marriage, which has prevailed for centuries over many cultures, is that marriage is an exclusively opposite-sex institution inextricably linked to procreation and biological kinship. The newer, "consent-based" view of marriage is that it is the solemnization of mutual commitment—marked by strong emotional attachment and sexual attraction—between two persons. Proponents of same-sex marriage argue that because gender differentiation is not relevant to this vision, the exclusion of same-sex couples from the institution of marriage is rank discrimination. The Constitution does not enshrine either of these views of marriage. This silence should end

Continued on next page.

the matter as far as the judiciary is concerned. Instead, Windsor (P) asks the Court to resolve a matter better left to the people. Government, however, must decide between these competing visions, and is not required to be neutral about which vision it chooses, provided that the vision of the good that it adopts is not countermanded by the Constitution. Thus, both Congress and the states are entitled to enact laws recognizing either of the two understandings of marriage. The majority cobbles together a decision that neither wholly embraces Windsor's (P) argument, nor completely adheres to a single strand of doctrine. Insofar as the decision is clear that the question of same-sex marriage should be resolved primarily at the state level, the majority is entirely correct, and, in the future, if the case arises, the Court should permit the people of each state to decide this question for themselves. In any event, § 3 does not encroach on the prerogatives of the states and does not prevent any state from recognizing same-sex marriage or from extending to same-sex couples any right, privilege, benefit, or obligation stemming from state law. All that § 3 does is to define a class of persons to whom federal law extends certain special benefits and upon whom federal law imposes certain special burdens. Assuming Congress has the power under the Constitution to enact the laws affected by § 3, Congress has the power to define the category of persons to whom those laws apply.

ANALYSIS

Many consider this decision to be a landmark civil rights case. Some constitutional scholars have characterized the mocking tone of Justice Scalia's dissent as "intemperate," "extraordinary," and "at the very least, an exercise in jurisprudential cynicism." See Larry H. Tribe, "DOMA, Prop 8, and Justice Scalia's intemperate dissent," at https://www.scotusblog.com/2013/06/doma-prop-8-and-justice-scalias-intemperate-dissent/ [last visited March 2022]. Others have disagreed with Chief Justice Roberts's assessment that the majority relied on federalism, instead noting that the majority did not place any weight on this doctrine to reach its decision. In the wake of the ruling, the Obama administration and federal agencies started the process of conforming statutes and regulations to the Court's decision. Finally, as predicted by the dissenters, lower courts, faced with ambiguities in the decision, have interpreted *Windsor* in different ways to reach different results as to state regulation of marriage and the denial of marriage rights to same-sex couples.

Quicknotes

FIFTH AMENDMENT Provides no person shall be compelled to serve as a witness against oneself, be subject to trial for the same offense twice, or be deprived of life, liberty, or property without due process of law.

RATIONAL BASIS REVIEW A test employed by the court to determine the validity of a statute in equal protection actions, whereby the court determines whether the challenged statute is rationally related to the achievement of a legitimate state interest.

STATE SOVEREIGNTY The absolute power of self-government possessed by a state.

SUBSTANTIVE DUE PROCESS A constitutional safeguard limiting the power of the state, irrespective of how fair its procedures may be; substantive limits placed on the power of the state.

Obergefell v. Hodges

Same-sex spouse (P) v. State official (D)

135 S. Ct. 2584 (2015)

NATURE OF CASE: Consolidated actions challenging as unconstitutional a state's denial of the right of same sex couples to marry or to have their marriages, lawfully performed in another state, given full recognition. [The procedural posture of the case is not presented in the casebook extract.]

FACT SUMMARY: Fourteen same-sex couples (P) and two men whose same-sex partners were deceased claimed that state officials (D) violated the Fourteenth Amendment by denying them the right to marry or to have their marriages, which were lawfully performed in another state, given full recognition.

RULE OF LAW

The Fourteenth Amendment requires a state to license a marriage between two people of the same sex and to recognize a marriage between two people of the same sex when their marriage has been lawfully licensed and performed out-of-state.

FACTS: Obergefell (P) and Arthur were a same-sex couple living in Ohio, which did not recognize same-sex marriages. They travelled to Maryland, which does recognize such marriages, and they were married. Three months later, Arthur, who had an incurable disease, died. Following Arthur's death, and in accordance with Ohio law, Arthur's death record failed to record Obergefell as Arthur's "surviving spouse" and listed Arthur as "unmarried" at the time of his death. Obergefell (P) brought suit to be shown as the surviving spouse on Arthur's death certificate. Other similarly situated same-sex couples (P) made similar claims, asserting that state officials violated the Fourteenth Amendment by denying them the right to marry or to have their marriages lawfully performed in another state given full recognition. The United States Supreme Court granted certiorari, and the actions were consolidated. [The procedural posture of the case is not presented in the casebook extract.]

ISSUE: Does the Fourteenth Amendment require a state to license a marriage between two people of the same sex and to recognize a marriage between two people of the same sex when their marriage has been lawfully licensed and performed out-of-state?

HOLDING AND DECISION: (Kennedy, J.) Yes. The Fourteenth Amendment requires a state to license a marriage between two people of the same sex and to recognize a marriage between two people of the same sex when their marriage has been lawfully licensed and performed out-of-state. The plaintiffs (P) sought to marry someone of the same sex and have their marriages deemed lawful on the same terms and conditions as marriages between persons of the opposite sex. Marriage as a union between two persons of the opposite sex has been central to the human condition and throughout the annals of human history. The institution of marriage has existed for millennia and across civilizations. This history marks the beginning of this case. To the government defendants (D), it would demean a timeless institution if marriage were extended to same-sex couples. However, the plaintiffs (P), far from seeking to devalue marriage, seek it for themselves because of their respect—and need—for its privileges and responsibilities, as illustrated by the plaintiffs' (P) own experiences. The history of marriage is one of both continuity and change. Changes, such as the decline of arranged marriages and the abandonment of the law of coverture, have worked deep transformations in the structure of marriage, affecting aspects of marriage once viewed as essential. These new insights have strengthened, not weakened, the institution. This dynamic also can be seen in the Nation's experience with gay and lesbian rights. Well into the 20th century, many states condemned same-sex intimacy as immoral, and homosexuality was treated as an illness. Later in the century, cultural and political developments allowed same-sex couples to lead more open and public lives. Extensive public and private dialogue followed, along with shifts in public attitudes. The Court ultimately reflected these changed attitudes in its decisions. The Court has long held the right to marry is protected by the Constitution, and that marriage is "one of the vital personal rights essential to the orderly pursuit of happiness by free men." The Court has reiterated that the right to marry is fundamental under the Due Process Clause. Those prior cases describing the right to marry presumed a relationship involving opposite-sex partners, but it should be kept in mind that the Court, like many institutions, has made assumptions defined by the world and time of which it is a part. Other precedents have expressed broad constitutional principles that go beyond such assumptions. In assessing whether the force and rationale of its cases apply to same-sex couples, the Court must respect the basic reasons why the right to marry has been long protected, and such an analysis compels the conclusion that same-sex couples may exercise the right to marry. Four principles and traditions demonstrate that the reasons marriage is fundamental under the Constitution apply with equal force to same-sex couples. The first premise of this Court's

Continued on next page.

relevant precedents is that the right to personal choice regarding marriage is inherent in the concept of individual autonomy. This abiding connection between marriage and liberty is why the Court invalidated interracial marriage bans under the Due Process Clause. Decisions about marriage are among the most intimate that an individual can make, and this is true for all persons, whatever their sexual orientation. A second principle in this Court's jurisprudence is that the right to marry is fundamental because it supports a two-person union unlike any other in its importance to the committed individuals. Same-sex couples have the same right as opposite-sex couples to enjoy intimate association, a right extending beyond mere freedom from laws making same-sex intimacy a criminal offense. A third basis for protecting the right to marry is that it safeguards children and families and thus draws meaning from related rights of childrearing, procreation, and education. Without the recognition, stability, and predictability marriage offers, children suffer the stigma of knowing their families are somehow lesser. They also suffer the significant material costs of being raised by unmarried parents, relegated to a more difficult and uncertain family life. The marriage laws at issue thus harm and humiliate the children of same-sex couples. Fourth, and finally, this Court's cases and the nation's traditions make clear that marriage is a keystone of the nation's social order. States have contributed to the fundamental character of marriage by placing it at the center of many facets of the legal and social order. There is no difference between same- and opposite-sex couples with respect to this principle, yet same-sex couples are denied the constellation of benefits that the states have linked to marriage and are consigned to an instability many opposite-sex couples would find intolerable. It is demeaning to lock same-sex couples out of a central institution of the nation's society, for they too may aspire to the transcendent purposes of marriage and seek fulfillment in its highest meaning. The government defendants (D) argue that the plaintiffs (P) do not seek to exercise the right to marry but rather a new and nonexistent "right to same-sex marriage." Although liberty under the Due Process Clause must be defined in a most circumscribed manner, with central reference to specific historical practices, such an approach is inconsistent with the approach this Court has used in discussing other fundamental rights, including marriage and intimacy. If rights were defined by who exercised them in the past, then received practices could serve as their own continued justification and new groups could not invoke rights once denied. The right of same-sex couples to marry is also derived from the Fourteenth Amendment's guarantee of equal protection. The Due Process Clause and the Equal Protection Clause are connected in a profound way. Rights implicit in liberty and rights secured by equal protection may rest on different precepts and are not always co-extensive, yet each may be instructive as to the meaning and reach of the other. The Court has acknowledged the interlocking nature of these constitutional safeguards in the context of the legal treatment of gays and lesbians, and this dynamic also applies to same-sex marriage. The challenged laws burden the liberty of same-sex couples, and they abridge central precepts of equality. The marriage laws at issue are in essence unequal: Same-sex couples are denied benefits afforded opposite-sex couples and are barred from exercising a fundamental right. Especially against a long history of disapproval of their relationships, this denial works a grave and continuing harm, serving to disrespect and subordinate gays and lesbians. The right to marry is a fundamental right inherent in the liberty of the person, and under the Due Process and Equal Protection Clauses of the Fourteenth Amendment couples of the same-sex may not be deprived of that right and that liberty. Same-sex couples may exercise the fundamental right to marry, and the state laws challenged by the plaintiffs (P) are held invalid to the extent they exclude same-sex couples from civil marriage on the same terms and conditions as opposite-sex couples. There may be an initial inclination to await further legislation, litigation, and debate, but referenda, legislative debates, and grassroots campaigns; studies and other writings; and extensive litigation in state and federal courts have led to an enhanced understanding of the issue. While the Constitution contemplates that democracy is the appropriate process for change, individuals who are harmed need not await legislative action before asserting a fundamental right. Gays and lesbians have suffered pain and humiliation at the hands of state action, and the effects of these injuries no doubt have lingered. A ruling against same-sex couples would have the same effect and would be unjustified under the Fourteenth Amendment. The plaintiffs' (P) stories show the urgency of the issue they present to the Court, which has a duty to address these claims and answer these questions. The government defendants' (D) argument that allowing same-sex couples to wed will harm marriage as an institution rests on a counterintuitive view of opposite-sex couples' decisions about marriage and parenthood. Finally, the First Amendment ensures that religions, those who adhere to religious doctrines, and others have protection as they seek to teach the principles that are so fulfilling and so central to their lives and faiths. The Fourteenth Amendment requires states to recognize same-sex marriages validly performed out of state. Since same-sex couples may now exercise the fundamental right to marry in all states, there is no lawful basis for a state to refuse to recognize a lawful same-sex marriage performed in another state on the ground of its same-sex character.

DISSENT: (Roberts, C.J.) The plaintiffs' (P) arguments have appeal based on arguments rooted in social policy and considerations of fairness, but the Court is

Continued on next page.

not a legislature, and whether same-sex marriage is a good idea should not be the Court's concern. The Court can only say what the law is, not what it should be. The majority's decision is not a pronouncement of a legal judgment, and the right it announces has no basis in the Constitution or precedent. The core meaning of marriage has been that it is a union between a man and a woman, notwithstanding that this core has changed through history. The concept of marriage has been premised on the need for procreation as a means for the human race to survive, which is why at its core it is about a union between a woman and a man, and this singular understanding of marriage has prevailed in the United States throughout its history. The majority's decision is bald judicial policymaking, which previously has been rejected in favor of judicial self-restraint, and that is why the majority's position is indefensible as a matter of constitutional law. Allowing unelected federal judges to select which unenumerated rights rank as "fundamental"—and to strike down state laws on basis of that determination—raises significant concerns about the judicial role. Implied fundamental rights must be objectively and deeply rooted in the nation's tradition and history. The majority acknowledges none of this doctrinal background, and instead returns the Court to the long-discredited approach inherent in substantive due process from the ear of *Lochner v. New York*, 198 U.S. 45 (1905). Rejecting *Lochner* does not require disavowing the doctrine of implied fundamental rights, and this Court has not done so, but to avoid repeating *Lochner*'s error of converting personal preferences into constitutional mandates, modern substantive due process cases have stressed the need for "judicial self-restraint." No precedents, including those that have guaranteed the privacy rights of same-sex couples, support the right to same-sex marriage. Unlike criminal laws banning contraceptives and sodomy, the marriage laws at issue here involve no government intrusion. They create no crime and impose no punishment. Same-sex couples remain free to live together, to engage in intimate conduct, and to raise their families as they see fit. Nothing interferes with these couples' right to be let alone. In short, the "right to marry" cases stand for the important but limited proposition that particular restrictions on access to marriage as traditionally defined violate due process. These precedents say nothing at all about a right to make a state change its definition of marriage, which is the right the plaintiffs (P) actually seek here. Given that the majority redefines the core meaning of marriage, its opinion invites the question of whether that core meaning can be expanded beyond just two individuals to many, since from the standpoint of history and tradition, a leap from opposite-sex marriage to same-sex marriage is much greater than one from a two-person union to plural unions, which have deep roots in some cultures around the world. Expanding marriage to include same-sex couples, the majority insists, would "pose no risk of harm to themselves or third parties." This argument again echoes *Lochner*, and this "harm principle" again smacks of judicial legislation. A Justice's commission does not confer any special moral, philosophical, or social insight sufficient to justify imposing those perceptions on fellow citizens under the pretense of "due process." There is indeed a process due the people on issues of this sort—the democratic process. Respecting that understanding requires the Court to be guided by law, not any particular school of social thought. The majority's manner of deciding this case will, in the long run, be detrimental to the Court as an institution, since the majority repeatedly and unabashedly exalts the role of the judiciary in delivering social change—a role it clearly does not have under the Constitution. Nowhere is the majority's extravagant conception of judicial supremacy more evident than in its description—and dismissal—of the public debate regarding same-sex marriage. Those who founded our country would not recognize the majority's conception of the judicial role. They after all risked their lives and fortunes for the precious right to govern themselves. They would never have imagined yielding that right on a question of social policy to unaccountable and unelected judges. By deciding the question of same-sex marriage under the Constitution, the Court removes it from the realm of democratic decision, which will have significant consequences in the loss of respect for the Court. After all, the Court's power comes at the expense of the people's power, and the people know it. Finally, the majority needlessly sullies people of faith, who did nothing more than follow the understanding of marriage that has existed for our entire history, by characterizing them as bigoted and hurting gays and lesbians. In sum, the Constitution had nothing to do with the majority's decision.

DISSENT: (Scalia, J.) The majority's opinion is the furthest extension imaginable of the Court's power to create so-called liberties that do not exist in the Constitution. Thus, the majority usurps the power to govern, which should remain with the People and their elected officials. A system of government that makes the People subordinate to a committee of nine unelected lawyers does not deserve to be called a democracy. The Court's Justices do not represent a cross-section of America, and to let them decide the policy question of same-sex marriage violates a fundamental tenet of democracy: no social transformation without representation. The majority's opinion is both pretentious and egotistic, and lacking in logic and precision. This decision should have been left to the People. The Constitution does not remove the issue the majority now decides from the political process, and it has long been recognized that the regulation of domestic relations such as marriage is an area that is within the

Continued on next page.

exclusive province of the states. Not only does the federal government not have authority to intervene in this area, but history also indicates that at the time of the Fourteenth Amendment's ratification, every state limited marriage to one man and one woman, and no one doubted the constitutionality of doing so. Thus, as there is no constitutional basis for overturning this conception of marriage, the public debate over same-sex marriage must be allowed to continue.

DISSENT: (Thomas, J.) The doctrine of substantive due process is not defensible, but even if it were, the plaintiffs (P) have no claim here. To invoke the protection of the Due Process Clause at all—whether under a theory of "substantive" or "procedural" due process—a party must first identify a deprivation of "life, liberty, or property." The majority claims the petitioners are deprived of "liberty," but the majority's concept of liberty is not one that can be found in the Due Process Clauses. Based on the history of these Clauses, going back to the Magna Carta, "liberty" was construed to refer only to freedom from physical restraint. Even assuming "liberty" goes beyond such freedom, the American legal tradition has long understood "liberty" as individual freedom from governmental action, not as a right to a particular governmental entitlement. To the extent that the Framers would have recognized a natural right to marriage that fell within the broader definition of liberty, it would not have included a right to governmental recognition and benefits. Instead, it would have included a right to engage in the very same activities that plaintiffs (P) have been left free to engage in—making vows, holding religious ceremonies celebrating those vows, raising children, and otherwise enjoying the society of one's spouse—without governmental interference. The majority emphasizes that its decision will advance the "dignity" of same-sex couples, but the Constitution does not contain a right to dignity. Even if there were a "dignity" clause in the Constitution, the government would be unable to bestow dignity, which has long been understood to be innate. Slaves did not lose their dignity because the government allowed them to be enslaved, and, certainly same-sex couples do not lose their dignity because the government denies them certain benefits. Like liberty, dignity is to be shielded from government, not provided by it. The government cannot bestow dignity, and it cannot take it away.

DISSENT: (Alito, J.) The majority's view of marriage is not a traditional view, which rested for millennia on ideas tied to procreation. Admittedly, society's understanding of marriage is changing. However, there still are states that adhere to the traditional view of marriage and are afraid that departing from that view will erode the marriage institution. Although the views of citizens and states vary, what is clear is that it is far beyond the outer reaches of the Court's authority to say that a state may not adhere to the understanding of marriage that has long prevailed, not just in this country and others with similar cultural roots, but also in a great variety of countries and cultures all around the globe. The majority's decision usurps the constitutional right of the people to decide whether to keep or alter the traditional understanding of marriage and violates core federalism principles. The majority, by imposing its view on the entire country, and taking the issue away from democratic processes, marginalizes those Americans who have traditional ideas. In attempting to make up for the harsh treatment of gays and lesbians in the past, the majority will inflict bitter and lasting wounds on the nation.

ANALYSIS

The majority's decision will require states to issue marriage licenses to same-sex couples and to recognize same-sex marriages entered in other states largely based on a constitutional provision guaranteeing "due process" before a person is deprived of his "life, liberty, or property." The dissent characterizes this outcome as result of substantive due process, which has been discredited as permitting judges to stray from the Constitution's text, guided only by their personal views. The dissent (Thomas, J.) also views the majority's use of equal protection (which the majority indicates acts synergistically with due process) as only a means to shore up its substantive due process analysis, which the dissent claims is an analysis both based on an imaginary constitutional protection and a revisionist view of history and tradition.

Quicknotes

DUE PROCESS CLAUSE Language found in the Fifth and Fourteenth Amendments to the United States Constitution providing that no person shall be deprived of "life, liberty, or property without due process of law."

EQUAL PROTECTION CLAUSE A constitutional provision that each person be guaranteed the same protection of the laws enjoyed by other persons in like circumstances.

FOURTEENTH AMENDMENT Declares that no state shall make or enforce any law that shall abridge the privileges and immunities of citizens of the United States. No state shall deny to any person within its jurisdiction the equal protection of the laws.

JUDICIAL RESTRAINT Self-imposed discipline by judges making decision without indulging their own personal views or ideas that may not be consistent with existing law.

Bostock v. Clayton County, Georgia

Gay employee (P) v. Municipal employer (D)

140 S. Ct. 1731 (2020)

NATURE OF CASE: Appeal in action asserting that Title VII of the 1964 Civil Rights Act prohibits employment discrimination on the basis of sexual orientation and transgender status. [The procedural posture of the case is not presented in the casebook excerpt.]

FACT SUMMARY: [Employers (D) fired employees (P) merely because the employees (P) were gay or transgender. The employees (P) contended that they were discriminated against on the basis of "sex," in violation of Title VII of the 1964 Civil Rights Act.]

RULE OF LAW

Title VII of the 1964 Civil Rights Act, which prohibits employment discrimination because of an individual's "sex," also prohibits discrimination based on sexual orientation and transgender status.

FACTS: [Employers (D) fired employees (P) merely because the employees (P) were gay or transgender. In consolidated cases, the employees (P) contended that they were discriminated against on the basis of "sex," in violation of Title VII of the 1964 Civil Rights Act. The procedural posture of the case is not presented in the casebook excerpt.]

ISSUE: Does Title VII of the 1964 Civil Rights Act, which prohibits employment discrimination because of an individual's "sex," also prohibit discrimination based on sexual orientation and transgender status?

HOLDING AND DECISION: (Gorsuch, J.) Yes. Title VII of the 1964 Civil Rights Act, which prohibits employment discrimination because of an individual's "sex," also prohibits discrimination based on sexual orientation and transgender status. Title VII makes it "unlawful ... for an employer to fail or refuse to hire or to discharge any individual, or otherwise to discriminate against any individual ... because of such individual's race, color, religion, sex, or national origin." 42 U.S.C. § 2000e–2(a)(1). The straightforward application of Title VII's terms interpreted in accord with their ordinary public meaning at the time of their enactment resolves the issue presented. The parties concede that the term "sex" in 1964 referred to the biological distinctions between male and female. Also, the ordinary meaning of "because of" incorporates the but-for causation standard, which, for Title VII, means that a defendant cannot avoid liability just by citing some other factor that contributed to its challenged employment action. The term "discriminate" in 1964 meant what it means today: "[t]o make a difference in treatment or favor (of one as compared with others)." Further, the statute's repeated use of the term "individual" means that the focus is on a particular being as distinguished from a class of beings. The consequences of the law's focus on individuals rather than groups are anything but academic. The statute protects individuals of both sexes from discrimination, and does so equally, even when an employer terminates an individual in part because of sex. An individual's homosexuality or transgender status is not relevant to employment decisions. That's because it is impossible to discriminate against a person for being homosexual or transgender without discriminating against that individual based on sex. Thus, an employer violates Title VII when it intentionally fires an individual employee based in part on sex. It makes no difference if other factors besides the plaintiff's sex contributed to the decision or that the employer treated women as a group the same when compared to men as a group. A statutory violation occurs if an employer intentionally relies in part on an individual employee's sex when deciding to discharge the employee. Because discrimination on the basis of homosexuality or transgender status requires an employer to intentionally treat individual employees differently because of their sex, an employer who intentionally penalizes an employee for being homosexual or transgender also violates Title VII. There is no escaping the role intent plays: Just as sex is necessarily a but-for cause when an employer discriminates against homosexual or transgender employees, an employer who discriminates on these grounds inescapably intends to rely on sex in its decisionmaking; it is irrelevant what an employer might call its discriminatory practice, how others might label it, or what else might motivate it. The plaintiff's sex need not be the sole or primary cause of the employer's adverse action, and it is of no significance if another factor, such as the plaintiff's attraction to the same sex or presentation as a different sex from the one assigned at birth, might also be at work, or even play a more important role in the employer's decision. Finally, an employer cannot escape liability by demonstrating that it treats males and females comparably as groups. An employer who intentionally fires an individual homosexual or transgender employee in part because of that individual's sex violates the law even if the employer is willing to subject all male and female homosexual or transgender employees to the same rule. The employers (D) emphasize that homosexuality and transgender status are distinct concepts from sex, and that if Congress wanted to address these matters in Title VII, it would have

Continued on next page.

referenced them specifically. However, when Congress chooses not to include any exceptions to a broad rule, the Court applies the broad rule. For example, although "sexual harassment" is conceptually distinct from sex discrimination, it nonetheless falls within Title VII's sweep. The employers (D) also observe that since 1964, Congress has considered several proposals to add sexual orientation to Title VII's list of protected characteristics, but no such amendment has become law, even though Congress has enacted other statutes addressing other topics that do discuss sexual orientation. From this the employers would have the Court infer that Congress meant to exclude sexual orientation and transgender status from Title VII. However, no such inference can be made, because there is no authoritative evidence explaining why later Congresses adopted other laws referencing sexual orientation but didn't amend Title VII. Speculation about why a later Congress declined to adopt new legislation offers a "particularly dangerous" basis on which to rest an interpretation of an existing law a different and earlier Congress did adopt. The employers (D) additionally contend that few in 1964 would have expected Title VII to apply to discrimination against homosexual and transgender persons. However, resort to legislative history has no bearing here, where no ambiguity exists about how Title VII's terms apply to the facts. The Court has repeatedly explained that when the meaning of a statute's terms is plain, legislative history is superfluous. Instead, legislative history can be useful to clear up ambiguous terms. Although legislative history can never defeat unambiguous statutory text, historical sources can be useful shed light on whether a law's ordinary meaning at the time of enactment has taken on new meaning with the passage of time. To ferret out such shifts in linguistic usage or subtle distinctions between literal and ordinary meaning, the Court has sometimes consulted the understandings of the law's drafters as some (not always conclusive) evidence. Although it is possible that a statutory term that means one thing today or in one context might have meant something else at the time of its adoption or might mean something different in another context, the employers (D) do not seek to use historical sources to illustrate that the meaning of any of Title VII's language has changed since 1964 or that the statute's terms ordinarily carried some missed message. Rather than suggesting that the statutory language bears some other meaning, the employers (D) (and dissents) merely suggest that, because few in 1964 expected today's result, the Court should not dare to admit that it follows ineluctably from the statutory text. To take such an approach, and to refuse enforcement just because the parties before the Court happened to be unpopular at the time of the law's passage, would not only require the Court to abandon its role as an interpreter of statutes, it would tilt the scales of justice in favor of the strong or popular and neglect the promise that all persons are entitled to the benefit of the law's terms. Moreover, if the Court applied the statute's plain text only to applications expected when it was passed in 1964, many, if not most, of the applications made since then would have to be overturned. In fact, many now-obvious applications met with heated opposition early on, even among those tasked with enforcing the law. Over time, the breadth of Title VII's language has been applied to many situations that could not have been expected in 1964. Those applications now are accepted, and are no longer sought to be overturned. On separate grounds, the employers (D) express their fear that complying with Title VII's requirements may require some employers to violate their religious convictions. While free exercise of religion is a significant constitutional concern, that is not before the Court, since none of the employers (D) has represented that compliance with Title VII will infringe their religious liberties in any way. In sum, the language of Title VII is broad, and an employer who fires an individual merely for being gay or transgender defies the law.

DISSENT: (Alito, J.) The Court abuses its authority to interpret statutes, and instead engages in full-blown legislating, since it is preposterous to say that discrimination because of "sex" is discrimination because of "sexual orientation" or "gender identity," even today. Certainly, it is extremely doubtful anyone in 1964 would have thought so—the concept of "gender identity" was essentially unknown at the time. Title VII covers biological sex, not the sex to which one is attracted or identifies with. According to the majority, Title VII is unambiguous, but until 2017, every Court of Appeals to consider the question interpreted Title VII as prohibiting discrimination on account of biological sex, as did the Equal Employment Opportunity Commission (EEOC). "Sex," "sexual orientation," and "gender identity" are different concepts, as the majority concedes, and neither "sexual orientation" nor "gender identity" is tied to either of the two biological sexes. It is quite possible for an employer to discriminate on those grounds without taking the sex of an individual applicant or employee into account. An employer can have a policy that says: "We do not hire gays, lesbians, or transgender individuals," and an employer can implement this policy without paying any attention to or even knowing the biological sex of gay, lesbian, and transgender applicants. It is painful to be reminded of the way our society once treated gays and lesbians, but any honest effort to understand what the terms of Title VII were understood to mean when enacted must take into account the societal norms of that time. The plain truth is that in 1964 homosexuality was thought to be a mental disorder, and homosexual conduct was regarded as morally culpable and worthy of punishment. To its credit, our

Continued on next page.

society has now come to recognize the injustice of past practices, and this recognition provides the impetus to "update" Title VII. However, that is not the Court's job. The Court must limit itself to understanding what the terms of Title VII meant when it was enacted, taking into account the societal norms of that time.

DISSENT: (Kavanagh, J.) First, the question of whether Title VII should be expanded to encompass employment discrimination because of sexual orientation is one for Congress and the President, exercising their legislative powers. Second, even assuming that discrimination on the basis of sexual orientation entails making a distinction on the basis of sex, a plaintiff must show either that courts interpret statutes literally, rather than using ordinary meanings of words, or that the ordinary meaning of "discriminate because of sex" encompasses sexual orientation discrimination. Here, the plaintiffs cannot satisfy either of these alternatives. Courts must follow the ordinary meaning of words and phrases in statutes so that those words and phrases will be understandable to everybody for purposes of the rule of law and democratic accountability. Also, the ordinary meaning of the phrase "discriminate because of sex" does not encompasses sexual orientation discrimination. Both common parlance and legal usage treated sex discrimination and sexual orientation discrimination as two distinct categories in 1964, and that is still true today. By treating the two distinct harms as one, the majority "misapprehends common language, human psychology, and real life," and it also rewrites history. The women's rights movement and the gay rights movement are distinct and separate. Federal law reflects these separate categories of discrimination. Many federal statutes prohibit sex discrimination, and many federal statutes also prohibit sexual orientation discrimination. However, those sexual orientation statutes expressly prohibit sexual orientation discrimination in addition to expressly prohibiting sex discrimination. Congress has never defined sex discrimination to encompass sexual orientation discrimination. Instead, when Congress wants to prohibit sexual orientation discrimination in addition to sex discrimination, Congress explicitly refers to sexual orientation discrimination. Contrary to longstanding practice, the majority usurps the role of Congress, which likely will lead to confusion and cynicism in the public, as it may lead the public to believe that judges make policy and use their personal preferences to do so. That is why it is crucial for judges to decide cases on the ordinary meaning of statutes. Notwithstanding the majority's transgression of the separation of powers, the victory achieved by gay and lesbian Americans through the majority's usurpation of power needs to be acknowledged. These Americans have endured unequal treatment in fact and in law and have worked very hard for equality. They can take pride in today's result, which no doubt is an outcome of that hard work and advancement of powerful arguments.

ANALYSIS

Despite the important differences between the Fourteenth Amendment's Equal Protection Clause and Title VII, the Court's decision may have the effect of influencing cases brought under the Equal Protection Clause. Under the Court's precedents, the Equal Protection Clause prohibits sex-based discrimination unless a "heightened" standard of review is met. *Sessions v. Morales-Santana,* 137 S. Ct. 1678 (2017). By equating discrimination because of sexual orientation or gender identity with discrimination because of sex, the Court's decision likely will be cited as a ground for subjecting not only discrimination based on biological sex, but also sexual orientation and gender identity discrimination, to the same exacting standard of heightened review. Thus, the Court's decision may have effects that extend beyond the domain of federal antidiscrimination statutes.

Quicknotes

EQUAL EMPLOYMENT OPPORTUNITY COMMISSION Created by Title VII of the Civil Rights Act of 1964, its purpose is to end employment discrimination based on race, color, religion, age, sex, or national origin.

EQUAL PROTECTION CLAUSE A constitutional provision that each person be guaranteed the same protection of the laws enjoyed by other persons in like circumstances.

FOURTEENTH AMENDMENT Declares that no state shall make or enforce any law that shall abridge the privileges and immunities of citizens of the United States. No state shall deny to any person within its jurisdiction the equal protection of the laws.

TITLE VII OF THE CIVIL RIGHTS ACT OF 1964 States that it shall be an unlawful employment practice for an employer to fail or refuse to hire or otherwise discriminate against any individual with respect to his employment because of such individual's race, color, religion, sex, or national origin.

Masterpiece Cakeshop, Ltd. v. Colorado Civil Rights Commission

Bakery (D) v. State civil rights commission (P)

138 S. Ct. 1719 (2018)

NATURE OF CASE: Appeal, on First Amendment free speech and free exercise of religious grounds, from affirmance by state's intermediate appellate court of state civil rights commission determination that a public accommodation establishment discriminated unlawfully on the basis of sexual orientation, and of the commission's enforcement and remedial orders to cease and desist from continuing such discrimination.

FACT SUMMARY: After Phillips (D), the owner of a bakery, refused to bake a wedding cake for a homosexual couple, on the grounds that he was religiously opposed to gay marriage, he was found to have violated the state's anti-discrimination act and ordered to cease and desist from such discrimination. Phillips (D) contended that the order violated his First Amendment rights of freedom of speech and free exercise of religion.

RULE OF LAW

Where a government entity tasked with enforcing anti-discrimination laws seems to be hostile to a business owner's defense to an unlawful discrimination charge that is based on the owner's religious beliefs, the entity violates the owner's First Amendment free exercise of religion rights to a neutral decisionmaker that would give full and fair consideration to his religious defense, notwithstanding that the entity's rulings and orders are subsequently affirmed by a neutral court of law.

FACTS: Jack Phillips (D) owned and operated a Colorado bakery. In 2012 he told a same-sex couple, Charlie Craig and Dave Mullins, that he would not create a cake for their wedding celebration because of his religious opposition to same-sex marriages—marriages that Colorado (P) did not then recognize—but that he would sell them other baked goods, e.g., birthday cakes. The couple filed a charge with the Colorado Civil Rights Commission (the Commission) (P) pursuant to the Colorado Anti-Discrimination Act (CADA), which prohibits certain kinds of discrimination, including discrimination based on sexual orientation, in a place of business engaged in any sales to the public and any place offering services to the public. State law at the time also afforded storekeepers some latitude to decline to create specific messages they considered offensive. Indeed, while the instant enforcement proceedings were pending, the Colorado Civil Rights Division concluded in at least three cases that a baker acted lawfully in declining to create cakes with decorations that demeaned gay persons or gay marriages. Under CADA's administrative review system, the Colorado Civil Rights Division first found probable cause for a violation and referred the case to the Commission. The Commission then referred the case for a formal hearing before a state Administrative Law Judge, who ruled in the couple's favor. Both the Commission and the Colorado Court of Appeals affirmed. Phillips (D) appealed to the Supreme Court, asserting that the enforcement order in the case, which required him to cease and desist from discriminating against homosexuals in his business, as well as to engage in various remedial measures, violated his First Amendment rights of free speech and free exercise of religion. The Supreme Court granted certiorari.

ISSUE: Where a government entity tasked with enforcing anti-discrimination laws seems to be hostile to a business owner's defense to an unlawful discrimination charge that is based on the owner's religious beliefs, does the entity violate the owner's First Amendment free exercise of religion rights to a neutral decisionmaker that would give full and fair consideration to his religious defense, notwithstanding that the entity's rulings and orders are subsequently affirmed by a neutral court of law?

HOLDING AND DECISION: (Kennedy, J.) Yes. Where a government entity tasked with enforcing anti-discrimination laws seems to be hostile to a business owner's defense to an unlawful discrimination charge that is based on the owner's religious beliefs, the entity violates the owner's First Amendment free exercise of religion rights to a neutral decisionmaker that would give full and fair consideration to his religious defense, notwithstanding that the entity's rulings and orders are subsequently affirmed by a neutral court of law. The laws and the Constitution can, and in some instances must, protect gay persons and gay couples in the exercise of their civil rights, but religious and philosophical objections to gay marriage are protected views, and in some instances, protected forms of expression. While it is unexceptional that Colorado (P) law can protect gay persons in acquiring products and services on the same terms and conditions as are offered to other members of the public, the law must be applied in a manner that is neutral toward religion. To Phillips (D), his claim that using his artistic skills to make an expressive statement—a wedding endorsement in his own voice and of his own creation—has a significant First Amendment speech component and implicates his deep and sincere religious

Continued on next page.

beliefs. His dilemma was understandable in 2012, which was before Colorado (P) recognized the validity of gay marriages. Given Colorado's (P) position at the time, there is some force to Phillips's (D) argument that he was not unreasonable in deeming his decision lawful. State law at the time also afforded storekeepers some latitude to decline to create specific messages they considered offensive. Phillips (D) was entitled to a neutral and respectful consideration of his claims in all the circumstances of the case. That consideration was compromised, however, by the Colorado Civil Rights Commission's (the Commission's) treatment of Phillips's (D) case, which showed elements of a clear and impermissible hostility toward the sincere religious beliefs motivating his objection. As the record shows, some of the commissioners at the Commission's formal public hearings endorsed the view that religious beliefs cannot legitimately be carried into the public sphere or commercial domain, disparaged Phillips's (D) faith as despicable and characterized it as merely rhetorical, and compared his invocation of his sincerely held religious beliefs to defenses of slavery and the Holocaust. No commissioners objected to the comments. Nor were they mentioned in the later state-court ruling or disavowed in the briefs filed here. The comments thus cast doubt on the fairness and impartiality of the Commission's adjudication of Phillips's (D) case. Another indication of hostility is the different treatment of Phillips's (D) case and the cases of other bakers with objections to anti-gay messages who prevailed before the Commission. The Commission ruled against Phillips (D) in part on the theory that any message on the requested wedding cake would be attributed to the customer, not to the baker. Yet the Colorado Civil Rights Division (Division) did not address this point in any of the cases involving requests for cakes depicting anti-gay marriage symbolism. The Division also considered that each bakery was willing to sell other products to the prospective customers, but the Commission found Phillips's (D) willingness to do the same irrelevant. For these reasons, the Commission's treatment of Phillips's (D) case violated the State's (P) duty under the First Amendment not to base laws or regulations on hostility to a religion or religious viewpoint. The government, consistent with the Constitution's guarantee of free exercise, cannot impose regulations that are hostile to the religious beliefs of affected citizens and cannot act in a manner that passes judgment upon or presupposes the illegitimacy of religious beliefs and practices. Factors relevant to the assessment of governmental neutrality include the historical background of the decision under challenge, the specific series of events leading to the enactment or official policy in question, and the legislative or administrative history, including contemporaneous statements made by members of the decisionmaking body. In view of these factors, the record here demonstrates that the Commission's consideration of Phillips's (D) case was neither tolerant nor respectful of his religious beliefs. The Commission gave every appearance of adjudicating his religious objection based on a negative normative evaluation of the particular justification for his objection and the religious grounds for it, but government has no role in expressing or even suggesting whether the religious ground for Phillips's (D) conscience-based objection is legitimate or illegitimate. The inference here is thus that Phillips's religious objection was not considered with the neutrality required by the Free Exercise Clause. The State's (P) interest could have been weighed against Phillips's (D) sincere religious objections in a way consistent with the requisite religious neutrality that must be strictly observed. [Reversed.]

CONCURRENCE: (Gorsuch, J.) When government does not act with neutrality toward the free exercise of religion, it must satisfy strict scrutiny, showing that its restrictions on religion both serve a compelling interest and are narrowly tailored. The Court's decision respects this principle. The judgmental dismissal of a sincerely held religious belief is antithetical to the First Amendment and cannot satisfy strict scrutiny.

CONCURRENCE: (Thomas, J.) Although the Court correctly determined that the Commission violated Phillips's (D) right to freely exercise his religion, it failed to address his free-speech claim. Here, Phillips's (D) cakes were expressive, akin to works of art, and he typically interacted with his clients to create custom wedding cakes to ensure that each cake reflected the couple that ordered it. To Phillips (D), a wedding cake communicates that the couple should be celebrated. Indeed, historically, wedding cakes have been full of symbolism and communicate the celebration of a marriage. By forcing Phillips (D) to create custom wedding cakes for same-sex weddings, Colorado's (P) public-accommodations law alters the expressive content of his message. Forcing Phillips (D) to make custom wedding cakes for same-sex marriages requires him to, at the very least, acknowledge that same-sex weddings are "weddings" and suggest that they should be celebrated—the precise message he believes his faith forbids. The First Amendment right of free speech prohibits the government from forcing such speech.

DISSENT: (Ginsburg, J.) The majority is correct that religious and philosophical objections do not allow business owners and other actors in the economy and in society to deny protected persons equal access to goods and services under a neutral and generally applicable public accommodations law. The majority is also correct when it says that gay persons must be spared from indignities when they seek goods and services in an open market. These pronouncements, however, should have

Continued on next page.

led to a different outcome. The majority's finding that the Commission was hostile to Phillips's (D) religious beliefs is in part based on the Commission's not finding that other bakers did not discriminate on the basis of religion when they refused to create cakes that had messages demeaning to gays. These cases, however, are hardly comparable. The three bakers would have refused to make a cake with the requested demeaning message for any customer, regardless of the customer's religion, and they would have sold the requester any baked goods they would have sold anyone else. The bakeries' refusal to make demeaning cakes of a kind they would not make for any customer scarcely resembles Phillips's (D) refusal to serve Craig and Mullins, for no reason other than their sexual orientation, a cake of the kind he regularly sold to others. When a couple contacts a bakery for a wedding cake, the product the couple is seeking is a cake celebrating their wedding—not a cake celebrating heterosexual weddings or same-sex weddings—and that is the service Craig and Mullins were denied. Colorado (P), the majority does not gainsay, prohibits precisely the discrimination Craig and Mullins encountered. The requester of demeaning cakes, on the other hand, suffered no service refusal on basis of his religion or any other protected characteristic. He was treated as any other customer would have been treated—no better, no worse. The fact that Phillips (D) might sell other cakes and cookies to gay and lesbian customers was irrelevant to the issue Craig and Mullins's case presented. What matters is that Phillips (D) would not provide a good or service to a same-sex couple that he would provide to a heterosexual couple. In contrast, the other bakeries' sale of other goods to Christian customers was relevant: it showed that there were no goods the bakeries would sell to a non-Christian customer that they would refuse to sell to a Christian customer. Further, the statements made by commissioners at the public hearings, regardless of how one views them in historical context, should not be taken to overcome Phillips's (D) refusal to sell a cake to a homosexual couple. The proceedings involved several layers of independent decisionmaking, of which the Commission was but one. First, the Division had to find probable cause that Phillips (D) violated the Colorado Anti-Discrimination Act. Second, the Administrative Law Judge entertained the parties' cross-motions for summary judgment. Third, the Commission heard Phillips's (D) appeal. Fourth, after the Commission's ruling, the Colorado Court of Appeals considered the case de novo. What prejudice infected the determinations of the adjudicators in the case before and after the Commission? The Court does not say. Phillips's (D) case is thus far removed from the only precedent upon which the Court relies, where the government action that violated a principle of religious neutrality implicated a sole decisionmaking body, the city council.

ANALYSIS

Because the Court based its decision on its finding of hostility to Phillips's (D) religious views by the Commission, it left open the issue of whether the First Amendment's free speech or free exercise of religion rights would be violated by requiring a business to serve people on the basis of their sexual orientation or identification in contravention of the business owner's religious beliefs. Justice Thomas, in his concurrence, specifically addresses this issue, concluding that, at least where the product or service at issue can be construed as expressive, compelling the business to provide that product or service against the owner's religious beliefs would indeed violate the First Amendment's free speech protections.

Quicknotes

COMPELLING INTEREST TEST A standard employed by the court under strict scrutiny review to determine the constitutionality of a statute, whereby the proponent of the statute must demonstrate that classifications drawn therein serve a compelling interest and are necessary for the furtherance of a state objective.

DE NOVO The review of a lower court decision by an appellate court, which is hearing the case as if it had not been previously heard and as if no judgment had been rendered.

STRICT SCRUTINY Method by which courts determine the constitutionality of a law when a law affects a fundamental right; under the test, the legislature must have had a compelling interest to enact the law, and measures prescribed by the law must be the least restrictive means possible to accomplish its goal.

Fulton v. City of Philadelphia

Foster care parent (P) v. Municipality (D)

141 S. Ct. 1868 (2021)

NATURE OF CASE: Appeal in action challenging as violating the Free Exercise Clause of the First Amendment a municipality's refusal to contract with a religiously affiliated foster agency for the provision of foster care services unless the agency agreed to certify same-sex couples as foster parents. [The procedural posture of the case is not presented in the casebook excerpt.]

FACT SUMMARY: Philadelphia (the City) (D), which contracted with private foster care agencies to place children with foster families, refused to contract with Catholic Social Services (CSS) (P), a foster care agency, unless CSS (P) agreed to certify same-sex couples as foster parents. CSS (P) and foster care parents (P) to which CSS (P) made referrals, contended that Philadelphia's (D) refusal violated the Free Exercise Clause of the First Amendment.

RULE OF LAW

Where a municipality refuses to grant an exemption from the municipality's antidiscrimination policy to a religiously affiliated contractor that provides services to residents and that objects to the policy on religious grounds, the municipality violates the Free Exercise Clause of the First Amendment.

FACTS: Philadelphia's (the City's) (D) foster care system relies on cooperation between the City (D) and private foster care agencies. The City (D) enters standard annual contracts with the agencies to place children with foster families. One of the responsibilities of the agencies is certifying prospective foster families under state statutory criteria. Catholic Social Services (CSS) (P) had contracted with the City (D) to provide foster care services for over 50 years. Because CSS (P) believes that certification of a prospective foster family is an endorsement of the family's relationship, it will not certify unmarried couples—regardless of their sexual orientation—or same-sex married couples, because it is a tenet of the Catholic religion that marriage is a sacred bond between a man and a woman. However, other private foster agencies in Philadelphia (D) certified same-sex couples, and no same-sex couple had sought certification from CSS (P). Following an investigation into CSS's (P) practices, the City (D) informed CSS (P) that unless it agreed to certify same-sex couples the City (D) would no longer refer children to the agency or enter a full foster care contract with it in the future. The City (D) explained that the refusal of CSS (P) to certify same-sex couples violated both a nondiscrimination provision in the agency's contract with the City (D) as well as the nondiscrimination requirements of the citywide Fair Practices Ordinance (FPO). Section 3.21 of the contract required an agency to provide services defined in the contract to prospective foster parents without regard to their sexual orientation. That section also permitted exceptions to this requirement at the "sole discretion" of a City (D) official (the Commissioner). CSS (P) and affiliated foster parents (P) filed suit seeking to enjoin the City's (D) referral freeze on the grounds that the City's (D) actions violated the Free Exercise and Free Speech Clauses of the First Amendment. The United States Supreme Court granted certiorari in the case. [The procedural posture of the case is not presented in the casebook excerpt.]

ISSUE: Where a municipality refuses to grant an exemption from the municipality's antidiscrimination policy to a religiously affiliated contractor that provides services to residents and that objects to the policy on religious grounds, does the municipality violate the Free Exercise Clause of the First Amendment?

HOLDING AND DECISION: (Roberts, C.J.) Yes. Where a municipality refuses to grant an exemption from the municipality's antidiscrimination policy to a religiously affiliated contractor that provides services to residents and that objects to the policy on religious grounds, the municipality violates the Free Exercise Clause of the First Amendment. In *Employment Div., Dept. of Human Resources of Ore. v. Smith,* 494 U.S. 872 (1990), the Court held that laws incidentally burdening religion are ordinarily not subject to strict scrutiny under the Free Exercise Clause so long as they are both neutral and generally applicable. This case falls outside *Smith* because the City (D) has burdened CSS's (P) religious exercise through policies that do not satisfy the threshold requirement of being neutral and generally applicable. A law is not generally applicable if it invites the government to consider the particular reasons for a person's conduct by creating a mechanism for individualized exemptions. Where such a system of individual exemptions exists, the government may not refuse to extend that system to cases of religious hardship without a compelling reason. Additionally, a law lacks general applicability if it prohibits religious conduct while permitting secular conduct that undermines the government's asserted interests in a similar way. Here, the nondiscrimination requirement of the City's (D) standard foster care contract is not generally applicable because § 3.21 of the contract includes a

Continued on next page.

mechanism for entirely discretionary exceptions by the Commissioner, and this renders the nondiscrimination provision not generally applicable. The City (D) maintains that greater deference should apply to its managerial treatment of private contractors than when it regulates the general public, but the result here is the same under any level of deference precisely because the inclusion of a formal system of entirely discretionary exceptions in § 3.21 renders the contractual nondiscrimination requirement not generally applicable. Similarly unavailing is the City's (D) contention that the availability of exceptions under § 3.21 is irrelevant because the Commissioner has never granted one. That misapprehends the issue. The creation of a formal mechanism for granting exceptions renders a policy not generally applicable, regardless whether any exceptions have been given, because it permits the government to decide which reasons for not complying with the policy are worthy, which, again, renders the policy not generally applicable. The City (D) also contends that foster care agencies are public accommodations for purposes of the citywide FPO and, therefore, are forbidden from discriminating on the basis of sexual orientation when certifying foster parents. However, foster care agencies are not public accommodations under state law, and certification as a foster parent is not readily accessible to the public. The contractual nondiscrimination requirement burdens CSS's religious exercise and is not generally applicable, so it is subject to heightened strict scrutiny, which a government policy can survive only if it advances compelling interests and is narrowly tailored to achieve those interests. The City (D) asserts that its nondiscrimination policies serve three compelling interests: maximizing the number of foster parents, protecting the City (D) from liability, and ensuring equal treatment of prospective foster parents and foster children. The City (D) states these objectives at a high level of generality, but the First Amendment demands a more precise analysis. The question is not whether the City (D) has a compelling interest in enforcing its nondiscrimination policies generally, but whether it has such an interest in denying an exception to CSS (P). Maximizing the number of foster families and minimizing liability are important goals, but the City (D) fails to show that granting CSS an exception will put those goals at risk. Although the interest of the City (D) in the equal treatment of prospective foster parents and foster children is a weighty one, the creation of a system of exceptions under the contract undermines the City's (D) contention that its nondiscrimination policies can brook no departures. Under the circumstances here, the City (D) does not have a compelling interest in refusing to contract with CSS (P), which seeks only an accommodation that will allow it to continue serving the children of Philadelphia (D) in a manner consistent with its religious beliefs; it does not seek to impose those beliefs on anyone else. The refusal of the City (D) to contract with CSS (P) for the provision of foster care services unless the agency agrees to certify same-sex couples as foster parents, therefore, cannot survive strict scrutiny and violates the Free Exercise Clause of the First Amendment.

CONCURRENCE: (Barrett, J.) Textual and structural arguments against retaining *Smith* are compelling, but there is no clear answer as to what standards should replace those announced in *Smith*. One flawed possibility is a categorical rule that strict scrutiny should apply whenever a neutral and generally applicable law burdens religious exercise. The approach adopted should be more nuanced, as it is when the Court confronts conflicts between generally applicable laws and other First Amendment rights, like speech and assembly. Some questions that would need to be resolved include whether an arm of a religious organization, such as CSS (P) here, should be treated differently than individuals; whether there should be a distinction between indirect and direct burdens on religious exercise, and what forms of scrutiny should be applied. Those questions need not be addressed here because the law at issue cannot in any event satisfy strict scrutiny, which is applied to laws that burden religious exercise and give government officials discretion to grant individualized exemptions.

CONCURRENCE: (Alito, J.) *Smith* was wrongly decided and should be overruled. It should be replaced by strict scrutiny review for any law that imposes a substantial burden on religious exercise. However, whether that test should be fine-tuned is not an issue that requires resolution in this case because the actions taken by the City (D) do not further any interest that can properly be protected. Protection from CSS's (P) policy, which to some is offensive and hurtful, is not an interest that can justify the abridgment of the free exercise of religion. The same principles apply in free speech cases. In an open, pluralistic, self-governing society, the expression of an idea cannot be suppressed simply because some find it offensive, insulting, or even wounding. The same principle applies to religious practices that give offense; the preservation of religious depends on it. An open society should respect the dignity, worth, and fundamental equality of all its members.

CONCURRENCE: (Gorsuch, J.) The Court should have overruled *Smith* and replaced it with a rule that requires strict scrutiny review for any law that imposes a substantial burden on religious exercise. That would have ended potential litigation for CSS (P). Instead, it is quite possible that it is only the beginning of litigation for CSS (P), if CSS (P) wants to pursue providing child fostering services in Philadelphia (D) without forfeiting its truly held religious beliefs. The Pennsylvania Supreme

Continued on next page.

Court can effectively overrule the majority's reading of the Commonwealth's public accommodations law; the City (D) can revise its FPO to make even plainer still that its law does encompass foster services; or, municipal lawyers can rewrite the City's (D) contract to close the § 3.21 loophole. This lack of definitive legal resolution for CSS (P) is a result of the majority's reluctance to overrule and replace *Smith.* Those who cannot afford endless litigation engendered by *Smith's* regime will continue to be forced to forfeit religious freedom protected by the Constitution, and there is no possible benefit that can arise from the majority's indecision about *Smith. Smith* was wrongly decided, and only the Court can fix its error. It should have done so in this case.

ANALYSIS

Because this decision was narrowly decided on the basis of the exemption language in Philadelphia's (D) foster care contract, it would likely not apply to a government regulation that lacks such an exemption. Nevertheless, the decision can be viewed as permitting those holding certain religious beliefs to opt out of nondiscrimination requirements when their discrimination arises from those beliefs. On the other hand, it can also be viewed as promoting religious liberty and prohibiting government discrimination against religious groups. Regardless of the view taken, it is clear that the decision does not announce broad constitutional principles.

Quicknotes

FIRST AMENDMENT Prohibits Congress from enacting any law respecting an establishment of religion or prohibiting the free exercise of religion; abridging freedom of speech or of the press; the right of peaceful assembly; and the right to petition for a redress of grievances.

FREE EXERCISE CLAUSE The guarantee of the First Amendment to the United States Constitution prohibiting Congress from enacting laws regarding the establishment of religion or prohibiting the free exercise thereof.

STRICT SCRUTINY Method by which courts determine the constitutionality of a law when a law affects a fundamental right; under the test, the legislature must have had a compelling interest to enact the law and measures prescribed by the law must be the least restrictive means possible to accomplish its goal.

District of Columbia v. Heller

Federal district/city (D) v. Handgun registration applicant (P)

554 U.S. 570 (2008)

NATURE OF CASE: Appeal from reversal of dismissal of a constitutional challenge to a city's gun regulations.

FACT SUMMARY: The District of Columbia (D) contended that its general ban on the possession and registration of handguns, its prohibition on the possession of usable handguns in the home, and its requirement that lawfully owned firearms (such as long guns) be kept unloaded and disassembled or bound by a trigger lock or similar device in a residence, did not violate the Second Amendment.

RULE OF LAW

The Second Amendment protects an individual's right to possess a firearm unconnected with service in a militia, and to use that arm for traditionally lawful purposes, such as self-defense within the home.

FACTS: The District of Columbia (the District) (D) bans handgun possession by making it a crime to carry an unregistered firearm and prohibiting the registration of handguns and requires residents to keep lawfully owned firearms (such as long guns) unloaded and disassembled or bound by a trigger lock or similar device. Heller (P), a District (D) special policeman, applied to register a handgun he wished to keep at home, but the District (D) refused. He filed suit seeking, on Second Amendment grounds, to enjoin the city from enforcing the bar on handgun registration, the licensing requirement insofar as it prohibits carrying an unlicensed firearm in the home, and the trigger-lock requirement insofar as it prohibits the use of functional firearms in the home. The district court dismissed the suit, but the court of appeals reversed, holding that the Second Amendment protects an individual's right to possess firearms and that the city's total ban on handguns, as well as its requirement that firearms in the home be kept nonfunctional even when necessary for self-defense, violated that right. The United States Supreme Court granted certiorari.

ISSUE: Does the Second Amendment protect an individual's right to possess a firearm unconnected with service in a militia, and to use that arm for traditionally lawful purposes, such as self-defense within the home?

HOLDING AND DECISION: (Scalia, J.) Yes. The Second Amendment protects an individual's right to possess a firearm unconnected with service in a militia, and to use that arm for traditionally lawful purposes, such as self-defense within the home. The District (D) argues that the Second Amendment protects only the right to possess and carry a firearm in connection with militia service, whereas Heller (P) claims that the right to carry a firearm is unconnected with militia service and protects use for traditionally lawful purposes, such as self-defense within the home. The Amendment is divided into its prefatory clause and operative clause. The prefatory clause announces a purpose but does not limit or expand the scope of the second part, the operative clause. The operative clause's text and history demonstrate that it connotes an individual right to keep and bear arms. The first salient feature of the operative clause is that it codifies a "right of the people." Based on other provisions of the Constitution, this right is an individual, rather than collective, right. This contrasts markedly with the phrase "militia" in the prefatory clause, which identifies a class that is a subset of "the people." That subset was comprised of able bodied males of a certain age. Thus, reading the Second Amendment as protecting only the right to "keep and bear Arms" in an organized militia therefore fits poorly with the operative clause's description of the holder of that right as "the people." The right protected by the Amendment is therefore exercised individually and belongs to all Americans. The terms "Arms" refers to weapons not specifically designed for military use but that could assist with self-defense. To "keep and bear Arms" means to possess and carry weapons for purpose of being armed and ready. The meaning in no way connotes participation in a structured military organization. Contrary to the dissent's opinion, no dictionary has ever adopted a definition of "bear arms" that connotes the carrying of arms only in the service of an organized militia. Under such an idiomatic interpretation, the Second Amendment would protect only the right to be a soldier and wage war. The Amendment's historical background confirms that it was intended to protect the individual right to possess and carry weapons in case of confrontation. The Second Amendment codified existing rights—which had nothing to do with service in the militia and permitted Englishmen to never be disarmed. The prefatory clause comports with this interpretation of the operative clause. The "militia" comprised all males physically capable of acting in concert for the common defense. Congress had the power to create an army, but the militia was already in existence. The power to organize it was the power to order it, not to create it. The Antifederalists feared that the federal government would disarm the people in order to disable this citizens' militia, enabling a politicized standing

Continued on next page.

army or a select militia to rule. The response was to deny Congress power to abridge the ancient right of individuals to keep and bear arms, so that the ideal of a citizens' militia would be preserved. If merely an organized militia was intended to be the sole institutional beneficiary of the Second Amendment's guarantee, that would not assure the existence of a "citizens' militia" as a safeguard against tyranny. This interpretation is supported by analogous arms-bearing rights in state constitutions that preceded and immediately followed the Second Amendment. The next step is to determine whether any of the Court's precedents foreclose the conclusions reached thus far. None of the Court's precedents refute the individual-rights interpretation or limit the right to keep and bear arms to militia purposes. Instead, some of those cases limit the type of weapon to which the right applies to those used by the militia, i.e., those in common use for lawful purposes. Like most rights, the Second Amendment right is not unlimited. It is not a right to keep and carry any weapon whatsoever in any manner whatsoever and for whatever purpose: For example, concealed weapons prohibitions have been upheld under the Amendment or state analogues. The Court's opinion should not be taken to cast doubt on longstanding prohibitions on the possession of firearms by felons and the mentally ill, or laws forbidding the carrying of firearms in sensitive places such as schools and government buildings, or laws imposing conditions and qualifications on the commercial sale of arms. The Court's precedent, holding that the sorts of weapons protected are those "in common use at the time," finds support in the historical tradition of prohibiting the carrying of dangerous and unusual weapons. Applying these principles to the case at bar requires the conclusion that the handgun ban and the trigger-lock requirement (as applied to self-defense) violate the Second Amendment. The District's (D) total ban on handgun possession in the home amounts to a prohibition on an entire class of "arms" that Americans overwhelmingly choose for the lawful purpose of self-defense. Under any of the standards of scrutiny the Court has applied to enumerated constitutional rights, this prohibition—in the place where the importance of the lawful defense of self, family, and property is most acute—would fail constitutional muster. Similarly, the requirement that any lawful firearm in the home be disassembled or bound by a trigger lock makes it impossible for citizens to use arms for the core lawful purpose of self-defense and is hence unconstitutional. Because Heller (P) conceded at oral argument that the District (D) licensing law is permissible if it is not enforced arbitrarily and capriciously, the Court assumes that a license will satisfy his prayer for relief and does not address the licensing requirement. Assuming he is not disqualified from exercising Second Amendment rights, the District (D) must permit Heller (P) to register his handgun and must issue him a license to carry it in the home. Affirmed.

DISSENT: (Stevens, J.) The issue presented by this case is not whether the right protected by the Second Amendment is an individual right, but rather, what the scope of that right is, and whether the Amendment protects the right to possess and use weapons for nonmilitary purposes. The Amendment's history indicates that it was intended to protect state militias, not to enshrine the common-law right of self-defense. The Court's precedent, requiring that the possession of a weapon have a reasonable relationship to the preservation of a militia, is the most natural reading of the Amendment's text and the interpretation most faithful to history. The Amendment's preamble makes clear that it is intended to preserve the militia. The majority overlooks that the Framers used "the people" to refer back to the object announced in the preamble. Those words mean that it is the collective action of individuals having a duty to serve in the militia that the text directly protects. The words: "To keep and bear Arms" refer to the unitary right to possess arms if needed for military purposes and to use them in conjunction with military activities. Different language would have been used to protect nonmilitary use and possession of weapons. Contrary to the majority's position, there is no language in the Amendment that is intended to protect the right of law-abiding citizens to protect themselves in their homes.

DISSENT: (Breyer, J.) The District's (D) regulation of handguns and weapons is consistent with the Second Amendment, even if interpreted as protecting citizens' interest in self-defense, because it focuses upon the presence of handguns in high-crime urban areas and is thus a permissible legislative response to a serious, indeed life-threatening, problem. The right protected by the Second Amendment, even assuming it is an individual right to possess and carry weapons for self-defense purposes in keeping with the majority's position, is not absolute and is subject to government regulation. Any attempt in theory to apply strict scrutiny to gun regulations will in practice turn into an interest-balancing inquiry, with the interests protected by the Second Amendment on one side and the governmental public-safety concerns on the other, the only question being whether the regulation at issue impermissibly burdens the former in the course of advancing the latter. Statistics show that for every intruder stopped by a homeowner with a firearm, there are four gun-related accidents within the home. While Heller (P) argues that the handgun ban will not reduce these types of accidents, and that crime and homicide rates are higher since the ban went into effect, the question is whether it was reasonable for the District's (D) legislative body to reject such empirically based arguments. Here, the District's (D) decision represents the kind of empirically

Continued on next page.

based judgment that legislatures, not courts, are best suited to make, and the interests that the District (D) properly seeks to further are "compelling." The handgun ban is a proportionate response to very high rates of crime in urban areas. There is no less restrictive alternative, because the objective is to eliminate handguns, with some exceptions. Moreover, the popularity of a particular weapon, such as the handgun, should not be dispositive of whether its use and possession is protected, since it is feasible that very dangerous weapons could be invented that would become the preferred choice of American citizens for self-defense. In essence the majority determines what regulations are permissible by looking to see what existing regulations permit. There is no basis for believing that the Framers intended such circular reasoning.

ANALYSIS

Some commentators have argued that the District's (D) ban on one class of weapons (handguns) does not violate the Second Amendment even under an individual rights view, since individuals are not barred from possessing or using all weapons for self-defense. Others would take a property approach to the regulation of guns, whereby such regulations are analyzed in the same way as other regulation of property under modern constitutional law and are permitted as long as they are rationally related to achieving a legitimate government purpose—essentially the approach taken by Justice Breyer in his dissent. Judge Posner, of the Seventh Circuit, believes that the majority opinion created new constitutional rights that did not previously exist. He has said, "The text of the amendment, whether viewed alone or in light of the concerns that actuated its adoption, creates no right to the private possession of guns for hunting or other sport, or for the defense of person or property. It is doubtful that the amendment could even be thought to require that members of state militias be allowed to keep weapons in their homes, since that would reduce the militias' effectiveness." Finally, others have criticized the opinion as circumventing the legislative process and being a form of judicial legislation.

Quicknotes

SELF-DEFENSE The right to protect an individual's person, family or property against attempted injury by another.

McDonald v. City of Chicago

Citizens (P) v. City (D)

561 U.S. 742 (2010)

NATURE OF CASE: Appeal from affirmance of judgment that the Second Amendment does not apply to the states.

FACT SUMMARY: [Several plaintiffs (P) challenged a ban on handguns in Chicago, contending that the ban was unconstitutional because the Second Amendment applies to the states.]

RULE OF LAW

The Second Amendment applies to the states by incorporation through the Due Process Clause.

FACTS: [The cities of Chicago (D) and Oak Park (D) in Illinois had gun bans. Several lawsuits were filed against the cities challenging those bans after the United States Supreme Court decided *District of Columbia v. Heller*, 554 U.S. 570 (2008), wherein the Court held that a District of Columbia (D.C.) handgun ban violated the Second Amendment because the D.C. law was enacted under the authority of the federal government and, therefore, the Second Amendment was applicable. The plaintiffs (P) in this case argued that the Second Amendment also applies to the states, and because it does, the Chicago (D) handgun bans were unconstitutional. The district court dismissed the suits, and, on appeal, the court of appeals affirmed. The United States Supreme Court granted certiorari.]

ISSUE: Does the Second Amendment apply to the states by incorporation through the Due Process Clause?

HOLDING AND DECISION: (Alito, J.) Yes. The Second Amendment applies to the states by incorporation through the Due Process Clause. As a threshold matter, the Privileges or Immunities Clause does not incorporate the Second Amendment. The issue, then, is whether the Amendment is incorporated through the Due Process Clause. In *Heller*, it was decided that the right to self-defense is a right that is "fundamental to the Nation's scheme of ordered liberty" and "deeply rooted in this Nation's history and tradition." Throughout the nation's history, Congress has upheld the right to bear arms as a fundamental right, and arguments to the contrary are not supported by history. The question is not whether a civilized society can exist without recognizing this particular right; it's whether the civilized society of our nation (as opposed to those of other nations) must recognize the right. If this were not so, for example, many of the criminal protections of the Bill of Rights, which are unique to our country, would not be incorporated against the states. The Due Process Clause of the Fourteenth Amendment incorporates the Second Amendment right recognized in *Heller*, a fundamental, deeply rooted right. [Reversed and remanded.]

CONCURRENCE: (Scalia, J.) While it is not clear that the Court should rely on principles of substantive due process, the decision here is supportable because the Court's incorporation of certain guarantees in the Bill of Rights is both long established and narrowly limited.

CONCURRENCE: (Thomas, J.) The judgment is correct, and the Fourteenth Amendment incorporates the Second Amendment against the states, but the Due Process Clause is not the appropriate mechanism for incorporation. Instead, the Privileges or Immunities Clause is the more appropriate avenue for incorporation. The framers of the Privileges or Immunities Clause and the ratifying-era public understood that the right to keep and bear arms was essential to the preservation of liberty. A constitutional provision that guarantees only "process" before a person is deprived of life, liberty, or property cannot define the substance of rights not mentioned in the Constitution. Neither the Due Process Clause's text nor its history suggests that it protects the many substantive rights this Court's cases now claim it does. However, reexamining the issue under the Privileges or Immunities Clause leads to the conclusion that the right to keep and bear arms is a privilege of American citizenship that is guaranteed by the Fourteenth Amendment.

DISSENT: (Stevens, J.) The core issue to be resolved here is whether the Second Amendment guarantees individuals a fundamental right, enforceable against the states, to possess a functional, personal firearm, including a handgun, within the home. That is a different question than the incorporation question, which was already decided in the late 19th century, and which is why the Court is correct in rejecting the argument that the Second Amendment is incorporated via the Privileges or Immunities Clause. The Second Amendment has not been incorporated. Thus, the issue is whether the right to bear arms applies to the states through the Fourteenth Amendment as encompassed by the idea of "liberty." First, firearms have a fundamentally ambivalent relationship to liberty. Just as they can help homeowners defend their families and property from intruders, they can help thugs and insurrectionists and other criminals murder innocent victims, thus lessening the liberty interests of those victims. Second, owning a handgun or any particular type

Continued on next page.

of firearm is not critical to leading a life of autonomy, dignity, or political equality. Further, the experience of other advanced democracies, including those that share our British heritage, undercuts the notion that an expansive right to keep and bear arms is intrinsic to ordered liberty, as those countries place stricter restrictions on firearms than does the United States. Finally, the Court's imposition of a national standard is unwise because, as part of the democratic process, elected officials have shown they are perfectly capable of safeguarding the interest in keeping and bearing arms. Gun control matters should be left to the states and localities, where citizens will be able to decide through the democratic process whether certain gun control measures are "improvident" or not.

DISSENT: (Breyer, J.) There is nothing in the Second Amendment's text, history, or purpose that would render it a fundamental right, insofar as carrying arms for personal self-defense is concerned. There is also nothing in the Constitution that warrants transferring regulatory authority over firearms from the legislative branch to the judicial branch or from the states to the federal government. Therefore, the Fourteenth Amendment does not incorporate the Second Amendment's right to keep and bear arms.

ANALYSIS

Most scholars agree that when the Bill of Rights was adopted, it was intended to limit the federal, not state, government. After the adoption of the Fourteenth Amendment in 1868, the Supreme Court held that rights from the Bill of Rights may be selectively applied, or "incorporated," through the Due Process Clause. In *McDonald*, the Court stated that provisions of the Bill of Rights may be incorporated only if they are "fundamental to *our* scheme of ordered liberty," or "deeply rooted in this Nation's history and tradition." The case therefore represents a restriction on the application of the Due Process Clause.

Quicknotes

DUE PROCESS CLAUSE Clauses, found in the Fifth and Fourteenth Amendments to the United States Constitution, providing that no person shall be deprived of "life, liberty, or property, without due process of law."

FOURTEENTH AMENDMENT Declares that no state shall make or enforce any law that shall abridge the privileges and immunities of citizens of the United States. No state shall deny to any person within its jurisdiction the equal protection of the laws.

PRIVILEGES OR IMMUNITIES CLAUSE Section 1 of the Fourteenth Amendment of the U.S. Constitution; prohibits state laws that abridge the privileges or immunities of U.S. citizens.

CHAPTER **10**

The Constitution in the Modern Welfare State

Quick Reference Rules of Law

Harper v. Virginia Bd. of Elections

Residents (P) v. State (D)

383 U.S. 663 (1966)

NATURE OF CASE: Suits challenging the constitutionality of Virginia's poll tax.

FACT SUMMARY: Harper (P) and other Virginia residents brought this suit to have Virginia's (D) poll tax declared unconstitutional.

RULE OF LAW

A state violates the Equal Protection Clause whenever it makes the affluence of the voter or the payment of a fee a condition for voting.

FACTS: Harper (P) and other Virginia residents brought these suits to have Virginia's (D) poll tax declared unconstitutional. The three-judge district court, feeling bound by the Court's decision in *Breedlove v. Suttles*, 302 U.S. 277 (1937), dismissed the complaint. Harper (P) appealed. The law at issue conditions the right to vote in state elections upon the payment of a poll tax.

ISSUE: Does a state violate the Equal Protection Clause when it makes the affluence of the voter or the payment of a fee a condition for voting?

HOLDING AND DECISION: (Douglas, J.) Yes. A state violates the Equal Protection Clause whenever it makes the affluence of the voter or the payment of a fee condition for voting. The right to vote is a basic and fundamental one, especially since it preserves other rights. Any alleged infringement on the right to vote must be carefully scrutinized. A state's interest, when it comes to voting, is limited to the power to fix qualifications. Wealth, like race or creed or color, is irrelevant to one's ability to participate intelligently in the electoral process. Further lines drawn on basis of wealth or property, like those of race, are traditionally disfavored. The requirement of the payment of a fee as a condition of obtaining a ballot causes invidious discrimination. *Breedlove v. Suttles*, 302 U.S. 277 (1937), sanctioned this use of the poll tax, and to that extent it is overruled. Reversed.

DISSENT: (Black, J.) So long as a distinction drawn is not irrational, unreasonable, or invidious, it must be upheld. There are certainly rational reasons for Virginia's poll tax, such as the state's desire to collect revenue and its belief that voters who pay poll tax will be interested in furthering the state's welfare. Hence, the tax must be upheld. If it is to be struck down, it should be done by the legislature, rather than the courts.

DISSENT: (Harlan, J.) The Equal Protection Clause does not impose upon this country an ideology of unrestrained equalitarianism.

ANALYSIS

If, as the dissenters in *Harper* argue, the poll tax classification is not wholly "irrational," the case represents a greater intervention than the courts undertook under old equal protection. There is some question as to whether this greater scrutiny was because the "fundamental rights" of voting are affected or because "lines drawn on basis of wealth" are traditionally disfavored. In *McDonald v. Board of Election Commissioners*, 394 U.S. 802 (1969), the Court sees wealth as an independent ground (apart from impact on fundamental rights) for strict scrutiny. There is a series of cases preceding and following *Harper* (among them *Reynolds v. Sims*, 397 U.S. 533 [1964]) that support the invoking of strict scrutiny when voting rights are affected.

Quicknotes

EQUAL PROTECTION CLAUSE A constitutional guarantee that no person should be denied the same protection of the laws enjoyed by other persons in like circumstances.

FUNDAMENTAL RIGHT A liberty that is either expressly or impliedly provided for in the United States Constitution, the deprivation or burdening of which is subject to a heightened standard of review.

POLL TAX A tax imposed upon each person within a certain class (e.g., all males of a certain age) irrespective of ownership of property, occupation, or ability to pay.

STRICT SCRUTINY The method by which courts determine the constitutionality of a law, when a law affects a fundamental right. Under the test, the legislature must have a compelling interest to enact the law, and measures prescribed by the law must be the least restrictive means possible to accomplish its goal.

Dandridge v. Williams

State official (D) v. Welfare recipients (P)

397 U.S. 471 (1970)

NATURE OF CASE: Appeal from judgment that a state's welfare program's maximum grant regulations violated the Equal Protection Clause.

FACT SUMMARY: Williams (P) and other welfare recipients contended that Maryland's (D) welfare regulation setting a limit on the total of aid any family could receive, regardless of family size or need, unconstitutionally discriminated against welfare recipients with large families, and violated the Equal Protection Clause.

RULE OF LAW

Generally, in the area of economic and social welfare legislation, a state does not violate the Equal Protection Clause as long as the classifications made by its laws have some "reasonable basis."

FACTS: Welfare recipients, including Williams (P), challenged the constitutionality of Maryland's (D) welfare program's maximum grant regulations, which set an upper limit of $250 per month on the amount any family could receive, regardless of the family's size or its needs. Like every other state, Maryland (D) participated in the Federal Aid to Families with Dependent Children (AFDC program). Under this jointly financed program, a state computed the so-called "standard of need" of each eligible family unit within its borders. Some states provided that every family would receive grants sufficient to meet fully the determined standard of need. Other states provided that each family unit would receive a percentage of the determined need. Still other states provided grants to most families in full accord with the ascertained standard of need but imposed an upper limit on the total amount of money any one family unit could receive. Maryland (D) followed this last course. Thus, the effect of the Maryland (D) maximum grant provision was to reduce the per capita benefits to each of the members of the largest families. Williams (P) argued that this regulation discriminated against those with large families in contravention of the Equal Protection Clause. Maryland (D) countered that the regulation was justified on basis of legitimate state interests in encouraging gainful employment, in maintaining an equitable balance in economic status as between welfare families and those supported by a wage-earner, in providing incentives for family planning, and in allocating available public funds in such a way as fully to meet the needs of the largest possible number of families. The district court held the regulation unconstitutional on its face as "overreaching" and cutting too broad and arbitrary a swath as applied to the entire group of AFDC-eligible families. The United States Supreme Court granted review on a direct appeal.

ISSUE: Generally, in the area of economic and social welfare legislation, will a state's statutory classifications pass muster under the Equal Protection Clause as long as they have some "reasonable basis?"

HOLDING AND DECISION: (Stewart, J.) Yes. The general rule with regard to economic and social welfare legislation is that the classifications it creates do not violate the Equal Protection Clause as long as they have some "reasonable basis." The concept of "overreaching" has no place relative to state regulation in the social and economic field that does not affect freedoms guaranteed by the Bill of Rights. The era when the Court thought the Fourteenth Amendment gave it power to strike down state laws "because they may be unwise, improvident, or out of harmony with a particular school of thought" has long passed into history. Although the cases that announced the rule that a discriminatory regulation will survive under the Equal Protection Clause if it has a reasonable basis primarily involved state regulation of business or industry, there is no basis for applying a different constitutional standard to economic or social welfare legislation. It is enough that such regulations be rationally based and free from invidious discrimination, as is the one at hand. Here, it is enough that a solid foundation for the regulation can be found in Maryland's (D) legitimate interest in encouraging employment and in avoiding discrimination between welfare families and the families of the working poor. By combining a limit on the recipient's grant with permission to retain money earned, without reduction in the amount of the grant, Maryland (D) provides an incentive to seek gainful employment. By keying the maximum family AFDC grants to the minimum-wage a steadily employed head of a household receives, Maryland (D) maintains some semblance of an equitable balance between families on welfare and those supported by an employed breadwinner. Reversed.

DISSENT: (Marshall, J.) The majority emasculates the Equal Protection Clause, given that the only difference between children with respect to whom assistance is granted and those children who are denied such assistance is the size of the family into which the child is born. The class of individuals with respect to whom payments are actually made is grossly underinclusive in

Continued on next page.

terms of the class that the AFDC program was designed to assist, namely, all needy dependent children. Such underinclusiveness manifests a prima facie violation of the equal protection requirement of reasonable classification, which requires Maryland (D) to come forward with a persuasive justification for the classification. The majority avoids asking for such a justification by focusing instead on the abstract dichotomy between two different approaches to equal protection problems the Court has previously applied. This case simply defies easy characterization in terms of one or the other tests employed under the Equal Protection Clause (the traditional rational basis test or the stricter compelling state interest test employed when fundamental rights are affected). Unlike cases involving business regulation, this case involves the vital interests of a powerless minority—poor families without breadwinners—but the majority fails to provide a reason for failing to distinguish the types of cases involved, other than merely saying, without explanation, that social and economic regulations are to be assessed pursuant to the same standard as used for commercial regulation. Equal protection analysis of this case is not appreciably advanced by the a priori definition of a "right," fundamental or otherwise. The focus, instead, should be placed on the character of the classification in question, the relative importance to individuals in the class discriminated against of the governmental benefits that they do not receive, and the asserted state interests in support of the classification. Here, upon close scrutiny of the record, even the stated justifications for the maximum grant regulation do not hold up as rational. For example, the alleged employment incentive that the regulation provides must assume that an appreciable number of AFDC recipients are in fact employable. Even if this were a reasonable assumption—which it is not—a state may not deprive certain needy children of assistance to which they would otherwise be entitled in order to provide an arguable work incentive for their parents. The record indicates that of Maryland's (D) more than 32,000 AFDC families, only about 116 could be classified as having employable members, and further indicates that not only has Maryland (D) failed to establish that there is a substantial or even a significant proportion of AFDC heads of households as to whom the maximum grant regulation arguably serves as a viable and logical work incentive, but it is also indisputable that the regulation at best is drastically overinclusive since it applies with equal vigor to a very substantial number of persons who are completely disabled from working. However, the challenged regulation is also grossly underinclusive because it singles out and affects only large families. No reason is suggested why this particular group should be carved out for the purpose of having unusually harsh work incentives imposed upon them. Not only has Maryland (D) selected for special treatment a small group from among similarly situated families, but it has done so on a basis—family size—that bears no relation to the evil that the state claims the regulation was designed to correct. There is simply no indication whatever that heads of large families, as opposed to heads of small families, are particularly prone to refuse to seek or to maintain employment. In sum, the maximum grant regulation involves a classification that is, upon examination, too arbitrary and unconnected to the asserted rationale, has too great an impact on those it discriminates against, and serves supposed interests which are too contrived and attenuated to meet the requirements of the Constitution.

ANALYSIS

The notion of welfare assistance as a fundamental right has not been accepted by the Court. As Justice Marshall notes in his dissent, this posture—that equal protection analysis turns on the basis of a closed category of "fundamental rights"—involves a curious value judgment, as it would be difficult to believe that a person whose very survival is at stake would be comforted by the knowledge that his or her "fundamental" rights were being preserved intact, even if their ability to survive was not.

Quicknotes

COMPELLING STATE INTEREST Defense to an alleged Equal Protection Clause violation that a state action was necessary in order to protect an interest the government is under a duty to protect.

EQUAL PROTECTION A constitutional guarantee that no person shall be denied the same protection of the laws enjoyed by other persons in life circumstances.

FUNDAMENTAL RIGHT A liberty that is either expressly or implicitly provided for in the United States Constitution, the deprivation or burdening of which is subject to a heightened standard of review.

RATIONAL BASIS TEST A test employed by the court to determine the validity of a statute in equal protection actions, whereby the court determines whether the challenged statute is rationally related to the achievement of a legitimate state interest.

San Antonio Independent School District v. Rodriguez

School district (D) v. School children (P)

411 U.S. 1 (1973)

NATURE OF CASE: Appeal from a finding that a school tax finance plan denies equal protection.

FACT SUMMARY: Rodriguez (P) argued that the Texas Public School finance system denied equal protection because students who lived in districts with a low property tax base received lower quality education than students who lived in high property tax base districts.

RULE OF LAW

School finance systems based upon diferring property tax rates in different school districts do not violate equal protection.

FACTS: Rodriguez (P) brought this class action suit on behalf of school children throughout Texas who are members of minority groups or who are poor and reside in school districts having a low property tax base. Texas finances its public schools through a system of state and local funding. The local funds are apportioned to reflect each district's relative taxpaying ability. Rodriguez (P) resides in Edgewood, one of seven school districts in the San Antonio metropolitan area. Edgewood has the lowest property value and highest tax rate of the seven districts and spends $356 per pupil. Alamo Heights, the most affluent of the seven, has the highest property value and the lowest tax rate and spends $594 per pupil. The district court found wealth to be a suspect classification and education to be a fundamental interest and held that the Texas system discriminates on the basis of wealth in the way education is provided. San Antonio (D) appealed.

ISSUE: Do school finance systems based upon differing property tax rates in different school districts violate equal protection?

HOLDING AND DECISION: (Powell, J.) No. School finance systems based upon differing property tax rates in different school districts do not violate equal protection. The wealth discrimination alleged here is unlike any other the Court has discussed. This is not a case in which poor persons are denied a desired benefit; they are receiving a lower quality version of that desired benefit. Equal protection does not require absolute equality or precisely equal advantages. As for a suspect class, the alleged discriminatory system has none of the traditional characteristics of suspectness, and it must therefore be concluded that the Texas system does not operate to the peculiar disadvantage of any suspect class. As for a fundamental interest, the determination of whether education is fundamental lies in assessing whether there is a right to education explicitly or implicitly guaranteed by the Constitution. Education is not explicitly guaranteed and no basis exists for finding it to be implicitly guaranteed. The action is a direct attack on Texas's method of raising and disbursing tax revenues, and the Court has traditionally disliked interfering with a state's fiscal policies under the Equal Protection Clause. Further, no scheme of taxation has ever been devised completely free of some discriminatory impact. The existence of some inequality in the state's manner of achieving its goal is not alone a sufficient basis for striking down an entire system. Any local taxation scheme requires creation of inevitably arbitrary jurisdictional boundaries. "Moreover, if local taxation for local expenditure is an unconstitutional method of providing for education then it may be an equally permissible means of providing other necessary (local) services." This decision does not approve of the status quo or deny the need for tax law reform, but any change must come from the legislature, not the courts. Reversed.

DISSENT: (White, J.) The Equal Protection Clause permits discrimination between class if the classification bears some rational relationship to a permissible goal sought to be attained by the statue. The system fails here because the means chosen is not rationally related to the end sought. It fails in maximizing local initiative and choice in districts with such low property tax bases that there is no real opportunity to the school district.

DISSENT: (Marshall, J.) The Court acknowledges that substantial interdistrict disparities in school expenditures exist in the state, and that these disparities are largely attributable to differences in the amounts of money collected through local property taxation. However, instead of scrutinizing the seriousness of these disparities and the invidiousness of this financing scheme, the majority focuses on how the state is attempting to close the gaps between its districts in terms of levels of district wealth and resulting educational funding. Yet, that is not the issue in this case; the issue is whether the scheme itself is in fact unconstitutionally discriminatory in the face of the Fourteenth Amendment's guarantee of equal protection of the laws. Here, it is evident that the financing scheme is discriminatory. Contrary to the majority's novel view, this Court has never suggested that because some "adequate" level of benefits is provided to all, discrimination in the provision of services is therefore constitutionally excusable. The Equal Protection Clause is not addressed to the minimal sufficiency, but rather to the unjustifiable inequalities, of state action. The overarching form of

Continued on next page.

discrimination in this case occurs between the schoolchildren of the state on basis of the taxable property wealth of the districts in which they happen to live. But, the quality of public education may not be a function of wealth, other than the wealth of the state as a whole. Under such a principle, the children of a district are excessively advantaged if that district has more taxable property per pupil than the average amount of taxable property per pupil considering the state as a whole. By contrast, the children of a district are disadvantaged if that district has less taxable property per pupil than the state average. The majority attempts to disparage such a definition of the disadvantaged class as the product of an "artificially defined level" of district wealth. A clearer definition of either the disadvantaged class of schoolchildren or the allegedly unconstitutional discrimination suffered by the members of that class under the present financing scheme could not be asked for, and, is not needed.

The majority, unlike the district court, finds neither that the financing scheme is subject to strict scrutiny, nor that the discrimination inherent in the scheme has to be shown necessary to promote a "compelling state interest." The lower court found that discrimination on basis of wealth is highly suspect, and that education is a fundamental interest, which, apparently, the majority does not. The majority seems to be saying that equal protection cases fall into one of two neat categories of review: strict scrutiny or mere rationality. However, such an approach is contrary to the Court's recent decisions, which have applied a spectrum of standards and taken a more reasoned approach that depends on the constitutional and societal importance of the interest adversely affected and the recognized invidiousness of the basis upon which the particular classification is drawn. For this reason, the majority is wrong in its effort to demonstrate that fundamental interests (and strict scrutiny) encompass only established rights that can be recognized from the text of the Constitution itself. Some rights, like the right to procreate, or the right to vote in state elections, are deemed fundamental even though the Constitution does not explicitly guarantee them. Although not all fundamental interests are constitutionally guaranteed, the determination of which interests are fundamental should be rooted in the Constitution's text. To do this, it must be determined the extent to which constitutionally guaranteed rights are dependent on interests not mentioned in the Constitution. That is, as the nexus between the constitutional guarantee and the nonconstitutional interest becomes more closely linked, the nonconstitutional interest becomes increasingly fundamental, with a corresponding increase in judicial scrutiny. Only by protecting the related interests from state discrimination does the Court ultimately ensure the integrity of the constitutional guarantee itself.

Although this Court has never held the provision of free public education to be constitutionally mandated, prior decisions indicate the fundamental importance of education in our society. In part this is because "some degree of education is necessary to prepare citizens to participate effectively and intelligently in our open political system . . . ," and because "education prepares individuals to be self-reliant and self-sufficient participants in society." Education is connected to constitutional guarantees because it affects the ability of children to learn to exercise their rights of free speech, to engage in political debate, and to vote. The majority's position is that the Court has "never presumed to possess either the ability or the authority to guarantee to the citizenry the most effective speech or the most informed electoral choice." This, however, misconstrues the issue, which is the disparity in the quality of education received by the state's different districts and that some districts cannot provide the same educational opportunity as other districts. While the majority insists that the wealth classification in this case is not the kind that it has previously struck down, because it does not completely deny all education to poorer districts, the Court previously held that the degree of discrimination is not relevant to an equal protection claim. The difference between this case and prior precedent is that in the prior cases, the wealth classification was based on personal wealth, whereas in this case, the wealth classification is based on taxable property wealth of a district where people happen to live. The issue, therefore, is whether such a classification, based on group wealth, merits strict scrutiny. The answer is that it does. First, while local district wealth may serve other interests, it bears no relationship whatsoever to the interest of school children in the educational opportunity afforded them by the state. Given the importance of that interest, the Court must be particularly sensitive to the invidious characteristics of any form of discrimination that is not clearly intended to serve it, as opposed to some other distinct state interest. Discrimination on basis of group wealth may not, to be sure, reflect the social stigma frequently attached to personal poverty. Nevertheless, insofar as group wealth discrimination involves wealth over which the disadvantaged individual has no significant control, it represents in fact a more serious basis of discrimination than it does personal wealth. Here, too, the state is completely responsible for the discrimination, not the private sector. These factors require strict scrutiny of the financing scheme and the state's justifications for it. Applying strict scrutiny in this case, as in all equal protection cases, requires consideration of the substantiality of the state's interest, and the reasonableness of the means employed to serve that interest. The only justification offered by the state to sustain the discrimination in educational opportunity caused by the financing scheme is local educational control. In the abstract, this is a very

Continued on next page.

substantial state interest. Here, however, local control is in reality offered as an excuse rather than a justification for discrimination. The state regulates the most-minute details of local public education, and there is no evidence of the state's dedication to local control over fiscal matters. If the state had a system truly dedicated to local fiscal control, one would expect the quality of the educational opportunity provided in each district to vary with the decision of the voters in that district as to the level of sacrifice they wish to make for public education. In fact, the state scheme produces precisely the opposite result. Local school districts cannot choose to have the best education in the state by imposing the highest tax rate. Instead, the quality of the educational opportunity offered by any particular district is largely determined by the amount of taxable property located in the district—a factor over which local voters can exercise no control. Thus, the state has selected means wholly inappropriate to secure its purported interest in assuring its school districts have local fiscal control. There are many alternatives that would serve this purpose.

ANALYSIS

In applying "traditional equal protection analysis," the Court, per Justice Brennan, held that a food stamp act provision, which prevented a person from obtaining food stamps if he lived in a household containing an individual unrelated to any other household member, was lacking any rational basis, *U.S. Dept. of Agriculture v. Moreno*, 413 U.S. 528 (1973). In another equal protection case, the Court, per Justice Douglas, upheld a zoning ordinance that defined a "family" as persons related by blood, adoption, or marriage, or no more than two unrelated persons living together. This was rational, *Village of Belle Terre v. Boraas*, 416 U.S. 1 (1974). The cases reached opposite conclusions as to rationality without broadening the scope of fundamental rights.

Quicknotes

EQUAL PROTECTION A constitutional guarantee that no person shall be denied the same protection of the laws enjoyed by other persons in life circumstances.

FUNDAMENTAL RIGHT A liberty that is either expressly or implicitly provided for in the United States Constitution, the deprivation or burdening of which is subject to a heightened standard of review.

STRICT SCRUTINY The method by which courts determine the constitutionality of a law, when a law affects a fundamental right. Under the test, the legislature must have a compelling interest to enact the law, and measures prescribed by the law must be the least restrictive means possible to accomplish its goal.

SUSPECT CLASSIFICATION A class of persons that have historically been subject to discriminatory treatment; statutes drawing a distinction between persons based on a suspect classification, i.e., race, nationality, or alienage, are subject to a strict scrutiny standard of review.

Plyler v. Doe

State (D) v. Children of undocumented aliens (P)

457 U.S. 202 (1982)

NATURE OF CASE: Constitutional challenge to a state educational restriction statute.

FACT SUMMARY: A class action suit challenged a Texas law that prohibited the use of state funds to educate the children of undocumented aliens.

RULE OF LAW

Absent a showing that such a policy furthers a substantial state interest, a state may not deny a public education to the children of undocumented aliens.

FACTS: In a class action suit, a Texas statute (Tex. Educ. Code Ann. § 21.031 [1981]) was sought to be invalidated on the ground it unconstitutionally denied equal protection to the children of undocumented aliens. The statute prohibited the use of state funds for the education of any children not legally admitted to the United States. Both the district court and the Fifth Circuit Court of Appeals held that § 21.031 violated the Equal Protection Clause of the Fourteenth Amendment. Texas (D) appealed, contending that the statute was not unduly discriminatory and was, in fact, justified for three reasons: (1) it was designed to protect the state from an influx of illegal immigrants; (2) it would relieve some of the special burdens that educating undocumented aliens imposes on the educational system; and (3) it would relieve the state of the burden of educating children who are less likely to remain in the state and contribute than other children.

ISSUE: May a state deny a public education to the children of undocumented aliens absent a showing that such a policy is justified by a substantial state interest?

HOLDING AND DECISION: (Brennan, J.) No. Absent a showing that such a policy furthers a substantial state interest, a state may not deny a public education to the children of undocumented aliens. To begin with, the proper standard of judicial scrutiny must be identified. As the people involved (undocumented aliens) are not members of a suspect class and as the right to an education, although clearly important, has not been held to constitute a fundamental constitutional right, the statute in question will be upheld if it is found to be rationally related to a substantial state interest. Upon examination, however, none of the three state interests advanced by Texas (D)—protection from an influx of illegal immigrants; relief from special burdens on the educational system; or relief from the burdens of educating children who will be more likely to leave the state—justify the statute in question. The legislative scheme found in § 21.031 cannot in any way be deemed as advancing the interests asserted by the state (even assuming these interests are "substantial state interests"). Denying children who are not responsible for their status a public education will stigmatize them with the heavy burden of illiteracy for the rest of their lives. They will be unable to participate in our civic institutions. The cost to the nation over their lifespans will be greater than the cost of providing them an education now. As such, the statute must fall, as it is in violation of the Equal Protection Clause.

DISSENT: (Burger, C.J.) The Court oversteps its bounds in striking down the Texas statute. Once it is conceded that neither a suspect class nor fundamental right is involved, only a rational relationship to a legitimate state interest need be found to uphold the law. Despite the fact it may not be the same course the members of the court would take if they were legislating, it cannot be said that the Texas law is irrational. As such, it is a valid law.

ANALYSIS

As mentioned in Justice Marshall's concurrence, the Court seems to be taking one step closer to the "sliding scale" approach of equal protection analysis that has long been advocated by certain legal theorists. Under this approach, a court would have greater flexibility than merely identifying the analysis required as being either "strict scrutiny" or "rational basis" and, as such, could better tailor the legal analysis to the facts of the case and the interests involved.

Quicknotes

ALIENAGE The condition or status of a foreign-born person who has not qualified as a U.S. citizen.

EQUAL PROTECTION A constitutional provision that each person be guaranteed the same protection of the laws enjoyed by other persons in life circumstances.

FUNDAMENTAL RIGHT A liberty that is either expressly or impliedly provided for in the United States Constitution, the deprivation or burdening of which is subject to a heightened standard of review.

STRICT SCRUTINY The method by which courts determine the constitutionality of a law, when a law affects a fundamental right. Under the test, the legislature must have a compelling interest to enact the law, and measures prescribed by the law must be the least restrictive means possible to accomplish its goal.

DeShaney v. Winnebago County Department of Social Services

Child (P) v. State (D)

489 U.S. 189 (1989)

NATURE OF CASE: Appeal from denial of damages for substantive due process violation.

FACT SUMMARY: After investigating claims of child abuse concerning Joshua DeShaney (P), the Winnebago County Department of Social Services (D) concluded there was insufficient evidence to establish a case against Joshua's (P) father, Randy, who subsequently beat Joshua (P) severely enough to cause him permanent brain damage.

RULE OF LAW

The language of the Fourteenth Amendment Due Process Clause does not require the state to protect the life, liberty, and property of its citizens against invasion by private actors.

FACTS: After his parents were divorced, Joshua DeShaney (P) was placed in his father's custody. Joshua's (P) father, Randy, remarried, and when Joshua's (P) stepmother later sought a divorce, she notified the Winnebago County Department of Social Services (DSS) (D) that Joshua's (P) father had abused him. Randy denied the accusations when interviewed by DSS (D). Over the next few months, Joshua (P) was admitted to the hospital several times with multiple bruises and a number of suspicious injuries on his head. He was placed in the temporary custody of the hospital, at the recommendation of the DSS (D). However, a "child protection team" determined there was insufficient evidence to retain custody, and Joshua (P) was returned to his father. Although a DSS (D) caseworker continued to suspect that Joshua (P) was being abused by someone in his household, the DSS (D) took no action. Finally, in March 1984, Randy DeShaney beat Joshua (P) so severely that he lapsed into a life-threatening coma. He suffered such severe brain damage that he was expected to be confined to an institution for the severely retarded for the remainder of his life. Through his mother, Joshua (P) filed suit for damages, claiming that the DSS (D) deprived him of his Fourteenth Amendment rights to liberty when it failed to protect him "against a risk of violence at his father's hands of which they knew or should have known."

ISSUE: Does the language of the Fourteenth Amendment Due Process Clause require the state to protect the life, liberty, and property of its citizens against invasion by private actors?

HOLDING AND DECISION: (Rehnquist, C.J.) No. The language of the Fourteenth Amendment Due Process Clause does not require the state to protect the life, liberty, and property of its citizens against invasion by private actors. The claim is one invoking the substantive rather than procedural component of the Due Process Clause. The purpose of the Clause was to protect the people from the state, not to ensure that the state protected them from each other. Thus, this Court has recognized that the Due Process Clause generally confers no affirmative right to governmental aid, even where such aid may be necessary to secure life, liberty, or property interests of which the government itself may not deprive the individual. If the Due Process Clause does not require the state to provide its citizens with particular protective services, it follows that the state cannot be held liable under the Clause for injuries that could have been averted had it chosen to provide them. Thus, a state's failure to protect an individual against private violence simply does not constitute a violation of the Due Process Clause. That DSS (D) once took temporary custody of Joshua (P) does not alter the analysis, for when it returned him to his father's custody, it placed him in no worse position than that in which he would have been had it not acted at all; the state does not become the permanent guarantor of an individual's safety by having once offered him shelter. Under these circumstances, DSS (D) had no constitutional duty to protect Joshua (P).

DISSENT: (Brennan, J.) Contrary to the majority opinion, this Court's cases stand for the much more generous proposition that, if a state cuts off private sources of aid and then refuses aid itself, it cannot wash its hands of the harm that results from its inaction. Through its child-protection program, the state actively intervened in Joshua's (P) life, and by virtue of this intervention, relieved ordinary citizens and other governmental bodies of any sense of obligation to do anything more than report their suspicions of child abuse to DSS (D). This opinion construes the Due Process Clause to permit a state to displace private sources of protection and then to shrug its shoulders and turn away from the harm that it has promised to try to prevent.

DISSENT: (Blackmun, J.) The question presented by this case is an open one, and Fourteenth Amendment precedents may be read more broadly or narrowly depending upon how one chooses to read them. Faced with a choice, a sympathetic reading, one that comports with dictates of fundamental justice and recognizes that compassion need not be exiled from the province of judging, is preferable.

Continued on next page.

ANALYSIS

Citing its prior rulings, the Court asserted that a state's affirmative duty to protect arises not from the state's knowledge of an individual's predicament or from its expressions of intent to help him, but from the limitation that it has imposed on his freedom to act on his own behalf. Thus, in the substantive due process analysis, it is a state's affirmative act of restraining an individual's freedom to act on his own behalf—through incarceration, institutionalization, or other similar restraint of personal liberty—which triggers the protection of the Due Process Clause, not its failure to act to protect his liberty interests against harms inflicted by other means.

Quicknotes

AFFIRMATIVE DUTY An obligation to undertake an affirmative action for the benefit of another.

DUE PROCESS CLAUSE Language found in the Fifth and Fourteenth Amendments to the United States Constitution providing that no person shall be deprived of "life, liberty, or property without due process of law."

SUBSTANTIVE DUE PROCESS A constitutional safeguard limiting the power of the state, irrespective of how fair its procedures may be; substantive limits placed on the power of the state.

Goldberg v. Kelly

State (D) v. Residents (P)

397 U.S. 254 (1970)

NATURE OF CASE: Appeal from order requiring hearing prior to termination of welfare benefits.

FACT SUMMARY: Kelly (P) and other residents of New York City, who had been receiving aid pursuant to a state welfare scheme, brought this action alleging that benefits had been terminated without prior notice and hearing.

RULE OF LAW

A state that terminates public assistance payments to a recipient without affording him the opportunity for an evidentiary hearing prior to termination denies the recipient procedural due process.

FACTS: Kelly (P) and other residents of New York City, who had been receiving aid pursuant to a state welfare scheme, brought this action alleging that welfare benefits had been or would be terminated, under New York law, without prior notice and hearing in violation of the Due Process Clause. The state contended that its post-termination notice and hearing procedure was constitutionally sufficient. Under the procedure a caseworker with doubts about a recipient's continued eligibility would first discuss the matter with the recipient, and then recommend termination of benefits if the recipient was still considered ineligible. Notification of termination was then sent in writing to the recipient together with information about the availability of a post-termination hearing. If the recipient prevailed he would be paid all funds erroneously held. The district court held that only a pre-termination evidentiary hearing would satisfy the Due Process Clause. Goldberg (D), as Commissioner of Social Services, appealed.

ISSUE: Does a state that terminates public assistance payments to a recipient without affording him the opportunity for an evidentiary hearing prior to termination deny the recipient procedural due process?

HOLDING AND DECISION: (Brennan, J.) Yes. A state that terminates public assistance payments to a recipient without affording him the opportunity for an evidentiary hearing prior to termination denies the recipient procedural due process. The extent to which procedural due process must be afforded the recipient is influenced by the extent to which he may be condemned to suffer grievous loss and depends upon whether the recipient's interest in avoiding that loss outweighs the governmental interest in summary adjudication. It is true, of course, that some governmental benefits may be administratively terminated without affording the recipient a pre-termination evidentiary hearing; however, when welfare is discontinued so is the means to obtain essential food, clothing, housing, and medical care. Termination of aid pending resolution of a controversy over eligibility may deprive an eligible recipient of the very means by which he lives. Moreover, important governmental interests are promoted by affording recipients a pre-termination evidentiary hearing. Public assistance promotes the general welfare by allowing the poor to have the same opportunity to participate in the community as others in a superior economic position. Affirmed.

DISSENT: (Black, J.) The Fourteenth Amendment is given too broad a construction. The amendment came into being primarily to protect Blacks from discrimination. The Court, however, relies upon the Fourteenth Amendment and in effect says that failure of government to pay a promised charitable installment to an individual deprives that individual of his own property. It strains credulity to say that a government's promise of charity is property belonging to a welfare recipient under the Due Process Clause.

ANALYSIS

The Court points out in *Goldberg* that the pre-termination hearing need not take the form of a judicial or quasi-judicial trial. It must be borne in mind that the statutory fair hearing will provide the recipient with a full administrative review. Accordingly, the pre-termination hearing has one function only: to produce an initial determination of the validity of the welfare department's grounds for discontinuance of payments in order to protect a recipient against an erroneous termination of benefits.

Quicknotes

DUE PROCESS CLAUSE Language found in the Fifth and Fourteenth Amendments to the United States Constitution providing that no person shall be deprived of "life, liberty, or property without due process of law."

NOTICE Communication of information to a person by an authorized person or an otherwise proper source.

PROCEDURAL DUE PROCESS The constitutional mandate that if the state or federal government acts so as to deny a citizen of a life, liberty, or property interest the individual is first entitled to notice and the right to be heard.

Shapiro v. Thompson

[Parties not identified.]

394 U.S. 618 (1969)

NATURE OF CASE: Appeal from decisions holding residency requirements for welfare applicants unconstitutional.

FACT SUMMARY: Statutory provisions denied welfare assistance to residents who had not resided within their jurisdiction for at least one year.

RULE OF LAW

A statutory prohibition of welfare benefits to residents of less than a year creates a classification denying such residents equal protection of the laws.

FACTS: A three-judge district court held unconstitutional certain state and District of Columbia statutory provisions. The provisions denied welfare assistance to residents of the state or district who had not resided within their jurisdictions for at least one year immediately preceding their applications for such assistance.

ISSUE: Does a statutory prohibition of welfare benefits to residents of less than a year create a classification denying such residents equal protection of the laws?

HOLDING AND DECISION: (Brennan, J.) Yes. A statutory prohibition of welfare benefits to residents of less than a year creates a classification denying such residents equal protection of the laws. The states justify the waiting period requirement as a protective device to preserve the fiscal integrity of their public assistance programs by discouraging needy families from entering their jurisdictions. However, this act of inhibiting migration by needy persons into the state is constitutionally impermissible since the right to travel from state to state is protected by the Constitution from laws or regulations that would unreasonably burden such movement. If a law has no other purpose than to chill the assertion of a constitutional right by penalizing those who choose to exercise them, it is patently unconstitutional. Further, the statutes create two classes of persons, different only in that one class has been in the area for one year. A state has a valid interest in preserving the fiscal integrity of its programs. But it cannot accomplish this purpose by invidious discrimination between classes of its citizens. The saving of welfare costs cannot be an independent ground for invidious classification. The states also assert that the waiting period serves certain administrative goals. They contend that a mere showing of a rational relationship and these permissible state goals will justify the classification. This is not true. As stated above, the right to travel is a constitutional right. Any classification that serves to penalize the exercise of a constitutional right is unconstitutional, unless it is shown to be necessary to promote a compelling governmental interest, rather than merely shown to be rationally related to a legitimate purpose. All of the administrative arguments advanced are either unfounded, irrational, or may be accomplished by a less drastic means. The district court's judgment is affirmed.

DISSENT: (Warren, C.J.) Since Congress has imposed a residency requirement in the District of Columbia and authorized the states, which receive federal funds for their welfare programs, to do the same, the real issue is whether Congress can create minimal residency requirements. Congress's right to enact a variety of restrictions upon interstate travel pursuant to its commerce power has been upheld in a number of prior cases. They require only that Congress have a rational basis for finding that a chosen regulatory scheme is necessary to the furtherance of interstate commerce. Congress had a rational basis for concluding that the insubstantial restriction imposed by residence requirements would, in the end, foster a climate more conducive to an enhanced flow of commerce and, in the long run, to personal mobility.

DISSENT: (Harlan, J.) The equal protection argument accepted by the majority has, in reality, two branches. Since any departure from equal protection requires a compelling governmental interest as justification under this theory, there are actually two separate types of equal protection violations. The "suspect classification" branch is well founded in the racial groupings from which the Fourteenth Amendment sprang. But the other branch is far more troubling since it looks to "fundamental rights." But the traditional equal protection approach required only that the state show a rational justification for its acts. To now require a "compelling interest" in these cases is to create in this Court a superlegislature somehow imbued with a special intelligence and expertise in regulating the internal affairs of the states. Using the traditional, and proper, approach to equal protection, there are perfectly adequate rational justifications for the states to impose a welfare residency requirement, and this Court has no authority to create new "fundamental rights," as it has done in this case.

ANALYSIS

Many agreed with Justice Harlan's dissent that the Court was simply resurrecting the judicial intervention of substantive due process under the guise of a new

Continued on next page.

stricter equal protection test. One commentator warned, "Looming down the path is the specter of economic due process, of judges riding to the rescue of Oklahoma's opticians or the Railway Express Agency." Supporters of the new doctrine answered that it was limited to minorities that seem permanently voiceless and invisible and whom the power structure in the political process tends to ignore. Subsequent decisions have shown the court to be willing to expand the number of suspect classifications to include national origin and sex as well as race.

Quicknotes

EQUAL PROTECTION A constitutional provision that each person be guaranteed the same protection of the laws enjoyed by other persons in life circumstances.

FUNDAMENTAL RIGHT A liberty that is either expressly or impliedly provided for in the United States Constitution, the deprivation or burdening of which is subject to a heightened standard of review.

SUBSTANTIVE DUE PROCESS A constitutional safeguard limiting the power of the state, irrespective of how fair its procedures may be; substantive limits placed on the power of the state.

Saenz v. Roe

[Parties not identified.]

526 U.S. 489 (1999)

NATURE OF CASE: Certiorari review of a state statute.

FACT SUMMARY: When California (D) discriminated against citizens who had resided in the state for less than one year in distributing welfare benefits, the state statute was challenged and held to be unconstitutional.

RULE OF LAW

Durational residency requirements violate the fundamental right to travel by denying a newly arrived citizen the same privileges and immunities enjoyed by other citizens in the same state.

FACTS: In 1992, California (D) enacted a statute limiting the maximum first-year welfare benefits available to newly arrived residents to the amount they would have received in the state of their prior residence. California residents who were eligible for such benefits challenged the constitutionality of the durational residency requirement, alleging their right to travel was violated. The district court preliminarily enjoined implementation of the statute and the court of appeals affirmed. Congress enacted the Personal Responsibility and Work Opportunity Reconciliation Act of 1996, which expressly authorized states to apply the rules (including benefit amounts) of another state if the family has resided in the state for less than twelve months. California (D) appealed, alleging that the statute should be upheld if it has a rational basis, and that the California's (D) legitimate interest in saving over $10 million a year satisfied that test.

ISSUE: Do durational residency requirements violate the fundamental right to travel by denying a newly arrived citizen the same privileges and immunities enjoyed by other citizens in the same state?

HOLDING AND DECISION: (Stevens, J.) Yes. Durational residency requirements violate the fundamental right to travel by denying a newly arrived citizen the same privileges and immunities enjoyed by other citizens in the same state. The first sentence of Article IV, § 2 of the Constitution, provides that "the Citizens of each State shall be entitled to all Privileges and Immunities of Citizens in the several States." The right of a newly arrived citizen to the same privileges and immunities enjoyed by other citizens of the same state is protected not only by the new arrival's status as a state citizen, but also by her status as a citizen of the United States. The Citizenship Clause of the Fourteenth Amendment protects all citizens' right to choose to be citizens of the state wherein they reside. Neither mere rationality nor some intermediate standard of review should be used to judge the constitutionality of a state rule that discriminates against some of its citizens because they have been domiciled in the state for less than a year. The state's legitimate interest in saving money provides no justification for its decision to discriminate among equally eligible citizens. Affirmed.

DISSENT: (Rehnquist, C.J.) If states can require an individual to reside in-state for a year before exercising the right to educational benefits, the right to terminate a marriage, or the right to vote in primary elections that all other state citizens enjoy, then they may surely do the same for welfare benefits. California has reasonably exercised its power to protect state resources through an objective, narrowly tailored residence requirement. There is nothing in the Constitution that should prevent the enforcement of that requirement.

DISSENT: (Thomas, J.) The majority attributes a meaning to the Privileges or Immunities Clause of the Fourteenth Amendment that likely was unintended when the Fourteenth Amendment was enacted and ratified. At that time, people understood "privileges or immunities of citizens" to be their fundamental right, rather than every public benefit established by positive law.

ANALYSIS

The Court in this case found that a state violated the Privileges or Immunities Clause when it discriminated against citizens who had been residents for less than one year. The Thomas dissent alleged that this was contrary to the original understanding at the time the Fourteenth Amendment was enacted. The Rehnquist dissent went on to point out that a welfare subsidy is as much an investment in human capital as is a tuition subsidy and their attendant benefits are just as portable.

Quicknotes

FOURTEENTH AMENDMENT Declares that no state shall make or enforce any law that shall abridge the privileges and immunities of citizens of the United States.

FUNDAMENTAL RIGHT A liberty that is either expressly or implicitly provided for in the United States Constitution, the deprivation or burdening of which is subject to a heightened standard of review.

Continued on next page.

PRIVILEGES AND IMMUNITIES CLAUSE Article IV, section 2, clause 1 of the U.S. Constitution, which states that a state cannot favor its own citizens by discriminating against other states' citizens who may come within its borders.

PRIVILEGES OR IMMUNITIES CLAUSE Section 1 of the Fourteenth Amendment of the United States Constitution; prohibits state laws that abridge the privileges or immunities of U.S. citizens.

RATIONAL BASIS REVIEW A test employed by the court to determine the validity of a statute in equal protection actions, whereby the court determines whether the challenged statute is rationally related to the achievement of a legitimate state interest.

STRICT SCRUTINY Method by which courts determine the constitutionality of a law when a law affects a fundamental right. Under the test, the legislature must have a compelling interest to enact law, and measures prescribed by the law must be the least restrictive means possible to accomplish its goal.

Glossary

Common Latin Words and Phrases Encountered in the Law

A FORTIORI: Because one fact exists or has been proven, therefore a second fact that is related to the first fact must also exist.

A PRIORI: From the cause to the effect. A term of logic used to denote that when one generally accepted truth is shown to be a cause, another particular effect must necessarily follow.

AB INITIO: From the beginning; a condition that has existed throughout, as in a marriage that was void ab initio.

ACTUS REUS: The wrongful act; in criminal law, such action sufficient to trigger criminal liability.

AD VALOREM: According to value; an ad valorem tax is imposed upon an item located within the taxing jurisdiction calculated by the value of such item.

AMICUS CURIAE: Friend of the court. Its most common usage takes the form of an amicus curiae brief, filed by a person who is not a party to an action but is nonetheless allowed to offer an argument supporting his legal interests.

ARGUENDO: In arguing. A statement, possibly hypothetical, made for the purpose of argument is one made arguendo.

BILL QUIA TIMET: A bill to quiet title (establish ownership) to real property.

BONA FIDE: True, honest, or genuine. May refer to a person's legal position based on good faith or lacking notice of fraud (such as a bona fide purchaser for value) or to the authenticity of a particular document (such as a bona fide last will and testament).

CAUSA MORTIS: With approaching death in mind. A gift causa mortis is a gift given by a party who feels certain that death is imminent.

CAVEAT EMPTOR: Let the buyer beware. This maxim is reflected in the rule of law that a buyer purchases at his own risk because it is his responsibility to examine, judge, test, and otherwise inspect what he is buying.

CERTIORARI: A writ of review. Petitions for review of a case by the United States Supreme Court are most often done by means of a writ of certiorari.

CONTRA: On the other hand. Opposite. Contrary to.

CORAM NOBIS: Before us; writs of error directed to the court that originally rendered the judgment.

CORAM VOBIS: Before you; writs of error directed by an appellate court to a lower court to correct a factual error.

CORPUS DELICTI: The body of the crime; the requisite elements of a crime amounting to objective proof that a crime has been committed.

CUM TESTAMENTO ANNEXO, ADMINISTRATOR (ADMINISTRATOR C.T.A.): With will annexed; an administrator c.t.a. settles an estate pursuant to a will in which he or she is not appointed.

DE BONIS NON, ADMINISTRATOR (ADMINISTRATOR D.B.N.): Of goods not administered; an administrator d.b.n. settles a partially settled estate.

DE FACTO: In fact; in reality; actually. Existing in fact but not officially approved or engendered.

DE JURE: By right; lawful. Describes a condition that is legitimate "as a matter of law," in contrast to the term "de facto," which connotes something existing in fact but not legally sanctioned or authorized. For example, de facto segregation refers to segregation brought about by housing patterns, etc., whereas de jure segregation refers to segregation created by law.

DE MINIMUS: Of minimal importance; insignificant; a trifle; not worth bothering about.

DE NOVO: Anew; a second time; afresh. A trial de novo is a new trial held at the appellate level as if the case originated there and the trial at a lower level had not taken place.

DICTA: Generally used as an abbreviated form of obiter dicta, a term describing those portions of a judicial opinion incidental or not necessary to resolution of the specific question before the court. Such nonessential statements and remarks are not considered to be binding precedent.

DUCES TECUM: Refers to a particular type of writ or subpoena requesting a party or organization to produce certain documents in their possession.

EN BANC: Full bench. Where a court sits with all justices present rather than the usual quorum.

EX PARTE: For one side or one party only. An ex parte proceeding is one undertaken for the benefit of only one party, without notice to, or an appearance by, an adverse party.

EX POST FACTO: After the fact. An ex post facto law is a law that retroactively changes the consequences of a prior act.

EX REL.: Abbreviated form of the term "ex relatione," meaning upon relation or information. When the state brings an action in which it has no interest against an individual at the instigation of one who has a private interest in the matter.

FORUM NON CONVENIENS: Inconvenient forum. Although a court may have jurisdiction over the case, the action should be tried in a more conveniently located court, one to which parties and witnesses may more easily travel, for example.

GUARDIAN AD LITEM: A guardian appointed by the court to represent a minor or incompetent person in a legal action.

HABEAS CORPUS: You have the body. The modern writ of habeas corpus is a writ directing that a person (body) being detained (such as a prisoner) be brought before the court so that the legality of his detention can be judicially ascertained.

IN CAMERA: In private, in chambers. When a hearing is held before a judge in his or her chambers or when all spectators are excluded from the courtroom.

IN FORMA PAUPERIS: In the manner of a pauper. A party who proceeds in forma pauperis because of his poverty is one who is allowed to bring suit without liability for costs.

INFRA: Below, under. A word referring the reader to a later part of a book. (The opposite of supra.)

IN LOCO PARENTIS: In the place of a parent.

IN PARI DELICTO: Equally wrong; a court of equity will not grant requested relief to an applicant who is in pari delicto, or as much at fault in the transactions giving rise to the controversy as is the opponent of the applicant.

IN PARI MATERIA: On like subject matter or upon the same matter. Statutes relating to the same person or things are said to be in pari materia. It is a general rule of statutory construction that such statutes should be construed together, i.e., looked at as if they together constituted one law.

IN PERSONAM: Against the person. Jurisdiction over the person of an individual.

IN RE: In the matter of. Used to designate a proceeding involving an estate or other property.

IN REM: A term that signifies an action against the res, or thing. An action in rem is basically one that is taken directly against property, as distinguished from an action in personam, i.e., against the person.

INTER ALIA: Among other things. Used to show that the whole of a statement, pleading, list, statute, etc., has not been set forth in its entirety.

INTER PARTES: Between the parties. May refer to contracts, conveyances, or other transactions having legal significance.

INTER VIVOS: Between the living. An inter vivos gift is a gift made by a living grantor, as distinguished from bequests contained in a will, which pass upon the death of the testator.

IPSO FACTO: By the mere fact itself.

JUS: Law or the entire body of law.

LEX LOCI: The law of the place; the notion that the rights of parties to a legal proceeding are governed by the law of the place where those rights arose.

MALUM IN SE: Evil or wrong in and of itself; inherently wrong. This term describes an act that is wrong by its very nature, as opposed to one which would not be wrong but for the fact that there is a specific legal prohibition against it (malum prohibitum).

MALUM PROHIBITUM: Wrong because prohibited, but not inherently evil. Used to describe something that is wrong because it is expressly forbidden by law but that is not in and of itself evil, e.g., speeding.

MANDAMUS: We command. A writ directing an official to take a certain action.

MENS REA: A guilty mind; a criminal intent. A term used to signify the mental state that accompanies a crime or other prohibited act. Some crimes require only a general mens rea (general intent to do the prohibited act), but others, like assault with intent to murder, require the existence of a specific mens rea.

MODUS OPERANDI: Method of operating; generally refers to the manner or style of a criminal in committing crimes, admissible in appropriate cases as evidence of the identity of a defendant.

NEXUS: A connection to.

NISI PRIUS: A court of first impression. A nisi prius court is one where issues of fact are tried before a judge or jury.

N.O.V. (NON OBSTANTE VEREDICTO): Notwithstanding the verdict. A judgment n.o.v. is a judgment given in favor of one party despite the fact that a verdict was returned in favor of the other party, the justification being that the verdict either had no reasonable support in fact or was contrary to law.

NUNC PRO TUNC: Now for then. This phrase refers to actions that may be taken and will then have full retroactive effect.

PENDENTE LITE: Pending the suit; pending litigation underway.

PER CAPITA: By head; beneficiaries of an estate, if they take in equal shares, take per capita.

PER CURIAM: By the court; signifies an opinion ostensibly written "by the whole court" and with no identified author.

PER SE: By itself, in itself; inherently.

PER STIRPES: By representation. Used primarily in the law of wills to describe the method of distribution where a person, generally because of death, is unable to take that which is left to him by the will of another, and therefore his heirs divide such property between them rather than take under the will individually.

PRIMA FACIE: On its face, at first sight. A prima facie case is one that is sufficient on its face, meaning that the evidence supporting it is adequate to establish the case until contradicted or overcome by other evidence.

PRO TANTO: For so much; as far as it goes. Often used in eminent domain cases when a property owner receives partial payment for his land without prejudice to his right to bring suit for the full amount he claims his land to be worth.

QUANTUM MERUIT: As much as he deserves. Refers to recovery based on the doctrine of unjust enrichment in those cases in which a party has rendered valuable services or furnished materials that were accepted and enjoyed by another under circumstances that would reasonably notify the recipient that the rendering party expected to be paid. In essence, the law implies a contract to pay the reasonable value of the services or materials furnished.

QUASI: Almost like; as if; nearly. This term is essentially used to signify that one subject or thing is almost analogous to another but that material differences between them do exist. For example, a quasi-criminal proceeding is one that is not strictly criminal but shares enough of the same characteristics to require some of the same safeguards (e.g., procedural due process must be followed in a parole hearing).

QUID PRO QUO: Something for something. In contract law, the consideration, something of value, passed between the parties to render the contract binding.

RES GESTAE: Things done. In evidence law, this principle justifies the admission of a statement that would otherwise be hearsay when it is made so closely to the event in question as to be said to be a part of it, or with such spontaneity as not to have the possibility of falsehood.

RES IPSA LOQUITUR: The thing speaks for itself. This doctrine gives rise to a rebuttable presumption of negligence when the instrumentality causing the injury was within the exclusive control of the defendant, and the injury was one that does not normally occur unless a person has been negligent.

RES JUDICATA: A matter adjudged. Doctrine which provides that once a court of competent jurisdiction has rendered a final judgment or decree on the merits, that judgment or decree is conclusive upon the parties to the case and prevents them from engaging in any other litigation on the points and issues determined therein.

RESPONDEAT SUPERIOR: Let the master reply. This doctrine holds the master liable for the wrongful acts of his servant (or the principal for his agent) in those cases in which the servant (or agent) was acting within the scope of his authority at the time of the injury.

STARE DECISIS: To stand by or adhere to that which has been decided. The common law doctrine of stare decisis attempts to give security and certainty to the law by following the policy that once a principle of law as applicable to a certain set of facts has been set forth in a decision, it forms a precedent that will subsequently be followed, even though a different decision might be made were it the first time the question had arisen. Of course, stare decisis is not an inviolable principle and is departed from in instances where there is good cause (e.g., considerations of public policy led the Supreme Court to disregard prior decisions sanctioning segregation).

SUPRA: Above. A word referring a reader to an earlier part of a book. (The opposite of infra.)

ULTRA VIRES: Beyond the power. This phrase is most commonly used to refer to actions taken by a corporation that are beyond the power or legal authority of the corporation.

Addendum of French Derivatives

CHATTEL: Tangible personal property.

CY PRES: Doctrine permitting courts to apply trust funds to purposes not expressed in the trust but necessary to carry out the settlor's intent.

IN PAIS: Not pursuant to legal proceedings.

PER AUTRE VIE: For another's life; during another's life. In property law, an estate may be granted that will terminate upon the death of someone other than the grantee.

PROFIT A PRENDRE: A license to remove minerals or other produce from land.

VOIR DIRE: Process of questioning jurors as to their predispositions about the case or parties to a proceeding in order to identify those jurors displaying bias or prejudice.